A SHORT HISTORY OF ECONOMIC PROGRESS

A SHORT HISTORY OF ECONOMIC PROGRESS

A Course in Economic History

Y. S. BRENNER

Routledge
Taylor & Francis Group
LONDON AND NEW YORK

First published in 1969 by
Routledge
2 Park Square, Milton Park, Abingdon, Oxon, OX14 4RN

Transferred to Digital Printing 2006

ISBN 0 7146 1277 4 (hbk)

ISBN 0 7146 4016 6 (pbk)

Preface

This book is based upon a series of lectures on the history of economic development given to students of economics at Cape Coast University in Ghana. It aims at providing an analysis of economic progress in the developed countries which will show which geo-economic, social, political and cultural forces assisted such progress, and which forces delayed or hindered it. It should incidentally explain why European nations took several decades to emulate the economic and industrial achievements of Britain; why nations in other parts of the world (e.g. Japan and Russia) were unable for a considerable time to match the advances of Western Europe and the United States, and why the developing countries are at present finding it so difficult to catch up with the economic progress of the more advanced industrial nations.

Y. S. BRENNER

August 1968

Contents

Figures

Chapter I

THE BEGINNINGS

INTRODUCTION: SOME GENERAL IDEAS

During the last hundred and fifty years there has been a substantial increase in productivity and affluence in some countries, and its effect has been increasingly felt by ever larger numbers of people in these countries. At the same time very little change of this kind has taken place in the rest of the world. In the following chapters an attempt is made to examine the conditions which made the increase in productivity and affluence possible and to trace its progress in the countries in which it is most evident.

For centuries mankind has been living on the borderline of starvation. Malthus blamed this on 'the constant tendency in all animated life to increase beyond the nourishment prepared for it'.[1] Yet, in the last century and a half the population of western Europe has grown faster than ever before in the history of mankind, and its growth has been accompanied by a very great improvement in the standard of living.[2] The reason why this outstanding accretion of population has not led to the dire consequences Malthus predicted is to be found in the socio-economic changes which arose out of the new organisation of society generally referred to as the agricultural and industrial revolutions. In other words, it arose out of the application of science to the problems of transport and production. Historical records show that formerly the peoples of Europe experienced death rates as high and as frequently subject to fluctuations, due to one type of catastrophe or another, as the economically more backward peoples in Asia and Africa today.[3] The available information[4] indicates that no more than one hundred and fifty or two hundred years ago mortality rates in Europe and the United States were little if any better than they are in most underdeveloped countries today and that the conditions which were responsible for the high mortality rate then are similar to those which still prevail in parts of Asia and Africa, namely poor health and malnutrition. Even as late as the middle of the nineteenth century lack of transportation made most small localities depend almost entirely upon their own harvests. When crops failed the people starved, although in other places not very far away there was food to spare.[5] In addition to such regional famines there were the even more disastrous continental crop failures which befell Europe from time to time. The famine of 1740–42 is a good example. During this famine death rates in several of the most affected areas rose to over fifty per thousand of population.[6] Finally, there was the chronic insufficiency of food of the late eighteenth and the nineteenth centuries. The extent of this chronic shortage appears to be the subject of a good deal of disagreement among economic historians. Some are of the opinion that in the years between one famine and the next the population was generally well fed;[7] others deny this by stressing the relative importance of the notoriously underfed poor in pre-industrial society. One authority on the subject concludes that by the middle of the nineteenth century one-third of the population of the United Kingdom and Ireland subsisted on nothing but potatoes and another third of the population had very little to add to this diet.[8] Both schools of economic historians are, however, agreed in the view that the productivity of agriculture in any society before the nineteenth century had never risen high enough to yield a sufficiently great surplus to permit more than a third of its number to consume foodstuffs without producing them.[9] The question arises why this should be so. Sir James Steuart, in the second half of the eighteenth century, provided the following explanation: unless the people who are not employed in agriculture produce an equivalent which may be accepted by the farmers in exchange for their surplus the latter will have no incentive to raise their output.[10] In his own words, 'every person who is hungry will make a demand, but every such demand will not be answered, and will consequently have no effect. The demander must have an equivalent to give: it is this equivalent . . . *the effectual demand* . . . which makes the husbandman labour. . . .'[11] The implication of this point of view is that only the growth of manufacture and industry, or trade with foreign markets, may increase agricultural production. Malthus had been concerned about the capability of mankind to find its nourishment, Steuart—with its will to find it. Since then world population has increased by approximately 29 per cent in the first half and 37 per cent in the second half of the nineteenth century (and almost 54 per cent in the first half of the twentieth century).[12] The rate at which the European population increased in the nineteenth century was far above the world average.[13] Normally a growing population is accompanied by increasing total output and, obviously, by a rise in the number of people among whom the output is divided. But the phenomenal rise in European population was attended by a no less phenomenal progress of science and technology. Had it not been for this progress, *per capita* output and consequently living standards would have been affected, depending in each case on the specific context and environment, in one of the following ways. Firstly, the effect could have been 'neutral'. Where land is abundant and fertile and the age composition of the society does not present particular problems the greater demand for victuals may be offset by the additional supply. This appears to have been the position in North America during the early days of the European settlement there.[14] Secondly, there could have been an increase in *per capita* output. A too thinly populated area may prevent the introduction of some simple or not so simple economies and improvements which can only be introduced if people are numerous and live in close proximity to each other. For example, the construction of a dam, a water reservoir, the draining of a swamp, which may all raise *per capita* output considerably but can only be accomplished if the number of people sharing in it is large enough. This is what happened in many parts of England in the later part of the eighteenth century.[15] Thirdly, a fall in *per capita* output could have taken place and with it a fall in living standards. The proportion of the poor and underfed members of society may increase until eventually those famous Malthusian checks on population 'misery and starvation' would turn the population growth into decline.[16] In fact something of this kind may well have taken place here and there in late seventeenth, early eighteenth and mid-nineteenth century Europe. Yet, the overall effect of population growth in Europe was positive. In England there had been a steady increase of efficiency in agriculture for a long time, and particularly since the early eighteenth century. Daniel Defoe tells of turnips and clover and of the fertilising of the soil by manure or by mixing marl with topsoil when it is too light. He also tells of great improvements in livestock breeding long before the days of Coke and Bakewell and the time which is now usually regarded as the age of improvement.[17] Thus it appears that an agricultural 'revolution' had been progressing in England long before the middle of the eighteenth century. This development, which was at the same time closely matched by the evolution and spreading of trade and commerce, was not confined to Britain alone. Progress in other parts of northern Europe was not dissimilar.

This then, the rise in agricultural productivity accompanied by the development of manufacture and trade, was the unique phenomenon of early modern Europe which laid the foundations and made possible the great industrial revolution which followed. Why it arose in Europe, and why at the time it did, are questions which cannot easily be answered. In his excellent study of the cultural changes which led up to the emergence of modern industrial society, the late R. H. Tawney wrote that the elements which combined to produce it were too numerous to be summarised in any neat formula and that 'history is a stage where forces which are within human control contend and co-operate with forces which are not'. [18] But, bearing in mind this reservation, he concluded that 'side by side with the expansion of trade and the rise of new classes to political power, there was a further cause, which, if not the most conspicuous, was not the least fundamental. It was the contraction of the territory within which the writ of religion was conceived to run. . . . When the age of Reformation begins', he wrote, 'economics is still a branch of ethics, and ethics of theology; all human activities are treated as falling within a single scheme, whose character is determined by the spiritual destiny of mankind; the appeal of theorists is to natural law, not to utility; the legitimacy of economic transactions is tried by reference, less to the movements of the market, than to moral standards derived from the traditional teaching of the Christian Church: the Church itself is regarded as a society wielding theoretical, and sometimes practical, authority in social affairs . . . by the Restoration the whole perspective, at least in England, has been revolutionised. Religion has been converted from the keystone which holds together the social edifice into one department within it, and the idea of a rule of right is replaced by economic expediency as the arbiter of policy and the criterion of conduct. From a spiritual being, who, in order to survive, must devote a reasonable attention to economic interests, man seems sometimes to have become an economic animal, who will be prudent, nevertheless, if he takes due precautions to assure his spiritual well-being.' [19] Thus by the eighteenth century man was not only better equipped but also more willing to improve his economic condition. Gradually he improved his means of communication and reduced the heavy toll of life from localised famines. Slowly, with the growth of towns, he learned to draw his victuals from greater distances which led to a rising degree of specialisation of food production in the areas most suited for it by their natural environment. Together with this he learned more about the storage of foodstuffs, which was no longer dismissed as the sole province of 'engrossers', and by all this he reduced death and starvation in the recurrent national and continental periods of dearth. Finally, the growing spirit of inquiry of that age which stimulated science spread into the contryside just at the time when a new kind of landowner was becoming more prominent—the man who had made his fortune in trade and manufacture and invested it in land. Having not only the financial resources but also the business experience required to make the best use of the land, these men were usually among the first to raise farm output. Thus with the emergence of the new capitalist ethic, the progress of rationalism, and the development of science, man also learned to raise *per capita* output in agriculture. Until then, increases in food production were primarily the consequence of enlargement of the cultivated area and the augmentation of its labour force.[20] This resulted in a kind of moving equilibrium between the rate of population growth and its means of subsistence. Whenever, in relation to population, land was abundant, birth rates rose in excess of death rates and people became more numerous.[21] But when the accretion of people reached the limits of 'the nourishment prepared for it' (at the prevailing level of technology) and poorer land was put to use diminishing returns from land set in. Sooner or later population growth abated and the trend reversed.[22] The unique phenomenon of the later part of the eighteenth century was that mankind was able to break away from this 'Malthusian' cycle of population growth followed by its diminution. Due to the better organisation of transport and production in agriculture, and the improved methods of husbandry, the old equilibrium of land and labour was superseded by another relating population growth to productivity. Consequently a new phase in human history evolved and with it the phenomenon of unemployment. Sometimes by choice and more often from necessity a surplus labour force moved from its agricultural background to the towns in search of other work. In other words, the rising productivity of land and labour provided both the food to feed the relatively greater number of consumers not directly concerned with its production, and the surplus labour force required to satisfy the needs of a growing trade and industry. It also provided a higher standard of living and made available the economic surpluses which were required to improve sanitary practices, and later also medical research and health education. The towns did not share in population growth in the same manner as rural areas until well into the eighteenth century. In the country as a whole growth normally originated from an excess of birth rates over death rates; in the towns it was due to migration. Before the middle of the eighteenth century there was no period in which towns experienced birth rates higher than their death rates. Consequently, it must be assumed that had towns 'continued to kill off each year 2 per cent of their total number in addition to the number born in them, as London probably did between 1700 and 1750, the population of all Western lands would soon have become stationary; for the ratio of the rural population to the towns, which was declining proportionally, could not have continued to supply the cities with the surplus that they would have needed to maintain their numbers'.[23] It can therefore be said that the rise in productivity removed two major obstacles to population growth, the lack of food and the heavy incidence of disease.[24] While the former affected the population as a whole the latter was particularly responsible for the rise of towns.[25] Another factor of no less importance was the development of transport. Again, it required both the surplus manpower and the rising numbers of people dependent on this service to stimulate its progress.[26] Throughout the period for which more or less reliable data are obtainable there was a persistent fall in the number of people directly concerned with the production of food and an equally impressive rise in the number of people engaged in its trade and transportation.[27] The connection between the latter and the growth of towns is only too obvious. Once a town had grown to the limits imposed upon it by the food produced within its immediate vicinity it could no longer expand. If none of the famous cities of antiquity ever approached in size the greater cities of the modern world it was precisely for this reason.[28] A city requires food, fuel and the raw materials for its manufacture. If it was located near the sea or upon a navigable river it had certain advantages. As Adam Smith observed, in the last quarter of the eighteenth century, it required only six or eight men to bring by water to London the same quantity of goods which would otherwise require 'fifty broad-wheeled waggons, attended by a hundred men, and drawn by four hundred horses . . .'.[29] Yet, even with the advantages of a harbour, it was only when mechanical means of transportation replaced manpower and domestic animals that the size of the cities was no longer restrained by their immediate rural surroundings. In addition to making the supply of cities more certain, and giving them an opportunity to draw their food and raw materials from wider and more varied areas, it also made it possible for them to sell their wares to a far greater number of people scattered throughout the world.[30] The growth of cities and their transport system was closely connected with a perhaps even more revolutionary innovation. This was the large-scale exploitation of a new source of energy. Until this time the main source of energy, apart from man's muscular work, had always been plants and animals or wind and water. This fact had set definite limits to the possible expansion of supplies of energy. The first two, plants and animals, were ultimately restricted by the supply of land. The remaining two, wind and water, were limited by their location. Progress in agriculture had increased the supply of biological converts, i.e. plants and animals, but scientific progress, which accompanied the growth of the towns, added a completely new source of inanimate converts to the supply of energy. The new supply of energy was not only free from the limitations which restricted the earlier forms of power but was also incomparably stronger. The most efficient water-wheel installation which existed in the late seventeenth century, the 'Machine of Marly', generated at its best about 75 h.p.; the best in the following century generated up to perhaps 105 h.p. But a steam-engine, exhibited in America in 1876, generated no less than 2,500 h.p., and a few years later 10,000 h.p. engines were used in the new electric power stations.[31] Only then did man indeed grow into a giant.

But urbanisation, particularly in England, had yet another effect. It encouraged the landed aristocracy, whose social and political status of leadership was now being threatened by the merchants and capitalists, to become more aware of profit. This encouraged them to extend enclosure, which in turn made possible the consolidation of holdings and greater efficiency in production. Obviously the new trend caused a great deal of hardship to those who were evicted from their land. But these hardships were accompanied by some ameliorating circumstances. The more efficient utilisation of land produced cheaper food and this helped to feed the rapidly growing urban populations. In addition to this the absorption of the new town populations became easier through the growing export market for industrial products. Finally, before long, England was able to feed her growing population by drawing food supplies from the newly settled countries. This led to more specialisation and to a re-allocation of agricultural resources. Thus the new countries not only helped to feed Britain, but were themselves drawing off part of her surplus population.[32]

Thus technological progress made possible the continuous increase of population in two ways: it provided the means of transportation necessary to convey relatively large numbers of people out of northern Europe to the less densely settled areas of the world in America, Africa and Oceania, and to bring back materials which were scarce; and, more important, it raised the productivity of land and resources in Europe itself. In Professor William Ashworth's words,[33] this technological progress made possible 'two types of economic change, extensive and intensive, which had to occur if the rapid growth of population was not to be disastrous'.

POPULATION GROWTH AND THE NEW AGRICULTURE

Taking the extensive process (i.e. migration) first, it originated following the famous voyages of discovery in the sixteenth century. However, until the nineteenth century its volume was relatively insignificant. Most emigrants were soldiers, adventurous traders, religious or political refugees or deported criminals.[34] In all cases migration involved a great deal of risk to health and life and it was only rarely supported by the mother country in furtherance of colonisation schemes.[35] All in all the numbers of people taking part in this movement during the seventeenth and eighteenth centuries were never large enough to influence developments in Europe.[36] The great change occurred only after the Napoleonic Wars. It was brought about on the one hand by the deliberate policies of some countries to attract immigrants from Europe,[37] and, more important, on the other hand, by the economic conditions in Europe —namely the scarcity of land and the unemployment of labour. These twin evils were the product of the improvements in preventive medicine which raised the rate of population growth above the rate and capacities of economic growth in Europe,[38] or, alternatively, the product of the 'capitalistic mode of production in agriculture and manufacture'[39] or even the result of a combination of both. Thus, in contrast to the 'new' countries, and in particular in contrast to America, which offered the immigrants free or cheap land and relatively well-paid employment in manufacture, Europe had very little to offer.[40] Therefore it is hardly surprising that, with the improvements in sea transport and the reduction in its cost and risks, the stream of emigrants from Europe increased. The flow was neither evenly distributed during the whole period nor was it growing at a steady rate, nor was it even shared in similar proportions throughout the period by the different countries of origin. It followed more or less the pattern of the change towards industrialisation which took place in nineteenth-century Europe, reaching a peak only in the early twentieth century.[41]

From a closer study of the emigration and population growth data[42] it becomes obvious, however, that the extensive (i.e. migration) solution to the population pressure problem was of relatively little significance. Not more than one-seventh, i.e. under 15 per cent, of the annual increments to Europe's population emigrated.[43]

The second, intensive, solution of the population problem was far more impressive. Here progress took place in two directions— through the decline of the relative role of agriculture in the occupational structure and through a reduction in the absolute number of people employed in food production. The first solution was somewhat delayed by the further occupation of virgin or thinly populated land; the second implied a rise in productivity.[44]

Today the growth of agriculture depends on both production and consumption. This has not always been so in the past. Melchor de Jovellanos,[45] writing in 1795, believed that the size of the cultivated area depended on the demand for foodstuffs alone. Most modern agricultural economists would give equal weight to the supply of raw materials for industry and to the demand for victuals.

But Melchor de Jovellanos' view was certainly correct in his own time. The change of emphasis from demand to supply was one of the factors which accompanied the growth of modern industry and its rising requirements for agricultural raw materials. Before the industrial revolution, agricultural production had already undergone several important transformations but none as profound as the change which took place in the nineteenth century. First, there was the period of subsistence farming, when each household was almost entirely self-sufficient and all its produce was locally consumed by the members of the family. Then followed the period of the 'direct barter economy'; people were still self-sufficient but produced enough to make some 'payments in kind' for services and goods which they received from persons no longer directly employed in agriculture. The rent collector, the priest, the barrel-maker, the salt merchant are examples of such persons who directly bartered goods and services for their food. After this followed the period of the rise of an impersonal market and its concomitant, the money or cash economy. Payments in kind were almost entirely restricted to the tenant-landlord relationship and ever-increasing numbers of people became dependent upon markets and middlemen to purchase their food. In this period prices began to play an important role in influencing the long-term decisions of farmers. Productivity had risen high enough to enable farmers to produce in normal years a surplus of food for sale, but the extent to which it was worth their while to produce on second or third best land was, in the long run, dependent upon the price the products fetched on the market. In this sense, therefore, Melchor de Jovellanos was right in relating the size of the cultivated area to demand alone. In his time it was indeed the strength of demand for food, as expressed in the food price movements, which more than anything else influenced farmers' decisions. Only in the course of the nineteenth century, with the progress of international transport and trade, the application of science to agriculture, and the rising competition between farm and industry for labour, did the change of emphasis from demand to supply become really evident. Better transport made possible the large-scale importation of food into Europe from wherever it was produced more cheaply.[46] One result of this was the increase in the total world food supplies because of the higher degree of specialisation; another result was the discouragement of the use of land of relatively low fertility in Europe. In addition to this, land use in Europe was affected in a not dissimilar way by the progress of chemistry, which led to the intensification of agriculture on some land and made other land not worth cultivating.[47] Finally it was during this period that it became possible to use land for other purposes than agriculture although there was still a wide discrepancy in the eighteenth century between the improvements discussed in the dissertations of learned societies and those actually introduced on more than a purely experimental scale in the field.[48] For a long time the new and the old continued to exist side by side. Most ordinary farmers kept to the traditional ways while an increasing number of greater landowners turned to the new methods. In some parts of Europe, however, the 'new agriculture' was almost universally adopted even before the middle of the nineteenth century.[49] The Netherlands are a good, though not the only, example. Here at a very early date the 'Malthusian' element, population pressure and scarcity of land, combined with the 'Steuartian'[50] element, 'effectual demand', the product of the growth of cities and manufacture, and revolutionised agriculture.

The Netherlands had been dependent for their supply of cereals on the Baltic trade since the sixteenth century.[51] No less than 10 per cent of the corn which was necessary to feed the population in the seventeenth century was imported, and the ratio of imported to home-produced cereals on the market was continually increasing. The rising demand for imported food was due not only to population growth but also, and even more so, to the growth of towns. It was matched by increased shipping. For it was during the eighteenth century that farming in the Netherlands passed through a period of revolutionary changes. It became less concerned with traditional crops and had to divide the land between food crops and raw materials for manufacture like flax for linen, hemp for ropes, tobacco, etc. In time the demand for industrial crops outweighed that for food crops, and, with prices becoming the main arbiter, even the farmers found it more desirable to buy imported corn than to grow it themselves on land which they could employ more profitably.

This trend of agricultural development was accompanied by yet another important change. This was the extraordinary rise in the volume of vegetable and fruit production which went together with the growth of towns. Within a few decades the rural map of the Netherlands was changed. Land in the vicinity of cities became almost entirely allocated to the production of vegetables, whereas the more remote areas were shared between fruits and industrial crops. The spreading of cultivation for these two crops at the expense of cereals foreshadowed the developments which took place throughout most of north-western Europe in the century that followed. This was the intensification of husbandry and of the exploitation of land. In other words the change was towards the employment of more men and more money per acre. The soil was dug more deeply and manured, livestock was kept in greater numbers, and transport to convey compost and ash from the towns improved.

Planting in rows and in pure stands quickly developed. The market gardens and industrial crops made this imperative. Coleseed made the replanting of seedlings increasingly widespread. Tobacco, hops and madder spread the planting in straight rows. Weeding became more important to safeguard young seedlings and new crops, and a great variety of new tools were invented which were more suitable for the new ways of farming the land. Moreover, as these new crops required a great deal of hard work, a gradual selection took place giving the advantage to the most expensive ones. In small holdings horticulture became predominant in many areas. But altogether the 'new agriculture' made it possible for a much greater number of people to make a living from a small area of land than had been the experience in earlier centuries. In addition more labour was employed in the processing of some of the industrial crops, so that before long oil presses, drying ovens and other similar home industries developed on, or nearby, many of the farms. Retting, hackling and flag spinning were among the new trades which helped to absorb a great part of the increasing labour force.[52] Thus, while agriculture adapted itself to the money economy, it also provided new employment for the growing population and more produce per acre of land.

A difficult problem is the dating of the stages in the spread of the 'new agriculture'. In order to be able to do this it becomes necessary to define the term 'new agriculture'. As this may cause a great deal of difficulty, it may be sufficient here merely to list the most obvious changes which were usually taken as a sign of 'new agriculture'. These were the transition from one cereal production to other crops and the introduction of crop rotations; the decline of the fallow, and better and more manuring, as well as the planting or sowing of purely industrial crops; the consolidation of agricultural holdings and their enclosure; the improved keeping and breeding of livestock and the more intensive use of land and of labour. Defined in this way it is apparent that there was very little really new in the 'new agriculture', as most of these improvements had already been adopted here and there even as far back as the middle ages. It was the spreading rather than the newness of the methods which made up the change. Yet they did not spread simultaneously. Taking each group of innovations or improvements separately, a very complex picture emerges from both the geographical and the chronological point of view. The transition from one-crop cereal production to other crops progressed, after the sixties of the eighteenth century, very slowly from the Netherlands to northern France,[53] but for a long time, even there, land used in the traditional manner lay next to land on which crop rotation was already practised successfully.

A similar mixture of new and old crops and new and old methods of cultivation continued to exist in many other parts of Europe. There is reliable evidence of this from eighteenth-century Scotland, England, Alsace, Schleswig-Holstein, Andalusia and southern France. An interesting point is that wherever the increase of the new at the expense of the old agriculture took place, it always coincided with population growth and also with rising living standards.[54]

Even the decline of the fallow is not easily traced and dated. It seems to be a fact that in northern Germany a method of three-crop rotation was practised on poor soils in the fifteenth and sixteenth centuries. But it disappeared almost entirely in the seventeenth century, and reappeared in the eighteenth, when it was almost universally adopted. The cause given in most books for this reversion to the older methods of cultivation which took place in the seventeenth century is the Thirty Years War and the decline of population. With less people, intensive farming became uneconomical and was abandoned.[55] Closely related to the decline of the fallow was the spread of manuring, but the history of its progress is almost as obscure. The practice of improving the soil by manure also dates back to the middle ages.[56] In the sixteenth and seventeenth centuries a system of rotation which included fodder-crops was sometimes introduced to keep the livestock on the land for manuring.[57] But again progress was not uninterrupted. It depended on the profitability of converting pasture into ploughland. Thus, when in the second half of the eighteenth century it became uneconomical to reserve land for livestock, the practice of manuring was much less widespread.[58] Yet again, the trend was not the same everywhere. When land use became more intensive in some areas a very severe shortage of manure arose and led to a variety of solutions. In the sixteenth century it was often the nearby city refuse which supplied the manure required by the neighbourhood. By the middle of the eighteenth century the demand in the Netherlands, for example, had risen so much that even city refuse had to be imported.[59] In the beginning of the nineteenth century the shortage was so severe that most farmers had once again to rely on their livestock for manure because there was little opportunity to buy any.[60] Only towards the middle of that century was some relief brought by the wider spread of the cultivation of clover. This made stall-feeding of greater numbers of livestock possible and thereby increased the supply of manure. Real progress, however, was delayed until after the middle of the nineteenth century, when botany and modern chemistry came to the rescue and totally revolutionised the whole process of manuring.[61]

The dating of the introduction of new crops is equally difficult and complicated. Rye, oats and wheat were grown in Europe for a very long time. The wider use in bread of the last of these three appears to have progressed only from the middle of the eighteenth century onwards.[62] Even then the wheat was often not grown separately but mixed with rye; indeed, various mixtures of the two cereals were commonly used in the making of bread. As early as the twelfth century buckwheat was sometimes grown on sandy soil; in the sixteenth its cultivation spread for a time very rapidly; then it declined once more until the late eighteenth and early nineteenth centuries. This suggests that its spread took place when cereal prices were high enough to make the cultivation of inferior soil profitable. After the middle of the nineteenth century its cultivation declined again until it was almost entirely replaced by the potato. The story of maize is no less obscure than that of buckwheat. Maize might have come to Europe from America and was initially used as a fallow crop. Its main advantages were that it yielded crops which were about three times larger than those of wheat, and that it could be used either as food for man or fodder for cattle. However, with the increasing production of wheat, it gradually became a cattle food crop. The most important new agricultural produce which spread throughout Europe on the eve of the industrial revolution was the potato. This was perhaps the only innovation which really deserved to be called new.[63] Like the yam, it originated in America. It was brought to Europe in the middle of the sixteenth century but did not gain much popularity until the following century. Then it began to replace cabbage roots and cereals in the diets of the people who lived in densely populated areas and in regions with poor soil. Elsewhere potatoes, though used for cattle and pigs, were not considered fit for human consumption until the early nineteenth century. In England potatoes gained great importance as human food from the time of the corn dearth in the middle of the eighteenth century.[64] When in the nineteenth century population pressure was mounting and land became relatively scarcer, potatoes were universally adopted as a staple food for all classes all over Europe. The outstanding success of the potato during this period was largely due to the fact that it is a relatively labour-intensive crop with a high yield per acre and that it can be grown on poor soil. How important potatoes had become by the middle of the nineteenth century is evident from the appalling consequences of the phytophthora epidemic which destroyed the potato crops in 1845, 1846 and 1848. Worst of all was the epidemic in Ireland, where absolute famine reigned in the summer of 1846, and where in the years which followed the famine the British

Government passed legal measures to evict the tenants who could not pay their outstanding rents and taxes, and to burn their homes.[65]

Among the 'new' industrial crops, flax, which was used in the manufacture of linen, was of particular importance. Being a very labour-intensive crop it had great possibilities in periods of rapid population growth and at all times in densely populated areas. Unfortunately, however, it is also a very soil-exhausting crop. Therefore it did not spread through northern Europe until the supply of corn became better organised. As flax was used for a great variety of purposes, such as making sacks, clothes, oil for lighting, cattle food, etc., and was very profitably cultivated by small farmers,[66] it played a similar role in the economic development of many continental cities to that which wool had done a century before for the English towns. The spreading of dye-plants followed the progress of the cloth industry. Hops were another 'new' plant which became very popular for beer in the eighteenth century. They too were highly labour intensive and dependent upon other developments to facilitate their wider spreading. Land had first to be consolidated and heavily manured, and this only became possible after stall-feeding of cattle was well established. Tobacco was yet another crop, imported from America, which made only slow progress in Europe until the eighteenth century, when governments recognised its possibilities as a source of revenue. Before that its production was officially discouraged and sometimes forbidden completely. With the growth of international trade in the second half of the nineteenth century, tobacco production in Europe diminished again because imported tobacco was usually both better and cheaper. Beet-sugar growing was greatly encouraged in France during the Napoleonic Wars but with no success. Its widespread cultivation did not start until after the middle of the nineteenth century. Fodder crops, turnips and clover in particular, spread from northern Europe to the rest of the Continent and to England in the course of the eighteenth century.[67] This was important because it helped to solve some of the problems, like winter and stall-feeding of cattle, which had held back progress in many other fields of agriculture until then.

Crop yields varied very widely. According to Slicher van Bath[68] 'if we compare the ratios of the modern period, after 1500, with those of the late Middle Ages, we see that in many parts there was but little progress from the sixteenth century to the late eighteenth, or even early nineteenth'. This was true of Germany, Scandinavia and most of France. It was certainly not true of English, Dutch and Flemish farming, which had progressed a great deal. On some well-run farms in these countries yields had already reached a mid-nineteenth century level in the early part of the eighteenth century.[69]

The close connection between the growth of towns and the spreading of trade on the one hand, and the uses to which land was put on the other, can also be traced in the changes which affected livestock breeding in northern Europe. Livestock was kept for one or more of the following reasons; to supply certain provisions (like milk and milk products, meat, hides or wool), for the household of the farmer himself or for sale on the market; to do heavy work, such as pulling carts or ploughing; and to produce manure for the better cultivation of the land. The stress put in different times and places on breeding livestock particularly suited for one or the other of these purposes often reflected the more general changes which took place in the economic history of the areas concerned. For example, the gradually rising standard of nutrition was reflected in the increasing production of milk and butter in north-western Europe between the years 1500 and 1800. Again, the differences between, say, Dutch yields (which rose by about 100 per cent) and German yields (which rose by no more than 20 per cent) throughout this period also tell their own story. Similarly, Slicher van Bath[70] believes that there was a trend towards keeping more cows and horses and less sheep in the eighteenth century.[71] Reclamation, he claims, 'ate into the heathland and waste, leaving less room for sheep to graze. The pig population, on the other hand, rose nearly everywhere during the eighteenth and nineteenth centuries. Before then peasants kept one or two pigs for their own use but by now they began to breed them for the market.' Even taking into consideration the increase in the number of pigs, the proportion of small to large animals was changing in favour of the latter, which could be used for both food and work. Another change in the same vein which took place in the seventeenth and eighteenth centuries was the concentrated effort of progressive farmers in the Netherlands and in England to breed animals which were particularly suited for meat. Great progress was made in raising the weight and enlarging the size of the edible parts of 'meat animals'.[72] This too may well have reflected either population growth, i.e. pressure on the available food supplies, or a rising standard of living which appeared in the form of a greater demand for meat and other relatively expensive foods. The first of these two possibilities finds a certain degree of support in the frequency of complaints about the overstocking of the common land and in the repeated outbreaks of cattle plagues which were worse than any that had occurred before the second half of the eighteenth century and which are sometimes associated with underfeeding of cattle.[73]

The higher yield of food per unit of land or livestock was, however, only one aspect of agricultural progress: the reduction of labour-time per unit of output was another. For centuries productivity of farm labour rose very slowly and sporadically. Many tasks required as much work in the eighteenth century as they did during the middle ages; some required less time, but the reduction was very slight indeed when judged by the progress which took place during the nineteenth century. In many places it was the number of workers which the farmer could expect to have at his disposal in harvest time that, more than anything else, decided the size of the area which he was going to sow with cereals. This was still so in the eighteenth century, but in the nineteenth century, with the rapid progress of mechanisation, such conditions were no longer important.[74] According to Slicher van Bath the production of 1800 litres of wheat on one hectare, using the ordinary plough, harrow, sickle and flails, took 144 man-hours in 1830. In 1896, with the aid of the machines which were in use at that time in the United States, labour-time had been reduced to 22 man-hours; and in 1930, with tractors and combine-harvesters, it was reduced again to 8¼ man-hours. In other words, between 1830 and 1896, 85·6 per cent of labour-time was saved and costs were reduced by 81·4 per cent.[75] A completely new dimension was added to agricultural progress in the course of the nineteenth century. While all the earlier innovations were primarily directed towards the land in the sense of raising its yield, the new dimension was directed towards reducing the labour required. If the former may be attributed to rising population pressure, then a difficulty arises in explaining the latter. It is hardly consistent with a surplus of cheap labour that labour-saving devices gain much popularity. The solution to this apparent contradiction may be found in the geographical location and the timing of the progress of one or the other of these trends.

Most labour-saving devices which were invented before the end of the eighteenth century were poorly constructed and not really suitable for the jobs they were designed for, but they already contained most of the basic ideas which were to bring about great progress in the century that followed. However, progress in the technology of agriculture was above all dependent upon basic changes which occurred in other contexts. Only when cheap cast-iron was available could agricultural machines be made of longer-lasting material and by craftsmen specialised in the production of such equipment.[76] Similarly it was only after the steam engine had come into use in factories and on the railway line that it was adapted 'to the stackyard and the field and, through the employment of the steamer for trawling, to the harvest of the sea. Pipe drainage of agricultural land and improvement by the use of superphosphate, basic slag, and other artificial fertilizers are further examples of the contribution of industry to agriculture.'[77] Without going into the details of these innovations, which are too numerous and complex to be discussed here, or into the details of the spreading of each new piece of labour-saving equipment, some landmarks must be mentioned. First among these is the small iron-framed plough which required fewer draught animals than the common heavy plough. This plough spread from the Netherlands to England in the second half of the eighteenth century. In England it was further developed into an all-iron plough, which was then turned into various other farm implements. It also gave rise to the first specialised plough-making firm, namely that of Robert Ransome of Ipswich, which played an important role in the development of farm machinery in the years that followed. It was this firm that in 1789 introduced the first cast-iron ploughshare with self-sharpening blades.[78] Elsewhere, at the same time a heavier implement, the cultivator, was introduced. This was a horse-drawn set of parallel iron wheels with strong curved prongs used for ploughing and clod crushing. At about the same time Jethro Tull's seed drill (originally invented in 1732) was improved and adapted for a number of new purposes such as manuring and the spreading of light seed. The horse-hoe, which replaced many single-row hoes, was another of Tull's innovations which spread by the end of the century. However, the most puzzling thing about agricultural progress was the late date at which the really important time-and-labour-saving machines began to spread. Though, for example, harvesting was the most labour-consuming operation, the reaping machine, invented by the end of the eighteenth century, did not gain widespread popularity before the last quarter of the nineteenth century.[79] Then it spread very rapidly indeed from America into northern Europe.[80] Other labour-saving machines which ought to be mentioned and which also came from America were the reaping machine (1848) and the mowing machine (1856). The fact that much of the labour-saving equipment spread first in America and only later in Europe may reflect the following two facts: first, that labour was scarce and land abundant in nineteenth-century America, which led to extensive cultivation and high labour costs, and therefore to the introduction of labour-saving machines, which became economical there at an early date; second, that labour was abundant and land scarce in Europe until the 1880s,[81] and therefore intensive cultivation and low labour costs meant that it would have been neither practical nor economical to introduce labour-saving equipment there until nearly the end of the century. This explanation is reasonable if invention is defined not only as the conception of an idea, but as its birth as a marketable product, i.e. as a product which can be sold at a price which covers its costs and reasonable profits.[82]

The United States and England took the lead in the application of new farming equipment, but the rest of western Europe followed only very hesitantly in the course of the latter part of the nineteenth century. The main reason for this difference between England and the Continent lay in the diversity of land ownership. On the Continent most farmers were tenants, not landowners, or had very small holdings. Often their rents were paid in kind as a share of the crop. Therefore, they had neither the money nor the incentive to invest in costly equipment. They could not borrow money because the land which could have served as security was not theirs, or not large enough. They had no reason to raise the yield as only a fraction of the extra produce was their gain, which might not suffice to offset the expense of the machine, while the real net profit would only accrue to the landlord. Where continental farmers were rich and might have had the incentive to buy the new inventions—that is near towns—they were just at this time abandoning cereal production and going over to the more intensively cultivated crops for which the new machines were not yet suitable. In England the situation was different. The fast progress of enclosures which rapidly brought large tracts of land under individual ownership made the introduction of agricultural machines both possible and profitable.[83] Also, in the southern United States and in Russia, machines began to play an important role with the abolition of slavery in the former (1862) and the abolition of serfdom in the latter (1881).[84]

So the spreading of agricultural machinery in mid-nineteenth-century Europe could only take place on large farms with wealthy owners.[85] Yet, even as early as 1817, there were several machines in use in England. Some were already causing social unrest. The best known among these was the steam thresher. During the Napoleonic Wars cereal prices in England had risen very significantly. Wages too had risen, though not quite as much as cereal prices.[86] The combination of high cereal prices and better wages made the introduction of a greater number of agricultural machines economical. One of these machines was the steam thresher, which caused a great deal of trouble after the war when labour was no longer as scarce as before. Threshing had been the farm workers' most important winter occupation because as much as 60 per cent of all winter work consisted of threshing.[87] Thus, with the spreading of the machine, a great many people found themselves without income during the winter months. It is hardly surprising therefore that the threshing machines were among the prime targets of destruction during the labour unrest in 1830.[88] After the middle of the nineteenth century the situation changed. Mechanisation of agriculture progressed almost unhindered as the migration of labour to the cities rapidly transferred the centre of gravity of unemployment to the urban areas and industries. By that time progress in the mechanisation of agriculture helped to reduce farm produce prices, which fell very markedly in the seventies and eighties.

In summary, then, population growth and the rise of cities brought with them new problems and new solutions. Starting from the Netherlands in the seventeenth century, where trade with the continent of Europe along the Rhine combined with the northern trade on the high seas, a profound change in agriculture took place. Farmers' decisions of what and how much to grow became progressively less subject to the immediate requirements of their households and more on the prices which crops were able to realise on the market. Once this change had taken place, several subsequent developments transformed the whole structure of agriculture in the Netherlands. Cereals were imported from countries which were less densely populated; and in the Netherlands itself land use became more specialised and intensive. Perishable products, vegetables, and other intensive foodstuffs with high yields per unit of land, which could neither be stored for long periods nor transported over long distances, became very popular with farmers around towns. Fruits became equally popular with farmers in the more remote districts and on poorer soil; and with the growth of manufacture in the cities, intensively cultivated industrial crops, like flax, were soon taking up the rest of the land. Thus the higher density of population produced its own remedies for food shortages and unemployment—namely the intensification of the use of both land and labour. From the Netherlands the trend spread to England, where conditions were not dissimilar. The concentration and intensification of production there in turn affected production in America. England provided a growing market for cereals which America could produce, and soon the demand was too brisk to be satisfied by the thinly populated farms with traditional farming equipment. Thus, while European conditions encouraged better use of land, American conditions led to the more productive employment of labour. Good corn prices on the one hand and the high cost of labour on the other made the introduction of farm machinery in America economical before this was the case in Europe. Only when the Napoleonic Wars produced a temporary labour shortage in England did some of the labour-saving equipment spread more rapidly there. Gradually, however, with the relative rise of importance of industry as compared with agriculture, the intensification of land use combined with the need to economise in the use of labour and transformed agriculture into an industry.

In the rest of Europe progress came only later. Social, legal and political conditions prevented an early growth of modern agriculture and delayed the development of modern industry until close to the last quarter of the nineteenth century. After that progress came very rapidly. In the eighteenth and early nineteenth centuries, however, most farms in France and in southern Germany were too small, and their farmers too poor, to introduce far-reaching improvements.[89] In addition to this, in both France (until 1789) and Germany (until 1807) a great variety and number of *seigneurial* privileges persisted which not only diminished farmers' incomes but made improvement virtually impossible. While the small farmer was thus unable to exploit his land more efficiently, the great landowner had little interest in doing so. Unlike their English counterparts, French great landowners never took much interest in the running of their farms. More often than not their incomes accrued from the legal privileges which went with the land rather than from the produce of the land itself. It is also relevant that there was less population pressure and less rapid urbanisation in France than in the Netherlands and England.[90] The Revolution of 1789 and the subsequent Constitutions brought little change. The confiscated church lands were soon broken up into very small holdings and the land which belonged to the fallen aristocrats was bought up by their relatives through fictitious buyers. Eventually even the plans for enclosure were modified to the point of abolition, so that in fact small landownership increased rather than diminished in post-revolutionary France.[91] In southern Germany conditions were similar to those in France. In northern Germany, however, a peculiar legal position enabled landlords to deprive farmers of their land while preventing them from leaving the district. Thus, on the one hand, great landed estates came into being while, on the other, a class of agricultural wage workers developed. In Prussia peasants had a degree of legal protection, for in 1807 they were freed from the laws which restricted their liberty to sell their holdings and seek work elsewhere. By 1811 rents and feudal dues could be converted into money payments or exchanged for one-third of the land and the renunciation of all traditional claims. The result of this law, which was originally designed to favour the peasants, was that within a very short period landowners managed to bring under their control more than one million hectares of land, thereby making about 100,000 farmers landless. During the depression which followed the Napoleonic Wars and continued until the late 1830s much of this land was converted into sheep-runs. The landless labourers were deprived of their means of subsistence in these regions and forced to move westwards in search of industrial employment, so that, in the later part of the century, when food prices improved and the Prusian landlords reverted to tilling their land, they were faced with a problem of labour shortage.[92]

URBANISATION, TRANSPORT AND THE GROWTH OF MARKETS

Having briefly traced the rise of agricultural production and productivity, in the parts of the world affected by it during the century which preceded the 'era of the Steam Engine', it now becomes necessary to examine the factors which were both its source and its consequence. Most important among these were population pressure and the growth of towns. On the latter subject Adna Ferrin Weber wrote in 1899,[93] 'population follows the line of least resistance in its distribution, and will consequently be affected by changes in the methods of production. . . .[94] If men were like other animals and had no further wants than bodily appetites and passions, there would be no large aggregations of people; for in order to produce food men must live either in scattered habitations . . . or in hamlets. . . .[95] Even with a comparatively high grade of wants man may live in these small groups, each of which is economically autonomous and self sufficing producing for itself and buying and selling little if anything.'[96]

However, when man finally discovered that it was more economical to leave certain tasks in the village to 'specialists', i.e. to those best adapted to do them by experience or inclination, self-sufficiency declined and the development of manufacture and trade began. From that time man's wants became increasingly sophisticated and even more divorced from agriculture. Two gradual but simultaneous processes were taking place: on the one hand human wants expanded, on the other man learned to increase his productivity. The former created the 'effective demand',[97] the latter rendered its satisfaction possible. Eventually the artisan no longer produced his food himself but received it in exchange for the product of his labour. Trade then became a necessary link. For 'without trade and commerce indeed, no towns or cities could come into existence; for they presuppose a non-agricultural population which buys its food supply'.[98] Even when the village was self-sufficient it was never entirely divorced from trade with the rest of the world. Salt and iron, to name but the most obvious commodities, had to be obtained from outside throughout the whole middle ages. Thus it was that even in the most bellicose times some kind of arrangement was usually in existence to safeguard trade and traders.[99] Some trading places derived their relative safety from the proximity of a shrine, others from the neighbourhood of a fort or castle, and others again from a nearby garrison or powerful feudal lord; but more often than not it was the primitive agricultural village or the coalescence of several such villages which eventually grew into a trading town for the people of the neighbouring area.[100] As trade facilities may well have been the main source of development of small communities into towns, it appears fairly obvious that such villages as were situated either at fording places or amidst some fertile region or upon good trade roads would have great advantages. It may, therefore, be said that the size of an inland city may well have been dependent upon the size and fertility of the plain or valley in which it was situated and for which it would be a distribution centre, and on the number of people who lived scattered throughout that valley or plain.[101]

However, the most important factor in the location and growth of cities is, what Weber called, 'the break in transportation', especially where the transfer of goods is accompanied by a change in their ownership. This is so because the transfer of goods from one means of transportation to another requires a great deal of labour, equipment and organisation, and because the transfer of ownership requires a complex system of storage involving great resources and many people. The townspeople have needs more sophisticated than those of people living in the village and they have the means to pay for the satisfaction of those needs. For this reason, the rising class of merchants and money changers was accompanied almost everywhere in Europe by a growing number of artisans who made a living by producing the goods the merchants required. Where cities were situated in the middle of a fertile plain or upon navigable rivers reaching into fertile regions, or near the sea, or in recent times near a railroad, they grew—being as it were both the cause and the result of their own attraction. Yet it invariably required certain specific social conditions to bring about this 'self sustained' growth of modern towns which had never come about in ancient times. The rising class of traders and money changers did not always attract the artisans to their trading centres, nor did their settlement invariably lead to a division of labour.[102] In ancient times it was quite common for the head or some important member of a family, tribe or household to live in town and deal in trade or some other urban business while the other members of his household provided his requirements in their rural surroundings. Only after a degree of specialisation, i.e. division of labour, was achieved within the household was it carried further in the town. When the craftsman realised that it was more convenient to keep his increasingly complex and numerous tools in the place where people would come to him for his services, he also discovered that the most convenient place for this was the market place or the town. Eventually 'the shoemaker, the smith, the weaver, the dyer, the brewer, the bricklayer, the carpenter, accumulated capital . . .',[103] increased the degree of specialisation, and at the same time freed himself from his former rural social dependence. In time the city replaced the social unit to which the man had formerly belonged. Thus the division of labour within the household or village gave rise to a further division of labour between town and country. The old allegiances to family, tribe or clan were transferred to the new collective structure of the town. It was therefore not unnatural for towns to develop by the old familiar pattern into a united whole, a complete financial and business system, managed in the exclusive economic interest of its citizens.[104] Gradually the division deepened and the town began to look upon its rural surroundings in much the same way as the lord of the manor regarded his tenants or the European national states in the nineteenth century their colonial dependencies, i.e. as their monopolistically controlled markets and sources of foodstuffs and raw materials.[105] But the division of labour did not stop there. When English wool or Flemish and Alsatian cloth, etc., proved to be better or cheaper than that which was produced elsewhere, a further kind of 'geographical' specialisation was added to the existing occupational divisions of labour. This gave rise to a new kind of conflict which required a wider organisation for its settlement. The towns with similar interests had to unite in order to exclude the competition of the others. The nation began to replace the town which had replaced the tribe, family or household as the focal point of man's loyalty and feeling of 'belonging'. Thus a new process of social and economic integration took place by which the towns and their rural hinterland were drawn together. The disintegration of the quasi-feudal links gave rise to a new form of social integration, namely nationalism. The objects of the individual's loyalty became even more abstract. As the town elders had replaced the feudal lord or pater familias as the focal point of the individual's loyalties, so did the nation take the place of the town, and the king the place of the elders. This process, by which whole regions were shut off against outsiders while their internal links were strengthened, is in fact the essence of Colbert's mercantilism. The tightening of the links, the construction of canals and other means of communications quickened the pace of economic activity and stimulated specialisation.[106] Thus mercantilism built roads and canals, promoted technical and artistic education and worked for a uniform customs system. By reforming the river tolls, etc., within the countries and by breaking down municipal and provincial autarchy, mercantilism made the various regional entities into nations. 'The effect of this gradual enlargement of the economic society upon the growth of cities', wrote Adna Ferrin Weber, 'must be clear to every student. How different is London a local market for the agriculturalists of Essex and Middlesex from London the world's financial and commercial centre'.[107]

However, the 'enlargement of the economic society' could not take place without the development of the necessary transportation system. This causal connection led some historians to the erroneous idea that the progress of transport was the cause of urbanisation.[108] Until the 'age of the railway', transportation developed together with, and as a result of, the cities' growing requirements. Even in the late eighteenth century most highways were little more than rights of way 'which had become well beaten tracks as a result of usage and which, over much of their length, were passable only by horse and foot traffic'.[109] Although travelling had increased since the middle ages it was mainly on foot or on horseback. There were few heavy goods to be transported and those were sent by water wherever this was possible. For this reason there was neither the wish nor the compulsion to improve the roads. In England, for example, the responsibility for their maintenance rested from 1555 until 1835 with the authorities of the parish through which the road passed. Where the parish was not directly interested in the road little if anything was done to maintain it.[110] Even when pressure was brought to bear upon the parish to do something about the roads, little progress could be made under the system prescribed by the 1555 Act for carrying out such work. Initially the labour for road-works was recruited in the usual feudal manner of so many days per household. The team of labourers was then made up of the 'choice workers of the household' who could best be spared—i.e. the most idle and useless, who would make 'a holiday of it, lounge about and trifle away their time'.[111] Later these 'day services' could be commuted into cash payments, but this did little to improve matters as long as no professionals were employed to supervise the work and as long as the responsibility continued to rest with the parish—sometimes merely with the owner of the field near which the road happened to pass. Thus as late as the eighteenth century the roads were still 'rocky lanes full of huge stones . . . and abominable holes'.[112] The change came gradually with the developments in agriculture and industry in the last century before the industrial revolution: that is, with the transition from subsistence to commercial farming, the progress of the manufacturing industries in the towns, and the consequent increase in the distances over which goods had to be conveyed.

As a result of the increased territorial division of labour and production the areas within which local exchanges were taking place expanded. The distances over which internal trade was carried on increased, and with them the number of people and communities who had a direct interest in the improved maintenance of roads and waterways. When, because of deforestation or for other reasons, charcoal was rapidly replaced by coal as a major fuel, road improvement became a problem of prime importance. Although, even in the seventeenth century, coal was increasingly used in the production of hardware and in particular of iron tools, the transport problem was still manageable; but when in the eighteenth century coal became the main fuel for the smelting of iron ore the whole pattern of inter-urban communications was revolutionised. The ancient towns had usually grown along the trade routes at places best suited for the 'break in transportation'. The new towns grew near deposits of coal and iron, which more often than not were to be found far away from natural avenues of trade. The old towns had developed because of their proximity to good routes of commerce, the new towns had to create such routes in order to be able to distribute the fruits of their productive efforts and to receive the foodstuffs they required. Once begun, the network of exchange and specialisation, and with it the network of communications, grew in ever wider circles. For example, in England 'the use of coal . . . led to the development of the iron industry on or near the coalfield areas of the Midlands and in the more remote counties such as Northumberland. The heavy clay of Staffordshire, together with the traditional skill of pottery workers in that area, made Staffordshire the natural centre of the expanding pottery industry. The cutlery industry was firmly rooted in Sheffield partly as a result of the suitability of the grit of the local grindstones. Silks were manufactured in London and in Derby. The woollen industry was becoming established in Yorkshire.'[113] Thus, the territorial division of labour stimulated transport improvements not only for the conveyance of finished products but also for the often more bulky raw materials. The improvements took the form of the creation of new waterways and the development of road-making techniques.

The two most important factors which helped to improve the network of roads were the turnpike system and the subsequent rise of professionalism in road construction. The former was a system of collecting money for the maintenance and improvement of roads from the people who used them; the latter was part of the general trend towards the use of science in all construction and engineering works.[114] Though turnpikes had been known in England since the middle of the seventeenth century, their spreading was delayed until close to the end of the eighteenth century. To put up a turnpike or toll gate it was necessary to have Parliamentary approval, which often met with strong opposition from vested interests. By the last quarter of the eighteenth century, however, economic pressure had become so strong that construction was no longer held back by opposition of this kind. Within half a century, that is in the last quarter of the eighteenth and first quarter of the nineteenth century, no less than 20,000 miles of roads were constructed by this system. Yet there were many deficiencies in the system. Christopher Savage summarised them as follows.[115] Firstly, there were no acquitable tolls. This was due to the fact that the trustees gave preferential rates to some people or groups of people while they themselves were not properly supervised and were not strictly guarded as to the acquisition of land and diversion of highways. Moreover, there was no audit of their accounts and there was no supervision of their borrowing power. Secondly, though initially turnpikes were thought to be a useful device for a temporary arrangement to repair exceptionally bad pieces of roads, they tended to become permanent institutions. In fact, renewal of turnpike authorities became a matter of course. Thirdly, far from producing a national network, it left road administration in a mess of scattered unconnected roads, broken down by an incredible number of turnpikes. Finally, even their primary aim of repairing particular sectors of the roads was not achieved. Many sections remained unrepaired and turnpikes were put up where roads were good and did not warrant any extra expenses. Even when repairs were made often the trustees were not required to be knowledgeable in roadmaking and were simply unable to do the repairs required of them. Above all this loomed high the major defect of the turnpike administration, namely, complete financial mismanagement.[116] The whole system of the turnpikes was scattered with endless cases of evasions, favouritism of all kinds, and of arbitrary exactions and other means of embezzlement, and with the great debts into which these companies and their trustees fell. Sometimes the trusts heaped up debts equal to, or higher than, the amount of tolls which could be expected. And then more debts were incurred and new tolls were levied, or old ones increased, while no more attention was paid to the repair of the trusts.[117]

Yet with all these shortcomings in the system, road construction made some progress under it. In 1810 the Board of Agriculture, which took an ever-increasing interest in road construction, adopted Macadam's suggestions for construction and administration, and with this a new era began. Basically Macadam's ideas were very simple, namely, to use small artificially broken stone of good quality for the road surface rather than a mixture of stones and sand; to engage only competent surveyors who were of proven honesty; to put the administration of the whole system under a mild form of Parliamentary control.[118] At the same time progress was made on the engineering problems of road construction, in which a great deal of experience was gathered in Scotland and Wales owing to the topographically more complicated problems there. These improvements and some administrative innovations are usually linked with the name of Thomas Telford and the road commission set up at the request of the Postmaster-General.

In France, Italy and the Netherlands, though not in Germany, the situation was very different from that of England. Both France and Italy inherited a number of good roads from Roman times which were kept in a reasonable state of repair. In Arthur Young's words, French roads were 'truly magnificent', while the English had no idea at all what such roads were like. Louis XV created the *Corps des Ponts et Chaussées* and Napoleon made very good use of the experience gathered by the *corps* in road and bridge building when this became a military and administrative necessity for his government. There were years in his reign when as many as 13,000 leagues of road connecting the various parts of France and connecting France with her neighbours were either built or repaired.[119] In contrast with the state of affairs in England, the maintenance and construction of the main national roads was the responsibility of the central government, whereas the maintenance of the departmental routes was left in the hands of the local authorities. This system put the responsibility for the roads into the hands of those most likely to be interested in their good repair. Although some of the 229 trunk roads of the Napoleonic era were badly neglected in the last three years of its govenment, they were quickly repaired during the Restoration period. Thus, although fewer new roads were constructed in the post-Napoleonic period than during his reign, the old roads were well maintained and continually improved. This left, however, the legacy of a peculiar geographical distribution of roads in France, by which almost half of the total 20,000 miles of good roads were concentrated in Alsace and Lorraine.[120] During the July Monarchy, 1830–48, the emphasis in road building moved away from the national and departmental roads and turned towards the 'feeder' or 'link' roads connecting the national and departmental ones into a whole system. These link or feeder roads were constructed jointly by the communes and the departments but were later maintained by the departments alone. The communes had, however, the sole responsibility for roads within their own areas, so that in fact each grade of road was administered by the organisation most interested in it. By the middle of the century almost all local roads were connected with the departmental roads, and through them with the national roads which were in turn connected with the road networks of the countries which had a common border with France with good roads of their own.[121] Foremost among these was Holland, where a great number of roads smoothly paved with bricks already existed in the eighteenth century. Second to them came the roads in other parts of Europe, where the ancient Roman roads continued to provide the foundations for the new road system. These were Flanders, Italy and Germany west of the Rhine. The condition of the roads in the rest of Europe was very similar to that of England. In Germany, where the foundations of the Roman civilisation were lacking and where political divisions made economic progress almost impossible, most roads were, until the second quarter of the nineteenth century, akin to those of England in the seventeenth, i.e. mere rights of way. Prussia inherited in 1815 a French road system with her new provinces in the Rhineland and Westphalia. Elsewhere there were very few roads indeed. Only with the progress of the *Zollverein* were new roads built, and even then most of these were in the same two provinces. After 1845, however, a period of rapid roadbuilding began in the eastern part of Prussia, which continued until 1870.

The early history of the navigable waterways in north-west Europe is similar to that of the roads. In England the rivers, unless they were privately owned, were regarded, like the King's highways, as free passages for whoever wished to use them. But, unless they were privately owned, they were little use as means of communications because of the great number of obstructions which made them impassable. As in the case of the roads, it was not until the second half of the eighteenth century that some effective legislation to improve river navigation was passed, and some real steps to improve inland navigation were taken. The latter took two forms; firstly, improvement of existing waterways, secondly, new canal construction. Until the middle of the seventeenth century most legislation concerning waterways in England was confined to safeguarding their maintenance as thoroughfares for whatever inland water transport there was. After the middle of that century, when increasingly greater quantities of goods like food and coal were being transported to the growing towns, new efforts were made to open up for navigation rivers which had hitherto been useless for this purpose. The method employed was by granting 'letters patent' either to the people directly interested in the traffic upon the river, or to companies, similar to the road trusts, which undertook to make the river, or section of the river, suitable for navigation; for this service they were entitled to collect tolls. The process of making more rivers navigable was greatly aided by the improvements which took place during this period in the construction of water locks.[122] Vallans, a Hertfordshire poet, was so impressed with the new water locks of his day that he described them in his poems:

> 'This locke contains two double doores of wood,
> Within the same a cesterne all of plancke,
> Which onely fils when boates come there to passe
> By opening of these mightie dores.'[123]

'By the middle of the eighteenth century, although England still had no true canals comparable to those of the Continent, the length of English rivers which had been made navigable by artificial means was roughly equal to the whole of that which was naturally navigable.'[124] Progress in this respect was most marked in Britain in three periods: from 1662 to 1665, when many Acts were passed in Parliament for the improvement of navigation on the rivers Stour, Salwarpe, Wey, Lugg, Medway, Avon and Itchen; from 1697 to 1700, when Acts were passed for the improvement of navigation on the Tone, Aire, Calder and again on hitherto unopened parts of the Trent, Lark and Avon; and from 1719 to 1721, when Acts were passed for the development of the Idle, Kennet, Douglas, Weaver, Mersey and Irwell. 'These measures were, however, only the first symptoms of the great change which was to follow. So far people had been content to deepen and improve certain waterways; nobody had yet thought seriously of making artificial ones.'[125] But then, after the middle of the eighteenth century, a new type of town began to develop near the sources of raw materials, and transport requirements became more pressing and of a different nature altogether. The population and the importance of manufacturing towns, as distinct from commercial towns, increased and revolutionised the nature of exchange. Trade began to move away from the traditional luxury or semi-luxury goods, with a few necessities like salt thrown in, towards the exchange of everyday commodities—foodstuffs and raw materials—which were required in quantities that were incomparably larger than anything the world had known since Roman times. Towns like Manchester, Liverpool, Birmingham and Sheffield had grown too big to rely upon their immediate neighbourhood for food, while some of the older towns required raw materials, and above all coal, in greater quantities. Food and coal prices rose sharply, and made the investment in the improvement of water communication highly economical.[126] Thus the demand for food in some areas, and for fuel and raw materials in others, combined to give rise to the great era of canal construction, which within half a century linked most of England by a magnificent network of waterways.[127]

The first important step in this direction was the construction of the Worsley Canal, 1759–61, built on the initiative of the Duke of Bridgewater, who owned some coalfields at Worsley and wished to transport his coal to Manchester some ten miles away.[128] Six years later the Duke of Brindley completed another canal which connected Liverpool with Manchester. By the time this canal was completed an even more ambitious scheme was well on its way to completion. This was the Grand Trunk Canal which linked the Trent and the Mersey and thus provided a continuous waterway from the Mersey and the Humber to London from 1777. Not surprisingly Josiah Wedgwood, whose potteries had been suffering very considerably from the lack of good transport facilities to the big markets, was one of the most persistent supporters of this scheme. But by that time canals were being built in many other places all over England, so that by the end of the century the system was almost complete. For the construction of the smaller or local canals money was usually raised locally from the people who seemed most interested in them, with the central government merely granting the required permission for their construction. The money was collected by setting up joint stock companies in which the interested parties could buy shares. Obviously not all schemes turned out to be financial successes, and sometimes people lost the money they invested in these ventures. This was particularly true of a great number of canal failures in 1797.[129] In most cases, however, the canals were completed successfully and the stockholders were reimbursed from the tolls collected from the canal users.[130] The canals reduced transport costs by more than half and sometimes by three-quarters in comparison with land transport; they contributed to the redistribution of population; they stimulated industry, trade and agriculture; and they had the additional advantage over river transport that they were independent of tides, winds and silting. Above all they could be drawn to where transport was most needed.[131] The main defect of the canals was that they were constructed without adequate supervision to ensure the required uniformity of width, depth and locks necessary if they were to become a national network of communications. This prevented the development of more through traffic and the more rapid growth of the size of boats. However, had it not been for these shortcomings, the rapid growth of rail transport in the second half of the nineteenth century might well have been delayed for many years.

In the northern plains of continental Europe a relatively good network of waterways existed for many centuries before the industrial revolution. In France some very important canals were built in the reigns of Louis XIV[132] and Louis XVI,[133] and the tradition of canal building was really never interrupted except for a relatively short period during the Revolution. When the St. Quentin canal, begun by Louis XVI, was completed in 1810 the future of Paris as an industrial centre was assured.[134] Coal, the mainstay of industrial progress in this period, could now be transported inexpensively and with relative ease from the northern mines, while food could continue to be supplied from the town's immediate surroundings. In Napoleon's time, in 1808, the Marne was linked to the Seine, but most of his other schemes proved to be too ambitious and were delayed until the Restoration.[135] Even then financial difficulties forced the governments to seek private funds for their realisation, which led to deficiencies not dissimilar to those experienced in England. Yet no less than 6,000 miles of canals were built during this period, and 1,200 miles between 1830 and 1848, all according to the original plan of 1818.[136] The most important of these were canals which linked the great rivers or ran parallel to rivers in sections where these were unsuitable for traffic.[137] They were mostly completed in the decade ending in 1848.

Holland had, of course, a very ancient and well-developed system of waterways. Yet, even there a whole series of canals was constructed after 1815 to link the coalfields with the inland ports and the sea.[138] Canal construction in Germany progressed at a much slower pace. Their total length never amounted to half the length of the French canals, though some individual canals were of equal size and importance. The best known of these was the Rhine–Elbe canal. Progress was held back by the political division of Germany, which made large-scale canal traffic schemes unworkable until the days of the *Zollverein*. Thus for a long time the rivers remained the only arteries of commerce in Germany. As most of the rivers in Europe flow through more than one country, very little was done to improve navigation upon them. It took the governments no less than sixteen years to regulate the international status of the Rhine (1816–31) and equally long to get rid of the innumerable toll and customs systems operating on the Rhine within Germany itself. Thus only the *Zollverein* and the coming of the steam engine, by the middle of the nineteenth century, transformed the Rhine into a good transport route.

The most noteworthy feature of the growth of river navigation and the rapid development of canals was the fact that it reflected a considerable change in the nature of commerce. From a luxury-trade it had become a trade in everyday necessities. More than that, it reflected the end of an era, the end of the era of mercantilism and the beginning of industrial society. To the mercantilist trade was the wealth of the world, and wealth meant national power. Power which could be gained by an 'increase of population, the protection of agriculture and industry, the economy of low wages, a favourable balance of trade, the development of colonial systems, the accumulation of capital with a resulting low rate of interest and a reform of the revenue system'.[139] The mercantilist notion of economic development was focused upon aggregate output; and not on the *per capita* rate of production and consumption—on power, and not welfare. The people for whom progress was desired were the 'people who mattered', namely the merchants, manufacturers and the rich landowners, and not all classes of society. That which was desirable in one class, the entrepreneurs' 'love of gain', was evil in another. They believed that the world's resources and domestic demand were strictly limited, which led them to the conclusion that low wages were the best incentive to hard work and maximum production. Consequently their trade was foreign trade and the goods they carried were for foreign consumption. As the middle of the eighteenth century drew closer and the relative labour shortage which had raised workers' wages abated and came to an end, the technological progress was already indicating the difference between total and *per capita* output differentials. Attitudes towards enterprise and labour changed. The protectionist restrictions were gradually relaxed and the belief that workers' wants were strictly limited withered away in the face of the expanding domestic market for both manufactures and foodstuffs. Gradually even mercantilist writers discovered that workers' wants are no less expansible than those of their 'betters', and realised the true significance of the new technological inventions. The nature of trade changed. Food, fuel, raw materials and common necessities to satisfy domestic requirements replaced luxuries and export goods at the top of the list of things which were to be transported. To the outward routes of the seas the inward routes of rivers and canals were added.[140]

MACHINES AND NEW SOURCES OF POWER

Thus, to the combination of population pressure, rising productivity of land and labour, division of labour within the traditional social units and between town and country, growing numbers of wage workers in the cities and in road and canal construction and the resultant development of the cash economy, and, no less important, the emergence of a new social ethic, a further dimension was added which took shape and grew with ever-increasing impetus from the middle of the seventeenth century—namely, the progress of technology. The latter, first in Britain and then in continental Europe and North America, very profoundly affected productivity and production, and totally revolutionised the whole structure of society. Indeed, it transformed Britain in under a century from a state which was predominantly agricultural and mercantile—'a nation of shopkeepers' as Napoleon still called it—into the 'workshop of the world'. In the early eighteenth century only a few processes in the manufacturing industries were mechanised. For example, in the woollen industry the following machines were in operation: the water-powered fulling mill,[141] the gig mill,[142] the knitting frame,[143] and the Dutch loom which could weave twenty-four narrow ribbons simultaneously.[144] Similarly there were some mechanised processes in the silk industry. For example, there was the silk-throwing machine which had been introduced into Britain from Italy in 1716 and resulted a few years later in the construction of the first modern factory in England. But there was still nothing really revolutionary about these machines. Technological improvements had been progressing for a long time, but neither the wool nor the silk market was capable of expanding at a pace which would have put exacting strains on either the nature or methods of production. However, the appearance of those innovations, and particularly the increasing use of the silk-throwing machine, was an important landmark in industrial history in that it was indicative of future possibilities, since it required only two or three 'operators to operate many hundreds of spindles and reels, which did the work that had previously been done by some hundreds of hand-throwsters'.[145] Here, indeed, for the first time was a machine with the capacity to create self-sustained growth through its impact on other stages of production; a machine whose 'appetite for energy was too large for domestic sources of power and whose mechanical superiority was sufficient to break down the resistance of the older forms of hand production'.[146]

All that was now required to transform traditional manufacture into modern industry was the application of the principle incorporated in the machine to a popular commodity with an elastic demand, i.e. a demand which swiftly reacts to changes in price. Cheap textiles fulfilled this condition. They were a popular commodity, which lent itself to mechanisation, and in which the mechanisation of one process led to a strain upon the other stages of production, so that as soon as one process was speeded up it stimulated progress in others. In addition to this, cheap textiles were the kind of product where the impact of improvements was soon felt through the economy as a whole. For these reasons it was cotton which ushered in the industrial revolution. As a raw material, cotton was more suitable for mechanisation than wool because it was both more uniform and less fickle.[147] Its supply was far more elastic than that of wool because it took less time to shift cultivation from one crop to another than it did to raise sheep.[148] Its market as a finished product was more elastic and expansive than that for woollen goods, because each fall in its cost of production or rise in incomes brought cotton goods into the reach of a greater number of people and because its tough, yet comfortable and light fabric opened for its sales the bulk of markets in the warmer areas, in southern Europe, America, India and Africa. 'The West Indies and mainland colonies (in America) together bought 10 per cent of English domestic exports in 1700–01, 37 per cent in 1772–73, about 57 per cent in 1797–98. Wool had played a big part in these gains: the sale of cloth in the new Atlantic market (America and Africa) grew sixfold from the beginning of the century to the eve of the American Revolution. Now it was cotton's turn.'[149] While Key's fly shuttle (1733)[150] and John Wyatt and Lewis Paul's spinning frame (1738)[151] had originally been designed for the woollen industry, they found their true importance in cotton. Once they were adopted, progress was swift, and produced a chain reaction in the form of an incessant sequence of 'challenge and response'. Under the pressure of an apparently unlimited demand for the new fabrics, the acceleration of one stage of production immediately caused bottle-necks in either the stage of production which followed or that which preceded it. Thus, for example, the fly-shuttle, which spread in the cotton industry during the third quarter of the eighteenth century, led to severe shortages in the supply of yarn, which in turn stimulated the introduction of Lewis Paul's spinning frame and a whole series of other improvements, culminating in Arkwright's water frame,[152] Hargreave's famous Jenny[153] and Crompton's Mule, so called because Crompton combined the rollers of the water frame with the movable carriage of the Jenny by placing the spindles on the carriage and the rollers where the spindles had stood in the Jenny.[154] By 1790 the mule had been improved very considerably. It had been adapted to take a greater variety of yarns and a greater number of spindles, so that it replaced no less than two hundred hand spinners. Consequently, carding was lagging behind and improvements had to be made in the preparatory processes to keep up with the demand of the spinners. In short, one innovation gave rise to another, and in the course of a few decades production was speeded up tremendously, while the quality of the product was also improved very considerably in the process.[155] The greater demand for yarn was followed by a rise in the demand for cotton,[156] while the greater supply of yarn led to a greater demand for weavers. Weavers' wages rose very sharply, and their working habits deteriorated equally sharply, until in the second quarter of the nineteenth century Roberts managed to improve Cartwright's power loom to such an extent that its use became economical. Then, when by 1822 the power loom could easily replace the work of two or three weavers, their prosperity began to diminish.[157] The success of the power loom was tremendous. According to David S. Landes' estimates[158] 2,400 power looms were operated in Britain in 1813, 14,150 in 1820, 55,500 in 1829, 100,000 in 1833, and 250,000 in 1850. From 1833 onwards each of these looms could replace the work of four manual weavers. Consequently by 1830 their wages had fallen to the 'irreducible minimum' of 6s. per week, and by the middle of the century there were barely three thousand hand weavers left in Britain. It goes without saying that the rapid improvement of the weaving and spinning techniques could not have taken place without an equally rapid growth in the development of the preliminary and finishing stages of cloth making. Here the gains were less spectacular but no less impressive. In addition to this there were also important improvements in the quality of the machines employed at all stages which resulted in equally significant improvements in the finished textile products.

The fact that the technological progress in cotton was not matched by an equally rapid one in similar industries—in woollens, for example—was partly due to the fact that the cotton markets could be easily expanded, but this was not the only reason. An even more important one can be found in the more intractable nature of the other raw material. For example, in 1840 cotton looms were working at approximately 150 picks per minute, while almost identical looms in the woollen trade could only do 46.

In iron making, as in the textile industry, there was a sequence of developments. Here too it was a case of 'challenge and response'. As iron making is basically a chemical refining process, i.e. the conversion of an ore into a finer compound or pure metal through the application of heat, the progress of the iron industry was closely dependent upon developments in the nature and supply of fuels. Fuels, however, are themselves compounds containing impurities, and from this point of view wood appears to be less harmful to iron than coal. Thus while coal was employed in various other industries, it was not used in the iron industry until the eighteenth century. Even then coal could not be easily employed because the right kind of coal was only seldom available near the iron ore deposits and its transportation from greater distances usually presented more insurmountable problems.[159] Moreover, the utilisation of coal in iron making requires a powerful forced draught, i.e. big furnaces, which had not been constructed, and could not have been constructed, before the last quarter of the eighteenth century.[160] In addition to this it also required an alteration in the character of the blast, i.e. the application of a hot instead of a cold blast in the smelting process of iron, and this was only understood in the second quarter of the nineteenth century.[161] Even had these improvements in the pig iron industry been realised at an earlier date, however, they would have had little effect, as pig iron is unyielding and cannot stand up to much pressure. Only after a way to remove the remaining impurities was found did it become a really useful, malleable form of iron. Small quantities of this iron were indeed produced from the fifteenth century onwards, but the product was not always satisfactory and was very costly. The change only came with Henry Court's invention of a technique which combined puddling and rolling in iron making into one process.[162] This not only produced a superior product—wrought iron—but made production far less costly and considerably faster, while the product itself became more suitable for the standardisation of the resultant products. With the new process all that was necessary in order to produce identical rails or bars or other similar iron goods was to shape or groove the rollers accordingly. As a result of this[163] iron consumption increased tremendously. [164] As the production of iron required coal, coal production had to rise similarly. According to the estimates summarised by Professor Landes[165] Britain was using perhaps 10 or 11 pounds of wrought iron per person in 1740 and about 20 pounds per person in the third quarter of the eighteenth century. While on the Continent iron consumption was less than 5 pounds per head even at the later date. One of the major causes of this difference was Britain's exceptionally good endowment of coal and iron resources.[166] As in the textile industry, the more spectacular advances in iron were accompanied by a host of minor improvements which widened the basis of the industry to a similar extent. The pioneers were hardly aware of the tremendous progress they were making; often their achievements were not the outcome of scientific research but of pragmatic experimentation. Indeed, many great ironmasters got excellent results without ever understanding why.[167] As it was, demand rose sharply with any new progress in the iron industry itself or in any other industry which could be improved by the substitution of iron for less lasting naterials. Industrial machines, agricultural implements and, from the middle of the nineteenth century, water and gas pipes and, above all, rails had an insatiable hunger for iron.[168] This insatiable demand called forth an equally brisk demand for coal. As with the weaving and spinning 'seesaw' a similar reciprocal relationship developed in coal and iron production. Yet, there was one significant difference. Coal is a material which cannot be replenished like cotton or wool. With each new demand mines had to be sunk more deeply and became progressively more expensive to exploit. For centuries this problem had been growing in the tin and silver mines and though, from the sixteenth century onwards, some very ingenious contrivances had been invented, especially for draining off underground water, they were all dependent on animate motive power which presented a great many logistic problems.[169]

The first important step forward towards a solution was the discovery of atmospheric pressure which eventually led to the invention of the steam engine.[170] In 1647 Pascal confirmed Torricelli's claim that pressure was inversely related to altitude by having a barometer carried to the top of a mountain. This showed that it was possible to use atmospheric pressure to work upon a piston underneath which a vacuum could be created.[171] The first successful attempt in this direction was achieved by Otto von Guericke, who in 1654 demonstrated in Ratisbon how, by sucking out the air from below a well-fitting piston in a cylinder, the piston descended in spite of the joint efforts of fifty men to hold it up.[172] The advantages of von Guericke's device were obvious for lifting heavy weights; all now depended on man's ability to create and to recreate the vacuum under the piston at will. After a number of not very successful attempts[173] Denis Papin in 1690 first got the idea of using steam for this purpose. 'Since it is a property of water that a small quantity of it turned into vapour by heat has an elastic force like that of air, but upon cold supervening is again resolved into water, so that no trace of the said elastic force remains', he wrote,[174] 'I conclude that machines could be constructed wherein water, by the help of no very intense heat, and at little cost, could produce that perfect vacuum. . . .' Papin's own engine was of little practical use but it demonstrated the principle upon which the more successful steam engines which followed were based. Eight years later Thomas Savery incorporated the idea in his 'Invention of Raising of Water and occasioning Motion to all sorts of Mill Work by the Impellent Force of Fire, which will be', according to his master patent of 1698,[175] 'of great use and Advantage for Drayning Mines, Serving Towns with Water, and for the working of all Sorts of Mills Where they have not the benefit of Water nor Constant Windes'. Indeed, it was Savery's interest in mining, his 'consideration of the difficulties the miners and colliers labour under by the frequent disorders, cumbersomeness in general of water engines', which, as he said, encouraged him, 'to invent engines to work by the new force'.[176] In the eighteenth century Savery's machines were replaced by others. Foremost among these was Thomas Newcomen's. Though apparently unaware of Savery's work, Thomas Newcomen invented and developed a machine similar to the former's. With the help of a plumber, named Calley, he invented 'a fire-machine for drawing water from the mines' to which he was induced[177] 'by considering the heavy costs of lifting water by means of horses as practised in the English tin mines.' In fact Newcomen's engine was greatly superior to Savery's; but, as the latter owned the patent for producing steam engines, the spreading of Newcomen's machine was delayed. By 1725, however, the Newcomen engine was used by mine-owners almost everywhere. On the continent of Europe Newcomen's machine was first installed in 1722 in Saxony and in 1726 in France.[178] In both areas it met with immediate success. Soon after this it spread into Belgium and Spain. When the Savery–Newcomen patent, which had in the meantime been bought up by a group of businessmen, expired in 1733, the machine spread very rapidly in coalmines throughout Europe. Thus deeper mining was made easier and less costly. Soon a great number of improvements to the machine followed, and the more convenient size of the cylinders, and improved workmanship,[179] made Newcomen's machine for almost half a century the most important single contribution to the exploitation of Britain's mineral resources and, thereby, to its industrial progress.

The next great step forward in the use of steam as a source of power came with James Watt's steam engine. Born in 1736, and having studied instrument making in London until 1757, Watt was appointed as 'Mathematical Instrument Maker' at Glasgow University. Unaware of the fact that his friend Joseph Black, the Professor of Chemistry at the University, had already observed the same phenomenon, Watt discovered that 'to make the best use of steam, it was necessary, first, that the Cylinder should be maintained always as hot as the steam which entered it; and secondly, that when the steam was condensed, the water of which it was composed, and the injection itself, should be cooled down to 100 degrees, or lower where that was possible. . . .'[180] The way to accomplish this did not immediately present itself, but early in 1765 he found that if a communication were opened between a cylinder containing steam, and another vessel which was emptied of air and other fluids, 'the steam, as an elastic fluid, would immediately rush into the empty vessel and continue to do so until it had established an equilibrium; and if the vessel were kept cool by an injection, or otherwise, more steam would continue to enter until the whole was condensed'. As Watt did not have the money to develop his invention, Black introduced him to John Roebuck, an industrialist with interests in coalmines, who obtained for him the famous patent of 1769 for 'A new Method of Lessening the Consumption of Steam and Fuel in Fire Engines'. In 1773 Roebuck went bankrupt and his share in

Watt's patent was bought up by a manufacturer named Boulton, whose works near Birmingham were suffering from a water shortage. By 1774, after successfully solving the problem, Watt's machines were installed, one in a Staffordshire coalmine, and another in a blowing blast-furnace in Shropshire. By that time Wilkinson had invented a superior boring-mill which enabled Watt to make use of a cylinder much better manufactured than the one available for his earlier machines. The effect was tremendous. It reduced coal consumption by more than 60 per cent. Not surprisingly, therefore, his machines were immediately in great demand in Cornwall, where mining for tin and metal was deep and coal very expensive. In 1782 Watt patented two additional improvements to his machine. One made the machine double-acting, by which he was able to get twice the original power from each cylinder. The other used the steam expansively instead of employing suction, as had previously been done. For the first improvement Watt replaced the chain connection between the beam and the piston-rod by a rigid connection constructed in such a way that the force was transmitted from the piston in both directions, i.e. up as well as down. For the second improvement he admitted steam into the cylinder only during the early part of the stroke, letting it drive the piston on by its expansion. One great advantage of the double-acting machine was its even motion, which characterised all rotative beam-engines which followed. However, his machines, though making some use of the expansive force of steam, remained essentially 'vacuum-engines', as Watt did not believe that steam could be used safely in any other way. These were more significant improvements than any which followed, until the middle of the nineteenth century.[181]

Yet, while Watt did not believe in the safe application of steam as an expansive force, others did. Jacob Leupold in Germany, and a little later Richard Trevithick in England, recognised the potentialities of an expansive steam engine, the first of which was operated by Trevithick in 1800 in a Cornish mine. A year later he designed a steam road-carriage which could carry some 30 cwt. at a speed of about nine miles an hour on an even road.[182] This road-carriage had surprisingly little commercial success. However, another steam carriage which he devised in 1804, and which ran on an iron tramway between the Pendarren ironworks and the Glamorganshire canal, was very successful. It could travel at four miles an hour carrying 25 tons of iron. Obviously it was highly economical. His next 'self-moving' machine was ordered by a colliery near Newcastle. There it influenced the design of another steam engine constructed by George Stephenson, at a nearby colliery,[183] and encouraged Trevithick to continue constructing stationary steam engines to drive, among other things, sugar and corn mills, water pumps and iron rollers. By this time, however, progress in the construction of expansive, or high pressure steam engines, was also being made in the United States by Oliver Evans. Most of the subsequent progress in steam engines during the first half of the nineteenth century took the form of improvements in the output of power and in fuel economy.[184]

'To summarise the state of steam-engine practice about 1830', writes H. W. Dickinson in his contribution to the *History of Technology*,[185] 'it may be said that the standard prime mover for larger mills and factories was the Watt jet-condensing steam-engine using steam at little more than atmospheric pressure. In smaller establishments, the "grasshopper" and the "table" engines were commonly employed. For pumping at mines and waterworks the high-pressure Cornish engine of Trevethick, usually working at about 70 lb. to the square inch, had no rival. For marine work, propulsion was by paddles always driven by side-lever engines, jet-condensing and working at about 4 or 5 lb. to the square inch. Locomotive practice was in its infancy.'

Thus the hunger for iron generated the hunger for more coal, and the latter the development of the steam engine which added to the already existent pressure for better tools and workmanship in related industries. This eventually led to an ever-increasing trend towards the substitution of inanimate energy for man and horse power whereby the power supply was increased many times and production costs greatly reduced. While progress in agriculture increased the productivity of land, progress in industry greatly increased the productivity of labour. Together they laid the foundation for the growth of national incomes.

Thus, for the first time, the possibility of a sustained growth of the volume of goods and services obtainable for each unit of human effort and accessible resources became a reality. The true beginning of this new stage in human history must be placed in eighteenth-century Europe, from where it spread, and is still spreading, throughout the rest of the world. It is true that there had been important developments even before the eighteenth century—but these were of a different nature and magnitude. They had never been important enough to break the close interdependence between population trends and living standards. The truly revolutionary change which took place in the eighteenth century in Europe was, therefore, that man's ability to produce material things was no longer strictly dependent upon his natural physical environment. By 1771 Arthur Young claimed, on the basis of a comparison of his national income estimates with those of Gregory King which were made in 1688, that average real incomes had doubled in England in the intervening time. Though the comparison may not be accurate it indicates the awareness of contemporaries of the undoubted rise in living standards which had taken place already. 'Whether the [British] economy was already launched on the path of sustained growth by the early 1770s is difficult to say', write W. A. Cole and Phyllis Deane, in their contribution to *The Cambridge Economic History of Europe*,[186] but 'the stream of British domestic exports had broadened to more than two and a half times their volume at the beginning of the century. Agricultural output is estimated to have expanded by about a fifth. The evidence for the textile industries suggests that their output may have doubled. The population of Birmingham (the centre for the metal industries) had quadrupled. In effect, there is a considerable weight of evidence in favour of the hypothesis that the process of economic development had gathered a formidable momentum in Britain before the industrial revolution took shape. By the turn of the century it was clear that, in spite of the wastes and distortions of war and inflation, what was happening to the British economy was something new in human experience. . . . National output was growing in global terms at a compound rate of 2 per cent per annum and in per head terms at nearly 1 per cent per annum.'

Next to Britain, in late eighteenth and early nineteenth century industrial development, came Belgium. Belgium was favoured by the abundance of suitable coal and by the great number of British 'expatriate' workmen and experts in manufacture. In the early part of the nineteenth century a very skilful engineering industry developed there, which was largely due to the integrated coal and iron works which had sprung into existence by that time. Yet within a short period the supply of coal could no longer keep pace with the demand of the fast-growing industry, and industrial growth was slowing down in the 1840s. In any case, Belgium was too small a country to serve as the industrial basis for all the rest of continental Europe. In the whole of France there were no more than 625 steam engines in operation by 1830 and about 5,200 by the middle of that century. The cause of this could hardly have been technological backwardness, for France was as scientifically advanced as Britain. The cause was economical—it was the high cost of coal more than anything else which held back France's industrial progress in the nineteenth century. In industries which were less dependent on the cheap supply of power, or which had water power readily available (such as the Alsatian textile industries), progress was similar to that in Britain. Yet this could not alter the fact that even by the middle of the century most French industries were still small workshops owned by their masters.

While industrial progress in France was held back by the lack of suitable natural resources, in Germany it was hampered by a host of legal, institutional, political—in short, man-made—impediments. Even as late as the year 1850 most German manufacture was still a subsidiary employment, and most iron making was still in the hands of small masters with workshops in the towns. Though coal was abundant in Germany, it could not be exploited before 1840 because of the political structure of the country (i.e. because of the division into small principalities which made it their business to impose all sorts of duties and other impediments on the flow of goods and raw materials). The rest of Europe was even less developed than Germany until the middle of the nineteenth century.

In the United States, mechanisation was never much in advance of Europe before 1850. There, too, most manufacture was 'home-made', usually by the familiar 'putting-out' or 'domestic' system. In fact, for a century after independence, America continued to have an almost typical colonial economy. Land, commerce, shipping and agricultural export crops, such as cotton, were the most attractive sectors for capital investments. Manufacture had very little attraction except during the years of war in Europe when trade became more difficult. By 1815, however, many of these war-time industries were no longer competitive and went out of business. Land was readily available and wages were high. And yet, by the middle of the century, the United States was again producing cotton goods equivalent to about a third of British production, making it the second greatest cotton manufacturing country in the world. In all other established industries, however, the United States was far behind Britain, although some industries, such as meat-packing, flour-milling and watch-making, which had not been 'industrialised' in Europe, were already being carried on in factories in the United States though few machines were employed. Under the pressure of high wages, much attention was given to the best possible organisation of labour and to the development of labour-saving devices. The latter, in turn, contributed to the development of the engineering industry, which, soon after the middle of the century, was to play a most important role in the production of agricultural equipment and in communications. Thus, the shortage of labour, the greater dispersion of population and the nature of the export crops, combined to turn American industrialisation, in its early stages, in a direction somewhat different from that which it had taken in Britain and Belgium.

In Britain, Belgium, France, Germany and the United States of America the new era of industrialisation and rising living standards had thus already begun by the middle of the nineteenth century, but it was still in its very infancy. The story of its growth and how it spread to other parts of the world is the subject of the following study.

NOTES

1. Thomas Robert Malthus, *An Essay on the Principle of Population*, 1798, Bk. I, Ch. 1.
2. United Nations *Population Studies*, No. 17, *The Determinants and Consequences of Population Trends*, New York, 1953, p. 12.
3. H. Gille, 'The Demographic history of northern European countries in the eighteenth century', *Population Studies*, Vol. III, No. I, June 1949, pp. 3–70.
4. United Nations *Population Studies*, *op. cit.*, Part II, Ch. IV.
5. F. A. Southard, 'Famine' in the *Encyclopedia of the Social Sciences*, Vol. VI, New York 1948, pp. 85–89. He mentions 450 localised famines which were recorded in Western Europe between the years 1000 and 1855.
6. H. Gille, 'The Demographic history . . .', *op. cit.*, pp. 3–70.
7. W. F. Ogburn, 'Malthusian theory and the population of Iceland 1750–1920', *Proceedings of the International Congress for Studies on Population*, Rome, 7–10 September 1931.
8. B. J. Stern, *Society and Medical Progress*, Princeton, 1941.
9. By comparison, in Ghana in 1960 the average farmer was producing enough food to feed 1½ working people, in the United States 12. *Vide* Ghana *Seven-Year Development Plan*, 1963–64 to 1969–70, pp. 8–10.
10. James Steuart, *Collected Works*, 1805, 'An Inquiry into the Principles of Political Economy', 1st ed. 1767, p. 35.
11. James Steuart, *op. cit.*, p. 153.
12. L. Dudley Stamp, *Our Developing World*, London, 1960, p. 19.
13. United Nations *Population Studies*, *op. cit.*, Tables II and III, pp. 11–12.
14. See Adam Smith, *Wealth of Nations*, 1776, Bk. IV, Ch. VII, Pt. II.
15. For some examples of this see T. S. Ashton, *An Economic History of England. The 18th Century*, London, 1955, pp. 30–62.
16. See for example Friedrich Engels, *The Condition of the English Working Class in 1848.*
17. Daniel Defoe, *A Tour thro' England and Wales* (Everyman ed.), Vol. I, pp. 277, 285, and Vol. II, p. 59.
18. R. H. Tawney, *Religion and the Rise of Capitalism*, Harmondsworth, 1948, p. 274.
19. R. H. Tawney, *op. cit.*, pp. 272–273.
20. A. P. Usher, 'The history of population and settlement in Eurasia', *The Geographical Review*, Vol. XX, No. 1, January 1930, pp. 110–132.
21. This, for example, took place in Europe during the century which followed the Black Death and the subsequent outbreaks of plague.
22. This may have been the case in the seventeenth century in Europe. *Vide* Y. S. Brenner, 'The inflation of prices in England, 1551–1650', *Economic History Review*, Vol. XV, No. 2, November 1962. See also F. J.

Fisher, 'Influenza and Inflation in Tudor England', *Economic History Review*, Vol. XVIII, No. 1, August 1965.

23. Warren S. Thompson, *Population Problems* (McGraw-Hill Series in Sociology), p. 77 and p. 106, Fig. 6–3, Percentage of the population urban and rural. It is interesting to note that the population of England and Wales was already distributed 60 per cent urban and 40 per cent rural as early as 1881.

24. M. C. Buer, *Health, Wealth, and Population in the Early Days of the Industrial Revolution*, London, 1926; M. G. Dorothy, 'Some Causes of the Increase of Population in the Eighteenth Century as Illustrated by London', *Economic Journal*, Vol. 32, 1922, pp. 325–352; A. Landry, 'La Démographie de l'ancien Paris', *Journal de la société de statistique de Paris*, No. 2, 1935, p. 37.

25. For the rise of towns see Warren S. Thompson, *op. cit.*, p. 389, Table 19–1. For example:

Town	*1800*	*Population in* *1850*	*1900*
New York	79,216	696,115	3,437,202
London	959,310	2,363,341	4,536,267
Paris	547,756	1,053,262	2,660,559
Moscow	188,654	332,878	1,174,673

26. Warren S. Thompson, *op. cit.*, pp. 390–391, Tables 19–2 and 19–3.

27. *Vide* Warren S. Thompson, *op. cit.*, pp. 390–391, Tables 19–2 and 3. It is interesting to compare the relationship between manpower in agriculture and in transport in India in 1931 and in the United States in 1820.

	India:	U.S.:
Agriculture, etc.	71·5%.	71·9%.
Trade and Transport	7·1%.	2·5%.

In 1950 the position in the U.S. was: Agriculture 12·5 per cent and Trade and Transport 32·5 per cent (with manufacturing and mechanical pursuits 32·0 per cent).

28. *Vide* Warren S. Thompson, *op. cit.*, pp. 388–389.

29. Adam Smith, *Wealth of Nations*, 1776, Vol. I, pp. 16–17.

30. Warren S. Thompson, *op. cit.*, p. 390.

31. T. K. Derry and Trevor I. Williams, *A Short History of Technology*, Oxford, 1960, pp. 311–312, 616.

32. Carl Eicher and Lawrence Witt, Eds., W. H. Nicholls, *Agriculture in Economic Development*, New York, 1964, p. 19.

33. William Ashworth, *A Short History of the International Economy Since 1850*, London, 1962, p. 3.

34. M. L. Hansen, *The Atlantic Migration 1607–1860*, Cambridge (Mass.), 1940.

35. M. R. Davie, *World Immigration*, New York, 1936, p. 305.

36. D. Kirk, *Europe's Population in the Interwar Years*, League of Nations, Geneva, 1946. (There are in fact no reliable statistics for this period.)

37. The American land policy is a good example.

38. J. Isaac, *Economics of Migration*, New York, 1947, pp. 21–22.

39. Karl Marx, *Das Kapital*, 1867, Vol. I, p. 594.

40. J. Isaac, *op. cit.*, p. 154.

41. For the data upon which this very simplified summary is based *vide* United Nations *Population Studies*, *op. cit.*, Table 16, p. 100. France, in the table given below, includes Switzerland and the Low Countries, while the Austro-Hungarian Empire, Russia, Poland, Portugal and Spain, which made up most of the emigration total after 1900, were excluded.

AVERAGE ANNUAL OVERSEAS EMIGRATION FROM EUROPE 1846–1910
(Thousands)

Year	*All Europe*	*Britain*	*Germany*	*Scandinavia*	*France, etc.*	*Italy*
1846–55	299·5	215·4	55·5	5·6	16·1	0·4
1856–65	208·2	133·6	46·4	7·1	6·7	6·1
1866–75	358·3	182·4	81·2	30·7	15·0	21·0
1876–85	458·2	171·4	108·9	40·8	15·7	46·5
1886–95	706·3	171·6	88·8	54·5	25·5	142·2
1896–1905	791·1	118·5	26·7	38·0	12·1	243·1
1906–10	1,436·7	234·6	26·4	43·7	17·6	402·4

42. *Vide* Abstract of Table No. 16, United Nations *Population Studies, op. cit.*, footnote No. 41, and United Nations *Population Bulletin* No. 1, December 1951.

43. *Vide* United Nations *Population Bulletin, op. cit.*, and footnote 41.

POPULATION AND MIGRATION FROM EUROPE
(Millions)

Year	*World Total Population*	*Europe and USSR Population*	*Annual (approx.) Overseas Migration from Europe. Total*
1650	470	103	
1750	694	144	
1850	1,091	274	0·257
1900	1,550	423	0·543 (1,039)
1950	2,403	594	0·400 (or more)

44. The following table constructed from the population data in the United Nations *Population Bulletin, op. cit.*, the *Annual Abstract of Statistics* No. 96, 1959, U.K., and Colin Clark's Table XXIII in *The Conditions of Economic Progress*, London, 3rd Ed., 1960, for production may illustrate this point though the data here cover only the United Kingdom in a later period of the industrial revolution.

Years	*Total Population*	*Males engaged in Agriculture and Fishing*	*Average hours in Agriculture*	*Product per Man-hour*
1861	24,525,000			
1867–69		1,556,000	3,200	0·142
1871	27,431,000			
1870–76		1,490,000	3,170	0·153
1881	31,015,000			
1877–85		1,408,000	3,120	0·159
1891	34,264,000			
1886–93		1,358,000	3,080	0·174
1901	38,237,000			
1894–1903		1,291,000	3,020	0·181
1911	42,082,000			
1904–10		1,327,000	2,970	0·188

45. Melchor de Jovellanos, *Informe de la sociedad económica al real y supremo consejo de Castilla*, 1795, p. 2.

46. Food and Raw Materials: British imports and exports since the time of the industrial revolution. (Thousands of pounds.)

	Imports		*Exports*	
Year	*Food*	*Raw Materials*	*Food*	*Raw Materials*
1890–94	169,985	110,209	10,233	23,316
1910–13	263,104	195,400	31,647	55,862
1924	543,051	324,267	56,928	106,489

Total British Exports and Imports 1815 and 1855 and 1895 (Thousands Pounds)

	1815	1855	1895
Imports	32,980	143,543	416,690
Exports	58,629	116,691	285,832

Source: Arthur Birnie, *An Economic History of the British Isles*, London, 1935, p. 289.

47.

YIELDS IN QUINTALS PER HECTARE OF LAND

	Wheat				
	1885–89	*1909–13*	*1925–29*	*1934–38*	*1949–51*
U.K.	20·3	21·3	22·5	23·1	27·3
Switzerland	14·1	21·3	22·0	24·1	27·7
Netherlands	18·8	23·5	29·8	30·3	36·9
Algeria	4·9	6·7	5·5	5·6	5·8

Source: Colin Clark, *op. cit.*, Table XXVIII, p. 296.

AREA OF LAND UNDER CULTIVATION IN ENGLAND AND WALES

Year	*1870*	*1880*	*1890*	*1900*	*1910*
Total (acres)	25,957,035	27,363,782	27,872,335	27,538,130	27,292,588
Corn crops	8,123,780	7,471,815	6,715,920	6,076,759	5,826,063

Source: W. Page, Ed., *Commerce and Industry: Statistical Tables*, 1919.

48. *Vide* G. E. Fussell and C. Goodman, 'Crop Husbandry in Eighteenth Century England', *Agricultural History*, Vol. XV, 1941, pp. 202–216; 1942, pp. 41–63.

49. For example, Flanders and Brabant in the Netherlands, and Norfolk, Suffolk and Essex in England.

50. James Steuart, *op. cit.*

51. C. Verlinden, *et al.*, 'Mouvements des Prix et des Salaires en Belgique au XVIe Siècle', *Annales*, Vol. X, 1955, pp. 173–198.

52. B. H. Slicher van Bath, *The Agrarian History of Western Europe A.D. 500–1850* (English translation Olive Ordish), London, 1963, p. 242.

53. G. Lefebvre, *Les Paysans du Nord pendant la révolution française*, 1924, pp. 207–208.

54. This apparently anti-Malthusian phenomenon was observed in the middle of the nineteenth century by J. H. Thünen, *Der Isolierte Staat in Beziehung auf Landwirtschaft und Nationalökonomie*, 1842.

55. G. Schröder-Lembke, 'Enstehung und Verbreitung der Mehrfelderwirtschaft in Nordostdeutschland', *Zeitschrift für Agrageschichte und Agrasoziologie*, 1954, pp. 123–133.

56. B. H. Slicher van Bath, *op. cit.*, pp. 176, 245.

57. B. H. Slicher van Bath, *op. cit.*, pp. 246–261.

58. B. H. Slicher van Bath, *op. cit.*, p. 261.

59. P. Lindemans, *Geschiedenis van de landbouw in België*, 1952, Vol. I, p. 58.

60. It is noteworthy that in 1800 Rotterdam sold her refuse to the

southern Netherlands rather than to the neighbouring farms. *Vide* A. Backhaus, *Entwicklung der Landwirtschaft auf den Gräflich Stolberg-Wernigrödischen Domänen*, 1888, pp. 131–136.

61. B. H. Slicher van Bath, *op. cit.*, p. 262, quotes Liveing's famous though premature eighteenth-century discovery of an artificial manure which was supposed to increase the seed, strengthen the plants, destroy weeds, moss and worms, kill insects, snakes and slugs, and was also easily transportable. It contained 12 lb. kitchen salt, 1 lb. salpetre and 20 lb. of finely sieved wood or coal ash.

62. E. Lipson, *The Economic History of England*, 1948, Vol. II, pp. 427–428; F. K. Riemann, *Ackerbau und Viehaltung im vorindustriellen Deutschland*, 1953; H. Sée, *Histoire économique de la France*, 1948, Vol. I, pp. 197–198.

63. *Vide* E. N. Salaman, *The History and Social Influence of the Potato*, 1949.

64. In England the potato achieved its widest expansion between 1770 and 1860, but with the growth of the corn trade with America and Russia people were once again using more cereals and less potatoes. *Vide* B. H. Slicher van Bath, *op. cit.*, pp. 267–268.

65. K. H. Connell, 'Peasant Marriage in Ireland after the Great Famine', *Past and Present*, 1957, XII, pp. 76–91. Irish population in 1841 was about eight millions and in 1911 it was only four and a half millions.

66. As little land as 0·65 hectare was sufficient to support a family, according to P. Lindemans, *op. cit.*, 1959, Vol. II, pp. 214–246.

67. Lord Townsend is largely responsible for the propagation of turnips in early eighteenth-century England. For the history of fodder crops, *vide* N. Riches, *The Agricultural Revolution in Norfolk*, 1937, pp. 84–85, 88.

68. Slicher van Bath, *op. cit.*, pp. 280–282.

69. *Vide* Slicher van Bath, *op. cit.*, Tables II and III, pp. 382–334.

70. Slicher van Bath, *op. cit.*, p. 294.

71. 'The German figures, which show a great increase in the number of sheep during the depression years from 1820 to 1845, form an exception. Before the rise of Australia as a wool-exporting land, the German states were the chief producers of wool during the first half of the nineteenth century' (p. 295).

72. R. Trow-Smith, *A History of British Livestock Husbandry*, 1957, Vol. I. Slicher van Bath, *op. cit.*, p. 296, writes: 'In the eighteenth century England won great renown through her livestock-breeders. The most famous was Robert Bakewell, but there were many others, such as Sir Thomas Gresley, Farmer Wester, Fowler, the Culley brothers, the Colling brothers, and others. In regard to breed improvement, we must remember that in the seventeenth and eighteenth centuries a great change took place in the qualities considered desirable in the animals. Sheep, formerly kept for their wool and manure ("four-legged dung-carts"), were now more valued for their meat. . . . By keeping a careful eye on the new requirements the stock-breeders [here the author means all kinds of stock not only sheep breeders] were able to achieve good results. The advances of the two hundred years consist more in the increased weight of the edible and most succulent parts of the animal than its greater total weight. The hides have grown thinner, the bones lighter.'

73. W. Jordan, *Viehseuchen im Bayerisch-Schwäbischen Voralpengebiet Während des 17., 18. und 19. Jahrhunderts*, 1951; Ch. F. Mullett, 'The Cattle Distemper in mid-eighteenth century England', *Agricultural History*, XX, 1946; W. G. Hoskins, *The Midland Peasant*, 1957, pp. 239–244.

74. L. Rogin, *The Introduction of Farm Machinery and its relation to the*

Productivity of Labour in the Agriculture of the United States during the Nineteenth Century, 1931, pp. 130–132.

75. B. H. Slicher van Bath, 'The Influence of Economic Conditions on the development of Agricultural Tools and Machines in History', *Mechanisation in Agriculture*, 1960, pp. 1–36. Quoted from Slicher van Bath, *The Agrarian History of Western Europe A.D. 500–1850*, p. 300.

76. Until that time the making of agricultural implements had been the monopoly of the local carpenter and blacksmith. *Vide* T. K. Derry and Trevor Williams, *A Short History of Technology from Earliest Times to A.D. 1900*, Oxford, 1960, p. 668.

77. T. K. Derry and Trevor I. Williams, *op. cit.*, p. 669.

78. In 1789 Ransome introduced the chilled cast-iron share, of which the under surface had been cooled more quickly than the upper surface, so that the blade was self-sharpening through wear.

79. Though reaping machines were invented both in Britain (Patrick Bell, 1780) and in America (Obed Hussey, 1833) they were not widely adopted before the middle of the nineteenth century.

80. In 1860, McCormick's firm in America produced 4,000 McCormick reaping machines a year.

81. *Vide* Appendix B in E. H. Phelps Brown and Sheila V. Hopkins, 'Seven Centuries of Building Wages', *Economica*, 1955, Reprinted in E. M. Carus-Wilson, Ed., *Essays in Economic History*, Vol. II, p. 196.

82. For a discussion of economic incentives for and consequences of technological inventions, *vide* C. F. Carter's contribution to the symposium on the history of science held in Oxford in July 1961 and published, A. C. Crombie, Ed., in *Scientific Change*, London, 1963, pp. 678–690.

83. According to Johnson, *Disappearance of the Small Landowner*, p. 90, the acreage which was enclosed between 1700 and 1760 was 312,363; between 1761–1801, 3,180,871; and between 1802–1844, 2,549,345. See also G. T. Griffith, *Population Problems in the Age of Malthus*, 1926.

84. The question of whether the end of slavery caused the progress of the machine or the machine led to the abolition of slavery cannot here be discussed.

85. This was so, firstly, because horses had to supply the haulage power for most of the machinery, and therefore the farmer who wished to employ machines must have been able to keep many horses; secondly, as the equipment was only efficient on level land of fair size which was reasonably well drained, only farmers who had such land could use machines; finally, as most of the machines were only good for cereal farming.

86. *Vide* Phelps Brown and Sheila Hopkins, *op. cit.*, Appendix B, p. 196.

87. B. H. Slicher van Bath, *op. cit.*, p. 307.

88. N. Gash, 'Rural Unemployment 1815–1834', *Economic History Review*, Vol. VI, 1935–36, pp. 90–93.

89. Probably 75 per cent of the farms in north-eastern France were of less than three hectares.

90. In 1880, town population in England and Wales amounted to 67·9 per cent, in Belgium to 43·0 per cent, in France to 34·8 per cent, and in Germany to 29·1 per cent of the total population. United Nations *Population Studies*, 17, *op. cit.*, p. 109. Total population (1900) U.K. 37·9 m., Belgium 6·7 m., France 40·1 m.

91. This will be discussed in a later chapter dealing with post-revolutionary France.

92. *Vide* F. Lütge, *Deutsche Sozial- und Wirtschaftsgeschichte*, 1952.

93. Adna Ferrin Weber, *The Growth of Cities in the Nineteenth Century.*

A Study in Statistics, 1899. Quoted here from the Cornell University Press edition, New York, 1963.

94. Adna Ferrin Weber, *op. cit.*, p. 157.

95. Adna Ferrin Weber, *op. cit.*, p. 160.

96. Adna Ferrin Weber, *op. cit.*, p. 161.

97. *Vide* p. 2. Quotation from James Steuart, *op. cit.*

98. Adna Ferrin Weber, *op. cit.*, p. 170.

99. *Vide* W. Cunningham, *Growth of English Industry and Commerce*, Cambridge, 1890–91, Vol. I, pp. 76–90.

100. For the growth of English cities see W. Cunningham, *op. cit.*, p. 23; For Continental cities see Robert S. Dickinson, *The West European City. A Geographical Interpretation*, London, 1951; for a good example see p. 54.

101. Adna Ferrin Weber, *op. cit.*, pp. 171–172.

102. For discussion of the growth of towns in the middle ages see H. Pirenne, *Economic and Social History of Medieval Europe.*

103. Adna Ferrin Weber, *op. cit.*, p. 176.

104. J. W. Ashley, *An Introduction to English Economic History and Theory*, Part II, *The End of the Middle Ages*, London, 1893, Bk. II, Ch. I, 'The Supremacy of the Towns'.

105. It must be noted that in comparison to the trade in everyday necessities with which we are concerned here the trade in costly luxuries, with which we are not concerned in this chapter, was insignificant.

106. See progress of specialisation in agricultural production, pp. 96–97.

107. Adna Ferrin Weber, *op. cit.*, p. 181.

108. This was indeed the case during the great railway expansion era in the United States.

109. A. M. Milne and J. C. Laight, *The Economics of Inland Transport*, 2nd ed., London, 1963, p. 24.

110. It is interesting to note that even today when one approaches the Swiss–Austrian border, for example, the last part of the road through 'no mans land' is usually much inferior to the rest of the road.

111. An eighteenth-century source quoted by Christopher I. Savage, *An Economic History of Transport*, London, 1959, p. 12–13. In the late nineteenth century this method was still employed in northern Ghana.

112. Arthur Young, quoted from S. Smiles, *Lives of the Engineers*, London, 1862–65.

113. Milne and Laight, *op. cit.*, p. 26.

114. Names like Metcalf, Telford and Macadam are usually mentioned as the pioneers in this field. The turnpike system is still in use in the United States and Italy for motorway construction in our time.

115. Christopher Savage, *op. cit.*, pp. 25–26.

116. A deficiency which is part of a *weltanschauung*, still very common, for example, in Ghana to this very day, that office is something to be enjoyed by the holder rather than a responsibility [Y. S. B.].

117. S. and B. Webb, *English Local Government—The Story of the King's Highway*, 1913, p. 141. Quoted from Christopher I. Savage, *op. cit.*, p. 26.

118. R. H. Spiro, 'Macadam and the Metropolis Turnpike Trust', *Journal of Transport History*, November, 1956, p. 208.

119. The most famous of these are the roads over the Simplon and Mont Cenis.

120. It is noteworthy that after 1870–71 these roads were added to the German system, which often causes some statistical difficulties when assessing the rates of road construction in France and Germany.

121. Lavergne, *L'Economie rurale de la France.*

122. See picture of water lock in Charles Singer, E. J. Holmyard, A. R. Hall and Trevor I. Williams, Eds., *A History of Technology*, Oxford, 1958, Vol. IV, p. 567, and in Derry and Williams, *op. cit.*, p. 186.

123. Vallans (1577) quoted from Derry and Williams, *op. cit.*, p. 186.

124. For history of canal locks in England, *vide* Derry and Williams, *op. cit.*, pp. 436–440.

125. Christopher I. Savage, *op. cit.*, p. 16. This is, of course, only true of England.

126. The Duke of Bridgewater believed that by a canal joining Worsley via the Irwell with Manchester he could reduce the price of coal from 5½d. or 7d. per cwt. to 4d. per cwt. *Vide* Christopher I. Savage, *op. cit.*, p. 17.

127. See Maps of canals and rivers in Singer, Holmyard, Hall and Williams, *op. cit.*, pp. 564–565.

128. For details, *vide* Trevor I. Williams and T. K. Derry, *op. cit.*, pp. 436–438.

129. The greatest boom in canal construction was in the years 1792–93.

130. D. T. Jackman, *The Development of Transportation in Modern England*, 2nd ed., 1962.

131. Christopher I. Savage, *op. cit.*, p. 23.

132. For example, the Canal de Languedoc connecting the Atlantic with the Mediterranean.

133. For example, the Canal de Picardy.

134. Louis XVI did not complete the canal because he ran out of funds. Roger Pilkington, in his contribution to Singer, Holmyard, Hall and Hill, Eds., *History of Technology*, Vol. IV, p. 556, tells the following little story: 'The St. Quentin canal incorporated two tunnels. The longer was 3¼ miles long, and when in due course the canal was opened no boatman dared to enter it. In desperation the authorities offered freedom from all canal dues in perpetuity to the first boat to pass through the tunnel, and one man volunteered. His boat . . .' was still navigating on the canal tax free near the end of the nineteenth century.

135. The most famous among these were the Amiens–Düsseldorf and the St. Denis–St. Martin projects.

136. After the allies evacuated France, a systematic plan for the construction of canals was drawn up and abided by until it was completed.

137. For example, the canals which linked the Rhone to the Rhine, the Marne to the Rhine, and the Aisne to the Marne.

138. Also in this period many port entrances were made deeper, such as the entrance to Amsterdam across the Zuider Zee.

139. Eli Heckscher, *Encyclopedia of Social Sciences*, p. 347.

140. For 'Mercantilism', see Eli Heckscher, *Mercantilism*, 1955, Vols. I and II, or the brief summary in Y. S. Brenner, *Theories of Economic Development and Growth*, London, 1966, Ch. I.

141. The fulling mills were introduced from the Continent in the thirteenth century.

142. They date from the sixteenth century. *Vide* Derry and Trevor Williams, *op. cit.*, p. 108.

143. Invented in 1598.

144. *Vide* Derry and Trevor Williams, *op. cit.*, p. 107.

145. *Vide* Derry and Williams, *op. cit.*, p. 100.

146. David S. Landes, 'Technological Change and Development in Western Europe', in *The Cambridge Economic History of Europe*, Cambridge, 1965, Vol. VI, Pt. I, p. 311.

147. A fact which must have played an important role when machines were still very poorly constructed.

148. See discussion of this point by D. S. Landes, *op. cit.*, p. 313.

149. D. S. Landes, *op. cit.*, pp. 313–314.

150. *Vide* Derry and Williams, *op. cit.*, p. 107 (picture).

151. *Vide* Derry and Williams, *op. cit.*, p. 105.

152. *Vide* Singer, Holmyard, Hall and Williams, *op. cit.*, p. 278.

153. *Vide* Singer, Holmyard, Hall and Williams, *op. cit.*, p. 279.

154. *Vide* Singer, Holmyard, Hall and Williams, *op. cit.*, p. 279.

155. *Vide* Singer, Holmyard, Hall and Williams, *op. cit.*, pp. 280–305.

156. This was approximately four million lb. in 1768–72 and forty-seven million lb. in 1798–1802.

157. The delay in the spreading of the loom was not only due to the normal technical and financial difficulties accompanying almost every new invention but also to the great fluctuations in demand caused by the Napoleonic Wars and the Continental blockade. *Vide* Singer, Holmyard, Hall and Williams, *op. cit.*, pp. 300–302.

158. *The Cambridge Economic History of Europe*, Vol. VI, Pt. I, p. 316.

159. This explains the earlier rise of the iron industries in Britain, Germany and Belgium, where coal and iron were found together in some places.

160. *Vide* Singer, Holmyard, Hall and Williams, *op. cit.*, pp. 103–104, 183.

161. *Vide* Singer, Holmyard, Hall and Williams, *op. cit.*, p. 109, 253.

162. Singer, Holmyard, Hall and Williams, *op. cit.*, pp. 106–107. 'Cort is also credited with the invention of grooved rollers, . . . patented in 1783. There too, however, he had predecessors. . . . Previously, bars had to be made either by hammering, or by cutting hot strips from a rolled plate with a slitting-mill. With grooved rollers 15 tons of iron could be dealt with in 12 hours, whereas it was difficult to produce one ton in the same time with the forge-hammer.'

163. David S. Landes, *op. cit.*, p. 325.

PIG-IRON OUTPUT OF GREAT BRITAIN (IN LOG TONS)

1740	17,350	1806	258,206	1835	940,000
1788	68,300	1825	581,367	1839	1,248,781
1796	125,079	1830	678,417	1848	1,998,568
				1852	2,701,000

Vide also Paul Mantoux, *The Industrial Revolution in the Eighteenth Century*, Revised Edition of 1961, London, pp. 271–310.

164. *Vide* Singer, Holmyard, Hall and Williams, *op. cit.*, Figure 62, p. 107.

165. *The Cambridge Economic History of Europe*, Vol. VI, Pt. I, p. 324.

166. It is possible that the initial rise in the demand for iron in Britain was stimulated by the war requirements of the Napoleonic Wars, but by 1815 the self-sustained nature of the demand is well apparent.

167. *Vide* W. G. Hoffmann, *British Industry 1700–1950*, Oxford, 1955. His tables give an excellent indication of the tremendous cumulative effect.

168. When Cort patented his new process in 1783 Britain was behind France in iron production. Sixty years later she produced more iron than the rest of the world taken together, though production had risen everywhere.

169. Because both men and horses have to be fed.

170. The accepted explanation of the rise of water was that 'nature abhorred a vacuum'. *Vide* Singer, Holmyard, Hall and Williams, *op. cit.*, p. 168.

171. Singer, Holmyard, Hall and Williams, *op. cit.*, p. 169.
172. Singer, Holmyard, Hall and Williams, *op. cit.*, p. 169, Figure 100.
173. Singer, Holmyard, Hall and Williams, *op. cit.*, pp. 170–171.
174. Quoted from Singer, Holmyard, etc., *op. cit.*, p. 171.
175. Quoted from Singer, Holmyard, etc., *op. cit.*, p. 172.
176. Thomas Savery, *The Miner's Friend*, 1702, quoted from Singer, Holmyard, etc., *op. cit.*, p. 172. H. W. Dickinson in Singer, Holmyard, etc., quotes the following advertisement of 1702 to show Savery's energetic business approach: 'Captain Savery's engines which raise Water by the force of Fire in any reasonable quantities and to any height, being now brought to perfection and ready for publick use; These are to give notice to all Proprietors of Mines and Collieries which are incumbered with Water; that they may be furnished with Engines to drain the same, at his Workhouse in Salisbury Court London . . . , where it may be seen working on Wednesday and Saturday . . .'
177. According to Marten Triewald, a craftsman who came to work with him.
178. In France the machine was first installed near Paris to supply the city with water from the Seine.
179. It is interesting to note that, as Dickinson, in Singer, Holmyard, etc., *op. cit.*, observes, the development of Newcomen's machine after his death was 'due to practical men, for the philosophers seemed to have considered machinery beneath their notice'. Smeaton, for example, designed an engine in 1775 for emptying the docks at Kronstadt (Russia) with a 66 in. diameter cylinder.
180. Quoted from Singer, Holmyard, etc., *op. cit.*, p. 182.
181. For an illustration, see Singer, Holmyard, etc., *op. cit.*, p. 187, Figure 107.
182. *Vide* Singer, Holmyard, etc., *op. cit.*, p. 188.
183. This was the famous Killingworth colliery steam engine constructed in 1813.
184. From the beginning of the nineteenth century more progress was made in the construction of compound engines. A beam-engine with two cylinders operating parallelly side by side, which showed a 50 per cent fuel economy, was constructed by Arthur Woolf in 1811. In 1815 Woolf managed to get a patent for the new design for France and soon many of these machines were made there and continued to be made there until well into the second half of the nineteenth century. By that time Trevithick's engines were being employed for corn threshing, meal grinding, etc., and were already causing some unemployment problems.
185. Charles Singer, E. J. Holmyard, A. R. Hall and Trevor I. Williams, Volume IV. See also pp. 195–196.
186. Vol. VI, Pt. I, Ch. I, p. 9.

Chapter II

POPULATION

WORLD TRENDS IN POPULATION GROWTH

'At least two periods of secular increase can be tolerably well identified in the demographic history of medieval and early modern Europe, the first extending from about the middle of the eleventh to the end of the thirteenth, the second from the middle of the fifteenth to the end of the sixteenth century. . . . In this sense the demographic development of the eighteenth century was not unique. What was unprecedented about it was the fact that the secular upward movement started from a higher level, and that it was able to maintain, and for some time even increase, its momentum. Population growth in the eighteenth and nineteenth centuries, unlike that of previous epochs, was not terminated and reversed by catastrophe.'[1] The trend of population growth in the rest of the world followed that of Europe.[2] From the middle of the nineteenth century onwards the populations of Asia, Africa and the Americas increased very rapidly, reaching an unparalleled rate of acceleration in the second quarter of the twentieth century, just at the time when, 'owing to the personal decisions of millions of human beings, not to Acts of God such as the Black Death of the fourteenth century',[3] the sharp rise in European population was slowing down.

Yet even in nineteenth-century Europe the pattern of accretion was neither uniform from a geographical point of view nor evenly spread in time. In the first half of the century it was most impressive in the north and west; in the second half in the south and east.[4] Until the thirties total population accretion in Europe progressed at the rates of between 6·5 and 9·4 per 1,000, from then and until the seventies it varied between 5·8 and 7·7 per 1,000, and from the seventies to the end of the century it rose steadily from 8·3 to 9·9 per 1,000.[5] After the turn of the century the rate of population growth abated in Europe and was overshadowed by the rates of growth experienced in other parts of the world.[6]

THE ACCRETION OF PEOPLE IN EUROPE

Our knowledge of *why* and *how far* European population grew in the seventeenth and eighteenth centuries is deficient. The source

FIGURE I

The Acceleration of World Population Growth

(The Rate of the rate of Growth)

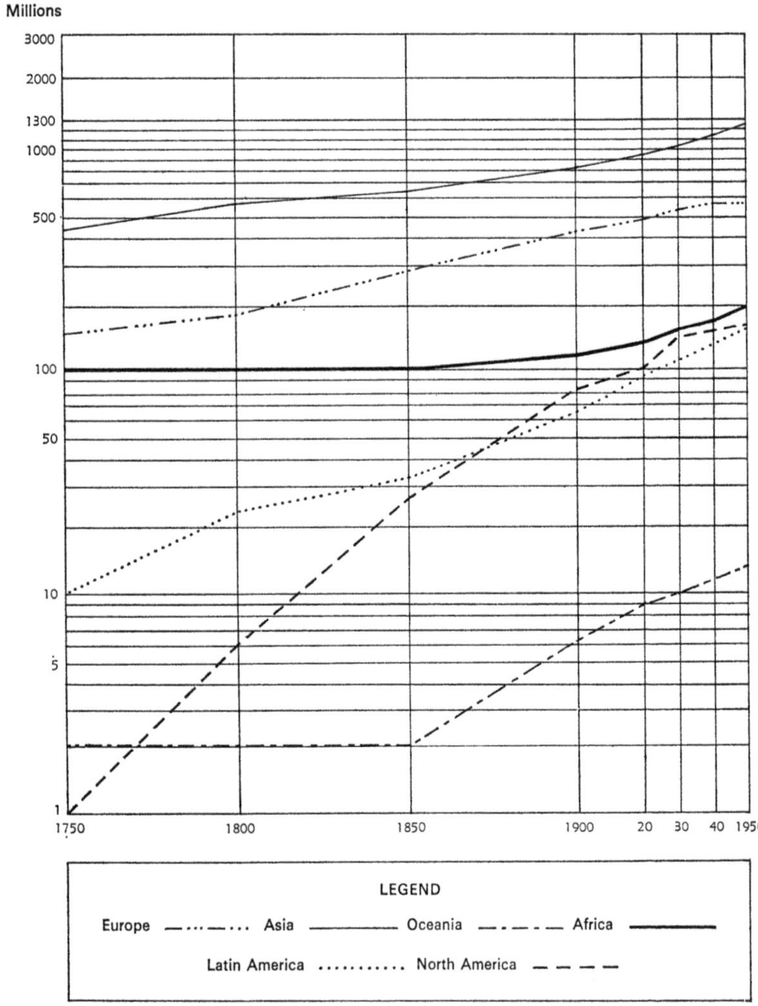

FIGURE 2

Rate of Population Growth
Selected Countries in Europe

(Annual per 1.000)

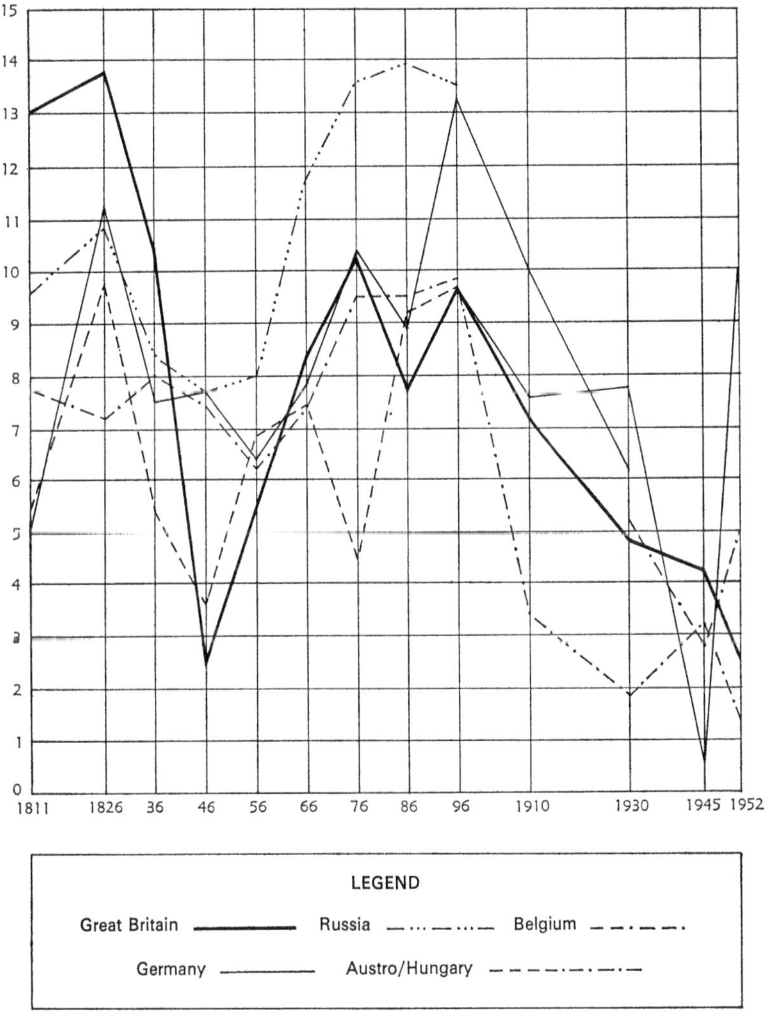

material is scarce and unreliable. Where the material is satisfactory from the statistical point of view, it is usually confined to limited groups of people who are not typical for the population as a whole;[7] where the records cover a wider range of society they normally fail to provide some rather essential data.[8] We do not even know whether it was a decline in the death rate or a rise in the birth rate which set off the increase in Europe's population. The traditional explanation is that there was a fall in death rates, and particularly in infant mortality, due to improvements in medicine and public health, which was followed by an inflated accretion of people when the greater number of surviving children reached maturity. This explanation can no longer be accepted without very severe reservations.[9] The evidence against it in Professor McKeown and R. G. Brown's article on the medical improvements during this period shows that little medical progress had actually taken place before the end of the eighteenth century and that little of it affected the greater majority of people.[10] In fact only in the case of vaccination against smallpox do the authors admit a substantial effect on the prevention or cure of disease earlier than the twentieth century.[11] Moreover, even after the great discoveries of Pasteur and Koch, in the last quarter of the nineteenth century, the contribution of medical care to population growth was far less direct than the traditional theory suggested. What is indicated by the evidence is a change in the causes of death rather than an outright reduction of mortality rates.[12] 'In the 1840s about a third of all deaths were due to infectious diseases, and almost a half to infectious and respiratory diseases taken together. In the 1940s infectious diseases had almost disappeared from the list; instead, over a third of all deaths were due to circulatory diseases—diseases of the heart and the coronary arteries—and just over half to circulatory diseases and cancer taken together.'[13] Population growth, in as far as it was the consequence of improvements in medical care and therapy, can therefore only be explained as a result of higher life expectation. This is so because the infectious diseases, which became less frequent, are more common with the younger age groups, and the circulatory diseases, which became more frequent, are more characteristic of the older age groups. Yet, with all these reservations in mind it is still generally accepted by historians of the eighteenth century that a reduction in the incidence of epidemics took place in the middle of that century which almost certainly led to a higher birth rate in the period which followed. In this sense, then, it still appears to be true that population growth may well have been the outcome of a decline in infant mortality.

The reason for the diminution of epidemics in the middle of the eighteenth century is not quite clear. The most frequently cited explanation is the 'ecological revolution among rodents', i.e. the disappearance from Europe of the rat carrying the plague flea. This explanation does, however, very little to dispel the mist which surrounds the whole problem. It merely substitutes one unknown for another. Instead of getting an answer to the question about the basic causes of the decline in mortality from epidemics, we are now faced with the problem of explaining the disappearance of the black rat from Europe.[14] The other evidence in support of the 'medical theory', the increasing concern with health—of which the spreading of inoculation among the aristocracy in the early eighteenth century and the growing volume of literature about personal cleanliness and child care in the later half of that century are taken to be indicative—is, like the elimination of the black rat, more likely to be the record of the symptoms rather than of the causes of the phenomenon. The more profound explanations appear to be climatic or economic. While little is known about the former,[15] the latter presupposes a sequence of events in which higher living standards have to precede population growth.[16] This proposition, however, which has not gone unchallenged since the days of Malthus, need not be universally true.

The general state of knowledge regarding the causes of early modern European demographic changes is too thin, and the information itself is too ambiguous to draw any clear conclusions about the links between population movements and economic changes. 'A vast range of possible connections between changes in nuptiality, fertility and mortality on the one hand, and the industrial and agricultural patterns of their regions on the other', has indeed been indicated by students of this problem, '. . . but they have also provided much evidence of the existence of movements in vital rates not visibly corresponding to economic patterns'. In the words of D. E. C. Eversley,[17] 'Apart from the autonomous variables of climate, we find that diseases do not always run their courses according to prevailing living standards or employment opportunities. Harvests and sickness fluctuate, but not always together. Marriage and fertility respond to changes in the levels of real wages, but the relationship is sometimes direct and sometimes inverse. In other words, social conventions, traditions and prejudices, political necessities and religious scruples supervene to blur the simple outline. The pattern may be highly complex, and allow no simple or unitary explanations. Each facet of the situation may have its own set of data and causal links.' What does emerge from the evidence is that epidemics and harvest failures became less frequent in the second half of the eighteenth century and that at almost the same time the Plague disappeared almost entirely from northern Europe. In addition to this it appears fairly evident that life expectancy had risen substantially since its trough in the middle of the seventeenth century, a fact which by itself should account for a cumulative accretion of people in the period that followed.[18]

As for the positive factors which might have contributed to population growth, such as earlier marriages and higher fertility, the position is no less obscure.[19] In so far as marriage is concerned it is fairly clear that the trend was away from rather than towards early marriages.[20] It is true that much of the evidence upon which this statement rests is taken from specific groups of population, the aristocracy and towns, but as it is well known that most marriages were, until late into the nineteenth century, arranged by the families of the partners with a clear and deliberate regard for the economic merits of the union, and as it is also well known that peasant societies were, and still are, more inclined than town people to act in this manner, it appears not unreasonable to believe that this trend towards later marriages was more or less representative of western Europe as a whole.[21] In fact, as Mr. Hajnal has shown, western European society in the eighteenth and nineteenth centuries differed from all other societies in its high ages at marriage and high proportion of people who never married at all.[22] To date the beginning of this pattern is again rather difficult. All that can be said with a degree of certainty is that it was already well established in the eighteenth century.[23] One authority,[24] by reference to the legal regulations regarding the age of puberty, places its initiation in the late fifteenth or early sixteenth century.[25] But legal arrangements are seldom the cause of change, more often they merely reflect it and must not be taken as reliable guides for the beginning of a new development.[26] Yet, one fact is fairly certain—that, as a rule, in the eighteenth and nineteenth centuries men in western Europe would not or could not marry before they owned land of their own or had completed their apprenticeship.[27] As François de la Rochefoucauld observed on his visit to England in 1784, 'Perhaps another reason for [late marriages in England] is because it is usual to set up house immediately after marriage. The young couple never stay with their parents and they must be sensible enough to avoid extravagance both in their conduct and in their expenditure.'[28] How far this evidence of late marriages is conclusive, and to what degree it can be extended to the other countries in which the great accretion of people took place in the eighteenth century, is difficult to assess. P. Deprez, for example, writing about eighteenth-century Flanders, mentions 'improved legitimate fertility' and ascribes it to 'the relatively low age of women at the time of their first marriage' and to the relatively advanced age of women at the time of their last confinement.[29] Yet his statistics of the average age of women at first marriage show an inclination towards later rather than earlier marriages in the period under consideration.[30] Apparently, therefore, neither the theory of 'medical improvements' nor that of 'earlier marriages' has adequate supporting evidence. Most other theories stress biological, economical and sometimes ecological factors, so that we learn of the existence of 'marked differences in fertility even when marriage rates were the same',[31] and that 'even in régimes in which there is little deliberate control of conception and in which age at marriage is not changing significantly, it does not follow that the number of live-births to a marriage in which both partners survive to the end of the child-bearing period is necessarily constant or extremely large. . . . Ability to conceive may be related to nutrition or health (gonorrhoea may, for example, be an impeding factor); foetal or conception wastage may change, and the probability of conception may be reduced by prolonged breast-feeding or by social or religious taboos on intercourse. . . .'[32] Thus, even if a higher fertility could be shown for the period following the middle of the eighteenth century, the question why this should have happened will still remain unanswered.

The answer which seems to present itself is a higher standard of living. This would account for a higher rate of survival, together with positive changes in human fertility. If, then, it were true that people married later in the eighteenth century because, as Cantillon tells us,[33] certain living standards, which were of course different from class to class, were required for setting up a new household, it is not unreasonable to assume that marital fertility was higher than before and that the children born of such economically more viable unions had a better chance of survival.[34] However, the economic explanation for the sustained increase in northern European population during the eighteenth and nineteenth centuries can be accepted independently. It need not depend upon the evidence of changes in the marriage patterns. Professor Utterström discovered that 'underlying Denmark's (and Skàne's) rapid population increase after the late 1700s was a series of comprehensive agrarian reforms which chiefly benefited the peasantry. In conjunction with the steep rise in grain prices, especially during the French Revolution and Napoleonic Wars, the reforms led to a great deal of new cultivation and a large increase in agricultural employment', and consequently to higher living standards and population growth.[35] Similarly, 'there was a relatively long period of mild winters during the first half of the eighteenth century' in

Sweden which coincided with a drop in epidemic diseases akin to that of the period 1820–50 which made it easier particularly for the poor to survive.[36] In Flanders too, 'the history of population cannot be separated from economic and social history'.[37] In the châtellenie du Vieuxbourg and the sandy parts of the north of Flanders, which had a highly developed linen industry in the eighteenth century, population growth was considerable from 1740 onwards; while in the Pays de Schorisse and the intermediate villages—that is to say in the industrialised areas in a state of transition, with mixed though mainly sandy soil—population increase was far less impressive in the second half of the eighteenth century. This is also true of the Pays d'Alost, where rural industry was then in decline and where the soil is mixed and for the most part clay. In the non-industrialised north of eastern Flanders population was actually diminishing after 1740 and birth-marriage ratios were very low.[38] In Finland, population was persistently declining in the eighteenth century, and again this may be traced back to bad economic conditions resulting from crop failures, war and foreign occupation followed by epidemics.[39] Wars, famine and epidemics are also held to be the cause for the low rate of population growth in pre-eighteenth-century France.[40] But the eighteenth century in France is of special interest because it appears to be the period when birth-control began to spread among the rural mass of the population.[41] Yet France did not experience the beginnings of industrialisation, as England did in this period, nor did it undergo a period of economic transition which could account for higher living standards and subsequent population growth. The climatic-economic explanation is therefore 'negative' (i.e. the absence of those major catastrophes which until the beginning, or even the middle of the eighteenth century, destroyed in a few years, if not months, the surplus accumulated during a few decades free from such calamities), rather than 'positive', i.e. through deliberate man-made economic improvements.[42] According to Louis Henry therefore, the 'reduction in the level of mortality in the period 1750–90 is enough to explain why the increase in population during this period was much more pronounced than it had been previously'.[43] In Britain calculations of life expectancy at birth in the eighteenth century show[44] an unmistakable and persistent climb from the low point to which the group born in 1650–74 had fallen.[45] The evidence for this was taken from the death rates among peers, but, as Professor Glass points out, the probability that the population as a whole also experienced a considerable fall in its death rates is evident. 'For given the different economic circumstances, it is hardly likely that the general population would have shown right back to the generations born at the end of the seventeenth century the relatively light mortality which was not achieved by the peerage until after the generation of 1725–49. As yet, however, there is little factual material available for groups below the peerage in economic and social status. . . .'[46] This explanation of population growth, i.e. by longer life expectancy, has of course the merit of combining both the higher fertility (longer ability to bear children) and lower mortality (wastage through epidemics and famine) theories. It only helps to see the mechanism of growth, however, and not the underlying, and in this context more important, causes of the process of population growth.

According to writers in the late eighteenth and early nineteenth centuries the 'long term changes in the size of population were primarily the result of changes in the supply of or demand for labour'.[47] This *par excellence* economic explanation argues that if the demand for labour were continually increasing, 'the reward of labour must necessarily encourage in such a manner the marriage and multiplication of labourers, as may enable them to supply that continually increasing demand by a continually increasing population'.[48] Thus the crux of the problem is whether the eighteenth-century accretion of people was brought about by extraneous factors, by ecological or climatic changes, which can therefore be regarded as the source of economic progress,[49] or was the result of economic progress and therefore indigenous to the economic development. Neither of these alternatives entirely excludes the other, but for the study of economic growth it seems extremely important to detect the aspect which needs to be stressed.[50]

Professor Habakkuk points out that a distinction ought to be made in pre-industrial society between the 'forces which determine the long-term changes in the size of the population and those which determine short-term fluctuations'.[51] Regarding the short-term fluctuations, it is obvious that those of death rates are more violent than those of birth rates. The causes of the former were diseases, harvest failures and wars (of which the first cause following upon the two others seems to have taken the greatest toll of life). The causes for the latter were alterations in fecundity, in the age distribution of women of child-bearing age, the age distribution of the total population, and the age of marriage.[52] In addition to this, fluctuations in the death rate may in themselves have brought about changes in birth rates. This is so because death from a variety of causes, like famines or wars, in no way destroys the general capacity of a region to feed its population. In fact a reduction in population may in many cases stimulate the rate of survival of the next generation by positively influencing the ratio of people to land and to other resources. Additionally, it is also likely that death under some circumstances may have resulted in an attitude which led to the deferment of marriages, with a result that many more marriages were contracted in the years following those of the high mortality; and—a point stressed by Professor Habakkuk as of great importance—people could afford to marry earlier after years of high mortality because 'some sons of peasants inherited their father's holdings earlier than would otherwise have been the case, [and] landless men found it easier to obtain holdings, and wage-earners gained from higher wages caused by the scarcity of labour'.[53] The high incidence of death in one period may also, of course, weed out the weakest, and thereby prolong the life expectancy of those who survive. Regarding the fluctuations in pre-industrial society from a more long-term perspective, Professor Habakkuk takes the view that 'the most important influence on the trend appears to have come from the side of the birth rate'.[54] He suggests that differences in death rates between countries in Europe and between one period and another should, in fact, be less pronounced and influential in the long run than those of birth rates.[55] His explanation then hinges upon differences in the 'age at and frequency of marriage', i.e. on economic opportunity. If this were true it could explain the slow progress of population growth in France where the landownership, that is the ownership of land by small peasants, was rather a factor which led to the postponement of marriages, because the peasant had an incentive not to marry until he inherited his father's land, and the rapid progress of population in colonial America where land was abundant and easily obtainable.[56] He is, of course, aware that in a society where everyone marries as soon as he is physiologically capable, as is the case of women in most economically backward societies today, little change would come as a result of economic improvements in the rate of marriage, but the evidence about the European marriage pattern is documented well enough to show that in fact Professor Habakkuk's argument for the eighteenth century is valid.[57] With this in mind the fall in the death rate by the end of the eighteenth century can be seen in a new light. If it were true, as the statistics indicate, that the death rate was rising in the 1770s and falling in the 1780s, this need not necessarily lead to the conclusion that 'the fall in the death rate was the most important cause of the population increase'. If T. H. Marshall's observation that 'the chief feature of the falling death rate was a rapid decline in infant mortality'[58] is also re-examined,[59] it may be suggested that neither the statistical nor the medical evidence need be interpreted in one way only. Professor Habakkuk's alternative explanation of the fall in the death rate is: 'That it was the result of changes in the age composition of the population brought about by the rising birth rate of earlier decades, and the result also, perhaps, of the existence of a smaller proportion of vulnerable people in the population.' On this reading of the evidence he concludes[60] that 'the fall in the death rate would be a fall of the type that often followed after a period of high mortality; it would register changes due to other causes, and be itself a prime cause of cumulative population increase . . .'.[61]

Though it would be foolish to place much confidence in the short-term movements revealed in such notoriously imperfect statistics, he still maintains that 'one could make out a case for the contention that the figures do betray some suggestion of the pre-industrial pattern of population growth. . . . The fall in the death rate from 1730 to 1760 and the much greater fall from 1780 to 1810 may, in some degree, have been reactions to periods of high mortality.'

Turning to the long-term changes, it is obvious that the birth rate rose to 1790 and remained at a rather high level for several decades afterwards.[62] Possibly this was due to a higher birth rate at an earlier period, but the length of time during which this high birth rate was then sustained is highly suggestive of the operation of additional forces besides the favourable age composition. From this point of view the long run of good harvests from 1730 to 1755 becomes, perhaps, more significant as a stimulus for the higher birth rate, through earlier marriages, than as the cause of the reduced death rate, through the absence of severe famines. More than this, Malthus, among other contemporaries, 'took the view that the cheaper food of these years did not produce a proportionate increase of population but that the labourers' increased corn wages, instead of occasioning an increase of population exclusively, were so expended as to occasion a decided elevation in the standard of their comforts and conveniency'.[63] Professor Habakkuk's conclusion from this is that if Malthus was right—and Ricardo's 'ratchet effect', for example, seems to justify such an assumption[64]—it may well be that the Industrial Revolution was stimulated by the increase in demand for comforts and conveniences released by this long period of low food prices.[65] Indeed, some eighteenth-century observers assumed that industrialisation by itself, rather than a higher demand for labour, was stimulating the accretion of people. This was supposed to be so because industrialisation tended to create 'new species' of demand among consumers, and a redistribution of income in favour of the poor, who were assumed to have a demand for goods upon which more labour had to be expended than upon the luxury goods for the less numerous rich.[66] That industrialisation tended to work less in favour of the rich may or may not be true, but that it worked in favour of a relatively increasing share of the population, at least until late in the eighteenth century, seems fairly certain.[67] If one compares the 'mercantilist' writers' attitude to labour (which reflected their inability to conceive of the growth of an internal popular market for goods and of technological progress) with that of the later classical economists, who were aware of the long-term trend towards higher living standards, there can remain little doubt about the reality of the case for the interdependence of industrial changes and population growth, and that the latter may well have taken the form of a higher birth rate.[68]

H. Gille, in his study for the research programme of the Population Investigation Committee, 'The Demographic History of the Northern European Countries in the Eighteenth Century',[69] reaches a different conclusion. Basing his view upon Swedish, Finnish, Danish, Norwegian and Icelandic statistics he claims that, looking at the period as a whole, the range of population movement was rather narrow. Death rates were slightly falling in the third quarter of the eighteenth century and continued to fall even more in the next century. This fall was matched by a fall in marriage rates during the first part of the period, but not by the end of the eighteenth and in the early nineteenth centuries. By then, the marriage rate had become almost stationary. Birth rates declined during the first part, and continued to fall until the twentieth century, with the possible exception of the two decades following upon the year 1840. Altogether the rate of population growth appears to have been relatively constant, both in the eighteenth end in the nineteenth century.[70]

Whether these differences between Professor Habakkuk's and Mr. Gille's conclusions merely reflect the inadequacy of the factual statistical evidence, or whether they show the true differences in the course of population growth in various countries, and in this case the close connection between the birth rate and industrial progress, neither answer really satisfies us on the question of the causal sequence of population increase and economic progress in the eighteenth century. Finally, both explanations need not be mutually exclusive. The long run of good harvests must have had an effect both on the rate of survival and, more important, on the rate of increase in births induced by widening economic opportunities and on the other short-term factors which were mentioned by Professor Habakkuk. Yet there may have been other causes: for example, changes in the eating habits and diet of the people which may have led to long-term improvements in nutrition and consequently to greater resistance to disease.[71] To accept such an assumption it would, however, be necessary to show that eating habits had really changed or that agricultural production increased even more rapidly than population—in other words, to prove the existence of profound dietetic changes and increased *per capita* production and consumption of agricultural produce. There is evidence of such changes having taken place, but they might have been both the cause and the result of population growth. As Professor Habakkuk argues, 'It might be that, because of social impediments to enclosure and because of technical ignorance, population increase, in the sixteenth century for example, tended to raise prices rather than increase production, and thereby provoked the application of the positive checks.'[72] By mid-eighteenth century, because of such developments as changes in the agrarian structure and the wider diffusion of technical knowledge, English agriculture was much more capable of responding to the demands of increasing population, and for this reason an increase of population, once started, tended to proceed much further.[73] In other words, '*We still do not know whether the reduction in disaster (or higher human fertility) in the eighteenth century was produced by man, the result for instance of economic progress, or whether it was just a piece of good luck, the continuation of which was made possible by the undeniable progress of a later period*'.[74]

For the nineteenth century 'we must pay as much attention to the forces which kept the birth-rate up as to those which pulled the death-rate down'.[75] As for the birth rate going up, there seems to be some contemporary evidence that farm workers 'tended to marry earlier where the practice of boarding them in the farmhouse was discontinued; and board wages became less common during the Napoleonic Wars because the labourers, being less plentiful than before, could make better terms; and there was no revival of the practice after the wars, partly because the farmer liked having the house to himself, partly because day labourers could be more easily subsidised from the rates.'[76] In addition to this, there is also the possibility that the increase in birth rates was due to a shift in the class structure of the population. In other words, that the number of people belonging to the classes which 'usually' bear more children increased at the expense of, or relative to, the other classes. That such differences between the habits of social groups with regard to the age of marriage existed, and that variations in fertility were considerable in the nineteenth century, is almost certain.[77] Since 'it is improbable that such differences were a secondary product of (1) differences in age composition, (2) differences in adult mortality (that is, differences in the number of marriages broken by death before the end of the childbearing period), or (3) differences of control of births within marriage, the main causes must be differences in age at marriage and in nuptiality.'[78] Although there is in fact no reliable evidence to show that the classes with the earlier marriage habits were those which were growing faster, relatively and absolutely, in the period under consideration, there is no reason to suppose that this was not the case. On the contrary, from a socio-economic point of view it appears most likely that they were. If it were true that the average age at marriage began to rise in the last quarter of the nineteenth century, there appears to be justification for the recent argument that marriage habits responded to economic conditions only within certain income groups, and that larger numbers of people did not enter these until the 1870s.

As for death rates, it appears that mortality was somehow lower after 1750 and that life expectancy by the middle of the nineteenth century was higher than in the 1770s and 1780s. Yet how far can these improvements be attributed to economic progress? Rickman,[79] writing in the second decade of the nineteenth century, believed that the fall in mortality during the preceding four decades was due to better nutrition and cleanliness. Whether or not his observations were correct is still a matter of dispute. As Professor Ashton has pointed out, the answer depends upon the size of the class which had an income well above subsistence level and therefore shared in the fruits of progress.[80] He himself tended to believe that it was rather large. Professor Habakkuk, on the other hand, dismisses this view, indicating that 'in view of the relatively slight increase in expectation of life in the later decades it is difficult to believe that the improvements in the standard of living can have had important demographic consequences.[81] Such developments as improvements in internal transport and marketing may have alleviated the demographic consequences of local shortages, but,' he argued, 'other economic developments, particularly the increase in urbanisation, would lead one to expect higher mortality.' Yet there is more evidence of technological progress than Professor Habakkuk seems inclined to accept as a population factor. There was increased agricultural production of a kind which tempts one to associate it with both total and *per capita* output—i.e. new and better methods of raising cattle and growing of grain, just at the time when better storage facilities and more overseas trade helped to overcome local food shortages. Why should these not have been reflected in the 'great dip in the death rate curve during the Industrial Revolution'?[82] Why indeed should not the improvements in nutrition have made the people less subject to a high death rate from epidemics? Why should not the greater consumption of vegetables, the more abundant use of coal to make dwellings less damp, the wider spread of washable garments and of the use of soap, taken together, have had the suggested cumulative effect on population growth? Griffith thought they had. And though he was probably wrong in dating the spreading of the medical improvements to the masses as far back as the eighteenth century, his views may still be correct if deferred to the nineteenth.[83] Truly it is a fact that the practice of inoculating against smallpox was spreading and that people like the students of Boerhaave of Leyden and von Haller of Gottingen, or like John and William Hunter, transformed British medicine even before the great days of Pasteur and Koch. So, in spite of the evidence collected by McKeown and Brown, there still remains the possibility that the collective effect, if not in the eighteenth then in the first half of the nineteenth century, may after all have been underrated. Again all depends upon the relative class structure of nineteenth-century society.

ECONOMIC CONDITIONS AND POPULATION TRENDS

According to T. H. Marshall,[84] 'The crude birth-rate during the whole period 1750–1830 was remarkably high as compared both with what went before and with what followed.... The maintenance of this high rate . . . during the last forty years of this period (1790–1830) is, however, very surprising, in view of three circumstances—the spectacular fall in the death rate which began about 1780, the decline in infant mortality . . . and the occurrence of a succession of acute economic crises. . . .[85] The marriage-rate may have risen up to the end of the eighteenth century, but it fell in the nineteenth, and . . . estimates make it lower in 1821 than it had been in 1801. This suggests that either fertility rose or illegitimacy increased, probably both. . . . The crude death-rate, having reached its lowest point about 1811, began to rise a few years later, and continued to do so until the late thirties. This rise coincided with a change in age-distribution favourable to a low death-rate, namely an increase in the proportion of those in healthy middle-life. It is therefore more serious than it appears. . . . It seems probable that this rise, most marked among infants and in the big towns, was the result of economic causes, using the term broadly to cover deficiency of food-supply, housing and sanitation. . . .' With this, Marshall believed that 'somewhere between 1820 and 1830 began a definite decline both of the marriage-rate and of the birth-rate. . . . This converging of the birth- and death-rates, with its consequent check on the rate of population growth, seems to be the result of economic pressure. Now observation has shown', Marshall continued, 'that the death-rate is not quick to respond to the fluctuations of economic prosperity whereas the marriage-rate and birth-rate are more sensitive. . . . The fact that the birth-rate did fall rapidly in the thirties indicates that it was responsive to economic pressure. The previous rise in the death-rate suggests that this pressure was present at least in 1815, probably sooner. This thought', Marshall concluded, 'again leads us to ask why it was that the birth-rate did not begin to fall earlier. Even if it suffered a check when the war began, it quickly recovered, and remained buoyant for another twenty years.' Here, then, is the essence of Marshall's whole argument: 'The economic pressure was in part a direct result of the rapidity of population growth. Urban concentration was a condition of this growth, and caused the high town mortality which drove up the national death-rate. The particular phenomena which acted most strongly to lower the birth-rate were, first, the burden of supporting the children saved by the declining infant mortality; secondly, the subsequent inrush of a wave of young adults into an already despondent labour market. These young people are unable to marry, and the birth-rate sags. . . .'

When he comes to the period which followed the 1830s, Marshall is less hesitant. He wrote, 'The first thing that strikes one about the population of England in the nineteenth century is the close symmetry between the rate of growth and the ebb and flow of economic prosperity'.[86] With this he divided the century into the periods of war boom, post-war depression, the Golden Years, the Great Depression and the pre-war recovery in the early twentieth century. The question he then asks is obvious: was there or was there not a causal connection between economic fluctuations and population trends? And, after answering this in the affirmative, though without giving enough consideration to the second side of the problem, he raises another problem which is: what happened in about 1880 to bring this causal relationship to an end? After disposing of international migration as a minor factor in population history (though he admits its indirect importance through its effect on the age structure of the society), he turns once more to the birth and death rates. He argues that the birth rate was falling when population was increasing most rapidly and began to recover before the rise of prices had had time to influence popular living standards, while the death rate until 1840 behaved as was to be expected, i.e. inversely to the rate of population accretion – rising when the total population of England and Wales was falling and declining when the total population increased. After 1840, however, it continued to be high during the Golden Years, when, according to the crude theory of economic causation, it should have fallen.

Turning to the birth rate first, Marshall begins from the assumption that it had fallen slightly in the last decade of the eighteenth century and had then remained fairly stable until it fell again more decisively during the 1830s. As the factors which could have influenced these trends were the age composition of the population, marriage rates and the age at marriage, together with voluntary birth control and 'physiological conditions affecting fertility' (about the last of which very little is known), he examined each, particularly the last two. Thus, regarding age composition and marriage, he suggested that, as population had been increasing towards the end of the eighteenth century, its age composition must have become younger. In the early nineteenth century, however, birth rates had to fall because the proportion of fertile adults to growing infants was diminished. This would also account for the lower marriage rate. There was therefore no cause to seek an economic explanation for these developments. After a time the infants would reach maturity and reinflate both the birth and the marriage rate. This should have happened by 1840. It did not. In fact, as Marshall pointed out, it was then that the fall was deeper than ever. What is the explanation for this? Here, he explained, was for the first time 'a clear possibility of economic causation . . . people abstained from marriage because, for the moment, they could not afford it'.[87] Since the marriage rate recovered very quickly and was distinctly buoyant for the better part of the third quarter of the nineteenth century, the idea of deferred marriages gains some degree of credibility. 'Naturally', Marshall concludes, 'the birth-rate rose too'. The problem which remains to be explained in this case is why the check on births appeared in the thirties and not before at the beginning of the slump. Marshall's answer here is that 'the fall in the thirties did not correspond with a period of low prices. Prices were high but wages were low and unemployment was considerable, and these conditions lasted for five or six years. It is a unique phenomenon in the nineteenth century.'[88] But, he added, 'we cannot rule out the other answer, that social policy mitigated the effects of the slump'. In other words, the new Poor Law and the Factory Act withdrew two sources of maintenance for young families.[89] The only alternative explanation, in Marshall's view, was one which excluded the economic factor from being decisive here; unless, of course, his premise was altogether erroneous, i.e. that economic conditions were not as he supposed they were in the late twenties or thirties. Finally, when birth rates fell again at the beginning of the last quarter of the nineteenth century, there is little doubt that it was due to 'voluntary control by contraception'. Thus Marshall arrived at the conclusion that as far as the alterations in the birth rate were concerned 'a theory of simple economic causation will not do'. The explanation should be sought in changing social habits. As he himself admitted: 'The solution of the problem remains obscure'.

As for the death rate, the evidence indicates a rise in mortality lasting from about 1820 to 1870, particularly in the towns and among children. This Marshall attributed to the 'illorganised, unhealthy urban environment' rather than to the spreading of new diseases.[90] It was, so he wrote, 'a product of economic civilisation'. He supported this argument by reference to the observation that 'the close correlation between death-rates and poverty', during this period, did in fact break down with regard to agricultural labour.[91] 'Not poverty', he concluded, but 'illdesigned expenditure of the national wealth' was the economic cause of the higher death rate. From the beginning of the last quarter of the century, improvements were progressing at an accelerated pace. *Per capita* output improved from both the quantitative and the qualitative point of view. So did consumption. Gradually people became acclimatised to the urban environment, and the environment itself was transformed by 'the growth of science and a service of public health and . . . the increasing advance of medical knowledge' which raised human vitality and prolonged human life. Eventually, even in the cities, although they were still unhealthy by modern standards, an excess of births over deaths reinforced growth from migration. The towns had ceased to siphon off the excess births over deaths from the rural areas.[92] Following T. A. Welton's example,[93] Marshall divided urbanisation in nineteenth-century England into four periods, each more or less corresponding to a quarter of the period. In the first quarter the old-established towns were taking in a great number of new citizens; in the second, the towns in areas which until then had not been influenced by the rise of modern industry were growing fast; in the third, new towns created by the Industrial Revolution itself—near the sources of power or raw materials—were taking the lead; and in the fourth period, the whole process was slowing down everywhere while people began to spread away from the big cities into suburban residential districts. The conclusions are obvious: the rising death rate of the twenties 'may have been caused by this sudden inrush into the old towns, which were physically and mentally unprepared to receive it'. The high death rate was then continued, though less severely, throughout the second and third period, when people concentrated in the new towns and crowded areas which were initially equally badly suited for the new way of life. A change for the better began in the last decade of the century. Partly, this was due to the spreading of the towns back into their hinterland. Briefly, Marshall believed that urbanisation, or rather the lack of preparation to receive the rapid influx of industrial labour into the towns, must be held a major cause for the high death rates in the period from the second to the last decades of the nineteenth century.

Yet, on the whole, it was Marshall's view that population in economic history has to be regarded not merely as an effect but no less as a cause.[94] He believed that it had its own vitality, which is not always resultant or related to economic conditions. This, he thought, was particularly true for the nineteenth century, when birth rates reacted almost independently, while death rates were affected by the medical developments. He attributed much more importance to economic progress as a cause for population growth, through high birth rates, than to the control of population because of economic reasons through high death rates. In fact, he assumed that high death rate for economic reasons affected only a very small portion of the population, namely only those living on the subsistence margin. Regarding migration, he noted that it was far from well adapted to the needs of industry. Thus, while population growth may well have stimulated economic development, it also caused temporary frictions and localised distress. For example, early in the century the higher rate of survival of infants burdened their parents with extra mouths to feed. Later, when the children grew up and reached maturity, a surplus of labour ensued and caused a great deal of hardship. It was in this period that child labour competed at its worst with that of adults. However, the rapid accretion round the year 1870 went beyond the productive powers of the relatively diminished working population, and once again incomes rose very rapidly until the pre-war decade, when an oversupply of labour caused renewed hardships. In Marshall's own words, 'ideally the industrial machine can adapt itself to any population, growing or stable, young or old, but in practice, the population has more than once proved itself to be a master who sets severe tasks to his puzzled servant'.

Against this reading of the events Professor Habakkuk raised the following objections. Firstly, that there is no 'evidence, that the frequency and severity of deficient harvests in the eighteenth century were determined by population pressure'. Although the effect of famine on mortality is almost certainly related to living standards, harvest failures by themselves merely 'reflected ascertainable vagaries of the climate, not the density of population in relation to resources'.[95] In other words, Professor Habakkuk is inclined to believe that even if death rates could be traced back to economic factors, i.e. harvest failures, it would still not prove the correctness of the Malthusian connection between over-population and economic capacity. It would merely stress the fact that in the eighteenth century a factor which was exogenous to both the economic and the demographic system, namely the climate, may well have been the source of their vagaries. Secondly, and Professor

Habakkuk held this to be the major point of his argument, 'deficient harvests were not the main agents of mortality'. They were, so he thought, judging from the evidence produced by Chambers,[96] overshadowed by 'outbreaks of disease which were not associated with dearth'.[97] He illustrated this point both by the example of the smallpox and influenza epidemics during the good harvests in the late 1720s, when epidemics could not have been 'a Malthusian punishment inflicted on an overexpanded population', and by the observation that they were not an exclusively English phenomenon, but general throughout northern Europe. Habakkuk therefore reached the conclusion that the harvest failures reflected weather and not population pressure, and that weather usually affected mortality directly without the mediation of a poor harvest. 'Indeed', he added, 'the weather that was good for the carriers of disease might also be good for the crops.'[98]

Thus we are faced with at least three alternative explanations for the fall in the death rate. Firstly, the best known and best refuted one of Talbot Griffith[99] and Buer,[100] which related the fall to improvements in health and medicine. Secondly, the economic explanation of T. H. Marshall and others,[101] which explained the fall in death rates in terms of a general rise in living standards. And thirdly, Habakkuk and Helleiner's explanation, that 'it was not so much a reduction of mortality in "normal" years that produced the secular downward trend of the death rate, but an unmistakable abatement of the "great crises".'[102] This abatement was itself the result of changes for the explanation of which, in Professor Habakkuk's words, 'we must look to the historians of climate and disease'. 'So far as the early decades of the nineteenth century are concerned —the period when population growth in England unambiguously diverged from that of Continental Europe—' Professor Habakkuk concluded,[103] 'substantial weight has . . . to be attached to the effect of the industrial changes in explaining the persistence of high levels of fertility. How far these changes offered positive opportunities for early marriage and how far they simply weakened the older restraints on marriage—these are questions which can be answered only when the evidence of the parish registers has been more systematically analysed.'

While in England the study of eighteenth- and nineteenth-century population trends developed in the form of the higher birth rates versus the lower death rates controversy, in France it took the shape of an argument about the causes of urbanisation—whether the rural population was forced from the land or whether it was attracted by the cities. The first modern author to raise the problem in this form is Louis Chevalier in his examination of the relationship between social progress and population movements.[104] In an earlier contribution on the same subject,[105] he stressed the differences between France, Britain and Germany with regard to population growth, drawing from these some socio-economic inferences though not fully stating them. From an economic and social point of view, he wrote, 'the French Revolution of 1789 was not accompanied by the upheaval which characterised it in the political field. . . .' The economic evolution of nineteenth-century France, i.e. the industrialisation and the expansion of urban centres, was too slow and too steady to merit in his view the term 'Revolution'. 'On this point', he claimed, 'France is quite different from England, where the economic revolution in the middle of the eighteenth century produced changes far more important than did the thunder of our Revolutionary assemblies. It is different too from Germany, whose economic, political and demographic evolution assumes after 1870 such a new shape that the demographic study of Germany in the twentieth century can perfectly well begin from the industrialisation at the end of the nineteenth century, taking that as a safe starting point, the beginning of a new period.'[106] The history of France from this economic and demographic point of view is, so he thinks, a kind of seamless dress dating back to the first quarter of the nineteenth century.

Until the middle of the eighteenth century both the birth and the death rates were high in France.[107] Most historians attributed the high death rate to 'the poor harvests, the famines, and the absence of means of communication'. After the middle of the century, when communications improved, the death rate fell and birth rates remained as high as before. So far there is little new in the French explanation. It is in fact similar to Professor Ashton's explanation about the accretion of people in England during the same period. The real difference appears with the interpretation of developments during the first half of the nineteenth century. Following Ernest Labrousse's argument, Chevalier ascribes the diminution of the rate of population growth in the early part of the nineteenth century in France to a fall in birth rates. In other words, the effects of the depression which followed the wars of the Revolution and the Empire made themselves felt via the birth rather than via the death rate. In this sense Chevalier's explanation comes, of course, much closer to Professor Habakkuk's than to Professor Ashton's. In fact, Professor Chevalier believes that 'it is possible to detect the influence on the standard of living of the population and on the birth rate, of the system of property and land-development on the one hand, and on the other hand of the economic variations inherent in this framework, only if it is possible to get more accurate information about the pattern and volume of those internal migrations, about which the only available information is lacking in precision. . . .' But, with this reservation, he finds it 'surprising that fertility, which had considerably diminished from 1815 to 1848 [in France], increased again up to about 1861, a period of political stability, and only began to fall again in 1865; this is, indeed, one of the more curious problems of the demographic evolution. . . .' And so Professor Chevalier adds that 'these economic, social and political evolutions were accompanied by a moral evolution, an evolution in moral standards and behaviour, which some contemporary demographers . . . are very inclined to see as the essential cause of the demographic evolution of France in the nineteenth and twentieth centuries. This influence is at once easier and more difficult to define. The conflict between religious feelings and what Renan called material interests, and the improvements in education, both in quantity and in quality, might perhaps contribute important elements to this study.' [108]

Another no less important study of French population in the first half of the nineteenth century shows how in rural areas population growth reached its highest rate of acceleration during the third decade of that century and then gradually began to fall in the years that followed. The author, Professor Charles Pouthas,[109] explains this in the following way. By 1820 rural France, in the areas concerned, was already overpopulated from the point of view of agricultural labour requirements. The difference between the available and the required labour was filled by a widespread rural manufacturing industry in textiles, metallurgy and woodwork. But, in the fourth decade of the nineteenth century, when towns rose to their industrial predominance, rural industries were losing ground very rapidly. It was then that the problem of overpopulation in the countryside became real instead of potential, as it had been before. With poor harvests adding to the difficulties, rural population was forced off the land and into the towns. These, however, were ill-equipped to receive the great influx and, as had also happened in England, urbanisation raised the death rates while poverty in the rural districts kept birth rates down.[110] For one and perhaps for two regions of France, namely Picardy and Aquitaine, studies were made which do in fact indicate that this is what actually happened.[111] Yet on a more general close examination the picture becomes less clear. As Claude Fohlen pointed out,[112] relying mainly on the material produced by the Société d'Histoire de la Révolution de 1848, under the direction of Ernest Labrousse, 'the impression one gets . . . is one of very great diversity. At a time when the *départements* of the East and West were affected by famine and industrial unemployment, Marseilles and the Var were experiencing remarkable prosperity.'

In Germany industrialisation and urbanisation made little progress before the middle of the nineteenth century. The rate of town-population growth was just slightly above the rate of population growth for the country as a whole. As until the second half of the nineteenth century the share of town population was higher in France than in Germany, the relatively faster rate of the total accretion of people in Germany may, perhaps, be associated with the lower rate of loss of life through ill-prepared urbanisation. Indeed, one may detect signs of an inverse correlation between the growth of towns and total population growth in mid-nineteenth-century Germany.[113] However, if urbanisation was the prime cause of demographic retardation, it may be difficult to explain the relatively sharper rise in English population, which increased by approximately 200 per cent in the nineteenth century as against an increase of only 100 per cent in Germany and 45 per cent in France,[114] when urbanisation was affecting a far greater share of the total population in England and Wales than in either Germany or France.[115] Thus, unless one is prepared to accept the view that the great improvements in health-care had taken place during the eighteenth century in England, or that the general economic background was very considerably better in England than in the rest of Europe, it may be difficult to uphold the theory which places the major onus for the slowness of population growth on the rise of towns.

By the last quarter of the nineteenth century the rural districts began to feel the effects of the drift of population to both the towns and abroad which had been gradually gaining in strength since the sixties. The relative lateness of this trend must at least partially be attributed to the specifically German political and legal structure of the period. The *Gesinde-Ordnung* of 1810 turned the whole process of peasant emancipation, and with it the freedom of movement, into a farce.[116] It was not until well after the middle of the century that the number of peasants who could escape the *Gesinde-Ordnung* had grown large enough to be felt. As agricultural wages were notoriously low in Prussia, the stream of labour into the towns was increasing steadily in the sixties and seventies. By 1880 it had become a torrent and German landlords were complaining about depopulation in terms almost identical with those of their English counterparts four centuries earlier, in Tudor times. In fact, the loss of labour to the towns was quickly made up by the influx of cheap foreign workers and by the fast progress of mechanisation. As the labour shortage was mainly seasonal, and was soon reduced by the afore-mentioned compensatory developments, it did not lead to any true improvement in agricultural wages. Consequently there was no swinging back of the pendulum—the gap between town and country became permanent. How far the influx of foreign labour was offset by the emigration to America of German citizens is difficult to assess, but there is a distinct possibility that the influx of foreign agricultural labour made good the loss of life caused by the ill-effects of urbanisation. However, the growth of towns took place when modern health education and care was also making good progress.

For the rest of Europe, population estimates collected from various sources were presented by Professor D. V. Glass and E. Grebenik in their contribution to *The Cambridge Economic History of Europe*.[117] And for towns by Warren S. Thompson in *Population Problems*.[118] The following is a simplified extract from their table:

POPULATION OF EUROPE

(Millions)

	1800	*1850*	*1900*	*1950*
Russia	44·0***	58·6**	94·3**	200·0***
Italy	18·1	23·9	33·9	46·6
Spain	11·5	15·5	18·6	27·9
Holland	2·2	3·1	5·1	10·1
Hungary		5·0**	6·9	9·3
Belgium	3·0	4·3	6·7	8·6
Portugal	3·1	4·2	5·4	8·4
Bulgaria		2·8**	3·7	7·3**
Sweden	2·3	3·5	5·1	7·0
Austria		3·9	6·0	6·9
Switzerland	1·8	2·4	3·3	4·7
Denmark	0·9	1·6	2·6	4·3
Finland	1·0	1·6	2·7	4·0
Norway	0·9	1·5	2·2	3·3

Yugoslavia, Czechoslovakia: no data avilable before the twentieth century. ** Dates not for 1850 but 1870–80 or as close to date given as possible with the available data. *** Including Soviet Asia.

Taken together the statistics for England, France, Germany and the rest of Europe show that European population as a whole grew very rapidly during the nineteenth century, and so did European towns. As has already been observed, the pattern of this growth was not uniform. In the earlier part of the century it was more pros nounced in the north-west, whereas in the later part the emphasi- shifted to the south and east. In the United States of America the pattern of the natural rate of increase was similar to that of northern

FIGURE 3

Total Population and Town Populations in England, France and Germany

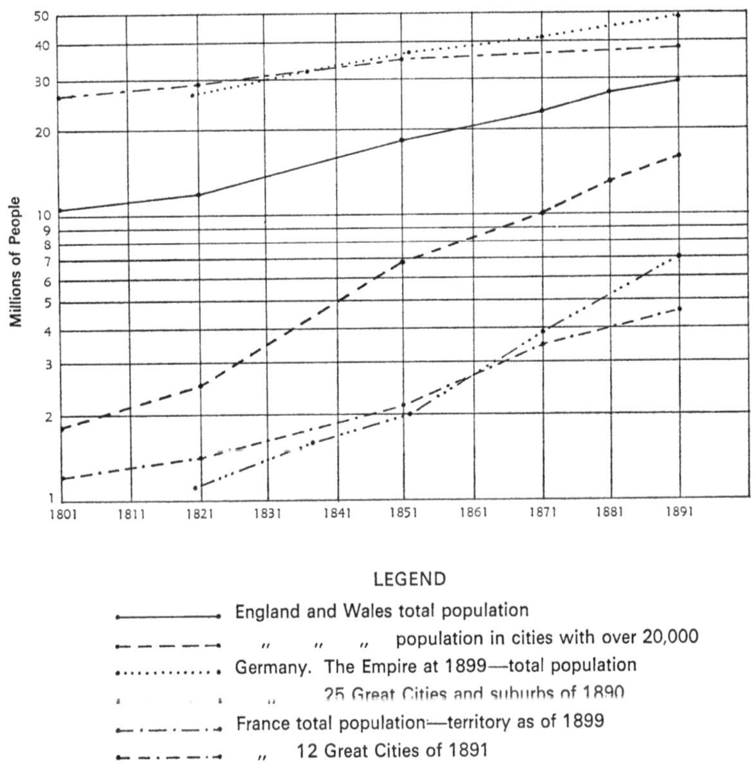

Europe; that is, it was greater during the early part of the nineteenth century. Towards the middle of the centurv the natural rate of increase began to fall; after the middle it continued to fall below the European rate.[119] At the same time, however, the country's population was inflated by the great influx of people from abroad. From 1800 to 1860 the overall increase of American population was approximately one-third per decade. After 1860 the rate of accretion decreased, though immigration continued to increase very appreciably. In 1891 F. A. Walker[120] attributed the slowing down of the natural rate of growth there during the second quarter of the nineteenth century to immigration. Immigration, so he argued, was threatening living standards and this had a psychological effect which in turn influenced the rate of natural accretion. J. Bertillon, two decades earlier, and H. P. Fairchild, two or three decades later,[121] held similar views, although theirs were less sophisticated and more in the traditional Malthusian vein. In fact both variations of the Immigration Theory were shown to be wrong by the statistical examination of the data by Thompson and by Whelpton.[122] Recently Walker's idea reappeared once more in an even more sophisticated form. Immigration, it is believed, can under certain circumstances have an indirect effect on the natural increase of native populations through the cultural impact of the immigrants.[123] It is, however, interesting to note that in the United States the heavy influx of immigrants followed the initial downward trend of fertility and did not precede it as was sometimes suggested.[124]

The following table shows the total accretion of population in the United States from 1790 to 1950.[125]

TOTAL POPULATION IN THE UNITED STATES
(Millions)

Year		*Year*	
1790	3·9	1880	50·2
1800	5·3	1890	62·6
1810	7·2	1900	76·0
1820	9·6	1910	92·0
1830	12·9	1920	105·7
1840	17·0	1930	122·8
1850	23·2	1940	132·5
1860	31·4	1950	150·7
1870	39·8	1960	178·0

Urban populations in the United States increased more rapidly than the population of the country as a whole. Their relative rate of increase was higher than that of France and Germany but only half of that of England and Wales in the nineteenth century.[126]

One important problem connected with inter-continental migration, which has never been properly solved, is the problem of motivation. For a long time American scholars in particular believed in the 'stereotype of the hungry denizen of the old world casting an envious eye on the wealth and opportunities of the new';[127] or, as Hansen wrote,[128] 'that America was a huge magnet of varying intensity, drawing the people of Europe from those regions where conditions made them mobile and from which transportation provided a path,' i.e. that 'American conditions determined the duration and height of the waves, European, the particular source'. In fact, out of 55 million Europeans who emigrated overseas between 1821 and 1924, 33 millions went to the United States.[129] Yet about one-third of these re-emigrated, and other receiving countries, for example Argentina with 5·4 millions, Brazil with 3·8 millions and Canada with 4·5 millions, had a relatively more important volume of immigration.[130] This calls to mind the possibility that European population was 'pushed' rather than attracted out of Europe in the nineteenth century; a point of view which gains additional support from the study of the various countries of origin of the waves of immigrants in different periods, and from the study of the variations in the intra-European patterns of population movements. As Frank Thistlethwaite pointed out, 'There were over a quarter of a million Italians in France by 1886 and nearly half a million in 1911. . . . France's slow and lagging industrialisation attracted not only Italian labourers, but Poles, Belgians and later Spaniards to the extent of about two millions by the 1920s, when France became the second most important and, after the United States Restriction Acts, *the* most important country of immigration in the world. . . .'

Thus, although it is obvious that nineteenth-century migration was economically motivated, its direction may well have been determined by transport conditions. The great influx of people into the United States may have been the result of the fact that trade routes to America were well established and that ships coming from there had little cargo to carry back, and their owners were therefore ready to take emigrants on the return journey at little cost.

Mr. Thistlethwaite appears to be of the opinion that 'the Atlantic economy was concerned with exploiting the grasslands of North America by means of European capital and labour in the interest of cheaper cotton and wheat for Europe and overseas markets for European manufactures'. He argues that 'the migration of the twin factors of capital investment and labour was the key to it and emigrants were essential to its operation', though he admits that 'the precise way in which this mechanism worked is still a matter for research and controversy. As far as emigration is concerned, the first attempt to refine the old crude assumptions about the push mechanism of over-population in Europe and the pull mechanism of American opportunity was made by American economists . . . as a by-product of research into the operation of the business cycle some thirty years ago. Jerome found a direct correlation between fluctuations in immigration into the United States and the short-term American business cycle, and, later, Kuznets and Rubin established three long swings in net immigration between 1870 and 1945 which tended to follow swings in income per head.'[131] Another view, of Brinley Thomas, is based on the one hand upon 'an inverse relation between home investment and the level of income' in Britain, and on the other, upon emigration and capital exports; i.e. upon 'a positive relationship between immigration, investment and income in the United States, and, correspondingly, disharmony between the rates of economic growth on the eastern and the western sides of the Atlantic'. The significant point here seems to be that the evidence may well be indicative of the positive relationship between population accretion and economic progress. If this view could be substantiated one would perhaps also come to the conclusion that the accretion of people in Europe was the source of economic development rather than its consequence. In any case, Thomas's statistics suggest that migration from Europe in the 1870s was primarily the result of events in Europe and not of the pull of American prospects. The upswing in the American economy came after, and not before, the great rise in immigration. And yet it would require a far greater degree of precision in determining the countries of origin of the emigrants before this view about the causes of the European 'exodus' can be accepted.

Generally, it can be said that emigration from Europe was initially directed towards the unoccupied grasslands in Australia, Argentina, North America and Siberia. Later this trend was overshadowed by the waves of migration towards the coal and iron centres. Consequently, inter-European migration became far more important than overseas migration. It appears to be proven that during the same time that some 16 million emigrants came from Europe, the population of the Continent itself increased even more. Its proportion of world population rose from 20 per cent at the beginning of the nineteenth century to 25 per cent at its end, while it never drew off more than 40 per cent of Europe's natural increase in any single decade.[132] Hence, the picture that emerges is not one showing the Europeans taking flight to the Americas and Australasia, but one depicting Europeans 'using their labour, capital and know-how to exploit the foodstuffs and raw materials of virgin lands', not only making possible the feeding of ever-growing populations at home, but also the industrialisation of the European continent. It is in this sense that William Ashworth is absolutely correct in writing that Europe took to 'two ways of overcoming the impending difficulties' created by the expanding populations, namely to 'take possession of the unoccupied or thinly occupied areas of the world' and/or improve the use of land which was already cultivated.[133]

One point concerning the 'push' mechanism of emigration from Europe is fairly well established. Neither the mass emigration from Ireland in the third decade nor from Greece in the last decade of the nineteenth century was caused by 'rural overcrowding'. In this sense, then, the implied explanation in the shortage of land and relative overpopulation theories acnnot be maintained as satisfactory solutions. It appears that, above all, migration was the result of man's *desire* to move—to break away from his traditional familiar background. With the rising living standards and the spreading of knowledge, with the decline of the habitual social and economic safeguards of European society, and with the growing of the recognition that man has rights as an individual and can make material progress, where hitherto he had been prevented from it by his socio-economic structural environment—in short, with the rise of individualism—man gained *hope*—the hope of bettering himself—and with it the desire to move wherever he was free from the traditional fetters of class and legal restrictions which prevented him from carving out a future for himself. The not really fortuitous coincidence of progress in transport and communication with this change in the Europeans' attitudes, and the equally not really fortuitous elimination of the feudal impediments to the freedom of movement in Europe, combined in the nineteenth century and made migration the big settlement movement it became. This, then, was the great difference between the colonial expansion of Europe and the European settlements in America, Australia and South Africa. The former was a clearly political and economic movement led from the top, the latter was a popular movement from below. Yet overseas migration was only one aspect of social mobility—urbanisation was another. Thus while one part of the uprooted population was either attracted or pushed abroad, another part went to the centres of industry. Soon urbanisation and the growth of industrialism counteracted the 'push' elements of emigration. By the middle of the century European industries were already absorbing the would-be emigrants. By 1850 the industrialisation of Britain had already progressed so much that it could absorb the potential emigrants, whereas by 1900 it could absorb in addition Irish potential emigrants as well. The same is true of Scandinavian countries. Timber in Norway and mining in Sweden had become already so important a factor in 1870 that it began to reduce the number of emigrants from there. From then on Scandinavian emigration was rather the result of the pull of the new world than of unemployment at home. On the eve of the First World War it almost ceased. In Germany the height of the emigration period had already passed by the middle of the century in so far as the south-west of the country was concerned. For the country as a whole it ceased by the mid-1880s. It therefore appears true that the overseas migration from Europe in the nineteenth and early twentieth centuries was above all the result of the breakdown of the European traditional rural pattern of life and the too gradual rise of modern industry. In other words, it was the time-lag between the waning of the old and the coming of the new society which more than everything else caused the migration to the new world.[134] Modern industrialism, however, is usually associated with urbanism, and urbanism does by itself change the whole structure of society. Though it is itself the outcome of changes, it tends to effect changes in return. The new cities of Europe not only developed beyond those known in antiquity, but spread their influence upon their hinterland, forcing upon agriculture new ways and improvements and creating new trade roads which encouraged more efficiency in production and in the exploitation of new sources of power. It is, therefore, the urban revolution that distinguished Europe in the nineteenth century.[135]

Turning now to the most densely populated continent, we find that even as late as 1947 estimates of population covered adequately no more than perhaps 50 per cent of Asia, and the farther one looks back in time, the evidence becomes progressively thinner.

In what used to be called British India, the first census was held in the third quarter of the nineteenth century. Then the estimated population of the sub-continent was about 203 millions, but this figure is almost certainly an underestimate.[136] Earlier estimates are even less reliable.[137] According to Carr-Saunders there was, however, 'a rapid growth of population in India during the hundred years before 1850'.[138] In 1911 India's population was approximately 300 millions. Yet most remarkable was the period 1921 to 1941. During this period the annual increase of population was '10 per thousand from 1921 to 1931 and 14 per thousand from 1931 to 1941'.[139] This trend of sharp increase has been interpreted as the result of a prolonged period of high birth rates, together with a fall in death rates due to a reduction in infant mortality and the gradual disappearance of cholera and plague.[140] This explanation is not really very helpful for our purpose. Geddes and Sovani, who studied regional variations, interpreted them as 'deviant expressions of common forces, under different geographical and economic conditions'.[141] In Geddes's view, poverty does not check reproduction in India (except perhaps through delay of marriage), and therefore population growth is mainly regulated there by the so-called Malthusian positive checks, i.e. 'the birth-rate varies somewhat, but not nearly as much as the death-rate'.

As for China, there appears to be a degree of correlation between economic prosperity and population growth from the middle of the seventeenth century onward.[142] After the middle of the eighteenth century, however, the rate of population growth receded markedly, and according to some authorities was gently stagnating.[143] It was then that high death rates more than anything else held back the accretion. This situation appears to have lasted until well into the present century. According to the best authorities available, the population of China numbered at least 148 million people in 1750, more than 342 millions in 1850, about 450 millions in 1910, and perhaps 582 millions in 1953.[144]

In Japan, registration was introduced in A.D. 646, but the first reliable statistics date back no more than about fifty years. All earlier information is based upon censuses which were held regularly but by very defective methods. In fact most estimates were made up by adding assumed birth rates and by subtracting assumed death rates. The best that can be said is that Japan's population numbered between 33 and 36 millions in 1872 and about 56 millions in 1920.[145] 'There is some disagreement among scholars as to the relative importance of abortion and infanticide as compared with famines and epidemics in checking the natural increase of the Japanese people in that era (1721–1850); both sets of factors were in operation. Following the opening of Japan to world commerce, the population increased to 56 millions in 1920, accompanying the increase of production, the growth of cities, and the extension of political power. Both birth and death rates appear to have risen during this period; but these apparent increases may have been due in part to improved registration.'[146]

It is also not irrelevant that the impulse towards expansion, which is generally assumed to have been transmitted from Europe to the other continents, need not in fact have been the true cause of the accretion. As has been shown, the increase in the population of parts of Europe in the last part of the seventeenth century may just have been a case of what may be called filling up the gaps created by the Thirty Years War. In other words, the definite growth in Europe's population did not begin before the eighteenth century. At the same time, however, the population of Japan increased fairly rapidly between the middle of the seventeenth and the first quarter of the eighteenth century, while the population of China also increased throughout the eighteenth century and perhaps even during the later parts of the seventeenth century. The significance of this observation, then, is that populations increased in at least two Far Eastern countries either before or coincidental with the expansion of the population in Europe. Yet there is no chance that either of these countries was at that time influenced by events in Europe. Apart from this, it is of course a fact that population growth in other countries outside Europe such as India, Egypt, Java, etc., began only much later, which calls to mind the possibility that it might have been the result of European influences.[147]

According to Professor Notestein, the experience so far has shown that as each 'backward' country progresses from the primitive to a higher stage of development population increases alarmingly and in excess of the country's ability to raise its food production. But once this stage is overcome an easier period lies ahead when family limitation takes effect.

In summary, 'the art of measuring man's numbers and their changes' is still in its infancy. The areas best covered by statistical information for the last two centuries are Europe, North America and Oceania, i.e. Europe and the regions of European settlement. Coverage for Latin America is incomplete, and for most of Asia and Africa even more fragmentary. As for earlier periods in history, the evidence is even for Europe very thin and of rather limited reliability. What is evident, however, is the fact that 'the numerical expansion of the human race has been sporadic' rather than continual, and that the 'diversity in the pattern of economic and social change has been matched by a diversity of population trends'. It further appears that the period following the middle of the nineteenth century has been one of outstanding increase in the total world population. This was due, at least since the last quarter of the century, to a considerable reduction in death rates. The question whether this was in fact 'one of the main achievements of modern civilization' even in earlier decades, i.e. whether it was the result of man's ability to produce more food, clothing and shelter for himself, and of the great progress in medicine and health care, or whether all these were merely the results of population growth—an extraneous factor in human history—must still remain unanswered. Most probably it was the result of both, with one factor being predominant in one period and place and the other in another. What is fairly certain is that the modern trend of population increase almost surely 'originated in Europe and later spread to other regions following European economic development. Recently, population growth appears to have slowed down in many parts of the European cultural sphere, while it has gathered momentum in other areas.'[148] Whether cause or effect, population growth was everywhere accompanied by relatively rapid cultural and socio-economic change. This change makes up the history of modern economic growth, which is the subject of the following chapters.

NOTES

1. K. F. Helleiner, 'The Vital Revolution Reconsidered', *Canadian Journal of Economics and Political Science*, Vol. XXIII, No. I, 1957. Reprinted with minor revisions in D. V. Glass and D. E. C. Eversley, Eds., *Population in History*, London, 1965, p. 86.

2. *Vide* A. M. Carr-Saunders, *World Population*, Oxford, 1936, and W. Willcox, 'Population of the World and its Modern Increase', *Studies in American Demography*, Ithaca, 1940.

3. K. F. Helleiner, *op. cit.*, p. 86.

4. Holland being the exception in this pattern.

5.

ANNUAL RATES OF POPULATION GROWTH IN A NUMBER OF EUROPEAN COUNTRIES

(Average annual rates of growth per 1,000)

	1801–20	*1821–30*	*1831–40*	*1841–50*	*1851–60*	*1861–70*
Britain	13·0	13·7	10·4	2·5	5·5	8·3
Belgium	7·7	7·2	8·0	7·4	6·2	7·4
Holland	5·5	9·6	9·3	6·7	7·2	8·4
Germany	5·2	11·2	7·5	7·7	6·4	7·8
France	5·5	6·2	4·6	4·4	2·4	2·8
Italy	2·4	9·3	6·8	7·0	4·9	6·0
Austro-Hung.	5·3	9·8	5·3	3·6	6·8	7·5
Balkans	4·2	3·3	6·3	6·3	5·2	6·2
Russia	9·6	10·8	8·3	7·7	8·0	11·7
Europe	6·5	9·4	7·1	5·8	6·2	7·7

	1871–80	*1881–90*	*1891–1900*	*1900–20*	*1920–40*	*1940–50*
Britain	10·2	7·8	9·6	7·1	4·9	4·2
Belgium	9·5	9·5	9·9		5·3	2·9
Holland	11·7	11·8	12·7	14·9	13·3	13·1
Germany	10·3	8·9	13·2	10·0	6·1	
France	2·0	2·2	1·6	−1·4	1·0	4·8
Italy	6·0	7·6	6·2	5·7	8·5	6·1
Austro-Hung.	4·4	9·1	9·6			
Balkans	4·6	11·0	10·5			
Russia	13·6	13·9	13·5			
Europe	8·3	9·0	9·9			

Based upon D. V. Glass and E. Grebenik, *The Cambridge Economic History of Europe*, Vol. VI, Pt. I, pp. 61–62, and G. Sundbärg, *Aperçus statistiques internationaux*, Stockholm, 1906, p. 31.

6. The highest average growth rates in the nineteenth century seem to have been experienced in Europe, America and Oceania. *Vide U.N. Demographic Yearbook*, New York, 1956, p. 151.

ESTIMATED WORLD POPULATION BY CONTINENTAL DIVISION

(In millions)

	Year							
	1750	*1800*	*1850*	*1900*	*1920*	*1930*	*1940*	*1950*
Europe and Asiatic U.S.S.R.	144	193	274	423	485*	530*	579*	594*
Asia ex. Asiatic U.S.S.R.	437	595	656	857	997*	1,069*	1,173*	1,272*
Africa	100	100	100	(120)	136*	155*	177*	199*
North America	1	6	26	81	115*	134*	144*	166*
Latin America	10	23	33	63	92*	110*	132*	162*
Oceania	2	2	2	6	9*	10*	11*	13*

Based upon United Nations *Population Studies*, No. 17, *The Determinants and Consequences of Population Trends*, New York, 1953, p. 11.

7. 'Births and Deaths among Europe's Ruling Families since 1500', by Sigismund Peller. Reprinted in D. V. Glass and D. E. C. Eversley, Eds., *Population in History*, London, 1965. Also 'A Demographic Study of British Ducal Families', by T. H. Hollingsworth, *op. cit.*

8. D. E. C. Eversley, 'Population, Economy and Society', in Glass and Eversley, Eds., *op. cit.*, p. 32, gives a number of examples, such as that ages at marriage are not always recorded, and when recorded are often unreliable.

9. G. T. Griffith, *Population Problems of the Age of Malthus*, Cambridge, 1926; J. M. Plumb, *England in the Eighteenth Century*, 1950; J. R. Hicks, *The Social Framework*, Oxford, 1942. A good summary of these views is given by H. J. Habakkuk, 'English Population in the Eighteenth Century', *Economic History Review*, 2nd Series, Vol. VI, 1953, pp. 117–118 and in the *Journal of Economic History*, Vol. XVIII, 1958, No. 4, p. 486.

10. *Population Studies*, Vol. IX, 1955, pp. 119–141.

11. McKeown and Brown, 'Medical Evidence . . .', *Population Studies*, Vol. IX, 1955, pp. 38–41.

12. *Vide* Table XII, on p. 77 (Chapter II) in D. V. Glass and E. Grebenik's contribution on World Population in *The Cambridge Economic History of Europe*, Vol. VI, Pt. I.

13. Glass and Grebenik, *op. cit.*, p. 78.

14. The explanation given by L. F. Hirst, *The Conquest of Plague*, 1953, was summarised by Phyllis Deane, *The First Industrial Revolution*, Cambridge, 1965, as follows: 'As far as the Plague was concerned the reasons seem to lie in "an obscure ecological revolution among rodents". Being mainly a flea-borne disease of rats it was bound to decline to some extent as living standards rose, so that wattle and daub walls began to be replaced by brick, thatched roofs by tiled, piles of rushes by carpets and systematic scavenging of the streets moved some of the piles of rat-breeding rubbish. . . . But, so it has been argued, it was the displacement of the small domesticated black rat, with its predilection for settled living in human habitations and its free-wandering flea, by the outdoor brown rat with its wandering habits and its nest-loving flea, that eventually freed western Europe from its recurrent susceptibility to Plague. The new species is said to have reached England by sea *circa* 1728 and to have steadily driven out its smaller rival.'

15. Such changes may have increased the yield of the land and thereby improved nutrition or reduced diseases like malaria which also declined in eighteenth-century Europe, a fact usually attributed to the draining of swamps.

16. The examination of economic progress in certain areas in West Africa today leaves little doubt about the fact that under-population, i.e. the shortage of manpower in a too thinly populated area, can no less prevent economic progress—the construction of a dam for water conservation for example—than over-population in an industrial society.

17. 'Population, Economy and Society', an introduction to Glass and Eversley, Eds., *Population in History*, London, 1965, p. 67.

18. 'A Demographic Study of the British Ducal Families', by T. H. Hollingsworth, *Population Studies*, Vol. XI, No. I, 1957, Tables No. 2 and 5. Reprinted in Glass and Eversley, Eds., *op. cit.*, pp. 358, 360.

19. *Vide*, for example, P. Deprez' article on Flanders, reprinted in Glass and Eversley, *op. cit.*, p. 614.

20. *Vide*, for examples, T. H. Hollingsworth, *op. cit.*, Tables 18 and 21,

Table 18

MEAN AGE AT MARRIAGE (BRITISH DUCAL FAMILIES)

Cohort born	*1330–1479*	*1480–1679*	*1680–1729*	*1730–1779*	*1780–1829*	*1830–1879*	*1880–1939*
Males	22·4	24·3	28·6	28·6	30·5	30·0	30·0
Females	17·1	19·5	22·2	24·0	24·7	24·2	24·9

and J. Hajnal, 'European Marriage Patterns in Perspective', in Glass and Eversley, *op. cit.*, Tables 8, 6, 5, 7 and 11. Table 8, for example, gives the age at first marriage of a Württemberg (Germany) family:

MEAN AGE AT MARRIAGE

Century	*16th*	*17th*	*18th*	*19th*
Males	25·3	26·3	28·9	31·1
Females	21·4	20·8	24·0	25·3

See also Daniele Beltrami, *Storia della popolazione di Venezia dalla fine del secolo XVI alla caduta della reppublica*, Padova, 1954, for Venice; Leonie van Nierop, 'De bruidegoms van Amsterdam', in *Tijdschrift voor Geschiedenis*, 1933, 1934, 1937, for Amsterdam; O. K. Roller, *Die Einwohnerzahl der Stadt Durlach im 18. Jahrhundert, etc.*, Karlsruhe, 1907, for Durlach in Germany; Roger Mols, *Introduction à la démographie historique des villes d'Europe du XIVe siècle au XVIIIe siècle*, Louvain, 1954–56; C. C. Morrell, 'Tudor Marriages and Infant Mortality', *Journal of State Medicine*, Vol. 43, 1935, for England; and J. D. Chambers, 'The Vale of Trent 1670–1800', *Economic History Review*, Supplement No. 3, 1957; E. Gautier and L. Henry, *La Population de Crulai Paroisse Normande*, Institut National d'Etudes Démographiques, Cahier No. 33, Paris, 1958, for France; and others mentioned in the References Appendix of Mr. Hajnal's article.

21. *Vide* J. Hajnal, *op. cit.*, pp. 101–143.

22. 'Marriage' is here to be understood 'as a union which is regarded as appropriate for the bearing and rearing of children'.

23. 'The reason why four women out of six do not bear children every year is that they cannot marry because of the discouragements and difficulties in their way.' Quoted from J. Hajnal, *op. cit.*, p. 106, in Richard Cantillon, *Essai sur la nature du commerce en général*, 1755.

24. Gaston Backman, 'Die beschleunigte Entwicklung der Jugend', *Acta Anatomica*, Basel, 1947–48, Vol. 4.

25. In ancient (Biblical) Hebrew society a boy was considered adult at the age of 13, and a girl marriageable at about the same age (three hairs under the shoulder). Yet Jacob had to wait for Rachel 14 years and for Leah 7. In Israel today the age of consent is 18 years.

26. There seems to be a gradual transition in western Europe beginning from the twelfth century from a society in which property rights arose out of the tenure of a given piece of land towards rights transferred through blood relationship—a kind of 'Jus sanguineus' taking the place of 'terrae'.

27. Assuming that land only changed hands on the death of the head of the family, the result would have been earlier marriages during the middle ages, when life expectancy was shorter than in more modern times. But there is considerable evidence that land was given to children while the head of the family was still alive. It is therefore more likely that throughout the middle ages people had been marrying within their own 'extended' families, and as long as this arrangement persisted there was no reason to postpone marriages for economic considerations. The land remained in the

family—there was no individual land ownership in the modern sense of the term—and there was no risk of losing it through marriage. Only with the widening of the area from which people were choosing their partners, from both the geographical and the social point of view, was the property situation altered. The newly-wed could no longer rely on the family and had to be able to support themselves.

28. *Mélanges sur l'Angleterre*, quoted from Glass and Eversley, *op. cit.*, p. 133.

29. P. Deprez, *The Demographic Development of Flanders in the Eighteenth Century* (translated by Margaret Hilton), Glass and Eversley, *op. cit.*, p. 626.

30. P. Deprez, *op. cit.*, p. 615.

31. Gustaf Utterström, 'Two Essays on Population in Eighteenth-Century Scandinavia', in Glass and Eversley, *op. cit.*, p. 528.

32. D. V. Glass, in Glass and Eversley, *op. cit.*, pp. 15–16.

33. Richard Cantillon, *Essai sur la nature du commerce en général*, 1755.

34. 'As far as the period before 1850 is concerned (except possibly for France), the positive correlation between marriage and economic activity and opportunity is clearly the most important. The standards of what was considered adequate wealth or income for marriage vary greatly, as Malthus himself repeatedly showed, at different times and in various countries. The general assumption was that the lower the customary standard, the earlier and more general marriages would be, hence the greater tendency of population to increase. This form of argument, however, fails to convince either in its Malthusian or in more modern form. If the standard of life is so low and hopes for the future no higher, the additional children which might be produced as a result of such a system will have so low an expectation of life as to make this type of marriage convention ineffective as a factor in increasing population by itself.' D. E. C. Eversley, 'Population, Economy and Society', in Glass and Eversley, *op. cit.*, pp. 43–44. In one sense, however, Dr. Eversley accepts the possibility that early marriages, even under conditions of dire poverty, may be conducive to population growth—that is, when the original life expectations of the children thus born in poverty become in fact 'falsified': i.e. if positive economic changes take place between the time the children are born and the time they should have died had conditions remained unaltered. However, in view of the observation that 'quite heedless marriages were not found to any large extent in western Europe', and that the age of marriage in the eighteenth and nineteenth centuries changed very little, the whole argument seems rather irrelevant.

35. Gustaf Utterström, 'Two Essays . . .', in Glass and Eversley, *op. cit.*, p. 529.

36. Gustaf Utterström, 'Two Essays . . .', *op. cit.*, pp. 546–547. 'It is also clear . . . that the mild winters 1721–35 must have made it easier for the poor to survive. Small fluctuations in climate may not have had any great effect on population development in the countries south of Finno-Scandia. Statistics relating to births and deaths in various parts of Denmark suggest that neither in 1721–35 nor in 1751–60 was there any increase in Danish population of magnitude comparable to that in Sweden. Denmark does not lie as near the "climatic margin" for grain production as do the other three Scandinavian countries. The majority of farmers elsewhere in Scandinavia, even after a normal harvest, had little grain to spare, but many Danish farmers grew grain for sale and even after a bad harvest they seem to have had enough, at any rate on the islands. This may well be one of the main reasons why the death rate fluctuated less violently in Denmark

than in the other Scandinavian countries, though even in Denmark the marriage, birth and death rates were markedly influenced by the yield of the harvest.'

37. P. Deprez, 'The Demographic Development of Flanders in the Eighteenth Century' (translated by Margaret Hilton), in Glass and Eversley, *op. cit.*, p. 627.

38. P. Deprez, *op. cit.*, pp. 621–622. 'It is obvious that this explanation is not an exclusive one: the fluctuations in the births-marriage ratios can of course be partly due to the effects of migration.'

39. *Vide* Eino Jutikkala, 'Finland's Population Movement in the Eighteenth Century', in Glass and Eversley, *op. cit.*, pp. 549–562, especially pp. 556–562.

40. J. Meuvert, 'Demographic Crisis in France from the Sixteenth to the Eighteenth Century', in Glass and Eversley, *op. cit.*, p. 521, suggests that 'the pursuit of evidence on births and deaths should be supported by parallel studies on grain prices and on the severity of food shortages. . . .'

41. J. Meuvert, *op. cit.*, p. 434.

42. Louis Henry, 'The Population of France in the Eighteenth Century', in Glass and Eversley, *op. cit.*, pp. 447–448. Henry's provisional conclusions are that the progress of France's population was retarded in the first half of the eighteenth century by the last great famine in 1709–10 and the bad years which followed it until 'the end of the reign of Louis XIV. A bad year in 1719 . . . the plague of 1720 . . . bad years during the decade 1740–49 . . . bad years, famines and epidemics from 1750 to 1789. But none as intense as the earlier crises.'

43. Louis Henry, *op. cit.*, pp. 447–448.

44. D. V. Glass, Glass and Eversley, *op. cit.*, p. 16.

45. 'For women . . . the increase was from 32·7 years . . . to 49 years for the generation born in the last quarter of the eighteenth century. . . .' D. V. Glass, *op. cit.*, p. 16.

46. D. V. Glass, *op. cit.*, p. 17. 'William Morgan's calculations for the whole life assurances of the Equitable . . . (1768–1826) almost entirely of males the mortality rates show declines around 50 per cent between 1768–87 and 1815–26 the main fall occurring by the end of the eighteenth century.'

47. Quoted from Professor H. J. Habakkuk's excellent article, 'English Population in the Eighteenth Century', in the *Economic History Review*, 2nd series, VI, 1953, pp. 117–133.

48. Adam Smith, quoted by Professor Habakkuk in *op. cit.*, reprinted by Glass and Eversley, *Population in History*, p. 270.

49. This statement has, of course, to be taken as a simplification, as it deliberately for the sake of clarity overstresses one factor—population—and ignores the others.

50. It must be borne in mind that what was true in one period and in one place need not be so in other periods and in other places.

51. Habakkuk, *op. cit.*, p. 271.

52. *Vide* Habakkuk, *op. cit.*, p. 272.

53. Habakkuk, *op. cit.*, pp. 272–273.

54. Habakkuk, *op. cit.*, p. 274.

55. Professor Habakkuk shows this as follows: '. . . the relatively slow rate of population increase of France in the later eighteenth century can most plausibly be attributed, as it was by some writers of the time, to a low birth rate; there is no reason to suppose that the French death rate was unusually high. (*Vide* J. J. Spengler, *French Predecessors of Malthus*, 1942.)

The rapid natural increase of population in colonial America was fairly clearly due in the main to a high birth rate. (*Vide* A. J. Lotka, in *J. American State Assoc.*, 1927, XXII, p. 169.) Mr. Connell places the weight of his explanation of the rapid rise of Irish population upon factors influencing the birth rate (K. H. Connell, *The Population of Ireland*, 1950). Mr. Aries suggests that the high density of population of modern Brittany is due to high birth rates. . . .' See p. 274 in Glass and Eversley, *op. cit.*

56. Habakkuk also quotes other examples: for Finland from Eli Heckscher, *Econ. Hist. Rev.*, 1949; for western and eastern fringes of Europe, Aries, *op. cit.*, pp. 23–25; for Ireland, Connell, *op. cit.*, p. 280 and others.

57. See J. Hajnal's earlier quoted article on this subject in Glass and Eversley, *op. cit.*, pp. 101–143.

58. T. H. Marshall, *op. cit.*, reprinted in Glass and Eversley, p. 435. (Quoted from Habakkuk, p. 276.)

59. As indeed is done by Professor Habakkuk, *vide op. cit.*, pp. 276–278.

60. Habakkuk, *op. cit.*, p. 279.

61. Professor Habakkuk partially withdrew this statement in 'The Economic History of Modern Britain', *Journal of Econ. Hist.*, 1958, p. 497.

62. Habakkuk, *op. cit.*, p. 279.

63. Malthus, *Principles*, pp. 228–229, quoted by Habakkuk, *op. cit.*, p. 280.

64. *Vide* Y. S. Brenner, *Theories of Economic Development and Growth*, London, 1966; 'The Classical Economists', David Ricardo.

65. Habakkuk, *op. cit.*, p. 280.

66. Habakkuk, *op. cit.*, p. 281.

67. *Vide* E. H. Phelps Brown and Sheila V. Hopkins, 'Seven Centuries of Building Wages', *Economica*, 1956. Reprinted in E. M. Carus-Wilson, ed., *Essays in Economic History*, London, 1962, Vol. II, pp. 168–196. See Appendix B. Also W. G. Hoffmann, *British Industry 1700–1950*, Oxford, 1955.

68. 'Mercantilist notions of economic development focused upon aggregate output and not on *per capita* rate of production and consumption, on power, and not welfare. The people for whom progress was desired were the "people who mattered", namely merchants, manufacturers and the rich land owners, and not all classes of society. That what was desirable in the one class—the entrepreneurs' "love of gain", was evil in another. They believed that the world's resources and domestic demand were strictly limited, which led them to the conclusion that low wages are the best incentive to hard work and maximum production, unlike modern economists they paid little attention to the expansion of domestic demand. . . . The classical school, and particularly Ricardo, believed in a sort of ratchet effect by which each general increase in the demand for labour and consequent rise in real wages would raise the working-man's subsistence level, so that the following downswing could never reduce them as low as they had been before. In time, Ricardo believed, the oscillations around the upward trend would gradually raise *per capita* production and consumption and would be helped and help education to restrain undue acceleration of population growth. . . .' As Ricardo puts it: '. . . many of the conveniences now enjoyed in an English cottage would have been thought luxuries at an earlier period of our history. From manufactured commodities always falling and raw produce always rising, with the progress of society, such a disproportion in their relative value is at length created, that in rich countries a labourer, by the sacrifice of a very small quantity only of his food, is able to provide liberally for all his other wants.' *Vide* Y. S. Brenner, *op. cit.*, Chapters I and II.

69. *Population Studies*, Vol. III, No. 1, June 1949, pp. 3–65.

70. Quoted from Contents Summary of Mr. Gille's article in *Population Studies*, Vol. III, No. 1, June 1949, pp. 1–2.

71. M. Pierre Goubert, 'Recent Theories and Research in French Population between 1500 and 1700'. Reprinted in Glass and Eversley, *op. cit.*, pp. 457–473.

72. This is also the author's view, *vide* Y. S. Brenner, 'Prices and Wages in England 1450–1550', *Economic History Review*, Vol. XIV, 1961, and 'Prices 1551–1650', Vol. XV, 1962.

73. Habakkuk, *op. cit.*, p. 284. For the connection between economic opportunity and fertility see W. Stys, 'The Influence of Economic Conditions on the fertility of Peasant Women', *Population Studies*, Vol. II, 1957–58, pp. 136–148.

74. See Louis Henry, *op. cit.*, in Glass and Eversley, p. 448.

75. T. H. Marshall, 'The Population Problem during the Industrial Revolution', *Economic History* (Supplement to *Economic Journal*), I, 1926–29. Reprinted Glass and Eversley, *op. cit.*, p. 247.

76. A. Redford, *Labour Migration in England*, Manchester, 1926, pp. 63 ff., quoted here from a summary by Professor Habakkuk in 'The Economic History of Modern Britain' in *The Journal of Economic History*, Vol. XVIII, 1958, p. 494.

77. Krause, 'English Fertility and Mortality', *Economic History Review*, Vol. XI, 1958; D. V. Glass, 'Changes in Fertility . . .', in L. Hogben, Ed., *Political Arithmetic*, London, 1937, pp. 173–194. Quoted by Habakkuk, *Journal of Econ. Hist.*, 1958, p. 494.

78. Habakkuk, *Journal of Economic History*, 1958, p. 494. This is so unless one could add evidence of changes in human fertility arising out of conditions like certain kinds of food or work, which were specific to some classes. There is, however, none [Y. S. Brenner].

79. Rickman's 'Second Series of Eighteenth-Century Population Figures', *Journal of the Royal Statistical Society*, XCII, 1929, pp. 256–263.

80. T. S. Ashton, *An Economic History of England. The 18th Century*, London, 1955, pp. 1–29. 'The Standard of Life of the Workers . . .' in F. A. Hayek, *Capitalism and the Historian*, Chicago, 1954, pp. 127–159.

81. Habakkuk, *Journal of Economic History*, 1958, p. 497.

82. T. H. Marshall, 'The Population Problem during the Industrial Revolution', *Economic History*, I, 1929. Reprinted in E. M. Carus-Wilson, Ed., *Essays*, London, 1961.

83. G. Talbot Griffith, *Population Problems in the Age of Malthus*, Cambridge, 1926, pp. 241–260.

84. T. H. Marshall, *op. cit.*, pp. 326–330.

85. The Napoleonic Wars, Speenhamland, Luddism, Peterloo, etc.

86. T. H. Marshall, 'The Population of England and Wales from the Industrial Revolution to World War', *Economic History Review*, V, 1935, No. 2, reprinted in E. M. Carus-Wilson, Ed., *op. cit.*, p. 331.

87. T. H. Marshall, 'The Population of England and Wales . . .', in Carus-Wilson, Ed., *op. cit.*, p. 335.

88. T. H. Marshall, 'The Population of England and Wales . . .', *op. cit.*, p. 336. Marshall's facts appear to be out of tune with other evidence about wage-price relationships. See, for example, the article of E. H. Phelps Brown and Sheila V. Hopkins, 'Seven Centuries of Prices of Consumables Compared with Builders' Wage-Rates', in *Economica*, 1956, Appendix B (Years 1780–1850). Also compare with W. G. Hoffmann, *British Industry 1700–1950*, Oxford, 1955, Total Production Tables (1780–1850). And see the present author's explanation for temporary spells of

unemployment, particularly in agriculture, due to technological progress in the Introduction, pp. 32–42.

89. Marshall himself admits that 'other countries had similar birth-rates and no Poor Law' at this time.

90. Though he does mention the appearance (1831) of the cholera epidemics (1848–54), he does not stress their importance.

91. This is, in fact, the point of view of Adna Ferrin Weber in *The Growth of Cities in the Nineteenth Century*, claiming that taking into consideration the relative growth of city populations to the growth in the country as a whole, the continuation of the higher death rate in the towns beyond the middle of the century would have led to a net fall in population. *Vide* Introduction, p. 5.

92. See Warren S. Thompson, *Population Problems*, pp. 390–391, Tables 19–2, 19–3.

93. See footnote No. 13, T. H. Marshall, *op. cit.*, p. 339.

94. T. H. Marshall, 'The Population of England and Wales . . .' *op. cit.*, pp. 341–342.

95. Habakkuk, *Journal of Economic History*, 1958, p. 498.

96. J. D. Chambers, 'Three Essays on the Population and the Economy of the Midlands'. Reprinted in Glass and Eversley, *op. cit.*, pp. 308–353.

97. Habakkuk admits, however, that there is 'some evidence that over the country as a whole severe dearth did cause higher mortality' and that mortality in towns, especially in London, where prices had already become the main dividers between life and starvation by this time, was particularly great in years of dearth. Obviously, if the second reservation was true, then it should help to explain the first. See William Farr, in *Journal of the Statistical Society*, 1846, IX, pp. 158–174, and D. M. George in *Economic Journal*, 1908. Quoted by Habakkuk, p. 498, footnotes 27 and 28.

98. Habakkuk, *Journal of Economic History*, 1958, p. 499.

99. G. Talbot Griffith, *Population Problems in the Age of Malthus*, Cambridge, 1926.

100. M. C. Buer, *Health, Wealth and Population in the Early Days of the Industrial Revolution, 1760–1815*, London, 1926. This view was best summarised by the economist J. R. Hicks in *The Social Framework*, Oxford, 1942, Ch. IV.

101. T. H. Marshall, *op. cit.*, and T. S. Ashton, *An Economic History of England. The 18th Century*, Ch. I.

102. K. F. Helleiner, *op. cit.*, p. 7. Quoted here from Habakkuk, *Journal of Economic History*, p. 499.

103. Habakkuk, *Journal of Economic History*, 1958, pp. 500–501.

104. *La formation de la population parisienne au XIXe siècle*, Paris, 1950.

105. 'Towards a History of Population', *Population*, 1946, pp. 245–256. Reprinted in Glass and Eversley, *op. cit.*, pp. 70–78 (translated by Peter Jimack).

106. Louis Chevalier, in Glass and Eversley, *op. cit.*, p. 73.

107. Louis Chevalier, in Glass and Eversley, *op. cit.*, p. 74.

108. Louis Chevalier, in Glass and Eversley, *op. cit.*, pp. 74–75.

109. Charles H. Pouthas, *French Population during the first half of the nineteenth century*, Paris, 1956.

110. This is more or less the view which T. H. Marshall and others adopted about the effects of urbanisation in England. See also Warren S. Thompson, *Population Problems*.

111. See studies of Philippe Pinchemel, *Structures sociales et dépopulation*

rurale dans les campagnes picardes de 1836 à 1936, Paris, 1957, and also David Pinkey, *Napoleon III and the Rebuilding of Paris*, Princeton, 1958.

112. Claude Fohlen, *Journal of Economic History*, 1958, pp. 507–508.

113. It appears that the rate of urban accretion increased from about 1840, when the rate of total population increase began to slow down. The inverse correlation breaks down, however, in the 1870s, when both the towns' rate of growth and that of the rural areas rise very rapidly together. In the 1880s the old pattern returns once more.

114. English Population (approx.). 1801—10,506,000; 1821—12,000,000; 1851—17,928,000; 1871—22,712,000; 1881—25,974,000; 1891—29,003,000. French Population (approx.) (Territory of 1899). 1801—26,931,000; 1821—29,871,000; 1851—34,902,000; 1872—36,103,000; 1891—38,343,000. German Population (approx.) (Territory of Empire, 1899). 1819—25,917,000; 1837—31,590,000; 1852—35,930,000; 1871—41,000,000; 1890—49,428,000.

115.

ESTIMATED PROPORTION OF PEOPLE LIVING IN TOWNS COMPARED WITH TOTAL POPULATION

(England and Wales cities with population over 20,000; France, the 12 great cities of 1891. Germany, the 25 great cities of 1890 with suburbs)

	England and Wales %	*France* %	*Germany* %		*England, and Wales* %	*France* %	*Germany* %
1801	16·9	4·5		1851	37·7	5·9	5·7*
1811	18·1			1861	38·4	8·9	6·5
1821	20·8	4·7	4·7**	1871	43·4	9·8	9·5=
1831	25·0	5·0	4·9***	1881	50·0	11·2	11·6=+
1841	29·4	5·4	5·0++	1891	55·5	12·0	14·4=+++

* (1852) ** (1819) *** (1837) +(1880) ++(1840) +++(1890)
= Including suburbs.

116. *Gesinde-Ordnung* was the Ordinance regulating the relationship between the master and the other members of the household. *Vide* J. H. Clapham, *Economic Development of France and Germany 1815–1914*, Cambridge, 1921 (in 1961 edition, pp. 278–279 and 205). Clapham writes: 'Every agricultural labourer who could in any way be regarded as living with his employer came within its [*Gesinde Ordnung's*] scope; and it remained the basis of the Prussian law of master and servant throughout the nineteenth century. Under this law, a contract once entered into could not be terminated prematurely from the workman's side; striking was a crime punishable with imprisonment; obedience was due to the point of absolute servility . . . the typical labour system of the east made these conditions applicable to most labourers. . . .' It is interesting to compare these relationships with the situation in parts of West Africa today.

117. Vol. VI, Pt. I, p. 61. For the Statistics for England and Wales, France and Germany see pp. 186, 189 and note 115.

118.

GROWTH OF THE GREATER CITIES IN EUROPE
(Millions)

	1800	*1850*	*1900*	*1950*
Moscow	0·2	0·3	1·2	4·1
Leningrad	0·2	0·5	1·4	3·2
London	1·0	2·4	4·5	3·3+
Berlin	0·2	0·4	2·7	3·2
Paris	0·5	1·0	2·7	2·9+
Vienna	0·2	0·4	1·7	1·8
Rome	0·2	0·2	0·5	1·7

Data from Warren S. Thompson, *Population Problems*, 1953, Table 19–1, p. 389. These are actual city populations to the nearest hundred thousand. A different basis of classification would yield different results. See particularly data marked +.

119. The estimated annual number of births per thousand women (age 15–44) in the United States, 1800–30, were 276, 267, 250 respectively for each decade; 1840–50, 208; 1880–90, 146. (Source: Thompson and Whelpton, *Population Trends in the United States.*)

120. F. A. Walker, 'Immigration and Degradation', *Forum*, Vol. XI, August 1891, p. 634.

121. J. Bertillon, 'Migration', *Dictionaire encyclopédique des sciences médicales.* Vol. VIII, 1873; H. P. Fairchild, *The Melting Pot Mistake*, New York, 1925.

122. Thompson and Whelpton, *op. cit.*, 1933, pp. 304–307.

123. *Population Studies*, No. 17, United Nations, p. 137, '. . . it is possible that in societies where birth control is practised fairly generally . . . the ascent of natives on the occupational scale resulting from large-scale immigration of cheap labour may have the effect of lowering their fertility. . . .'

124. United Nations *Population Studies*, No. 17, p. 139.

125. J. F. Dewhurst, *America's Needs and Resources*, New York, 1947, 1955, United States *Bureau of Census*, and Adna Ferrin Weber, *op. cit.*, p. 22.

126. Adna Ferrin Weber, *op. cit.*, p. 22, Table II.

DECENNIAL PERCENTAGE RATES OF INCREASE OF URBAN POPULATIONS

Decades	*Percentage increase of total population*	*Percentage of people living in cities of 8,000+*	*Percentage of the increase of people living in 124 cities*
1790–1800	35·1	3·97	74·4
1801–10	36·4	4·93	51·1
1811–20	33·1	4·93	36·4
1821–30	33·5	6·72	52·0
1831–40	32·7	8·52	61·6
1841–50	35·9	12·49	82·2
1851–60	35·6	16·13	60·8
1861–70	22·6	20·93	46·9
1871–80	30·1	22·57	38·8
1881–90	24·9	29·20	47·7

127. Dudley Kirk, 'Demographic Trends in Europe', *Annals of the American Academy of Political and Social Science*, 1949, p. 46.

128. Marcus Lee Hansen, *The Immigrant in American History*, 1941, p. 192. Quoted here from Frank Thistlethwaite, 'Migration from Europe overseas

in the 19th and 20th Centuries', *XIe Congres International des Sciences Historiques*, Stockholm, 1960.

129. Imre Frenczi, 'A Historical Study of Migration Statistics', *International Labour Review*, XX, 1929. Quoted from Thistlethwaite, *op. cit.*

130. Figures from F. Thistlethwaite, *op. cit.*

131. F. Thistlethwaite, *op. cit.*

132. F. Thistlethwaite, *op. cit.*

133. William Ashworth, *A Short History of the International Economy since 1850*, 2nd ed., 1962, p. 2.

134. Frank Thistlethwaite, 'Migration from Europe Overseas in the Nineteenth and Twentieth Centuries', in *Population Movements in Modern European History*, Herbert Moller, Ed., Boston, 1964.

135. Kingsley Davis, 'The Origin and Growth of Urbanization in the World', *The American Journal of Sociology*, March 1955, LX, No. 5. Reprinted in Herbert Moller, *op. cit.*, p. 67.

136. K. Davis, *The Population of India and Pakistan*, Princeton, 1951.

137. A. M. Carr-Saunders, *World Population—Past Growth and Present Trends*, London, 1936, p. 274. (In England and Wales the density of population in the same year was 695 persons per square mile, in Baluchistan 6·5, in the Dacca division of Bengal 935. Source: Carr-Saunders, 1936. Part of the difficulty is of course that India's population is unevenly distributed.)

138. A. M. Carr-Saunders, *op. cit.*, p. 38.

139. United Nations *Population Studies*, No. 17, p. 16.

140. United Nations *Population Studies*, No. 17, p. 16.

141. N. V. Sovani, *The Population Problem in India: A Regional Approach*, Poona, 1942; A. Geddes, 'Half a Century of Population Trends in India . . .', *The Geographical Journal*, London, 1941, Vol. 98, Nos. 5–6.

142. W. F. Willcox, 'The population of China and its modern increase', in *International Migration*, Vol. II, New York, 1931.

143. For critical assessment of this point see A. J. Jaffe, 'A review of the censuses, etc.', in *Population Studies*, I, 1947.

144. See also different estimates in United Nations *Demographic Yearbook*, 1951, p. 97, and 1956, p. 143; I. B. Taeuber and L. A. Orleans in *Population Index*, XXII, 1956, p. 274; J. S. Aird, *The Size Composition and Growth of the Population of Mainland China*.

145. R. Ishii, *Population Pressure and Economic Life in Japan*, London, 1937.

146. Quoted from United Nations *Population Studies*, No. 17, p. 17.

147. A. M. Carr-Saunders, *op. cit.*, p. 43.

148. United Nations *Population Studies*, No. 17, New York, 1953, *The Determinants and Consequences of Population Trends*. Summary of Historical outline of world population growth. Chapter II, p. 20.

Chapter III

AGRICULTURE

PROGRESS IN AGRICULTURE: GENERAL OBSERVATIONS

When Malthus first published his celebrated *Essay on the Principle of Population* in 1798, the stated object of the work was 'to investigate the causes that have hitherto impeded the progress of mankind towards happiness and to examine the probability of the total or partial removal of these causes in future'.[1] When he found that it was 'much beyond the power of an individual to enumerate all the causes', Malthus restricted his work to the one which he considered to be the principal and most important—'the constant tendency in all animated life to increase beyond the nourishment prepared for it'. At about the same time that these words were originally written, at the end of the eighteenth century, the population of England numbered close to 10 million, of Europe 192 million, and of the world close to 919 million people. A century later, by the end of the nineteenth century, the population of England had increased to about 30, of Europe to 423, and of the world to perhaps 1,608 million people; while the share of Europeans had risen from 21·2 to 26·9 per cent, and the share of North Americans from 0·7 to over 5 per cent of world population. With this, living standards and food consumption had also risen almost everywhere during the century and most of all in Europe, North America and Oceania. How did this come about? Firstly, it was due to the occupation of hitherto thinly populated or unpopulated land in America, Africa and Oceania; and, secondly, to the great rise in the productivity of land and labour. The first solution to the Malthusian problem was closely connected with the progress made in the development of means of transport and communication, with migration, with the spreading of international trade and, later, in the sphere of politics, with colonialism. The second solution was connected with the progress in botany and chemistry and with the wider use of mechanical equipment in agriculture. The former increased the area of cultivation; the latter raised its productivity per acre and per man-hour employed on it.[2] Both these processes of widening and 'deepening' the area of production were closely related to, and conditioned by, the immense socio-economic or cultural structural changes which accompanied them, and in the course of which the more or less predominant subsistence farming civilisations in Europe and of European origin were transformed into highly industrialised economies.

The first countries to share in the new methods of agricultural production were the Netherlands and England. The first step in the new direction seems to have been the reduction of the fallow. This became possible with the increasing use of clover and rye-grass. These have the great advantages that they derive most of their nourishment from the air and not from the earth. Their roots are packed with little knots of bacteria which absorb nitrogen from the air by means of which they enrich the soil when they decay. With their help, fallow need no longer remain in its traditional form and the land can be re-used for a crop while it is actually being improved.[3] The winter roots, i.e. turnips, swedes and mangolds, did the same, while in addition they could be used as cattle-fodder, and weed killer. In fact, their spreading brought about a revolution in animal husbandry. Clover and turnips made it possible to feed cattle throughout the winter and thereby remove the main restriction on their numbers.[4] Consequently an increase in the supply of meat and manure followed, the rise in the latter helping considerably to raise the yield of the arable land. Yet although it appears that in fact many farmers regarded these innovations with much suspicion, and thought them fit only for 'gentlemen who had money to burn', progress was gradually taking place, though most ordinary farmers were for a long time still holding on to their traditional ways.

In fact, the average yield per acre of wheat rose from about 16 bushels in the late sixteenth century to about 20–22 bushels an acre in the late eighteenth.[5] Yet even the early progress of improvements in agriculture, that is the introduction of the new crops of 'artificial' grasses and winter roots, depended to a greater or lesser extent on the progress of enclosure. It became even more dependent during the nineteenth century with the introduction and spreading of better soil drainage, agricultural machines, and artificial, chemical, fertilisers. All these required consolidated and, in the case of machines, large-scale holdings. In addition to this they required security of tenure. The innovations cost money, and without security of tenure there was no point in investing in them. For these reasons enclosure and innovations went together and were indeed the business of the rich, of the 'gentlemen with money to burn'. Therefore it is probably true that, until close to the middle of the nineteenth century, the progress of enclosure reflected the rate at which the new farming practices were spreading throughout England. Thus, paradoxically, whenever food was scarce and its prices high, enclosure proceeded only very slowly, but when the farmers' prosperity abated, enclosure, and with it new agricultural techniques, spread most rapidly. The reason for this apparent paradox is fairly obvious; when victual prices were high the small landowners found it easier to resist the pressures or temptations of the rich. However, after the middle of the nineteenth century, the great landowners diverted their attention away from the traditionally cultivated small village holdings and turned towards the large tracts of waste which were still to be found scattered throughout England. By the end of the century the trend was reversed and increasingly greater quantities of food were imported; part of the arable land reverting to permanent grass.[6] By that time, however, urbanisation, the growth of the manufacturing industries, and improvements in transport, food preservation and the application of industrial machinery and chemistry had already transformed British agriculture into a highly developed modern industry.

The rising food prices which accompanied the process of urbanisation and industrialisation in the first half of the nineteenth century increased farmers' incomes and those of the most efficient farmers most of all. This in turn not only stimulated the wish for improvements but also provided the necessary capital to carry them out. Thus while the rise of the manufacturing industries stimulated the demand for farm products and thereby raised the farmers' incomes, the farmers' higher incomes also raised the demand for manufactures which stimulated the development of the manufacturing industries. Both sectors of the economy were therefore pushing each other forward. Though it is difficult to trace the exact sources of the capital which financed industrial development in the early nineteenth century, there is some evidence that a good part of it, and perhaps even the best part of it, came out of agricultural earnings. Yet, it is also true that some of the money which went into the innovations in agriculture was earned in industry. A not unrealistic assessment of the process may therefore be that 'the landed aristocracy—seeing its traditional socio-political dominance threatened by the rising urban class of merchant capitalists—became more profit-minded, giving new impetus to the enclosure movement by which land was consolidated into larger and more efficient holdings'.[7] While, on the one hand, this process must have caused a great deal of hardship for the evicted and bought-off tenants, it was, on the other hand, providing industry with its necessary labour force. At the same time it provided the farmers and landlords who were able to hold on to their land with a continuously expanding cash market for their produce. Thus it was the rise in demand for agricultural products, and above all for foodstuffs, which became *effective* through the rise of industry, which came to be the prime mover for the ascent in agricultural efficiency in England during the first three decades of the nineteenth century.[8]

In the rest of Europe, population growth remained essentially rural until the middle of the century. With the exception of France, and for different reasons with the exception of Ireland,[9] Europe's population was increasing rapidly at one time or another in the nineteenth century. However, after the forties the rural population no longer participated in the accretion to the same degree as the population as a whole. In fact rural population remained stagnant in many parts of Europe as its natural increase was rapidly siphoned off overseas or into the towns. According to Professor Folke Dovring,[10] the agricultural population of Germany numbered '18·7 million in 1871 and 18·5 million in 1895 which means 45 and 35½ per cent of the total population respectively'. In the three Scandinavian countries, the agricultural population also increased throughout the nineteenth century, but the much sharper rise in the non-agricultural population reduced the share of the former to less than 50 per cent of the total by the end of the century. Developments in Austria were not dissimilar. There too about half of the total population was employed in agriculture by 1900. In eastern Europe the trend was somewhat different. There the rise in population during the nineteenth century was not matched by the growth of towns and industry to the extent it was in north-western Europe, and consequently the number of people employed in agriculture continued to increase. Therefore, as Professor Dovring expressed it, 'Much of eastern Europe was thus the scene of a demographic explosion with little more than agriculture to take care of the increase'. In the Mediterranean countries, where population pressure had already been high, the accretion in the nineteenth century was less striking than in northern and eastern Europe. The cause may well have been the combination of poverty and the specifically Mediterranean cultural environment, which prevented landless labourers from getting married, while at the same time it greatly reduced illegitimacy. Though it is of course true that urban development had come much earlier in the Mediterranean area than in northern and in eastern Europe, its nature and its occupational structure were very different. The rise of northern towns was accompanied by both industrial and agricultural prosperity, whereas the Mediterranean peoples were in the nineteenth century experiencing a period of depression due to the loss of trade and the poverty of their quasi-feudal over-populated agricultural sector.

In summary, therefore, the shift away from the predominance of agriculture in the employment structure of the growing European population had its origin in eighteenth-century England and Belgium and continued in Germany before, in France during, and in the Scandinavian countries after, the middle of the nineteenth century. In eastern Europe, however, farming remained the foremost occupation until well into the twentieth century, and the same is true of the Mediterranean area. Even in predominantly agricultural societies there had always been a surplus of produce (in normal years) to feed perhaps 20 per cent of the population which was not productive in agriculture (such as soldiers, priests, administrators, artisans, merchants, etc.). Therefore any increase in the total number of people which was not accompanied by a similar increase in the number of people who were not productive in agriculture—assuming that no drastic changes were taking place in the age or sex distribution of the population—must have increased the agricultural surplus. As this was the case in eastern Europe in the later part of the nineteenth century, this too helped to feed the industrial populations of western Europe, in much the same way as America helped to feed the industrial population of England in an even earlier period. By that time, however, *per capita* output in agriculture had risen everywhere, including eastern Europe, and surpluses had increased considerably above the rate of population growth.

THE WIDENING OF THE WORLD'S CULTIVATED AREA AND THE RISING PER-CAPUT OUTPUT OF PEOPLE EMPLOYED IN AGRICULTURE

It is possible to outline the changes in European agriculture as follows. Firstly, Europe's agricultural population increased while industry had not yet reached the state in which it could absorb the full rate of population accretion. In the second phase, that is by the middle of the nineteenth century, the number of people who were engaged in agriculture remained relatively stable. And in the third phase, the number of people employed in agriculture was diminished in both relative and absolute terms. However, this phase was not reached anywhere in Europe (with two possible exceptions—England and Belgium) before the first half of the twentieth century.

If, as we have seen, the progress of agriculture may well have played a major role in facilitating the development of industry in the first of the three phases, then industry fully repaid its debt to agriculture during the second and third phases. The rapid increase in mechanisation, the application of inanimate power and of chemistry in industry, was by this time spreading to transport and agriculture, and at the same time revolutionising farming and farm produce. The directions from which experience gained in industry invaded agriculture were various; firstly, it took the form of labour-time saving mechanical equipment; secondly, it introduced better means of transport and food preservation and refrigeration; thirdly, it brought about the application of chemistry; fourthly, the production of new industrial raw materials; and fifthly, new forms of organisation and finance. The spreading of the use of mechanical equipment greatly reduced the labour-time required for the production of food, i.e. it increased *per capita* output, and on many occasions improved the quality of the work itself. The improved transport and preservation facilities made possible the importation of foodstuffs from where they could be best and most cheaply produced, i.e. it increased specialisation and the division of labour. The application of chemistry and the better understanding of the nature of plant and animal growth increased the output per acre. The greater demand for industrial raw materials from agriculture raised farmers' incomes and helped to bring about better utilisation of certain lands which were hitherto thought unproductive. The new forms of organisation helped to reduce further wastages of both man-days and land, while the new methods of finance, i.e. agricultural and co-operative banks, helped to finance improvements even on relatively small farms.

It is, of course, almost impossible to separate these factors from each other. A reduction in transport costs will influence the movement of labour, while it will also affect the production of goods in different parts of the world, and both will together influence the way land and labour are used and the application of machines and chemicals, etc. Clapham, for example, illustrated the complexity of this interdependence by showing that the cost of shipping greasy New Zealand wool half way round the world to London had already dropped to about 1d. or less, per one shilling worth, before 1886, and never fell below ½d. until 1914; and that, therefore, the fall of 26 per cent in the average cost of imported wool, from the decade of 1877–86 to the decade 1887–96, cannot be explained by the lowering of the distance barrier. 'But wheat, which on the average of the twelve years 1868–79 had cost 11s. a quarter in carriage from Chicago to Liverpool, and still cost 9s. 1½d. in 1880, could be brought for 6s. 2½d. in 1886. By 1892 the figure would be 4s. 3d., and by 1902, 2s. 10½d. The carriage costs of grains, on equally well-organised trade routes, had fallen, and would fall, similarly.'[11] With regard to fresh meat, the situation was again different. Imports of frozen meats grew only slowly in the eighties, 'while the processes for handling them were being worked out'.[12] For this reason pigs' meat, which came cured, could stand the competition of other meats until close to the end of the century. But, with the progress of refrigeration in the decade which followed, pig meat imports fell to no more than a third of the total.

During the same time, i.e. in the last four decades of the nineteenth century, an area about ten times as large as that of England was opened up for cultivation in the United States and linked by the great transcontinental railways with the eastern ports. In the course of their construction the working crews who built the lines were living on the native bison, the buffalo herds, which were consequently wiped out. Free land thus became abundant and labour became relatively even scarcer than it had been already. Two solutions presented themselves to this problem. Stimulated by the rapidly increasing demand for foodstuffs in the eastern United States and in Europe, both cattle grazing and the introduction of agricultural machinery became highly lucrative. Most important for the first solution, cattle raising, was the striking development of the open range. Here, in the period 1866–86 the cattle, 'descendants of stock imported by the Spaniards, roaming freely and controlled only by cowboys, multiplied rapidly in the room of the almost exterminated bison. Great herds were driven northwards from Texas to the railways and as far as Montana. On them was founded the meat-packing industry, centred on Chicago, which by the seventies was already supplying the European market. . . . The cattle-population of the range was doubled in two decades, to reach 45 million about 1886.'[13] In addition to this, grazing was also extended in other parts of the United States, where cattle were frequently fattened instead of being taken directly to the slaughter-house. In time 'blue grass', maize, timothy-grass and in some areas even wheat, oats, rye, barley, buckwheat and even potatoes were grown as cattle food, and much attention was given to the improvement of stock.[14]

The second solution, that is the substitution of agricultural machines for labour, was ushered in by the increasing utilisation of the steel mould-boards, the horse-hoe and the seed-drill. As Derry and Williams wrote,[15] 'Since harvesting was the most labour-consuming operation in agriculture, it is rather surprising that the reaping-machines invented in Britain and America from 1780 onwards were left ineffective for half a century'. But it was only after the railroads and the opening up of the West had revolutionised the demand for American agricultural products that the need for such equipment became truly pressing. In 1833, an American named Obey Hussey had invented a horse-drawn reaping-machine. A few years later the machine was improved by Cyrus McCormick, who also set up a factory in Chicago in 1848 for its production; ten years later this factory was producing 4,000 'McCormick reaping-machines' annually. By 1856 a machine which was equipped with a flexible cutter-bar was becoming popular for haymaking. As had been the case in the British cotton industry, the speeding-up of one process of production caused maladjustments in others and thereby stimulated the introduction of an ever wider range of innovations. Soon the improvement of reaping and haymaking equipment led to similar progress in the other stages of farm production. The first successful machine for the separation of the grain from the husks and straw was invented in 1784; a drum was rotated inside a curved shield, 'arranged like a mudguard on a wheel but with only a very small clearance: grain was fed in between drum and shield so that the husks were rubbed of'.[16] Until about 1842 the machine was usually driven by horse-power, but in that year Ranson won a prize from the Royal Agricultural Society in England for the application of locomotive steam-engines to threshing. 'Meanwhile, a winnowing machine had been developed for the further separation of the corn from the chaff by the use of a fan and sieves, which were respectively turned and shaken by rotating a handle outside the box through which the grain was passed. The way was thus prepared for a more complicated type of machine, which combined threshing with cleaning apparatus and screens for grading the corn; in the later nineteenth century these were usually engine-driven and were moved from farm to farm under their own steam according to the contractor's arrangements.'[17] In time similar steam-driven machines were also introduced with 'chopping knives and crushing rollers for the treatment of chaff, root crops, and cattle cake' to prepare the winter feed for cattle.

The net result of the introduction of these and similar pieces of labour-saving farm equipment was a rapid increase in *per capita* output.[18]

Conditions in Australia, New Zealand and Argentina were basically similar to those in the United States, although in fact cultivation in Australia developed less rapidly than on the open prairies of the United States. The land was less fertile and in many areas lacked phosphates, which were not imported until the last quarter of the nineteenth century. Yet labour shortage there was no less acute and its solution not dissimilar. Large numbers of cattle were kept for home consumption on the open ranges, and after Harrison, the editor of the *Melbourne Age*, saw the 'enormous source of wealth that lies still undeveloped in the export of meat from the Australian pastures', refrigeration began to be considered as a solution to the marketing problem. In fact, canned meat had been exported from Australia for some time, but the processes involved proved too expensive to be competitive on the European markets. In 1861 the first meat-freezing plant was set up in Sydney, in 1874 another, and yet another in 1875, and though these were constructed for the supply of the local market, the possibilities for extension were also recognised. Then, in 1877 the S.S. *Paraguay*, which was fitted with an ammonia-compression machine which could freeze meat to 17°F., arrived in France from Argentina after a six-month voyage with its cargo in excellent condition. This proved the possibility of conveying meat over long distances. Two years later a Bell-Coleman refrigerator plant was installed on another vessel, and Australian meat was sent to London and arrived there on 2 February 1880. Its quality was indistinguishable from freshly killed English beef and mutton.[19] The world had become 'smaller', and soon the same conditions which had stimulated meat production only two or three decades earlier in the United States encouraged it in Australia, New Zealand and even more strongly in Argentina.

In New Zealand, too, flocks had increased from under a quarter of a million in 1850 to over a million by 1880, but with the installation of the Bell-Coleman plants their number increased even more rapidly. According to T. N. Morris,[20] the New Zealand trade in frozen mutton and lamb amounted to 2 million carcasses in 1892 and to almost 4 million carcasses by the end of the century. At first the meat was frozen on board ship, but later it was placed in cold storage on land ready for immediate loading. Similarly some 3,571 carcasses of mutton and lamb (no beef) were shipped from Argentina in 1880, and two decades later the volume had risen to 2,332,837 carcasses of mutton and lamb and to 414,376 cwt. of frozen and chilled beef.

As for the introduction of labour-saving machines, progress was less impressive than in the United States. The stripper and the stump-jump, a kind of combine-harvester and a plough suitable for land cleared by burning, appear to have become fairly widespread by the last quarter of the nineteenth century. By the end of that century, with the development of the Australian railway system and the importation of superphosphates, Australia was able to join the major wheat-producing, and exporting, countries of the world. Wheat was also grown on a large scale for export in parts of New Zealand. Here the double-furrow plough, the binder and the grain-drill were used to replace scarce labour. After 1880, when artificial fertilisers were more frequently applied, wheat yields in New Zealand rose from 325,000 bushels in 1870 to 16¾ m. in 1891 and 19¼ m. in 1899.[21]

In summary, the rapid accretion of people in Europe, and the relative decline in the number of people employed in food production particularly in the north and west of Europe during the nineteenth century, not only produced a stream of emigrants to settle in some under-populated parts of the world,[22] but at the same time raised the demand for the victuals which could be grown there. Therefore, the twofold result of population growth in Europe was that, on the one hand it provided the labour force and on the other the market for the produce of the newly settled areas. As the market grew relatively faster than the labour force, economic progress had to adjust itself to the specific conditions. One way in which it adjusted was by turning to open-range cattle and sheep farming; another way was by introducing labour-saving mechanical equipment and by specialising in labour extensive crops. Both processes were accompanied by progress in the management, preservation and transportation of foodstuffs and stimulated by the rapidly decreasing portion of the European population who were able or willing to provide their own victuals. Indeed, as T. S. Mort had said in 1875,[23] 'God provides enough and to spare for every creature. . . . He sends into the world: but the conditions are not often in accord. Where the food is the people are not, and where the people are the food is not. It is however. . . within the power of man to adjust these things. . . .'

While Mort's efforts for 'adjusting these things' may have been highly commendable (he tried to freeze Australian meat for shipment to Europe), other efforts were not. One example of the latter kind was the slave trade. In temperate regions labour could be attracted to good land by the prospects of high yields or profits. This was not true of the tropics. Here conditions were more difficult and less inviting for settlers. In the seventeenth and eighteenth centuries, when the demand for tropical products was still relatively small, the employment of slaves, or 'gatherers', under white supervision, was the most common solution. However, with the growth of the European markets, 'gathering', i.e. the establishing of trading posts where the local population could exchange the uncultivated tropical fruits for things they wanted, was in many places replaced by deliberate efforts to grow the products in plantations staffed with slave labour. In some parts of the tropics both systems existed side by side, and in some 'gathering' even survived slavery.[24] Yet, with the development of agricultural machines, slavery proved to be too costly and inefficient on plantations where machines could be employed. As the operation of machines required a certain level of education, and education does not agree with the status of slaves, the white planters could not have it both ways. A cynic may conclude that with slavery becoming less profitable, civilisation discovered that it was immoral and the humanist campaign for its abolition became more successful. But for almost a century the struggle continued, while machines and contract labour were gradually replacing slaves. In time contract labour, i.e. workers brought from outside the area of the plantation, often from China for a specific period and for a specified rate of pay, transformed the whole structure of tropical agricultural production. The contracted or indented labourers were deprived of their traditional social security as members of an extended family or tribe and of their means of production, that is, land, by the fact that they were too far away from their original homes. They were therefore no less dependent for their livelihood on the owner of the plantation (the means of production) than their industrial counterparts in Europe—the proletariat.

With this, tropical agriculture was in places profoundly influenced by the progress in international transport. Here and there European trades were sometimes successfully removed to new areas. Tea was being produced in India and Ceylon, while an attempt to plant coffee in Ceylon ended in failure. Sugar was introduced into Queensland because of the labour shortages which arose in the traditional sugar-growing parts of the world after the emancipation of the slaves. This is perhaps particularly significant because, by the end of the nineteenth century, half of the world's sugar supply was still coming from canes. Another crop which, incidentally, also raised the demand for sugar was cocoa, which also spread with the wider consumption of coffee and tea. And although cocoa was known in Europe since the end of the eighteenth century, it was only after the middle of the nineteenth that it became one of the most important exports from the West Indies, the Gold Coast and later also from Nigeria.[25]

And with the changes in the products of the various tropical regions, organisational changes also took place. The old-style colonialism of the trading companies, which combined the merchant with the 'gatherer' and the plantation owners with the slave, began to break down and gave way here and there to a new kind of alliance between the local, and usually traditional leaders, and the European civil servants or government representatives, who gradually spread their 'protection' over the tropical enterprises of their nationals. In time the local traditional leadership was either replaced, made into or supplemented by the colonial administration. Thus a pattern was formed which introduced the tropics into the structure of European-centred international trade. This trade, however, was of a peculiar nature. Being structurally tied to European markets and geared to the export of primary products, it promoted an international division of labour between industrial countries in Europe and non-industrial ones in the tropics. In fact, the differences in education, skill, and social organisation[26] made industrial production in Europe more efficient than in the tropics. For this reason wage differentials, that is the cheaper colonial wage rates in the tropics, were more than offset by the savings in wages through the application of labour-saving machines in Europe. Thus the progress of technology in Europe, and the rising living standards which were almost everywhere accompanied by a higher level of education, made it more profitable for the investors in industry to use their capital in Europe than to risk it overseas in the tropics. As a result of this, investment in the tropics took place only in industries that were by their very nature not transplantable to Europe (i.e. mineral extraction and tropical agriculture) or during the short intervals when there were capital surpluses, i.e. gluts, in Europe and in the United States. A vicious circle caused the low level of capital to breed a low level of efficiency of labour, etc., and the low level of efficiency prevented the importation of industrial capital except for the purely Europe-orientated extraction and primary producing agricultural industries. Consequently, even local capital, wherever specific conditions made its accumulation possible,[27] usually went into commerce or short-term finance rather than to industry which could hardly compete with its European rivals. This would have been true even had local markets been protected, which was of course out of the question while such territories retained their colonial status. Tropical markets were never sufficiently attractive to entice foreign industrial capital because the local cash market, i.e. the effective demand, was nowhere large enough. Therefore an unwritten political bond came into being between the local (usually commercial) capital represented by the traditional leaders of the natives and the colonial governments, who were both interested in the maintenance of the economic *status quo*. The former served the 'mother country' by supplying it with cheap raw materials and tropical fruits—the latter helped the local elites to maintain their position and become rich. An intermediate status was held by the locally recruited civil service, which became the outlet for the relatively educated class which could not be absorbed in industry. Thereby the colonies were not only deprived of their natural reservoir of skilled labour but also 'delivered' from a potentially revolutionary element. It is because of the combination of these factors that each national movement for independence in the primary producing countries had at once a social content.

On the whole the increased supplies which were required from the tropics came from European settlers and from European-owned plantations, while only here and there the local people followed the European examples. The main constructive contribution of European agriculture to the colonial territories was the improvement of land clearing and the introduction of crops which had hitherto been unknown there. Rubber is a good example for this. Though later on small farmers produced much of the rubber for export, the trade had its origins in the great European-owned plantations.[28] Yet none of these export industries developed into a source of local market demand. They never became a source of cash-demand-forming employment.

'If we take cocoa farming as an example, we may be inclined' (as I have shown elsewhere),[29] 'to think that it has all the necessary ingredients for stimulating market-demand; it is fairly labour-intensive; a cash crop; defies the notions of risk avoidance and lack of long-term foresight in investment decisions, which is a frequent cause of complaint in under-developed countries and yet does not really stimulate demand. The cause appears to be twofold; firstly, most of the staple foodstuffs can be grown close to or in between cocoa trees and, secondly, the social "family" system makes subsistence farming possible and providential savings not obviously necessary. The combination of these two not only narrows the scope of the food market but indirectly by keeping down wage-rates reduces the market for manufactured goods. Thus, with the exception of a small number of foodstuffs, such as fish, and some "semi-luxury" goods, mostly foreign-made, the numerically greatest labour employing export sector contributes but little to the demand which could stimulate the development of local market production. However, the mineral extracting industry is equally discouraging. Though employment here is "demand-forming" and wages relatively high, the number of consumers involved is seldom large enough to have a significant impact on production.'

For these reasons, therefore, the opening up of the tropics to an increasing European trade benefited Europe by supplementing its supply of food and raw materials. The process, however, failed to benefit the peoples of tropical countries in the way that the development of America, Australia and New Zealand improved the conditions of those countries' settlers.

Thus, while northern Europe found its extensive solution to the food and population problem in the 'Atlantic' and tropical economy, by forging close trade links over the oceans, central Europe turned south and east to supplement its food supplies. Of course, neither of these trends was exclusive. At times England got grain from the Baltic states and France and Germany fruit and meat from America, Oceania and the tropics, but on the whole England was 'Atlantic' and the Continent 'eastwards' orientated.

In France and Germany land clearance in the nineteenth century was in most cases merely the resumption of cultivation on land which had fallen into waste because of wars and devastation. In Holland and Scandinavia, however, some hitherto unused land was actually added to the cultivated area. In the course of the nineteenth century some 200,000 acres were reclaimed from the sea in Holland, and in Scandinavia too a great area was cleared of forest. But this deforestation was the result of population growth and did little to yield a surplus for export or for the feeding of a rapidly growing urban population. In many cases the area cultivated expanded at the expense of grazing land and adversely influenced cattle breeding. Only after progress in technology, which gave agriculture the advantage of heavy iron-made equipment, could the difficult job of draining the soil and permanently clearing the forest land be successfully accomplished and a net surplus of produce achieved. It is therefore possible that the accretion of people in Scandinavia followed, rather than preceded, the industrial revolution which made the feeding of more people possible.[30]

In eastern Europe cultivation expanded more significantly, and in many places in excess of population growth. The settlement of eastern Hungary in the late eighteenth and early nineteenth centuries transformed the vast grazing region in the Danube plain into arable land. And in the rest of the Balkans 'the peculiar changes in the political map (during the nineteenth and early twentieth centuries) and their repercussions on the distribution of population, must have meant also a large expansion of the cultivated areas especially in the lowlands and hills with some abandoning of cultivation in the highlands. The migration of the free cattle-thieves from the mountains into the valleys involved many changes, among others increased importance of arable farming and diminution of the traditional pastoral economy, when the population grew larger.'[31] A very good example of the expansion of cultivation at the expense of grazing land was the regulation of the Tisza, a tributary river of the Danube, which used to flood large areas during the high-water season. By its regulation a vast plain became arable and for a time very fertile.[32]

DELAYS IN THE EMULATION OF MODERN FARMING TECHNIQUES IN EASTERN EUROPE

A convenient starting point for an examination of the agricultural developments which made Russia, for a time, into a major source of agra-produce is the year 1861, i.e. the year when serfdom was abolished there.

Essentially, the emancipation of the serfs, like so many other economic decisions in Russia, was a political decision consequent upon a military defeat. The Crimean War drove home the realisation that, without the development of an adequate railway system and a degree of industrialisation, Russia was unable to get on an even footing with the more advanced countries of Western Europe.[33] It was for this reason that even before the railroads made farming more profitable, and even before the productivity of free labour had risen so much above serf labour as to make the latter's unpaid services unprofitable, that a deliberate though strictly limited policy of industrialisation was envisaged by the Russian Government. However, the implementation of such a policy was fraught with a great number of complications. First, there was no class or group of people who were directly and vitally interested in industrial progress and upon whom the government could rely for support. The nobility could not be relied upon because it was bound to see its social and economic position threatened by the progress of industrialisation. The intelligentsia could not be relied upon because it was radical, opposed the autocratic régime, and questioned the very foundations of the social system. Yet at the same time the government had also to contend with considerable pressure from below, and was never free from the fear of unrest among the serfs which was particularly rife after each military defeat. Thus, the government was faced with the dilemma of having, on the one hand, 'to lay the ghost of peasant rebellions', and, on the other, to prevent the future menace of urban revolutions. The solution as it presented itself to the rulers of Russia was to promote just that degree of progress and liberty which was not inconsistent with the preservation of the traditional socio-economic structures. They had, therefore, to reduce the opposition to the growth of commerce and banking and to the spreading of the railway system, both of which had hitherto been regarded as the 'harbingers of the revolution'. These were the first steps towards turning Russia into the country which was able to produce a great share of western Europe's food supplies during the period of the latter's industrialisation. The liberation of the serfs helped to increase productivity in agriculture, the development of commerce and banking helped to stimulate production, and the linking-up of Russia with the rest of Europe by means of the growing railway system formed the connection between the increasing output and rising effective demand.[34]

On the eve of emancipation the number of serfs was about 22 millions, that is about half of the total peasant population of Russia. In many respects the position of the serfs was similar to that of slaves. The owner could transfer them from one kind of work to another, send them to the army or have them deported to Siberia for insubordination. The landlord could employ his serfs in industry, on his own land, or permit them to work in towns, provided they did not overstay his permission. There was always the police to return the serf to his master. The status of serf was attached to his person and not to the land he held. Even the children born to serfs in the city belonged to their master. The only way in which the serf could change his status was to purchase his freedom from his owner.

Thus Russian serfdom was very different from that of western European countries. It arose under the protection of a modern, well-organised central government which accepted it as a useful system for securing the labour force required to cultivate the land which was owned and administered by the nobility. There was neither the force of tradition nor the danger that peasants would escape and find shelter with another lord, nor even the freedom of the cities, to restrain the lords' autocracy. The Imperial police were ready to enforce the law everywhere. When the serf purchased his freedom in an industrial setting it meant a transfer of industrial capital to the nobility. As a result of this, industrialisation was not only held back by the shortage of labour but also by the additional cost of paying quitrents. Consequently, the margin of profitability in most industrial enterprises was too small to be attractive to investors and become competitive with western Europe.

In addition to this, serfdom had a harmful educational effect. Firstly, because they were deprived of any safety-valves for giving vent to their dissatisfactions, the Russian peasantry were left with only one means to free themselves from their oppression—namely by armed rebellion (and for this reason the government had to maintain continuous vigilance through a widespread network of secret informers).[35] Secondly, the Emancipation Act was above all an effort to strengthen Russia politically by raising its economic potential without opening up the floodgates to the pressures which were threatening the whole socio-political framework of society. In other words, the personal juridical status of the serfs was to be raised just high enough to suit the rulers' political ends and no more. They were to be settled with new obligations and given land, but without causing any significant losses to the nobility. They were, in fact, to be given precisely the degree of freedom which would increase total agricultural production and supply the trickle of labour to the cities which appeared desirable to a government which was eager to prevent the rise of a new source of social danger. With all this, however, the change in the *de jure* status of the peasantry was great indeed. They could henceforth acquire land, enter into legally binding agreements, and borrow funds and sue in the courts of law. Yet, *de facto*, those peasants who were rich enough to avail themselves of all these newly gained liberties had had them already, through all sorts of intermediaries, before 1861. So that in reality the new Act merely added greater security of tenure and title to property, and, what may have been more important, it created a new kind of atmosphere. The actual extent of the lands assigned to the peasants, under the system employed by the Ministry for the division of titles to land between the nobles and the freed serfs, was strikingly small.[36] How much land was actually divided by mutual consent is difficult to say, but the adverse educational effect of the whole situation was considerable. As Professor Gerschenkron pointed out,[37] 'Great emphasis has justly been placed in processes of industrialisation of backward countries on the need for improvements in the standards of honesty and in the willingness to abide by the obligations assumed. The flagrant breach of good faith and the disregard for property rights involved in the respective stipulations of the Acts of 1848 and 1861 certainly were a very inadequate way to instil respect for property and inviolability of contracts into a population among which very vague views of proprietary rights and a firm tradition of fraud were only too widespread.' In fact, the peasants had never really accepted the lords' titles to the land. The land had always been considered as belonging either to the tiller, the community, or God, though for all practical purposes the lord exercised full control over it. Moreover, many peasants must have felt that the new Act was rather favouring the landlord by giving him a title to the land—especially as wealth in Russia had been reckoned by the number of 'souls' the lord owned rather than by the acres under his control.[38] If to this is added the fact that the lord's forests and orchards, etc., were always considered 'fair game' for the poachers, and that the many traditional labour services were, in Russia as elsewhere, a large field for carelessness, evasion and deceit, it can be seen that the Emancipation could hardly have provided the best conditions for industrial responsibility. What the Emancipation did do was to create a new climate of social and occupational mobility which put Russia's economic development on a completely new foundation. Yet, at the same time, the allotments of land given to the freed peasantry were inadequate in size, and had to be paid for at disproportionately high rates.[39] Furthermore, the institutional system which was imposed upon the peasants with regard to the open and communal lands was conducive neither to the consolidation nor to the improvement of the land. The Act did in fact suggest that each commune should retain its rotative system for almost half a century after the land had been bought and paid for by individual farmers. It is therefore fairly certain that the prevailing attitude towards agricultural progress within the peasant economy was that 'it was not needed as the extent of arable land was fully sufficient to feed the population'. The export of grain was taken to be sufficient evidence of this.

It appears, therefore, that the Emancipation was to put the 'entrepreneurial leadership' and the leadership in raising the country's output into the hands of the gentry.[40] The peasant economy was to be left as a mere subsidiary to the gentry's, and the insufficiency of the peasants' allotments, together with the high obligations imposed upon them, were to make sure of a cheap labour supply. The way in which the Act disposed of the common land, the *mir* and the *obshchina*, made certain that peasants could not leave the land altogether and seek alternative employment. They were given just enough legal claim to the common land to make them feel that they were losing something by forfeiting it, while at the same time the area of land allotted to each was too small to make him economically independent. The peasant was made free to leave the land at the cost of relinquishing for ever his rights to it and to the use of the commons; he was required, in addition to this, to pay off all tax arrears to the end of the current year for all members of his household before he could leave, and then he also needed his parents' consent; finally, if the land he held had been bought from the landlord by the commune, he was to pay half of the debt which was incurred by the purchase of his allotment, and the village had to agree to guarantee the payment for the rest. In other words, the peasant who wished to make use of his new right to move had to pay half of the price of the land which he was abandoning and which he had always considered his own before the Act. So, in effect, the peasant found it almost impossible to leave the land, and even if he did so he was usually too poor to start anything else of his own. Thus, by design and in practice, the Emancipation made sure of a cheap supply of labour to the nobility whether the emancipated serf managed to move to the town or remained on the land. The one realistic avenue out of the village was to leave on a temporary passport which was given to peasants who left in order to earn the money required for paying arrears in government taxes. Such passports were issued for periods of between six months and three years. The applications had to be supported by the recommendation of the head of the *mir*, and the permit was granted by the local authorities at their discretion. Only in 1894 were these regulations somewhat modified, when a general change regarding industrialisation was adopted by the Russian Government. But even then, workers who wished to move to the town were required to bring formal permission from the head of the village commune and from the head of the family. Usually this meant paying a bribe to one or both. It is obvious that such practices did not help to reduce the cost of industrial production and to accelerate the rise of industry. They were even more effective in preventing the growth of an effective demand for industrial products in the rural areas—perhaps worst of all, they prevented the gentry from introducing agricultural machinery. As long as the peasants did not get enough land and were prevented from leaving the little land they had, farm labour was cheap and the gentry not hard pressed to introduce technological innovations. To some extent the discrimination in favour of the gentry could hardly have been avoided under the political and socio-economic reality of mid-nineteenth-century Russia, because the separation between the gentry's and the peasants' economies was not a matter to be settled by the stroke of the pen; but a better policy might have made the operation less painful. As Professor Gerschenkron sees it, the charters and the redemption procedure could have made a great difference. In reality, however, things were different. The peasants' allotments were too small, the obligations imposed on them too high, and the restrictions on their mobility too pressing, to make a clear change in the economy.[41]

Thus the Emancipation did not usher in the industrial revolution, but it helped to create some of the conditions required for it in the future. For example, it laid the foundations for its legal framework, and it increased the size of the gentry's estates and thereby their marketable share of Russia's agricultural product. It opened at least one legal avenue, redemption, for peasants to quit the land and settle in the towns, and thereby it helped, at least to some extent, to supply a labour force for industry. It reduced the objection to the construction of more railroads and increased the use of money. first through the institution of quitrents and then by the necessity to buy food after the quitrents were paid and the man had moved to the town. Finally, the combination of the railroads, the greater quantity of saleable farm produce and the wider use of money in the economy helped to raise the volume of food exports abroad; these brought in funds of which a part could be utilised for purchasing foreign industrial equipment. Yet, although all of these pointers to progress were, at least for the first two or three decades following the Emancipation, almost totally ineffective, they had a tremendous impact on the outlook of a section of the population, who gained the feeling that *things can be done* and that they were going to do them. In other words, it produced the 'cultural' revolution, the spirit of enterprise and hope which may well be the crucial factor in all economic development. It is for this reason that when, in the last decade of the nineteenth century, Russia eventually experienced her first spurt of industrialisation, the process took a rather unique form. Restricted by the shortage of labour on the one hand, and by the shortage of capital on the other—as most capital earnings were in the agrarian sector and not available to industry—the urge for industrialisation was leading towards the installation of the most highly labour-saving equipment; and this could only be made profitable when growth was maintained at an accelerating rate. This, then, appears to be the explanation for the fact that a country as short of capital as Russia was during this period was able to contrive in the 1890s a modern industrial structure which in a number of cases compared favourably in its capitalisation and level of technology with that of some of the most advanced countries.[42]

During the intervening period, i.e. between the Emancipation and the end of the century, pressure towards change was also mounting in the rural sector. Population growth had worsened the land-to-size-of-family ratios, which had already been inadequate even under the original allotments, and tax arrears had grown out of all proportion. Then, following a series of terrorist bomb attacks in the early part of the 1880s, which well reflected the general mood of the country, a number of economic reforms were finally introduced. Some of the more obnoxious taxes were abolished, others reduced, and some of the arrears struck off. In addition to this, a bank was set up to assist the farmers to purchase their land from the gentry. But again the results were not very significant. It appears that purchases made by the peasants themselves were on the whole more important than the mere 1·2 per cent of land which was acquired with the help of the bank during the crucial nine years.[43] On the whole, therefore, the reforms did little to change the actual economic conditions, though they gave the régime a short period of relative political stability. Altogether, Russia's rural population increased rapidly and Russian agriculture, like agriculture everywhere in Europe, suffered a series of severe setbacks in the last decades of the century. As a result of this *per capita* production on peasant lands was decreasing, while on those of the gentry, who were in the position to reallocate plots more freely and who were less restrained by circumstances from introducing better husbandry, it continued to increase.[44] However, the fall in the peasants' share of total output was too large to be offset by the far less significant rise in the gentry's share. Adding to this that under the pressure of government policies corn was exported during this period, and taking into account the increase in urban populations, it is obvious that *per capita* consumption in Russia was appreciably reduced towards the end of the nineteenth century. Yet at the same time that famine reigned, in the years 1891–92, for example, or that farm produce prices were falling due to developments beyond the control of the Russian Government, prices of industrial products were kept stable, and after 1891 were even raised under the protection of tariff barriers. Consequently there was little progress towards the mechanisation of agriculture. Moreover, rural unrest was bound to follow.

How, then, did the Russian Government go about improving the situation? The spurt of industrialisation in the nineties met with an exhausted local market which was not only too poor to accommodate the per force rising industrial output, but also had nothing to offer in exchange. As if this were not enough, the rural market was made even poorer; directly through excessive taxation, and indirectly through the labour and tariff policies concerning industry. The financial crash and the general depression in western Europe, which coincided with Russian 'overproduction', did not make things much easier. The government did nothing about it and the result of the economic disasters was rebellion and violence in the countryside and strikes and riots in the cities. These came to a head with the great transport strike which paralysed the country after Russia's defeat in the war against Japan in 1905.

In the following years the government managed to regain some of the positions it had lost by taking recourse to 'a combination of physical and judicial brutality that was unprecedented in the modern history of the country' and which was to leave its 'educational' legacy upon it for many years to come. With this there were, however, a number of institutional changes for the better which resulted from this pre-1905 period of violent opposition, and which the government was not able to withdraw or was forced to introduce. These were:[45] the abolition of joint responsibility for the payment of taxes which were henceforth the business of the individual households; the abolition of all the accumulated arrears of the land redemption and state land taxes; the abolition of corporal punishment (1903); the abolition of the restrictive provisions concerning the right to property and the right of the community to send an individual into forced employment without his consent, and the right of the commune to prevent an individual from choosing his place of residence (1906); and finally the abolition of the redemption payments themselves (1907).

Taken together, these laws gave the peasants at least legal equality, although officially the 'estate' of 'peasantry' was not yet abolished.[46] P. A. Stolypin, who was made Prime Minister after the dissolution of the first elected Parliament—the Duma—in 1906,[47] who had been governer of a rural district before his rise to prominence in St. Petersburg and who was familiar with the real situation of the peasantry, brought with him a new approach to the problem.

Whereas it had been the fashion in government circles to ascribe all rural discontent and unrest to the activities of radical agitators, he realised that it was rather the reality of the peasants' situation, that is their poverty, which made successful agitation possible. His solution for the problem was to 'create a class of small proprietors'. He believed that this class was the best safeguard for social stability. As he himself expressed this idea a few years later when, speaking of 1905–06, he said: 'It was necessary to destroy the cause of the causes . . . [of the political unrest] . . . to establish for the peasantry a new socio-economic order. . .'.[48] As usual, those who held power in Russia recognised the need for change when their old system could no longer hold out even by the use of terror. As had been the case in 1861, and as was to be the case in the era that followed, economic conditions were to be changed from above, by political decisions regarding the structure of the country's economy, and as a result of the threat of violence from below, which was very unlike the developments in western Europe, where the growing economic strength of the lower classes of society was reflected in and gave rise to political changes.[49] Thus, it was only in the twentieth century that the retarding force of the *obshchina*, that is the collective responsibility of the village community, was finally destroyed and the door opened to individualism in agriculture and industry.[50] Thus, that which all previous régimes had valued most as a stabilising force in Russian society and as being in the best tradition of its cultural inheritance—the *obshchina*—was lost and that which all previous régimes were most fearful of—the rise of an urban proletariat—was ushered in.

By the beginning of the century there were less than 48,000 miles of railroads in existence in Russia. By 1914 it had increased to 50,000 miles. At the same time less than 15 per cent of the population lived in towns and no more than 10 per cent derived their livelihood from industry. Many of them used to return to the villages in the summer to help their families with the harvest. But on the whole Russia had an economic system that was dependent on the West no less than the colonial territories in America, Asia, Africa and Australia were in the early nineteenth century. In fact Russia's agriculture and mineral extraction industry had developed under the strong influence of her export markets. In 1914 'she led the world as a grain exporter, and supplied nearly a third of the wheat imports and nearly half of the imports of other grains of western European countries. Cereals and other foodstuffs accounted for over half of Russia's total exports . . . and goods classified as raw materials and semi-manufactured goods for a further 36 per cent.'[51]

In summary, then, it was at the very time that the industrial revolution was making some headway in England that the Tsarist régime in Russia abolished the last freedoms of the peasantry which might have given the serfs some incentives to increase their production (1762). However, the increased demand for agricultural products which accompanied industrialisation in western Europe during the nineteenth century stimulated Russian trade, and with it the rapacity of the greater Russian landlords and bureaucrats. Only the disastrous defeat of the régime in the Crimean War brought a change in the conditions of the serfs and marked the beginning of their emancipation. The first step in this direction came in 1861, and was followed elsewhere in eastern Europe, in Rumania for example, a few years later (1864). In time the legal emancipation was also followed by a number of agrarian reforms, such as the separation of the peasants' from the landlords' lands; but this, which left the peasants with too little land per household to use it economically, was in the first place in the interest of the capitalistically minded landlords. As a result of this, and given the substantial agricultural overpopulation of the peasants' land, the reforms merely tended to increase what has been described as 'unwanted leisure' or underemployment. The premature application of the idea of the marginal substitution principle to the Russian economy, in place of the more appropriate application of the principle of 'maximising total agricultural output, may have been a hindrance on the road to a better expansion of production'. The requirements for money to pay taxes and to redeem their land under the new laws may also, however, have forced some peasants who were able to do so to increase their output for exports. By this they helped not only to increase the industrial output of western Europe, which paid Russia in industrial goods, but also to feed the industrial workers in Germany, France, Belgium and England. Yet, having failed to recognise the amount of discontent which this ruthless exploitation of the peasants in the interest of other classes had caused in the country, the régime was faced with such a rising wave of violence that it was forced to introduce a whole series of agrarian reforms to restore some degree of order.

THE INCREASING PER ACRE YIELD OF CULTIVATED LAND

So far in this discussion of agricultural progress we have been concerned with only two aspects of development, namely the rising *per capita* output of the people employed in agriculture, and the growing area of land which was opened up for cultivation. To some extent both these aspects were the result of technological industrial progress; the former because mechanical equipment and new sources of power enabled one man by the end of the nineteenth century to do what had required many hands at the beginning of it; the latter because progress in technology had given man the means of transporting the fruits of his labour and land from where it was abundant to where it was scarce, and because an international division of labour in agriculture had developed. There is, however, also a third aspect; namely, the increase in the yield per acre of the cultivated land. In the course of the eighteenth century some progress had been made in northern Europe in this direction by crop rotation and the use of nitrogen collecting plants which restored some of the fertility to exhausted soils. In addition to this, there had also been an increase in the use of animal manure. With the better understanding of botany and chemistry in the nineteenth century, and with the great improvements in world communication, another source of fertiliser greatly increased or restored the fertility of great areas of land. This source of the chemical fertiliser industry developed almost simultaneously in England, France and Germany, while at the same time new sources of natural fertilisers were discovered and exploited in South America.[52] Yet though the advantages of the most valuable fertilisers were already known in the first half of the nineteenth century, they did not come into general use until nearly the end of the second half. In the first half of the century, and indeed throughout most of it, Peruvian guano was the most popular of the new fertilisers in England which, at that time, was the leading country in modern agricultural methods. However, by 1870 the Peruvian guano sources were nearing exhaustion, and the experiments with alternative fertilisers became more and more economical. The first person to make superphosphate on a commercial basis was James Murray, of Dublin, in 1842. He treated not only bones with sulphuric acid (a process known and used occasionally since 1808),[53] but also mineral phosphate stone, which made production much cheaper and also increased the supply of its 'raw material' very considerably. It appears that to get the required superphosphate he mixed 'mineral phosphate with an equal weight of sulphuric acid in an earthenware vessel, and well agitating the mixture for two or three days. At the end of this time, it was mixed with some absorbent material, such as bran or sawdust. This yielded a dry, powdery fertiliser, easy to handle, which was sold in 280-lb casks.'[54] Less than thirty years later, in 1870, John Bennet Lawes' superphosphate factory in London, which had been established just one year after Murray patented his method, in 1843, was manufacturing about 40,000 tons of this fertiliser annually.

Yet superphosphate was only one of the new chemical developments in the service of food production. Nitrogen and potassium were two others of considerable importance. In the eighteenth and during most of the nineteenth century the most common source of nitrogen plant food was natural sodium nitrate. This was gained from Chilean saltpetre. In 1900 almost a million and a half tons of it were imported by European countries alone and some 170,000 tons by the United States of America. There it was used either directly or in the production of finer fertilisers.[55] As for potassium, most of it was gathered from the ash of plants until well into the nineteenth century. However, from 1870 onward, deposits of potassium salts rapidly replaced ash as the main source of potassium fertilisers.[56]

Thus within the last quarter of the nineteenth century artificial fertilisers became an essential feature of European agriculture.[57] The degree to which they were applied in these countries depended, of course, on specific conditions. In countries such as the Netherlands, Belgium and the western regions of Germany (and to a lesser degree Britain), where land was relatively scarce and population highly concentrated, and where a cash-demand for agricultural products was brisk, artificial fertilisers were in much greater demand than in the rest of Europe. In time, however, other countries like Norway, Switzerland, Sweden, France, Austria, Portugal and Italy also joined those at the top of the list.[58]

The importance of chemical fertilisers in some countries was even greater than it appears to be at first sight, because, together with other crops, the use of fertiliser also increased the production of fodder for cattle, which led to an increase of livestock and subsequently to an increase in the supply of manure.[59] Hand in hand with the increasing use of chemical fertilisers went the general process of intensification and commercialisation of agriculture. The great accretion of population in Europe during the nineteenth century provided a relatively abundant, and therefore also (in comparison with, for instance, North America) a relatively cheap, supply of labour, together with a growing demand for food. Yet had it not been for the growth of urban industries, which were dependent for their supplies of food, and sometimes also for their raw materials, upon a cash market of agra products, population growth might well have led to underemployment of labour, as it still does in many parts of the world today, rather than to the wider use of fertilisers and better utilisation of the land.[60] As it happened, however, the rapid growth of the cash market for agricultural products in nineteenth-century northern and central Europe made the application of chemical fertilisers very profitable; whereas in southern and eastern Europe, where either transport facilities to the cash markets or the markets themselves were missing, and where the supply of labour was too small in relation to the available land to cultivate it intensively, the wider use of fertilisers only followed in the wake of a belated industrial development. In addition to this the output *per acre* was also raised by other factors: better methods of land utilisation, soil conservation, protection of crops against insects and fungi, modern irrigation and drainage, land clearing techniques and better weeding.

The development of agronomy and the improvement of communications made possible a greater degree of specialisation when utilising different grades of soil for the crops best suited for them. The greater labour supply and the modern mechanical equipment made possible more terracing and levelling, which not only made previously unsuitable land fit for cultivation, but also prevented further erosion and washing away of plant nutrients from top soils. This was of particular importance in regions with heavy rainfall and in mountainous areas in the south of Europe.

Progress in genetics and in the other natural sciences greatly contributed to the improvement of plant and animal production, and to the struggle against plant and animal diseases and pests. While it is true that to some extent the spreading of the latter was a result of agricultural progress, as, for example, the Colorado beetle (a potato pest) seems to have been unknown in America before the introduction of the potato in Colorado, it is also true that the new chemicals which were discovered to fight it helped not only to keep this particular pest at bay but also to fend off a number of other pests. Not very different from the fortunes, or rather misfortunes, of the Colorado beetle were those of phylloxera. This disease, also imported from America in the 1860s, caused terrible devastation in European vineyards during the last quarter of the nineteenth century. The solution in this case came from botany rather than chemistry: the introduction of new hybrid varieties of grapes which were better resistant to the disease. At the same time a great number of new insecticides were discovered, which step by step reduced the losses of crops through pests and fungi in both field and storage.[61] In this the greater number of silos and other storage facilities also played an important role, although their greatest contribution was not felt before the twentieth century.

While it is a fact that progress in the improvement of the 'strains of cultivated plants and domestic animals' has been going on for ages,[62] the results of the deliberate and conscious effort of the nineteenth and twentieth centuries were far more important than all the previous achievements taken together although, *quantitatively*, their effects could not be seen until the middle of the twentieth century. According to Professor Dovring, 'modern plant genetics added something of the order of one-tenth to what might have been produced, *ceteris paribus*, by using the kinds of seed that were available around 1900'.[63] This is also true regarding the selective breeding of domestic animals; except that because of the much longer time required for the reproduction of these animals the full advantages cannot be truly appreciated even today.

Another problem which was brought nearer solution in this period was that of irrigation and drainage of farm-land. Though man had been struggling with these vital problems for at least 3,500 years,[64] it was not until the nineteenth century that, as a result of other industrial changes, it became possible to pump water from where it was not required to where it was. It was only 'the cylindrical clay-pipe, the pipe-making machines, and the provision of government drainage loans—all three innovations of the mid-forties—that at last made possible the general drainage of heavy land'.[65] During the same century much engineering skill was devoted to land-reclamation in the newly settled lands and in the colonies. One of the best-known early ventures was the Jumna (first the Western and then the Eastern Jumna) irrigation scheme in India. The cross-drainage works of the Eastern Jumna in particular involved some 'masonry weirs equipped with hinged gates that could be dropped to allow the passage of floods and raised to restore the canals'.[66] The reconstruction of the Jumna canals was followed by others in both India and Egypt.

In Britain, too, costly schemes were being put into effect in an effort to drain swamps and regulate rivers. There, however, it was the steam engine which began to replace the earlier and frequently not very successful drainage methods.

> 'These *Fens* have oft times been by Water drown'd.
> Science a remedy in Water found.
> The powers of *Steam* she said shall be employ'd
> And the *Destroyer* by *Itself* destroy'd.'[67]

wrote a late nineteenth-century poet, commenting on what he observed. Yet the most impressive achievement of this kind, the conversion of the Zuider Zee in Holland into an inland lake, was only accomplished in the twentieth century.

As for the irrigation of farm-land, this was merely one aspect of the more general problem of the rising requirements for a greater and more regular water supply during the later part of the nineteenth century. The rapid growth of towns and industries and the changing social habits which accompanied them[68] made a good and steady supply of water indispensable in Europe and North America. Initially, this led to a diminution and pollution of the near-at-hand supplies through over-exploitation. In time, however, many towns took deliberate and well-conceived action to solve this problem, and this resulted in something like a major revolution in the treatment and ownership of water resources. The outcome, by the end of the nineteenth century, was that almost all water supply systems and urban waterworks, in Europe and in the United States of America, provided a constant and reliable supply of water to whoever wanted it and was ready to pay for it. The supply systems were either owned or controlled by the local authorities. In some towns the requirements were too great to be met by the mere harnessing of springs or by wells and bore-holes,[69] and big dams and reservoirs had to be constructed. Yet the most important progress only came with the better exploitation of surface water, when man had learned to build large dams and discovered a good method for conveying the stored water supplies over great distances. Initially the water was allowed to run down from the mountain reservoirs in open channels by the force of gravitation. Later the aqueduct-like channels were replaced by tunnels lined with masonry. But in the last quarter of the nineteenth century, when iron and steel pipes became readily obtainable, the latter replaced masonry almost everywhere. With the development of steam engines, there came into use a steam-driven pump which helped to overcome another problem—the often topographically unfavourable location of the source of water supply in relation to where it was to be used. Most of these developments took place as a result of urbanisation, but they were soon successfully employed in rural areas as well, where their possibilities for agriculture were recognised almost immediately. Their most important contribution to agriculture was, however, reserved for the twentieth century, when cultivation spread into the dry areas of countries where climatic conditions made irrigation imperative during the summer months.[70]

Finally, the output of farmland per acre was also increased, especially but not only in Europe, by the greater diversification of crops and the higher degree of specialisation in the production of each of them. The number of farm-produced species of raw materials increased with the growth of industry; with the scientific progress in the rearing of livestock the variety of feed crops grew; and the quantity and diversity of land-and-labour-intensive crops of vegetables and fruit increased with the rising number of people who could afford a higher standard of nutrition. This progressive diversification not only brought about a more even distribution of employment throughout the farming year—because some crops required more work just at the time when others needed but little attention—but also a much more intensive utilisation of the land. A similar development also took place with livestock production.

When the new fertilisers made the keeping of livestock for manure no longer as necessary as before, whole regions became increasingly specialised, raising only the animals most profitable under their specific land conditions. The improvements in the food-processing industry thus further increased the intensity of the demand for labour, while the higher milk and meat output per animal was also rising for each acre of feed.

Finally, food supplies were further augmented by the harvest of the seas. Fishing and whaling increased, and though various kinds of fresh-water fish were consumed, they remained rather expensive. However, the exploitation of the most important source of fish, the great seas and oceans, was dependent upon progress in ship-building and food-preservation.[71] This progress came in the course of the nineteenth century, when almost simultaneously the efficiency, speed, power and range of fishing boats increased, and when they either became large enough to carry big water tanks capable of keeping fish alive throughout a lengthy voyage, or when they were steam-powered and capable of bringing in the trawl fast enough to stand another overland railroad voyage before it decomposed. Eventually, by the end of the century, the use of ice, cold storage and factory ships totally revolutionised the fishing industry and made it into a major factor in supplying the world population with high protein foods.[72]

CAPITAL AND ORGANISATION

Two other important aspects of this growth of *per capita* and per acre increase of food production were the new methods of financing the improvements, and the changes in the organisation of agricultural labour.

The methods varied from one country to another and often from one region to another in a single country. For the United Kingdom as a whole the main items of output in the third quarter of the nineteenth century were wheat, beef and veal, milk, mutton and lamb, pig meat, barley, potatoes, oats, hay and straw, and wool,[73] with a tendency towards a relatively sharper increase in meat and milk production. To some extent this tendency was due to the growth of towns and rising living standards, but in part it was also the result of the division of responsibility for improvements between landlords and tenants arising out of the peculiar heritage of British socio-economic history. Most of the land in nineteenth-century England was owned by a small number of very rich landlords[74] and most of their tenants were 'tenants at will', often with no more right to the land than a six months' lease. The situation, however, differed from that on the Continent; for in the majority of cases tenants' holdings were indeed too large to be cultivated by the farmer and his family alone, and often required either hired labour, or labour-saving equipment, or even both to cultivate it. Yet as the farmer had only a short lease of the land, it was usually the landlord who was responsible for the fixed capital, i.e. for drainage, roads, buildings, etc., while the farmer provided the 'removable' capital, stock, implements and machines, in effect, everything he could take away with him if he were to quit. It was therefore dependent upon the particular landlord whether capital investments took place which made crop cultivation attractive for the tenant-farmer, or whether the landlord invested little, leaving the tenant to invest in whatever appeared to be most profitable for him and could be taken away if he had to quit the land. The greater landlords usually invested heavily in their land and the smaller did very little. The combination of these two elements in the social and economic structure of English agriculture—the large and very rich landlord who could afford the most advanced schemes, on the one hand, and the small tenant-farmer whose holding was still large enough to permit him to buy the movable equipment he wanted, on the other—brought about England's leadership in modern agriculture. In effect the system, as if by design, not only put the responsibility for improvements into the hands of those who had most to gain from them—the landlords because by investing they could raise their incomes from the higher rents, and the tenants because they could increase their revenue by using the latest innovations—but also placed the responsibility for progress in the hands of those who had the necessary capital. As a result of this, by the last quarter of the century, English agriculture had made 'commonplaces of the most striking innovations developed over the previous century and a half'. This was not all. Her peculiar socio-economic legacy left England with a relatively strong class of farmers who had more 'to lose than their chains' and, therefore, were a stabilising political factor. In fact they provided the masses which were able to support the small number of great landlords and their interests against the pressures from the fast rising class of industrialists and the even faster increasing class of proletarians. Moreover, even the poorest class among the rural population of England—the landless farm labourers—did not become as poor as their continental counterparts in countries such as Russia or Germany. This was so not only because of the earlier and better employment alternatives in industry, the pressure from trade unions,[75] and the higher efficiency of labour wherever the farmer could afford the modern equipment and the landlord was able and willing to make capital improvements, but also because of the greater ease by which traditional practices could be changed to suit the changing situation in world food transportation. In fact the number of persons employed in agriculture changed very little during the last quarter of the nineteenth century in England,[76] but their identity altered very considerably. The depression in the 1870s weeded out the least efficient of their number, and those who survived had learned to concentrate upon the more profitable products. Most profitable of all was livestock and its produce, the share of which in the total agricultural output rose from 55 per cent in the sixties to 75 per cent by the end of the century.

Conditions in other countries were rather different. In France and in Belgium the landlords had very little interest in agricultural improvements. The political structure which survived in France until close to the end of the eighteenth century led the greater landlords to seek their fortunes through office rather than through the slow and socially 'not quite distinguished' interest in the 'peasants'' occupation. It was both more profitable and more 'respectable' to try to gain the favours of the Royal Court in Versailles than to live away from Paris and try to gain influence and riches through better exploitation of the land; unfortunately, in the process of waiting for favours at court, farms often had to be sold piecemeal to small farmers who could not afford to make any improvements. Thus, by the continuation of a feudal socio-political system, which led the aristocracy to prefer military, diplomatic and political careers, and by the continuation of a feudal legal system, which despite the landlords' legal advantages gave the tenant security of tenure and certain economic safeguards, a situation was created where in the words of Arthur Birnie,[77] 'instead of the lord dispossessing the peasant, it was the peasant who dispossessed the lord'.

Thus, with no great landlords to invest in agriculture, and no peasantry with holdings large enough to be able to exploit them effectively—with, on the contrary, a peasantry harassed by feudal jurisdiction and 'vexatious dues and charges'—the aristocracy was practically isolated both economically and politically, and was swiftly swept away by the great revolutionary tide of 1789. Yet while National Assemblies could divest the aristocracy, clergy and lawyers of their legal privileges, they were unable to reform the economic factors which prevented agricultural progress and prosperity. When in 1793 the National Convention abolished all the remaining feudal payments, the peasants finally gained complete ownership of their holdings, while at the same time they were delivered of the tithe and of a good part of the heavy national taxation. As this coincided with the sale of land confiscated from the church and nobility, some of the money that was saved was spent on the augmentation of the peasants' holdings. Still, most French peasants, approximately 97 per cent of them, never owned farms of more than 100 acres,[78] and the number of small farm owners was, and still is, greater than the number of hired agricultural labourers.[79] And yet the slight augmentation of the size of holdings, the abolition of some of the taxes which drained capital away from rural districts, and the decreasing rate of rural population growth[80] laid the foundations for the kind of progress which was to follow when the growth of urban industry and the expansion of the railway system gave agriculture, in the second half of the nineteenth century, the effective market which was powerful enough to revolutionise it.

From the beginning of the nineteenth century until 1850 urban population in France had grown very little,[81] but in the second half of the century the increase was considerable.[82] It was then that rural population decreased in France, not only in relative, but also in absolute terms.[83] Obviously, individual farm holdings grew in size, and as the farmers learned more about modern agricultural machinery and fertilisers, and also about foreign competition, they managed not only to increase the yield from their by now somewhat larger holdings in terms of per acre and *per capita* output, but also to concentrate upon the production of the most profitable instead of the most crop-yielding products. Soon their growing prosperity increased their political influence and they were able to defend their class interests in a way which only too often put impediments upon the industrial development of the country in the years to come.

Yet it would not be true to say that all great estates had disappeared from post-revolutionary France. Some of the old landlords had somehow managed to survive, and their descendants had even managed here and there to increase the size of their estates. Indeed, some of the largest estates were later bought by rich businessmen from the towns for their sporting pleasures, as had been the mode in England a century before. Still, a number of large agricultural estates survived and exerted a certain degree of influence upon French farming practices.

In the sixties, even in the north of France where agriculture was most advanced, the only machine which was in more or less general use was the horse-driven threshing machine. Its popularity in the north was due to the early progress of industry in these parts and the consequent relative labour shortage and the particular scarcity of seasonal labour. By the end of the century, mechanisation had spread south and had generally advanced very considerably, though it was still far behind that of the United States and England.

The main reason for this was that holdings were too small and too dispersed in France to make the new power-driven equipment economical for the individual farmer.[84] The branch of agriculture which could, and indeed did, compete successfully with the other well-advanced countries was market gardening and the dairying industry. It developed very rapidly during the last quarter of the nineteenth century, probably under the influence of the depression in cereal farming which visited France at that time and was largely due to rapid progress in international trade and communication. It was this trend, the rise of the dairying industry and the concentration on market gardening near the growing towns, which saved the French peasantry from being expropriated in the last quarter of the nineteenth century. It was the kind of farming which still required what Clapham called 'the patience and the touch of artistry' which the farmer with only a few acres of land could give. Yet while intensive farming and dairying helped him and his family to survive, it also prevented the mechanisation of agriculture and its 'depopulating tendencies' in rural France. The small peasantry was able to survive as a considerable social and political factor, while industrialisation and the growth of the urban proletariat progressed only gradually and never really managed to tip the scales.

The transition from medieval farming routines to those of modern France was also rather slow. In the third quarter of the nineteenth century there was a very considerable increase in wheat and wine production.[85] In the last quarter, international competition and the ravages of a vine pest and bad harvests of wheat all combined together, causing a series of severe setbacks to French farming. This led to a campaign for protectionism which resulted in the introduction of a whole list of tariffs, duties and taxes. In fact, it might have been this huge wave of foreign imports, which was the expression of the new international division of labour, and to which the European economies did not yet have time to get adjusted, that in the last quarter of the nineteenth century gave rise to that vogue of nationalism which never left Europe until more than half a century later.

However, while tariffs prevented more rapid progress in agricultural specialisation (and by this, perhaps, the more rapid increase in *per capita* consumption and per acre production), it also prevented the expropriation of the French peasantry. And although it may well be true that this was the reason for the belated growth of the 'cheap' labour supply in France—and therefore also of the slow development of French industry—it is equally true that it spared the French working class some of the sufferings and deprivations to which the British working class had been subjected a few decades earlier in the 'heroic' period of England's Industrial Revolution.

No less important were the changes which took place in the organisation of French agriculture during the eighties. In the seventies farmers' co-operatives had grown and met with considerable success in Denmark and northern Germany. Now they reached France. One indigenous source of co-operation was the ancient common fields and the so-called syndicates for sharing the cost and labour for drainage and irrigation works. Another source was the concerted action against the phylloxera pest in the seventies and, even more so, the concerted action against foreign imports and falling prices in the eighties, which gave rise to the *Société des Agriculteurs de France* and the *comices*. In 1884 trade unions (*syndicats*) were legalised in France and with them the door opened for the organisation of farmers and farm labourers. As Clapham wrote,[86] 'Growth was extraordinarily rapid. The figures are difficult and uncertain, but the general movement is clear. The syndicates were not alone in the field. The old agricultural societies and *comices* kept up the work of discussion and exchange of ideas. Some of the *comices*, besides helping to found syndicates, developed active policies.' They collectively purchased manures, seed and other requisites for their members and set up daughter societies: co-operative banking, mutual insurance work against loss of cattle, losses by frost and hail and other farmers' risks; co-operative dairies, egg societies, etc.[87] Some of the syndicates were local, others were departmental, and others again a federation of both local and departmental ones; some joined together syndicates of whole regions like the *Union du Sud-Est*, which combined fruit and vegetable growers into a powerful economic and political pressure group. However, for raising the *per capita* and per acre production on the farm the most important were the communal and strictly local syndicates and their specialised societies.[88] Initially, it appears, they considered wholesale purchasing for their members their main function. Some of them indeed acted as rural co-operatives' retail stores, distributing manures, seed, cattle cake, insecticides, compressed fodder, American wine stocks, and sometimes pots, pans, clothes and soaps. Later some began buying with collective funds agricultural machinery, which they hired out 'per area' or 'per day' to members, earning back the money originally expended on it. Eventually they ventured into the distributive side of their business, organising the collection, handling and conveying of members' products.

Thus co-operatives not only saved labour-time (going to the market to buy and sell) and reduced purchasing and transport costs by buying wholesale rather than in small quantities, but also made expensive mechanical equipment obtainable on an hourly or daily basis to the small farmer with each 'user' paying a share of the total expense proportionate to the use he made of the machine. In this way co-operation in France filled the gap created by the absence of the 'improving capitalist farmers' who had been in the forefront of progress in Britain.

In time, some of the co-operatives concentrated increasingly upon selling, which led to a certain amount of reorganisation. The combinations came to be based on products rather than localities. The growing specialisation of agricultural production caused farmers to seek co-operation with others in the same line of production because, as markets became more and more universal, i.e. less dependent upon the nearby neighbourhood for supplies, the community of interests shifted away from the geographical and towards the occupational point of view. It was obvious that in many cases the dairy farmer had less in common with his nearby neighbour who produced wheat than with another dairy farmer several miles or perhaps even several hundreds of miles away. Naturally things were not always mutually exclusive. The farmer could co-operate with his neighbour in a purchasing co-operative and with his co-producer of a given product in price fixing. More often than not, however, it was the land and the climate that dictated to the farmer the product he was producing, and therefore both the locality and the produce-orientated interests coincided. Eventually agricultural progress was also aided by the spreading of co-operative insurance societies and banks, where farmers could get loans on the security of their land and at easy terms. These were, however, less important in France than they were in Denmark and northern Germany, where they originated two decades earlier and played a very important role in the development of agriculture.

In Belgium things were very similar to France. The French 'conquerors' in 1795 liberated the peasantry and freed them from all payments except for the ordinary rents and taxes. As in France, the Church lands were offered for sale and purchased by small farmers to augment their holdings. But the proximity of Holland and its early developed industry gave Belgian farmers certain advantages over the French.[89]

The farmers in Germany west of the river Elbe found themselves in a similar position to those in France and Belgium. Almost all the land in this part of Germany was held in hereditary or life tenancy, which gave the peasants a good deal of security; but the size of the holdings, like those of the peasants in France, was usually too small to give the farmer the necessary degree of economic independence and income to be able to introduce far-reaching improvements. In the provinces close to the French border, along the river Rhine, the emancipation of the peasants came in the wake of the French Revolutionary and Napoleonic armies. In the 'unoccupied' provinces the emancipation came more slowly following the wave of liberalism which swept over these parts of Germany during the second quarter of the nineteenth century and culminated in the 'spring of the nations', i.e. the Revolution of 1848. Still, the emancipation was not nearly as complete as in France even by the middle of the century. There was still a lot to be changed after 1850 before most peasants could feel themselves complete owners of their land.[90] One such example is the case of Wurtemberg, where the peasantry were still obliged to pay off the value of their land before they were able to claim full ownership over it. This process was only completed in 1873, and until then much money which might have been reinvested in the land was skimmed off in the form of redemption payments. Another example is that of Bavaria, where the process only started with the abolition of the feudal jurisdiction in 1848, and where the peasant was made to pay very large sums to gain his personal freedom and full ownership of his land. Bavarian peasants were still paying off their land in the twentieth century, in fact, until 1914. Yet with all this it is still correct to say that in the western parts of Germany, as in France and in Belgium, farming was the business of the small peasant landowner.

For this reason, then, in Germany as in France, co-operatives played an extremely important role in promoting and financing the improvements in farming. Here too the direct cause for the acceleration of their growth was the fall in the prices of farm products consequent upon the rapid progress of international trade in the last quarter of the nineteenth century. However, though an important stimulant for it, depression was not the source of the movement. It merely created good conditions for its fruition.[91] During the famine of 1846–47, Friedrich Raiffeisen, the mayor of a number of villages in the western part of Germany near the Rhine,[92] started a co-operative bakery. As this met with a degree of success he organised, in 1858, the first German rural mutual assistance society.[93] The object of the society was to enable farmers to borrow money at low or no interest. This was a matter of the highest importance, as a farmer has, as a rule, to pay for his seed, fertiliser and hired labour, as well as for his own and his household's running expenses, long before he has an opportunity to gather and sell his crop and thus retrieve his expenditures.

Traditionally it was the rich landlord who advanced the money to the farmer for his seed, etc., on the security of his land and at the highest rate of interest he could hope to get—or not to get if he wished to possess the farmer's land. In Germany, where the aristocracy did not like to be publicly associated with money matters, they used the Jews, whom they managed to exclude by law from almost any other occupation, to act as their representatives. So that while they, the aristocracy, could take all the credit for 'helping' the farmers, they left the unpleasant onus of usury to the Jews.

Raiffeisen's idea was to organise small societies with unlimited liability, for mutual financial and other assistance. The members of the societies had to be landowners so that their land could serve as security for the lenders, and the societies had to be of unlimited liability to bring down interest rates for money borrowed from outside, and to make the members more closely interested in the prosperity of all. In the decade following the unification of Germany, the 'Raiffeisen rural banks' spread very rapidly throughout most of western Germany. The banks had no regular subscribed capital but merely a loan fund made up of the members' savings which could be lent to members on their personal and on their land's security. In time the banks developed and came more into line with normal banking practices, partly because of certain legal requirements imposed on them by the State, and partly because of the recognition of the fact that by normal banking methods they could increase their loan capital far beyond the amount they actually held in farmers' savings.

As well as the practical side there was also, perhaps unrecognised, a very important educational side to the system. As all members were contributors, and of course part owners of the 'bank', they were also the people who were going to lose by defaults. It was therefore anybody's business to decide whether or not a loan should be given to any one of their number. In other words, advances and loans were dependent upon the personal standing of the borrower in the community, i.e. upon personal knowledge of the man, his integrity, responsibility and industry. This fact must have exerted a considerable influence in forming a new social behaviour pattern of village life. At its best it made for mutual help and co-operation; at its worst it bred the particular manner of the German middle class.

In 1876 Raiffeisen formed a Central Bank as a shareholding company to act as a sort of bankers' banker for the local banks. A few years later the bank entered into an agreement with the Delitzsch bank, which performed duties similar to those of the Raiffeisen banks for industrial societies. By that time, both the Raiffeisen and the Delitzsch organisations not only performed bankers' duties but also acted as wholesale buyers of fertilisers, feed, seed, oxen, raw materials, etc. They were already making use of experts and professional buyers to make sure that their members got the best quality at a good price; and in some places they were also erecting industrial enterprises to supply some of their members' needs.[94] It is, however, important that the Raiffeisen banks were not the only agricultural societies in nineteenth-century Germany, and others may have been of equal importance, though from a different point of view.[95] According to Clapham[96] the general position in this respect was, in 1914, that the Spar und Darlehnkassen stood in the centre of the organisation, which were the agricultural credit banks of the imperial union, which since 1905 included in one way or another also the Raiffeisen banks, and which had a membership of over a million. In addition, there were some local agrarian unions which reported some 200,000 members but were not associated with the imperial, and the mainly urban Delitzsch banks which supported the independent agriculturists amongst their members. Altogether in 1908 they may have counted just under 1½ million members. Almost all who joined agricultural producing societies had one or another kind of association with one or more of the different credit societies. This also applies to the various societies whose object was not specifically the supply of credit. The latter were, as in France, predominantly co-operatives organised by farmers who were mutually interested in a certain product rather than united by a given locality. These conditions were, however, never so powerful in Germany as in France; firstly, because the German nobility had never been so thoroughly shaken up as the French during the Great Revolution and were therefore able to retain a great deal of influence; secondly, because the division of Germany into so many separate little 'states', which lasted until 1866 or even 1871, had made large-scale co-operation extremely difficult; thirdly, because the relative smallness of these states without the lure of Paris brought the nobility into much closer contact with the peasants, and also brought the peasantry under much closer supervision by the nobility; finally, because almost all liberties were granted to the peasants from above, rather than captured from below by the peasants themselves. The only true advantage which the German farmer had over the French was that, once the rapid growth of industry had begun in the 1870s, the wider geographical distribution of its centres often compensated for the farmers' lack of national organisation.

Another country where small peasant-holdings and co-operation played an extremely important role in agriculture was Denmark. Because of its geographic position, and its suitable climate and soil, Denmark had been a corn exporting country long before the nineteenth century. Thus, when the industrial revolutions in England, Belgium, and later in Germany, and the rising demand for food which accompanied them, increased the pressure of demand, Danish agriculture was ready to respond to it. In 1660 Denmark had lost her provinces on the Scandinavian Peninsula, and since then the 'new type' monarchy had vigorously concentrated upon the country's economic development. The new nobility which was 'called into being by gifts of land to government officials and favourites and by sales of crown lands to immigrant Holstein and German nobles, to Danish wealthy townsmen and newly rich'[97] supplied the spirit of enterprise which was well rewarded. This group, according to Professor Youngson, came to own in the course of the eighteenth century 'about 60 per cent of all Danish agricultural land; only about 5 per cent remained in the hands of owner-farmers, the rest being about equally divided between non-aristocratic landlords and the crown'.[98] With this, however, the strong position of the crown prevented the eviction of the peasantry from their holdings.[99] On the one hand, this did, of course, prevent a more rapid agricultural development because progress normally commences on large holdings owned by landlords who have the money to make improvements; but, on the other hand, it prevented the Danish population from being subjected to a degree of misery similar to that experienced by the British workers in the early days of Parliamentary enclosures—misery which would have been much worse in Denmark, a country with practially no coal and iron to support alternative employment in industry. Therefore, being prevented from investing their profits in the extension of their land, the rich Danish landlords were forced, if they wished to increase their output, to intensify the exploitation of the land they already owned. This may well have been the source of the surprising increase in production per acre during the years that followed. At the same time, however, while the landlords were forbidden to evict their poor tenants, the latter were not permitted to leave their land even where it could barely support them.[100] The system lasted until the third quarter of the eighteenth century. Then, between 1769 and 1788, the policy was revised. Feudal labour services and payments in kind were commuted into contractual money payments, and what was left of the common land was enclosed and reallotted. As corn prices were rising during this period, and the government was actively assisting peasants by making available loans on easy terms, the new policy bore fruit. Soon tenant-farmers began to be more prosperous, to buy their farms, and to improve their farming equipment and techniques. Then, after 1788, while the Revolutions and Napoleonic Wars did some damage to Danish political and commercial interests, they did little to interrupt the country's agricultural progress. Corn prices soared and compensated farmers for losses otherwise sustained.[101] Eventually, during the deflation which followed 1815, agricultural progress was slower, but such improvement as had taken place already was continued and, obviously, none of the new machines had been destroyed. Then, after policies which were designed to encourage industry were tried out and failed, all efforts were directed towards the promotion ot trade and agriculture. In the thirties, partly because of higher prices but also because of the genuine increase in the volume of exports, Danish farming prospered. In the forties, and in fact until the sixties, when British duties on the importation of corn were being reduced and almost abolished, Danish corn exports reached an unprecedented peak. During this time provincial banks and credit associations developed which helped to prevent the farmers' savings from disappearing in idle hoards. In the seventies the prosperity abated a little under the pressure of the same circumstances that caused the agricultural reversal in France and Germany, i.e. the growth of international competition. In the eighties and nineties, however, after it underwent certain far-reaching technical and organisational changes, Danish agriculture recovered again, and, indeed, even improved upon its previous prosperity.

The first, though perhaps not the most important, of these changes was the relative decline of the number of people directly employed on the land. It fell from 57·5 per cent in 1834 to only 41·1 per cent in 1901. This reduced the share of agricultural primary production in the total national output (at factor cost, 1929 prices) from 41·4 per cent in 1870–79 to only 25·5 per cent in 1895–1904. At the same time, however, the income from agriculture had risen (at factor cost, 1929 prices) from 421 million kroner in 1870–79 to 564 million kroner in 1895–1904,[102] while the country's population increased from about 2·1 to 2·5 millions. But the true contribution of agriculture to the general economic progress of Denmark is, in fact, not adequately represented by these statistics[103] because, in the words of Professor Youngson, it played 'a peculiarly dynamic role in the economic history of the period'. Initially it adapted itself with surprising rapidity to the new world markets and sources of supply by effecting a transition from a predominantly grain-producing to a mainly livestock-orientated husbandry. Partly this was the result of the declining fertility of the soil, which had been over-exploited in the years of the corn boom. But more than this it was due to the fact that Denmark was near to, and had close connections and good trade facilities with, the countries which were at the time in the forefront of industrialisation and urban growth.

The second important factor which helped to stimulate the changes in the Danish economy was the invention and adaptation to the requirements of small farmers of a superior type of milk separator in the early 1880s. Previously, butter making on a commercial scale had always required a great deal of capital and a steady supply of milk which had neither been shaken in transport nor stored for more than a very short time. This naturally prevented any kind of co-operation between farmers. The new separator worked perfectly well even with stored and shaken milk and made such co-operation possible. Within a short period a great number of co-operative creameries came into existence which not only enabled small farmers to benefit from all the advantages of economies of scale, but also taught them a great lesson in co-operation which made them extend the system to other branches of production with equally profitable results. The principle of the co-operative creameries was that[104] 'Each farmer who joined contracted for a certain period of time—usually for from one to ten years—to deliver to the creamery all the milk produced on his farm, except that used on the farm itself. Transport was arranged by the creamery. Butter was produced under the direction of a hired creamery manager, technically trained, and the proceeds from sales, after the deduction of operating costs, were paid over to the farmers in proportion to the amount of milk which each had delivered. In addition, the skim milk was returned to the farms each day, every farm receiving as much as corresponded to its deliveries of whole milk. The plan was financed by a loan raised on the co-operators' joint and unlimited liability. The strictly local character of each enterprise, whereby all members knew one another and were in almost daily contact with one another, made this a less hazardous method of financing than it would otherwise have been, and the necessary capital was easily obtainable on such security. All rules were set out in the "co-operative contract", and the members were themselves collectively responsible for policy decisions. The co-operators did not attempt to retail their milk, and they did not, until about 1895, take part in the export trade.'

Over five hundred such creameries developed between the years 1885 and 1890, and by the end of the century their number reached 940. It is relevant that they were greatly improved thanks to the help given to them by the government in initiating research in special research laboratories and at the universities. The fact that the creamery manager had to be a trained expert in his field also helped to improve both the production and the produce. Within two decades scientific knowledge had so far advanced that the amount of butter gained from a given quantity of milk was more than doubled. At the same time progress took place in the utilisation of the 'by-products' of the butter industry. The skim milk which was returned in great quantities to the farm was soon increasingly exploited to feed hogs which, in turn, marked the beginning of a considerable bacon industry. In 1887, when pasteurisation of milk eliminated the risks involved, the first co-operative bacon factory was started.

The third factor which greatly contributed to the progress of Danish agriculture was the relatively high level of rural education. Since the 1830s a great number of Folk Schools had been started, with the intention of raising the general level of education, particularly in the humanities, throughout the country. This movement met with considerable success and had a very profound influence on what could be called the Danish way of life. In fact, it created a completely new set of social values based more upon other achievements than property relations, while it also brought into a more equal and personal contact members of various income groups under circumstances which gave the more wealthy little advantage.

In summary, Denmark is a good example of a country where agriculture rather than mineral resources was the crucial factor in the process of industrialisation and general economic progress. It earned foreign exchange, provided employment for a growing population and accumulated capital (at least from the middle of the nineteenth century, when it became increasingly labour- and capital-intensive) and by being labour-intensive in a country of many small holdings, it raised the level of consumption and thereby gave rise to the development of other consumer-goods industries based mainly on the processing of agra-products.

We may therefore conclude that the main changes in agriculture which accompanied the industrialisation of Europe and North America were, firstly, the increasing tendency towards market production and, consequently, towards regional specialisation and concentration upon the products which yield the highest cash profits. Secondly, the extension of the cultivated area, in Europe, by deforestation, drainage and irrigation, and in other parts of the world, by similar methods and by the invasion of hitherto under-populated and under-exploited regions. In the densely populated parts of the world this led to the intensification of husbandry, and in the thinly populated parts it led to the concentration on extensive methods of production. In both the thinly and the densely populated areas progress was helped, and perhaps only made possible, by the development of transport and industrial technology. Thanks to this there became available equipment which could replace human labour (such as the threshing machine or the combine-harvester), or improve upon the quantity of work itself (such as the steam-powered water pump and the bulldozer) by which both the total and the *per capita* output was raised very appreciably. Thirdly, the better exploitation of the cultivated land, which was made possible by the progress in chemistry and in the natural sciences (fertilisers and better varieties of grains and livestock, etc.), resulted in a very considerable increase in the quantity of food produced per acre of land. Fourthly, there occurred a shift in countries with a growing industry in the occupational structure of the population away from agriculture and towards urban industrial employment. And finally Europe was divided into the corn producing countries with their great landowners, Russia, Prussia, the Danube regions, etc., and into the countries with very intensive agriculture and a predominantly small-holder peasantry, parts of France, western Germany, Holland, Belgium, Denmark and Switzerland.

NOTES

1. *Essay*, Bk. I, Ch. I. Quoted here from the 7th edition (1872) reprinted by Everyman's Library in 1960, p. 5.

2.

MAN-HOURS REQUIRED FOR THE PRODUCTION OF ONE METRIC TON IN THE U.S.

Year	*Wheat*	*Maize*	*Cotton*
1800	137	135	2,645
1840	86	109	1,932
1880	56	71	1,338
1900	40	58	1,248
1950	9·6	13·4	581

YIELD IN QUINTALS PER HECTARE IN THE U.S.

Year	*Wheat*	*Maize*	*Cotton*
1885–89	7·1		
1909–13	9·8	16·3	65
1925–29	9·5	16·9	77
1934–38	8·7	14·0	78
1949–51	10·6	23·5	159

Source: Colin Clark, *The Conditions of Economic Progress*, 3rd ed., London, 1960, Tables XXIII & XXVIII.

3. Arthur Birnie, *An Economic History of the British Isles*, London, 1935. Quoted here from 8th edition, 1955, p. 255.

4. Arthur Birnie, *op. cit.*, p. 256.

5. G. E. Fussell, 'Agriculture: Techniques of Farming', in Singer, Holmyard, Hall and Williams, Eds., *A History of Technology*, Vol. IV, Oxford, 1958, p. 40.

6. Arthur Birnie, *op. cit.*, p. 258, gives the following figures:

	Arable land (Acres)	*Permanent Grass* (Acres)	*Imported Wheat* (Quarters)
1870	23,905,000	23,416,000	8,611,000
1895	19,957,000	27,799,000	25,028,000

7. William H. Nicholls, 'The Place of Agriculture in Economic Development . . .', *Agriculture in Economic Development*, New York, 1964, p. 19.

8. I stress the term *effective* because most of the early improvements which increased agricultural efficiency could have been introduced much earlier, since they were known and tested in various places several decades before; their wider application only became really 'worthwhile' from the farmers' point of view when industry was able to produce something which could be taken in exchange for the farm surplus, i.e. when demand was transformed into 'effective' demand. This point is frequently overlooked by the supporters of the modern Demonstration Effect theories for the development of under-developed countries. *Vide* Y. S. Brenner, *Theories of Economic Development and Growth*, London, 1966, Ch. VIII, pp. 248–279, and also 'Problems of Under-Employment in West Africa', in the *African Quarterly*, New Delhi, October–December, 1965.

9. In France, population growth abated by the middle of the nineteenth century, and about 50 per cent of the total population were still employed in agriculture by the end of the century. In Ireland, migration was a prime factor.

10. Folke Dovring, 'The Transformation of European Agriculture', *The Cambridge Economic History of Europe*, Vol. VI, Pt. II, Cambridge, 1965, p. 605.

11. J. H. Clapham, 'Machines and National Rivalries 1887–1914', *An Economic History of Modern Britain*, Cambridge, 1938. Quoted here from 1963 edition, p. 72.

12. For details, see Singer, Holmyard, Hall and Williams, *op. cit.*, Vol. V, Ch. II.

13. G. E. Fussell, 'Growth of Food Production', in Singer, Holmyard, Hall and Williams, *op. cit.*, Vol. V, p. 4.

14. *Ibid.*, pp. 4–5.

15. T. K. Derry and Trevor I. Williams, *A Short History of Technology from earliest times to A.D. 1900*, Oxford, 1960, pp. 671–672.

16. *Ibid.*, pp. 672–673.

17. Derry and Williams, *op. cit.*, p. 673.

18. Colin Clark, *The Conditions of Economic Progress*, 3rd edition, London, 1960, p. 287. Table No. XXIII illustrates this fact.

MAN HOURS REQUIRED PER ACRE AND PER UNIT OF PRODUCT IN THE U.S.

	1800	*1840*	*1880*	*1900*	*1920*	*1940*	*1950–53*
Wheat							
Per metric ton	137	86	56	40	32	17	9·6
Per acre	56	35	20	15	12	7·5	4·4
Maize							
Per metric ton	135	109	71	58	44	33	13·4
Per acre	86	69	46	38	32	25	13·1
Cotton							
Per metric ton of lint	2,645	1,932	1,338	1,248	1,240	840	581
Per acre	185	135	119	112	90	98	71
Potatoes							
Per metric ton					33	13	9·9
Per acre					89	88	68

It must, however, be remembered that Clark's figures are not based on national aggregates but tend to represent the 'best' methods, i.e. the best methods available in practice to an intelligent contemporary farmer. This does of course exclude many farmers who 'through lack of knowledge, or lack of money to buy equipment, or for any other reason, fall short of these standards'.

19. Singer, Holmyard, Hall and Williams, *op. cit.*, Vol. V, p. 49.

20. T. N. Morris, 'Management and Preservation of Food', in Singer, Holmyard, Hall and Williams, *op. cit.*, p. 49.

21. G. E. Fussell, 'Growth of Food Production', in Singer, Holmyard, Hall and Williams, *op. cit.*, p. 9.

22. See, for example, Brinley Thomas, *Migration and Economic Growth, A Study of Great Britain and the Atlantic Economy*, Cambridge, 1954.

23. Quoted here from Singer, Holmyard, Hall and Williams, *op. cit.*, p. 47.

24. For example, the Rose Lime Company operates in this way in Ghana even today.

25. Derry and Williams, *op. cit.*, p. 683.

26. The traditional social organisation served as a kind of social security which made, and still makes, the worker less dependent on his employer than the European worker.

27. For example, the cocoa planters in the Gold Coast.

28. *Vide* William Ashworth, *op. cit.*, pp. 46–47.

29. *African Quarterly*, New Delhi, October–December, 1965.

30. This point is of considerable interest as it shows the variety of conditions making for population or economic growth. Whereas earlier I speculated that improvements in agriculture in, for instance, the Netherlands had made industrial progress possible, it appears that in Scandinavia industrial progress had stimulated agricultural progress, so that net population accretion may have also been the indirect result of industrialisation.

31. Folke Dovring, 'The Transformation of European Agriculture', in *The Cambridge Economic History of Europe*, Vol. VI, Pt. II, p. 619.

32. F. Dovring, *op. cit.*, p. 620, writes: 'This important break with a natural cycle did not show its adverse effects at once. The lessening evaporation from the ground seems to have caused a long-term diminution of air humidity and made frequent droughts more disturbing than before.'

33. A Gerschenkron writes in *The Cambridge Economic History of Europe*, Vol. VI, Pt. II, p. 707, about the emancipation, that it was a political decision of the men in charge of the Russian Government.

34. There appears to be a great deal of similarity between the economic structures in colonial countries and in late nineteenth-century Russia.

35. Here, indeed, were the forces which prevented the more rapid rise of Russian industry, and also the seeds of the system of repression which was later inherited and brought to perfection by the Stalin–Beria régime.

36. Y. E. Yanson, *Sravnitel'naya statistika Rossii*, St. Petersburg, 1880, II, p. 147.

37. A. Gerschenkron, *op. cit.*, p. 720.

38. This is also evident from the linguistic distinction between 'barskaya zemlya' and 'krest'yanskaya zemlya' the lords' and the peasants' land.

39. This is the 'intermediary conclusion' of Professor Gerschenkron, *op. cit.*, p. 741, at the end of his excellent analysis of the Emancipation.

40. See A. Gerschenkron, *op. cit.*, pp. 751–752.

41. A. Gerschenkron, *op. cit.*, p. 756.

42. A. Gerschenkron, *op. cit.*, p. 767.

43. *Ibid.*, p. 770.

44. For example, the gentry were in a better position to improve their farming not only because they were more likely to hear of such improve-

ments and because they were more likely to have the capital to buy the equipment, but also because some of the more important innovations needed draught animals, for which there was not enough land on the peasants' allotments. According to Professor Gerschenkron, *op. cit.*, pp. 776 and 778, 'The *per capita* index of output of wheat and rye developed as follows (in fifty provinces)':

1870–74	100·0	1883–85	97·1	1886–90	92·3
1891–95	95·1	1896–1900	97·2		

Deducting the quantities exported abroad:

1870–74	100·0	1883–85	95·3	1886–90	86·1
1891–95	91·9	1896–1900	94·5		

45. For a more detailed discussion of these Acts, see Professor A. Gerschenkron, *op. cit.*, Part 3, 'Clearing the Decks After the Battle: The Great "Volte-Face" ', pp. 783–798.

46. *Estate*, or *Standt* in German, was the feudal definition of a class.

47. The *Duma*, which was elected in 1905, lasted in fact for three months only.

48. Written in 1910. Quoted here from Professor Gerschenkron, *op. cit.*, p. 790.

49. It may, of course, be argued that the changes in Russia were also the result of economic pressures, only that in the West these pressures were the result of a rising standard of living of certain classes, whereas in Russia it seems to have been the result of the growing poverty of the peasant class due to the relatively decreasing amount of land at the peasants' disposal.

50. It may be worth noting that Stolypin was not the only statesman in Russia in his time who favoured the abolition of the old village system (the *obshchina*). Witte, for example, had struggled against the conservative point of view; but, as Professor Gerschenkron pointed out (*op. cit.*, p. 792), 'Witte considered the *obshchina* as a problem for the industrial development of the country, Stolypin's interest in industrialisation was marginal . . . he was explicit in regarding the land as the only source of welfare'.

51. Maurice Dobb, *Soviet Economic Development since 1917*, 5th edition, London, 1960, p. 37.

52. The best known names connected with the the early days of the chemical fertiliser industry are: J. B. J. D. Boussingault (1802–87), in France; Justus von Liebig (1842–1914), in Germany; and Sir J. B. Lawes (1814–1900), in Britain.

53. Trevor I. Williams, 'The Chemical Industry', in Singer, Holmyard, Hall and Williams, *op. cit.*, p. 254.

54. *Ibid.*

55. Some of it was also used in the munition industry for gunpowder and explosives.

56. For example, the number of Canadian wood asheries was reduced from 519 in 1870 to 128 in 1891. *Vide* Singer, Holmyard, Hall and Williams, *op. cit.*, p. 255.

57. In the twentieth century the process was carried even further, when a way was discovered to synthesise nitrogen salts from the air by electricity.

58. 'It is customary to express the consumption of fertilisers in units of pure content of plant nutrients ($N+P_2O_3+K_2O$) per unit area. The following table gives the consumption so measured of chemical fertilisers, as kilogrammes per hectare of arable land . . .', Professor Folke Dovring, *op. cit.*, pp. 656–657.

Country	*1910–13*	*1949–50*
United Kingdom	28	125
Ireland		24
Denmark	25	81
Norway	14	152
Sweden	14	57
Belgium	69	255
Netherlands	164	378
France	20	49
Switzerland	15	102
Germany	50	152
Poland	17	17
Roumania	0·05	0·15
Italy	14	25
Spain	4	20
Portugal	9	29

'A minimum requirement for utilisation of chemical fertilisers, as calculated in the 1920s, has been said to be the equivalent of 60 kg. of pure nutrient content per hectare under cereals and 90 kg. per hectare under industrial crops.'

59. As Professor F. Dovring, *op. cit.*, p. 658, points out, it is of interest that 'Already at the beginning of the present century it was stated in England that, in that country, more plant nutrients were imported in the form of feed concentrates to be transformed in the country into livestock products and manure, than in the form of chemical fertilisers'. Since then, the proportions have again changed in England.

60. For underemployment and the use of fertilisers in Africa today, *vide* Y. S. Brenner, 'Under-Employment in West Africa', *African Quarterly*, December 1965, and 'Mechanisation in West Africa', *African Quarterly*, July 1966.

61. We know, for example, that in Ghana in 1966, between 5–10 per cent of corn (maize) was lost through weevils in the field (spraid) and another 20–30 per cent during the period of drying by traditional methods. The use of silos and good chemicals could reduce these losses very significantly.

62. Folke Dovring, *op. cit.*, pp. 662–663, writes: 'The Ardenne horses and the English thoroughbred, the Ayrshire cattle and the Merino sheep, and many others, have been produced by people who did not know any modern genetics but were aware of the elementary fact of biological heredity. Likewise, the sugar beet, the turnip and many other cultivated plants have been produced through crudely systematic massive selection. In still other cases, a higher-yielding strain may have gained prominence under the relatively protected conditions of cultivated land merely by producing higher yields, and thus contributing more seed for next year than the lower-yielding strains in the same mixture.'

63. Folke Dovring, *op. cit.*, p. 663.

64. For example, the *shaduf* pictured in a tomb at Thebes, Egypt, 1500 B.C.

65. Derry and Williams, *op. cit.*, p. 684.

66. J. Allen, 'Hydraulic Engineering', in Singer, Holmyard, Hall and Williams, *op. cit.*, p. 541.

67. Quoted here from J. Allen, *op. cit.*, p. 545.

68. For example, the common use of water-closets and bath-tubs, etc.

69. For these and other methods used, see F. E. Bruce, in Singer, Holmyard, Hall and Williams, *op. cit.*, p. 555.

70. For more details, *vide* F. E. Bruce, 'Water-Supply', Singer, Holmyard, Hall and Williams, *op. cit.*, pp. 552–560. A good example for the irrigation of land in the present century is Israel's Negev irrigation plan.

71. C. L. Cutting, 'Food Preservation', in Singer, Holmyard, Hall and Williams, *op. cit.*, p. 44.

72. For details, *vide* Derry and Williams, *op. cit.*, pp. 686–691, and Singer, Holmyard, Hall and Williams, *op. cit.*, pp. 44–63.

73. J. Caird, *The Landed Interest and the Supply of Food*, 1878, pp. 5–6.

74. 'In 1873, 18,546,000 acres of England and Wales—almost exactly half the total area of the country—were owned by only 4,217 persons. . . .' William Ashworth, *An Economic History of England, 1870–1939*, London, 1960, p. 49.

75. For example, Joseph Arch's new union of farm workers in the 1870s.

76. Lord Ernle, *English Farming Past and Present*, p. 507.

77. A. Birnie, *An Economic History of Europe 1760–1939*, London, 1930, reprinted 1964, p. 20.

78. Augé-Laribé, *Le Paysan Français après la Guerre*, p. 27. Quoted from Birnie, *op. cit.*, p. 22.

79. According to Arthur Birnie, *op. cit.*, p. 22, it was 5½ against 3½ millions.

80. This may have been the result of their poverty or, alternatively, of deliberate family planning. See chapter II on Population, pp. 73–74.

81. According to J. H. Clapham, *Economic Development of France and Germany 1815–1914*, Cambridge, 1921, quoted here from 4th edition reprint 1961, p. 159, it was from 6·75 to 10·6 per cent.

82. J. H. Clapham, *op. cit.* By 1891 it was 21·1 per cent and in 1911 26 per cent.

83. J. H. Clapham, *op. cit.*, p. 159, gives the following statistics:

Year	*Total Population*	*Rural Population*	*Percentage*
1876	36,900,000	24,900,000	67·6
1886	38,200,000	24,450,000	64·1
1896	38,500,000	23,500,000	60·9
1906	39,250,000	22,700,000	57·9
1911	39,600,000	22,100,000	55·9

84. It is surprising that agricultural co-operation did not progress much faster in France during this period.

85. With the exception of Russia, France was the leading wheat-producing country in Europe, and although the French wheat area declined in the second half of the nineteenth century, net production increased due to better farming methods.

86. J. H. Clapham, *op. cit.*, p. 185.

87. J. H. Clapham, *op. cit.*, p. 186.

88. This is true until the last decade of the century, when the syndicates became more closely organised along different lines, in particular by the crop they produced and were marketing.

89. Wheat Production in Quintals (Colin Clark, *op. cit.*, pp. 296–297).

In	1885–1889	France:	11·8;	Belgium:	18·5
In	1909–1913	,,	13·2;	,,	25·3
Potatoes:	1909–1913	,,	86·0;	,,	186·0
Sugar:	1909–1913	,,	29·7;	,,	44·5

90. J. H. Clapham, *op. cit.*, p. 197.

91. For a detailed summary, see J. H. Clapham, *op. cit.*, pp. 221–225.

92. In fact, this was part of Prussia, although it was a Rhineland region.

93. The idea had already been adopted in a number of urban regions a few years earlier and is usually mentioned in connection with the work of men like Schulze-Deltzsch and others. This aspect of co-operation will be discussed here in more detail in connection with the industrial growth of Germany, pp. 132–133.

94. J. H. Clapham, *op. cit.*, p. 223, wrote: 'By the end of the century there was a central factory for artificial manures, a machinery depot at Frankfurt, and in Cologne a wholesale warehouse from which the village societies could buy their more essential requirements. . . .'

95. We shall come back to this point in the discussion of industrial progress in Germany, Ch. IV, pp. 161–163.

96. J. H. Clapham, *op. cit.*, p. 224.

97. E. Jensen, *Danish Agriculture, its Economic Development*, Copenhagen, 1937, p. 41, quoted here from A. J. Youngson, *Possibilities of Economic Progress*, Cambridge, 1959, p. 192.

98. A. J. Youngson, *op. cit.*, pp. 192–193.

99. According to Professor Youngson, *op. cit.*, this legislation 'was motivated largely by fiscal considerations. The legislation of 1725 declared that to lay waste peasant farms . . . is highly detrimental to the country, since thereby it will cease to be occupied by inhabitants as might otherwise be the case and . . . the necessary men for our land militia will not be born and sustained. . . .' (p. 193n.)

100. 'Proprietors must not presume . . . to join such farms to their own demesnes . . . since we desire that all revenues from the people and family tax shall not be reduced.' Legislation of 1725. (*Vide* note 99.)

101. Denmark had entered the war on the side of Napoleon.

102. Data taken from A. J. Youngson, *op. cit.*, pp. 202–203.

103. This point is of particular interest to students in Africa who, because of the impression left by colonial economic policies in their countries, or under the influence of Stalin's agra-policy, tend to dismiss agriculture as a possible source of rapid economic development.

104. Quoted from Youngson, *op. cit.*, pp. 207–208, in detail, because of the particular importance of these organisational possibilities for agra-development in Africa today.

Chapter IV

INDUSTRY

THE COMING OF INDUSTRY: GENERAL OBSERVATIONS

Machines, inanimate sources of power, a wide range of raw materials, the concentration of labour, and mass consumption—these are the main characteristics of industrialisation. Every one of them can be found to have led an isolated existence in one place or another, or in one form or another in earlier periods, but their combination and rapid economic ramification and expansion over increasingly wider areas of the globe are the distinctive feature of the late nineteenth and twentieth centuries.

The machine, defined as 'a combination of solid parts so contrived that by means of it natural forces can be made to cause certain definite motions',[1] as distinct from the tool which is set to work by man's physical strength, had been in use for a very long time before the nineteenth century; but it was only after the technical difficulties of constructing safe and durable engines, and the machinery for them to drive, were overcome in the nineteenth century that machines began to exert their truly revolutionary influence. The same can be said of the inanimate sources of power. Prime movers such as water and wind had been used for centuries to drive various kinds of equipment, but it was only then, with the development of steam-engines, that a source of energy which was reliable and powerful, independent of natural environment, became available—one which, unlike the animate sources, did not compete with man for means of sustenance. The range of useful raw materials was greatly extended in the nineteenth century as a result of scientific progress and of the application of new sources of power and machines. Many material resources which were considered of little or no value before the nineteenth century became of tremendous qualitative and quantitative importance. For example, in some places stone had already replaced wood in the construction of houses and, where neither one nor the other was available, brick became the most common building material; but from the beginning of the nineteenth century artificial cements, the most famous of which was Portland cement (1838), became an increasingly popular addition to and substitute for both. However, as artificial cements are much more readily available in quantity than stone and timber, their use added a completely new quantitative dimension to the building industry. Another even better example is the textile industry, where wool was augmented by cotton and cotton by synthetic fibres. No less important than the addition of 'new' raw materials was the more efficient exploitation of the old ones, their by-products, and their wastages.[2] However, machines, new sources of energy, and the new range of raw materials also brought with them new organisational structures, the factory system and the high concentration of labour. Here, again, workshops in which a great number of people were employed under one roof, and towns, had been in existence before the time of the Industrial Revolution, but both qualitatively and quantitatively they were of a different order. The factories were few in number and had little influence on the total volume of production; the towns were administrative and commercial centres with some handicraft workshops and craft guilds here and there, but they were not centres of large-scale 'value producing' economic activity. The old towns of the pre-industrial period were, above all, providers of services; the new towns were equally, if not more, providers of goods. The share of the former in the population of a country seldom exceeded 15 per cent, the share of the latter was seldom below 32 per cent, and more often than not, above 50 per cent.[3] The difference between the value and volume of the goods produced in pre-industrial and in industrialised towns was even more striking.[4] The social organisation in the old towns somehow resembled the 'vertical' feudal structure, with elders and guilds taking the traditional place of the nobility. Society in the industrial towns was becoming increasingly 'horizontally', interest or class-orientated in its forms of organisation. Finally, it was the mass consumption of manufactures which, in the nineteenth century, was stimulated and accompanied by, and also itself animated, all the earlier mentioned changes in techniques, materials, sources of energy, and organisation of production. A manufacturing industry of luxury goods had been in existence in Europe since the later middle ages; but, even in England, and as late as the eighteenth century, it was only producing for a limited clientele. Most people produced whatever they wanted themselves within their own households. Only a few items had to be bought or exchanged for local products. It was only after technological progress and the division of labour had reduced the cost of manufactures produced outside the household so much that their prices fell below the alternative-labour-cost of members of the rural household that a change began to take shape. Then, with the rate of exchange between the less rapidly developing agricultural sector and the rapidly growing industrial sector changing in favour of the former, a rapidly growing variety and volume of industrial goods were in demand and as their prices continued to fall in terms of other products, the production of which was less easily increased and made cheaper by industrialisation, their demand continued to grow. This self-sustaining process, which on the one hand created the demand, while on the other, by virtue of the same, it stimulated the supply, was further reinforced by competition among the producers. This competition, i.e. the 'crushing of the weaker', led to the deliberate application of science to production; while at the same time the opposition of the workers to their exploitation, wherever and whenever this was possible, led to the gradual increase of their purchasing power which kept the supply-stimulating demand going. This 'virtuous' circle was the motive power behind the forces which changed economic conditions in the developed countries from the middle of the nineteenth century onwards.

The first countries to take part in the industrial revolution were Britain and Belgium;[5] but even in these the process was far from being complete by the first half of the nineteenth century. In the words of the great historian of eighteenth-century industrial progress, Paul Mantoux,[6] even 'in the first decade of the nineteenth century . . . the use of machinery was still limited to certain industries, and these industries to certain specialities or certain districts. Side by side with great metal works . . . the small workshops . . . continued to exist, and survived for many decades. Side by side with the Lancashire cotton mills and the West Riding woollen mills, thousands of weavers went on working at home on their old hand looms. Steam, which was to multiply and generalize the results of all other mechanical inventions, had hardly begun its triumphant progress. Nevertheless the modern industrial system did already exist with all its essential features, and it is possible to detect in the developments which had taken place at that time the main characteristics of the great change.'

By the middle of the nineteenth century Britain was 'the very model of industrial excellence and achievement'.[7] She produced 'about two-thirds of the world's coal, more than half of its iron and cotton cloth' and her income *per capita* was very considerably higher than that of all other countries in Europe.[8] Yet, while Britain's industrial output continued to grow very significantly from the middle of the nineteenth century, that of some other countries grew even more. Foremost among these were Germany and the United States of America. This comes to light even in a superficial examination of the production or consumption data for the major sources of energy, minerals, or of other industrial materials.

COAL PRODUCTION

(Approximate output in million tons.)[9]

Year	*World Output*	*United Kingdom*	*Germany*	*United States*
1860	135	84·9	15·4	16·7
1870		120·7	31·8	43·1
1880		156·4	51·3	88·7
1890		180·3	72·0	155·3
1900	700	226·8	110·7	281·0
1913		292·0	190·1	478·4
1927		255·3	150·8	517·8
1955	1,700	221·6		464·6

It should be noted that in spite of the development of new sources of power—hydro-electricity, oil, gasoline, and most recently atomic energy—gas-coal retained its commanding position. According to Professor Landes[10] it still accounted for about 88½ per cent of the world's energy output in 1913, for 75½ per cent in 1925, and for 66½ per cent in 1931. In addition to this it must also be noted that the efficiency of the exploitation of each unit of coal had also increased very considerably.

STEEL PRODUCTION

(Approximate output in million tons)[9]

Year	*United Kingdom*	*Germany*	*United States*
1870	0·5	0·3	0·1
1880	1·8	0·8	1·6
1890	3·2	2·8	4·3
1900	4·9	7·3	13·4
1913	9·0	18·7	31·3
1927	9·7	16·2	44·9
1938	10·6	23·2	28·3
1955	19·8		104·5

World production of manufactures increased between the years 1870 and 1913 more than fourfold. However, Britain's share in it fell from 32 to only 14 per cent, though, of course, this still shows an absolute increase of about 56 per cent in the production of British manufactures.[11] At the same time the combined share of Britain and the United States in world output of manufactures fell from 55 to only 50 per cent, and that of England, France, Germany and the United States taken together, from 79 to 72 per cent. Although this relative increase in the share of other countries (excluding England, France, Germany and the United States) may seem minute (only 7 per cent), it is in fact considerable because it means that by 1913 the other countries alone were already producing more than *all* countries taken together in 1870.

FIGURE 4

Rate of Growth in Coal and Steel Production

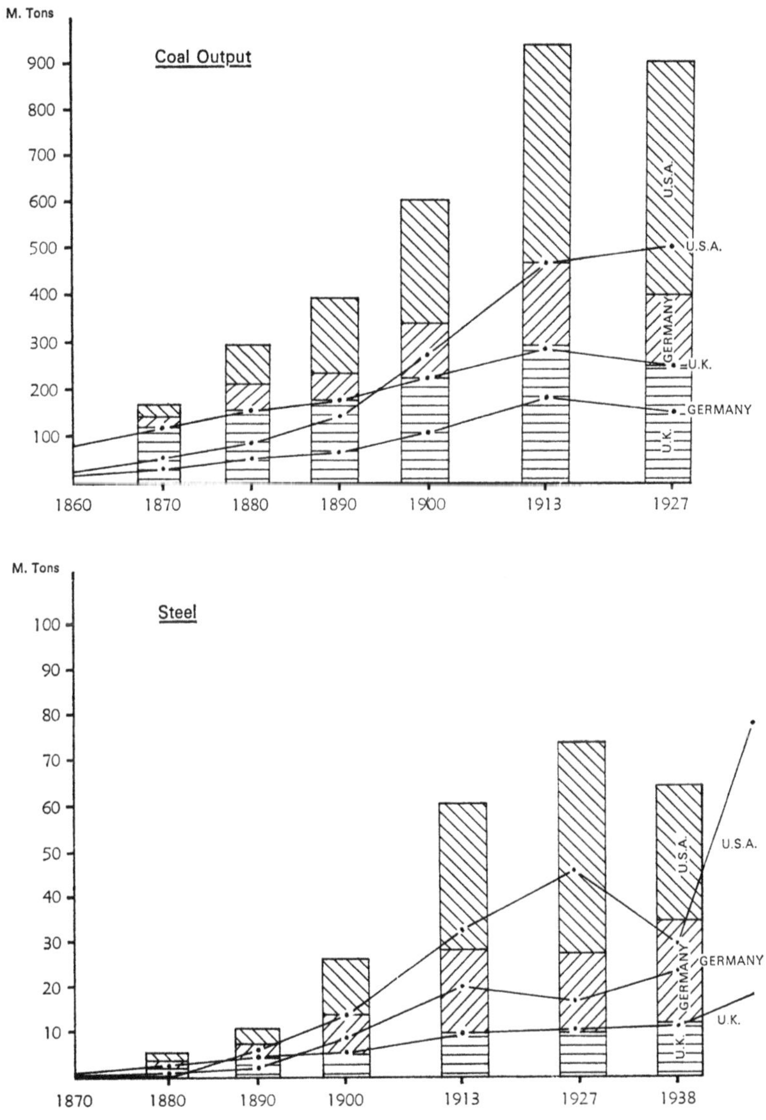

(a) The curves indicate national outputs and (b) the shaded rectangles total output for years indicated below.

FIGURE 5

World Output of Manufactures

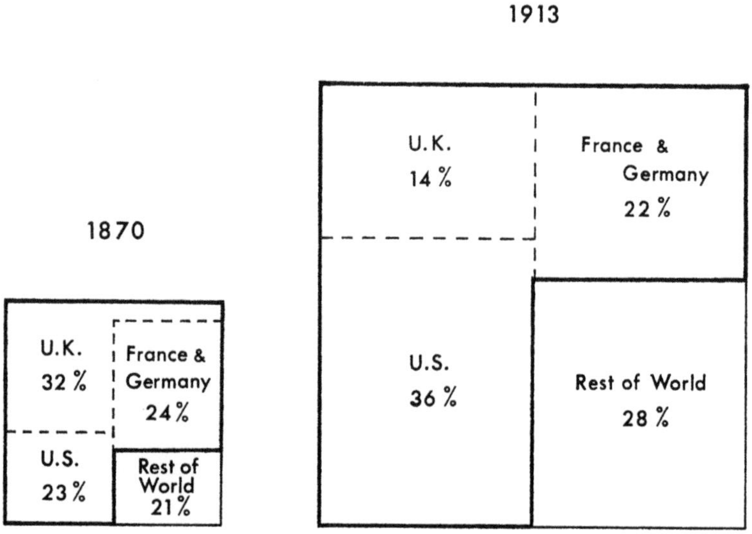

While the relative decline of Britain's share in world industrial output after 1870 can be fairly easily explained by the obvious fact that Britain is a comparatively small country, the delay in the continental emulation of her achievements is a rather more complicated problem. This is especially so because in scientific achievement the Continent was hardly less advanced than Britain. The explanation probably lies in the comparative advantages which Britain enjoyed in earlier periods; her unique geographic and demographic position, and her natural resources.

Geographically and demographically Britain, and particularly England, had an advantage over most countries on the Continent of Europe, for several reasons. Firstly, because her population was more concentrated, which made possible the undertaking of developmental tasks feasible only where enough people could benefit from them and where enough manpower was available to carry them out; for example, the construction of waterways or the erection of wind or water mills. Secondly, because being surrounded by the sea and well served with a good many rivers which could often be connected without too much cost into a close network of waterways, Britain was in a favourable position for both bringing together for industrial production different raw materials from various places, and for delivering the finished products to distant markets. Neither of these advantages, i.e. concentration of population and a useful network of communication, was to be found on the Continent. There, with few exceptions, the population was scattered over vast areas, and most rivers were not suitable for heavy all-year-round navigation. From the geological point of view, Britain's richness in natural resources of the kind required in the early stages of industrialisation gave her considerable advantages over the continental countries, which were relatively poor in this field. Those advantages lasted until the end of the nineteenth century, when new methods for the treatment of mineral resources were discovered and when, as a result of further exploration, more mineral deposits were found in continental Europe. Above all, however, Britain's coal and iron deposits were of superior quality and closely located to one another. This was seldom the case on the Continent.[12]

Politically Britain had been unified, free from internal customs frontiers, free from civil wars, and free from other wars on her own soil since the seventeenth century. On the Continent the situation was very different indeed. For example, neither Germany nor Italy achieved their economic or political unification before the late nineteenth century, while France, though outwardly more uniform than the two former countries, was still full of economic barriers and in the grip of civil and other wars until close to the century's end. Institutionally the early disappearance of serfdom, the uniform and more equitable legal system and its actual enforcement, gave Britain a not inconsiderable advantage. On the Continent industrial progress was often prevented by deliberate policies of 'landlord governments', which were eager to retain the labour force on their estates, and by the survival of feudal legislation affecting the personal status of the peasants.[13] Finally, there was the cultural or perhaps the socio-economic environment, which was far more suitable in Britain than on the Continent for economic change. For reasons which have their origin in historical developments, which often date back to the middle ages, poverty was never as dire in England as on the Continent, while class mobility was much more lively.[14] Because of the greater poverty on the Continent there was neither a market which could be stimulated by what initially could only have been marginal price reductions, nor was there enough alternative employment on the farm to place before the peasants a choice between working more on the land and purchasing, say, cloth, or making their own in their spare time. It was, indeed, not before the threshing machine made the distribution of work throughout the farming year more uniform, i.e. before the difference between the 'high' and 'low' seasons of employment in agriculture was appreciably reduced, that some of the jobs which industry could replace had any alternative cost or opportunity cost at all.

In addition to this, there was not even the possibility of turning the relatively greater poverty into an advantage by the development of an export trade. The little that could be saved by low wages was far less than what was added by the high cost of transport, insurance and loan capital current on the Continent owing to the geographical and political conditions.[15] No less, in fact probably more, important than these purely economic factors were the effects of the different cultural frameworks, and above all of the different social attitudes to business in Britain and on the Continent. In Britain, for a long time it was quite common for 'second sons' to find their way into trade and commerce. From there the next step to industry, when the opportunity arose, was but a small one. On the Continent, however, the class structure was much more rigid. Whether it was maintained by an undefined custom or merely by prejudice, as was the case in France, or by legal disabilities imposed by 'Estates', as in Germany or Russia, did not alter the basic fact that for a person of aristocratic descent trade or any other business activity was always associated with social degradation. A true gentleman, so it was held, did not concern himself with money matters, and least of all with commerce. Land and office, and sometimes marriage, were the only truly noble sources of income. In sixteenth-century England someone defined a gentleman as 'one who spends his money like a gentleman'. An apter definition of the continental nobility, even in the nineteenth century, might have been: a gentleman is one who gains his money like a gentleman. The stress in the former definition on spending and in the latter on the acquisition of wealth, which may in fact have been the result of the greater poverty on the Continent, is also symptomatic of another difference with far-reaching economic consequences where industrial and cheap mass-production is concerned. This is what Professor Landes called, the 'worship of thrift that on the Continent characterised the bourgeoisie as well as the peasantry to a degree unknown in Britain'.[16] Thus, while the nobility was socially prevented from taking part in business enterprise, ambitious members of other classes were equally discouraged, because in a society where prestige was more easily attained through government service or the professions, this major incentive for showing initiative in industry was missing. Consequently, as Professor Landes points out:[17] 'If the aristocrat was too high to stoop to trade, the ambitious, capable, *novus homo* preferred to by-pass it and seek eminence via the professions and government service.' Moreover, if some *novus homo* had after all made money in trade or industry, he was more likely to invest his profits in land than to plough it back into business where it did not enhance his social standing. There were also other and more practical difficulties in setting up industrial enterprises, as long as policy and tradition protected the old-established guilds. For centuries the guilds were very useful sources of government revenue; and, no less important, they were the only known method of quality control.[18] Over the centuries, too, their insistence upon quality had been the pride of their members. It had created a kind of class consciousness or class pride, a distinction which could seldom be matched by the trade marks of industrial producers and could hardly be upheld in the face of the less personal connection between the workman and his finished product. The worker, and even the owner, in an industrial enterprise where division of labour was practised, could no longer distinguish himself as a member of a separate class closed to all other members of society, which could only be entered by a combination of family ties (a kind of pseudo lineage), skill, and long years of experience gained through apprenticeship. Indeed, he had neither tradition nor social status to raise him above the rest of humanity even in his own esteem.

Even more important, though less direct, were the effects of social impediments on the flow of capital to industry in holding back industrial progress on the Continent. As Professor Landes observed,[19] the business in France and in the Low Countries, and even in Germany, was above all a family affair. It was so closely connected with the family that it became almost indistinguishable from it. The failure of the firm was as much a dark blot on the family name as if some seriously dishonourable action had been committed by one of its members. This was not the case with the British entrepreneur, who regarded his business as no more than a means to an end, and not an end by itself. The object of business was to make money, and not to glorify the family name. These different attitudes had very important consequences regarding the conduct of the enterprises. It made it much more difficult for the Continental entrepreneur to abandon traditional methods of production, to sacrifice quality for quantity and to engage in cut-throat competition than for his counterpart across the Channel. Moreover, it gave undue preference to security and discouraged risk-taking in new investment decisions on the Continent, while at the same time it discouraged borrowing or the acceptance of loan capital outside the family. In other words, it greatly restricted opportunities for expansion and more rapid capitalisation and development. In addition, the social identification of the family with a business enterprise and the tendency to look upon it as a source of prestige, with profits only as coincidental, also went a long way to prevent the growth of fruitful competition, i.e. it prevented the elimination of some of the less efficient enterprises, and thereby reduced efficiency. Continental manufacturing societies looked upon all competition as being unfair, and upon price competition particularly so. If wealth was based upon the ruin of others it did not enhance its owner's social prestige. It defied the purpose of the whole exercise. Of course, it helped to settle the price level in accordance with the least rather than the most efficient producers.

TRANSPORT AND THE TRANSFORMATION OF COMMERCE

How, then, were all these impediments on industrial growth in continental Europe overcome? Obviously it was a complex process, in the course of which one factor influenced some or all the others and was itself influenced by each and all of them. It is, however, extremely difficult, if not impossible, to extricate each individual factor and trace its intricate network of connections at each stage of the development. In the following pages an attempt is made to give an outline, and to explain the causes and effects, of the more obvious forces and changes which left their mark upon the various spheres of life and eventually resulted in the industrialisation of the Continent.[20]

From the geographical, or rather from the geo-economic and demographic point of view, the main changes came as a result of the revolution in transport and of the abatement of population growth 'owing to the personal decisions of the millions of human beings' living in Europe. These two factors completely transformed the economic structure and economic potentialities of Europe within the relatively short period of perhaps four decades. The transport revolution, which had its antecedents in the spurt of canal construction, in the improvement of river navigation, and in Napoleonic (mostly military) road building,[21] which was itself the result of progress in other spheres such as mineral extraction and the discovery and application of steam as a motive power, completely altered the whole economic structure of the Continent between the years 1860 and 1900. Within this period Europe was covered by a network of railroads, which not only connected the old sources of raw materials with the labour to exploit them, as well as the markets which could stimulate their exploitation, but also made completely new sources approachable, while at the same time it led to a profound geographical redistribution of population.

In the first quarter of the nineteenth century the growth of trade and industry in England had surpassed the improvements which had taken place in canal and road transport. Consequently, transport costs rose and the construction and modification of steam engines on rails to suit new transport needs became economical. Initially rails were used as feeder roads to canals. Their purpose was to enable the horses to pull heavier loads than they were able to carry on the normal roads. As this advantage of rails was particularly appreciated in the coal and iron mines, where the steam engine had been in use for some time as a means of extracting underground water, it is hardly surprising that the earliest applications of steam engines to rails took place in the quarries. There they were initially used to convey coal or iron to the canals for further transportation by means of waterways. Their wider use was, however, held back for some time by a number of technical difficulties. It was only in 1820, when more durable wrought-iron rails could be produced, that steam engines began very rapidly to replace horse power as the means of traction on the rails. In this sense the beginning of the railway age was in 1830, with the opening to regular goods and passenger transport of the Liverpool–Manchester line. Obviously, the new railroad, like many others which were to follow during the century, ran into a great deal of opposition from the canal companies and other vested interests, but their economic superiority was soon so obvious that their development could hardly be prevented for any length of time.[22] Indeed, once opened, the Liverpool–Manchester line proved itself immediately a most profitable venture for both its owners and users.

By 1838 some five hundred miles of railways, operated by steam locomotives, were open to the public in England.[23] The Birmingham railway, which was completed in this year and connected that town with London, demonstrated a most essential fact; namely, it showed that it was within the power of the new means of communication to break away from the checks which nature had put upon the means of transportation until that time. Not only was it obvious that the railways could free the economy from the increasingly extortionist tendencies of the managers of the monopolistic river and canal companies, but, more important, they could open up access to resources and potential markets which had so far been considered inaccessible. In fact, it demonstrated that economic development need no longer follow the veins of communication and be limited to the vicinity of rivers or sea-ports, but that the veins themselves could be drawn at man's will towards the economically valuable deposits or markets. In this sense, then, the railways caused a geographical revolution and a redistribution of Britain's population. The greatest shortcoming of the early spread of rail communication in Britain was the lack of a conception of a national railway system. Competing lines were being constructed in one and the same locality, and, at least initially, lines with different gauge rails were also being operated without due regard for the future needs of a unified system. In the 1840s, when business was prosperous and the rate of interest on loan capital in England rather low, railway construction was taken up with great enthusiasm, which did not abate until the great crisis of 1847. By that time, however, Britain had been provided with the main body of her modern railway system.[24]

On the Continent the State played a far more active role in railroad construction once its economic and political advantages had become obvious. The growth of trade and industry not having surpassed the improvements which had taken place during the eighteenth and early nineteenth centuries in the old transportation system, private investors were less inclined to risk money on large-scale railway schemes. As a result of this, it was in most cases the State that planned, supervised, and advanced the money for their construction. For this reason continental railways were constructed from the very beginning more in accord with a deliberate plan of economic development and political national ambitions. It can therefore be said that in a sense the development of continental railways was in many parts at least initially the promoter rather than the result of economic progress.

In Belgium the State took over railroad construction in 1834, and within a few years completed the two main trunk routes, one running north–south and the other east–west. These two lines not only provided the skeleton for local feeder lines but also linked the Belgian transport system to that of the neighbouring countries, and enabled it to profit from a considerable volume of northern European through-traffic. Thus, with the State having provided the major capital, the door was wide open for private capital to do the rest in its own local interests. In this way the Belgian railway system presents a good example of a mixed public and privately owned enterprise, in which the State provides the share which the private sector is either unable or unwilling to finance, and the private sector finances the rest of the enterprise in which it has a direct interest, i.e. the linking of its own businesses and towns to the main national network. The national lines in Belgium made little direct profit. The cost of their construction had been underestimated and the companies were forced by law to redeem debts rather early, but their indirect contribution to the development of the national economy was enormous. Although, as in England, railroad construction in Belgium suffered a severe reversal in 1847, the increasing participation of private investors can be taken as a measure of their success. By 1870 the share of the State operated railways had in fact fallen to less than 25 per cent, owing to the increasing number of privately owned lines. After 1886 the State began to buy up the private railways in order to increase the uniformity of the whole system and to prevent the lines from falling into foreign ownership.

The course of railway construction in France was similar to that of Belgium. Initially there was a considerable amount of public controversy about the financing and planning of the system, with economists propagating the view that development should be left to business interests, who vote with their money where railways are best placed, and the politicians, taking in this particular instance the more far-sighted view that the State should plan and finance the railways with the deliberate end of promoting political and economic aims. The outcome was a compromise by which private railway promoters were guaranteed government assistance in return for their acceptance of some overall State plan for the distribution of the trunk routes throughout the country and of a degree of State control over fares and freight charges. The compromise which was embodied in the Railway Law of 1842 in many ways reflected the mood of the times and the particularly French characteristics of combining State paternalism with the traditions of the *Corps des Ponts et Chaussées*, and concern with public utility. It also reflected cold logic in providing a skeleton of six major trunk lines radiating from Paris, the heart of France, to all the ends of the country, to which all the existing private lines and other new ones could be linked. In reality, however, the venture proved to be far too expensive, especially as the railroads were to be constructed of the finest materials, and to be financed by the State alone. For this reason private capital was invited to participate. Yet as the overall climate of the offer was discouraging, not much private capital was forthcoming until English investors, in the belief that railway construction had come close to its limits in Britain, began to invest heavily in France. Consequently, in France, as in England and Belgium, the forties witnessed a very rapid expansion of the railroad network. Progress continued until 1847, when it was brought to an abrupt halt by the crisis and the revolutions that followed. With the return to full power of the conservative elements in French politics in 1851, railway construction began once more, and the private companies were forced to reinvest a great part of their profits in the development of local and branch lines. In 1850 the French network consisted of some 2,000 miles of main and branch lines. In 1869, just on the eve of the Franco-Prussian war, the network had grown (partly as a result of this reinvestment policy) to over 11,000 miles.

In Germany, too, the economic and political significance of

railways was recognised almost immediately. Yet the fact of Germany's being divided into a great number of politically and economically independent States, and her industrial backwardness, prevented an early exploitation of the advantages which railroads were able to bestow. In fact, progress came very gradually, with the first lines being built by private investors, very cheaply, and for local use. Yet even this very limited progress brought with it a good deal of economic advantage to other industries in Germany. For example, the local iron industry was one of the first to reap the advantages of rail construction. In the beginning the governments took little action to support railway companies, being afraid of becoming financially involved and overburdening their budgets. However, they were not ready to leave them entirely in private control. From 1838 to 1847 rail communication increased very considerably. Then, in 1847–50, the crises caused a sharp fall in railway shares which made it possible for the governments to buy up a great many of them at a reduced price. Consequently, in 1850, approximately 55 per cent of all lines in Germany were State owned. Within a few years both the States and big private rail companies reached an agreement to give the whole system some uniformity. By that time the railroad mileage in Germany already exceeded that of France.[25] During the Empire this trend towards a uniform railway system was further reinforced by Bismarck's political ambitions for a unified Germany; but while his policy was proceeding well in Prussia, it met with considerable opposition in the southern States. There was, however, a compensating factor in the Railway Office, which was established in 1873 to co-ordinate the operation of German railroads, and which worked so well that from the outside it appeared that Germany had a uniform system. Outside Germany, and even before the middle of the nineteenth century, the country was linked with France and Belgium. In the eighties, new connections were added, with Genoa on the Mediterranean and with the Russian Empire in the east, and the famous Orient Express linked the whole European system from Paris to Constantinople.

Thus by the end of the nineteenth century the railway system of northern and western Europe was nearing completion, and in the process it swept away the geographical and demographical obstacles to economic progress one after the other.[26] The railways stimulated passenger traffic to an unprecedented extent by providing a cheap, rapid, safe and reliable means of transport,[27] which led not only to a more rapid spreading of knowledge but also to a far greater degree of mobility of labour. It led, in fact, to far-reaching changes in the geographical distribution of populations, a point which was well demonstrated by the political struggle of the sixties in England abou the Parliamentary representation of the Midlands, and even more so by the settlement of the West in America. In addition to this, the progress of the railways brought about an enormous expansion of freight transport. It was here in particular that railroads made their greatest contribution on the continent of Europe by making possible the bringing together quickly, cheaply and regularly of the different heavy and bulky raw materials required for industry which were widely dispersed in Europe. Moreover, the expansion of the railway system made possible the concentration and specialisation of labour in the places most suitable for a certain kind or stage of production, without the limitations formerly imposed by local food supplies. In other words, the expansion of locomotive-operated rail transport made possible a national, and, after the 1870s when steam shipping and refrigeration also developed, an international division of labour and regional specialisation. Man had not yet learned to change his geographical environment, but he had gone a long way towards overcoming the obstacles nature put in his path.

SCIENCE, NATURAL RESOURCES AND NEW SOURCES OF POWER

The next factor which helped the economies of continental Europe to emulate British progress in the second half of the nineteenth century was the scientific revolution that opened up completely new and hitherto unrecognised deposits of natural resources.[28]

It is impossible here to discuss the changes in detail, but the following examples will suffice to illustrate their importance, magnitude, and impact on the lives of millions of people. On the whole science was still in an era of specialisation, in the sense that each discipline was following its separate lines of research. However, technological development was already very rapidly transforming the way of life in Europe and in North America. The change was therefore rather quantitative than qualitative. The basis of the change, i.e. the invention and use of inanimate powered machinery, was the product of the eighteenth century. What followed in the nineteenth was the tremendous extension of its utilisation and the progressive increase in the efficiency of exploitation of the new sources of power and equipment. Initially most of these developments, which found a measure of expression in the reduction of production costs, were almost entirely confined to Britain; and even in Britain they were highly localised in places where fuel, that is, coal, was readily and cheaply available. One factor which therefore contributed to the spread of the new sources of power was the rapid growth of national and international transport,[29] which, of course, was itself a result of the new techniques. Moreover, it could not have taken place without parallel development in the metal and engineering industries. Here too, however, with the exception of Neilson's hot blast techniques (1828), there was little dramatically new in the nineteenth century. Certainly there were hundreds of minor technological improvements in the iron industry but no scientific change until the last quarter of the century, when first Bessemer, and then Siemens and Gilchrist, gave the industrial revolution the new dimension of steel. The new techniques for steel making which were discovered by them[30] provided Europe and its sphere of influence with a material which combined strength with hardness and malleability, three qualities of almost immeasurable advantage in industry. It also caused something like a 'reallocation' of Europe's national resources; or, more precisely, it gave rise to a better industrial exploitation of iron and coal deposits and particularly of those which had until this time been considered of little value. For example, Germany had little non-phosphoric iron ores as used in the Bessemer processes of steel production[31] but, in Lorraine and in Luxemburg there were rather large reserves of basic ore which, though unsuitable in earlier processes, were particularly good for the production of steel by Gilchrist Thomas' method.[32] As a result of this, when all over the world iron and steel producers were suffering a severe reversal during the depression of the eighties, the German iron industry was the only one which was making satisfactory progress.

In fact, not only Germany, but all countries which were rich in phosphoric ore and which had hitherto suffered some disadvantage in comparison with those who were rich in non-phosphoric ore, profited from the Gilchrist Thomas process. For example, France and Belgium belonged to the former group, as opposed to Britain which belonged to the latter. In this sense the new materials and new processes were bringing about a new allocation of the world's natural resources. The point is illustrated by Professor Clapham's tables of pig iron and steel output between the years 1880 and 1910.[33] It is, however, important to note that these dramatic increases in European iron and steel production were still relatively small in comparison with their growth in the United States of America.[34]

To illustrate the advantages of steel, one can point out that steel rails were not only less expensive than those made of puddled iron but also lasted fifteen to twenty times as long;[35] or that in the manufacture of boilers, steel plates could be made much thinner and better than iron ones. However, the 'redistribution' of natural resources (in the earlier stated sense) was not only the result of the progress in the iron industry but also due to the fast rise in the use of non-ferrous metals.[36]

Thus, taking the example of copper, the leadership in world

production was held successively by Spain, Chile and North America. On the whole, however, it must be said that the commonly employed indicators of nineteenth-century industrialisation in Europe and America, i.e. the output of coal and iron ore, tend to give too low an impression of the actual rate of growth. This is so not only because both coal and iron were increasingly augmented by a continually rising number and volume of other materials, but also because the exploitation of known resources became more and more efficient as the century progressed. Thus, for example, the greater supply of energy which was reflected in the rising consumption of coal, coke and lignite was underrated not only because of the additional sources of energy (oil and electricity) but also because of the rapidly improving efficiency of the burners and of the mechanical equipment they were driving.[37]

THE WANING OF THE POLITICAL AND INSTITUTIONAL IMPEDIMENTS TO ECONOMIC PROGRESS IN CONTINENTAL EUROPE

Politically, perhaps the most important factor which contributed to the emulation of British industrialisation on the Continent was the unification of Germany and the elimination of the traditional trade barriers in France, and the rise of the tide of European economic nationalism.

The acceleration of German economic growth since 1834 was undoubtedly promoted by the *Zollverein* (customs union), though it would be rash to attribute to it too much as the development of railways and the spreading of knowledge coincided with it. But, at the same time, there can be little doubt that without it progress would have been much slower.[38] The history of the *Zollverein* has been told too often to be repeated here. What is essential from the point of view of industrialisation was that by the beginning of the second quarter of the nineteenth century Motz had already recognised the potentialities of Maassen's Prussian tariff system (initiated in 1815) as an instrument for achieving German unity under Prussia's hegemony. As Prussia's provinces were too far scattered all over Germany to facilitate an effective collection of customs, they decided to fight the smugglers by making smuggling an unprofitable occupation. Thus, rather than relying on a high tariff collected from a small volume of trade, they adopted a policy of collecting a low tariff, by the standards of the time, of about 10 per cent *ad valorem*, from the much greater volume of trade which was bound to follow the tariff cuts. The cuts were, however, only designed to affect trade with Prussia, while mere through-traffic was made to pay as much as the Prussian revenue experts believed could be taken. And so, as Prussia lay, as Professor Clapham wrote, 'athwart most of the main trade routes of Germany', it held most of the rest of Germany to ransom. Soon the political possibilities arising out of this situation became obvious, and Prussia started upon a deliberate economic policy in furtherance of her political ambitions. The larger States were given to understand that if they joined the Prussian 'club' they would enjoy the Prussian privileges, whereas the minor princes were given money to construct roads and other public works as long as they fitted in with the overall Prussian scheme. In Prussia itself, this policy was welcomed in both aristocratic and industrial circles. The former saw in it a way of transferring the burden of taxation, and the latter a way of securing for themselves a market free from foreign competition. Finally, in 1833, central and southern Germany came to terms with Prussia, which left only the north-west apart. The north-west, being at that time a predominantly agricultural region, had little to gain from joining the *Zollverein*. Its markets were mostly overseas and its transport system independent of the Prussian tariff barriers. In addition, it had no difficulty in purchasing its industrial requirements from Britain, where they were cheaper than in Germany, and where it had a ready market for agricultural surpluses. Thus, with the exception of Hanover, Schleswig-Holstein, Mecklenburg, Oldenburg and Bremen in the north, and Alsace-Lorraine in the south-west, Germany was more or less economically united by the middle of the century. In fact, the revolutionary movements of 1848 and the developments which followed them, i.e. the liberation of agricultural labour and its subsequent transfer to the towns, and the struggle between the Prussian *Kleindeutsche* and Austrian *Grossdeutsche* policies, marked the end of the old era of division and the coming of the new era of industrially viable union.[39] The range and the volume of the industrial market was growing, protected by a high tariff wall against its old-established competitors across the Channel.

Then, while the struggle between the two factions for and against the inclusion of Austria in the German union was being waged, the Prussian industrialists found it politically expedient to press for a policy of low tariffs. As the Austrian industries were unable to accept such a policy, this was a certain way of preventing the *Grossdeutsche* party in Austria from gaining their powerful support. At the same time, however, as this policy discouraged Austria from joining the Prussian-led Federation, it opened the door for the inclusion of the north-western States. Their inclusion, in 1854, finally gave the free traders in the *Zollverein* a clear advantage. Before, the balance between the free traders in the agricultural north-east and the protectionists in the industrialist-led south-west was fairly evenly balanced with Prussia, where Delbruck was formulating economic policy with little public control over his decisions, supporting the abolition of tariffs. Now, with the joining of the predominantly agricultural north-west, the scales were undoubtedly tipped in favour of free trade. When, in addition to this, Austria was defeated in war and Prussia emerged victoriously in 1866, the policy of a *Grossdeutschland* was finally abandoned by one and all. During the five years that followed almost all that remained of Germany was united in the *Zollverein*.[40] At that time (1871) Germany, now the German Empire, felt economically strong enough to adopt an almost 'English' free trade policy. By 1877 even the last of the iron duties disappeared, although by that time the economic situation had already deteriorated. The economic depression which hit almost all the countries in Europe during the period 1873–82, and which was also reflected in the political difficulties the Empire had in collecting its revenue, eventually led to a gradual retreat from free trade and towards a renewal of protectionist policies in the German Empire. But by this time most of the political obstacles to the emulation of British industry had already been overcome.

In France, the political forces which had to be overcome before British industrial progress could be emulated were of a somewhat different nature from those in Germany. Nineteenth-century France had inherited a small industry from the eighteenth century which had been 'nursed into life' and kept alive by high protective tariffs and by the continental blockade. Even when the government changed, the Restoration did not abolish most forms of economic protectionism. On the contrary, the customs barriers were strengthened and made to include even non-industrial products like grains. Thus a premium was paid on industrial inefficiency while, at the same time, food prices were kept high; in consequence wages, and thereby production costs in industry, rose even higher.[41] Eventually the government of Louis Philippe introduced some almost radical liberal changes in the tariff system, but this new trend was only short lived. By the end of the first decade of his reign, in 1841, a new tariff law was introduced which returned the country to the old protective system. Moreover, the by now combined opposition of the great powers and some French and Belgian industrialists managed to prevent a Franco-Belgian customs union which might have given France access to the natural resources, coal and iron, she needed to stimulate her industrial progress. Even after 1848 there was little change in French trade policy. Only when close to the end of the fifties the political difficulties which until then had prevented the completion of the railway system were finally overcome did new opportunities for industrial development arise. But then the defeat of France in the Franco-Prussian war of 1870, the loss of Alsace-Lorraine, and the Paris uprising of 1871, plunged the country into a state of gloom which once again held back the progress which was just beginning to bear fruit.

Another no less important source of industrial inefficiency in nineteenth-century France, until the end of the sixties, was the labour legislation which banned all associations 'either of masters or of workmen'.[42] This rule, which remained in force in one way or another until 1868, effectively prevented the organisation of labour. Thereby it obstructed the only force left in France, under the prevailing 'hothouse' conditions of protective tariffs, which might have forced industry to introduce more and better mechanical equipment, i.e. to become more efficient. Thus, in effect, a policy which was designed to stimulate industry—by protecting it from foreign competition and by keeping down workers' wages—achieved precisely the opposite results.

From the institutional point of view the most important factor which prevented a more rapid emulation of the British industrial example on the Continent was the survival of feudal legislation and traditions regarding personal freedom and mobility. If the growth of towns may be taken as a measure for industrial development, it is obvious that before the middle of the nineteenth century Germany's industrial progress was very slow indeed. One cause for this was the sharp social division, usually reinforced by law, between town and country. For decades German rulers had been busy to 'keep the peasant at his plough and the burgher at his handicraft'.[43] Moreover, even within the towns, the number of craftsmen in a trade were more often than not legally restricted by royal decrees or by guild regulations. In Prussia, for example, the division went as far as having three different codes of law, each of which was specially reserved for a different class, or rather 'estate', of the population. The peasants were judged according to one law, the burghers according to another, and the nobility according to a third.[44] No aristocrat was lawfully able to buy free land and no peasant could acquire land in the city. In Prussia this legal 'trinity' was finally abolished in 1806, but for a long time after people continued to abide by what they traditionally believed to be right. In addition to this, and as distinct from France and the French-occupied regions of the Revolutionary period, i.e. in Prussia and in the east and north of Germany, the guilds still held a formidable position during the first half of the nineteenth century. In fact their domination of a great number of trades in towns remained almost entirely unchallenged in most of Germany until 1848, and in parts of it until 1862.[45] Their system of restrictive practices was a considerable obstacle on the path towards economic expansion. Such limited industries as had come into existence, by royal encouragement, during the later part of the eighteenth century, and had created their small working class which was free from the traditional restrictions, collapsed under the impact of Napoleon's Continental System. They left little institutionally valuable behind them upon which a new structure could be built. A new beginning was made in 1821 when the Prussian Government, now fully aware of the importance of industrialisation, set up the Gewerbe Institute: a school to teach the new industrial techniques to a new kind of craftsmen. Unfortunately, however, the Institute was badly located, being in Prussia, at a place with little water power and with virtually no suitable coal, at a time when steam was just about to become the very lifeblood of the new methods of production. Yet with all this the creation of the Institute was of considerable importance. It pointed to the new direction in which the government was going, at the time when the emancipation of the peasants was also opening a door towards a new institutional approach to the country's industrial labour problem.

The next step, in Prussia, was taken around the year 1848. Until then a great many villein services had survived though they affected only a small proportion of the population: those who had been excluded from the earlier emancipation Acts because they were considered 'below peasant status'. The Law of 1850 came to rectify this omission. Thus, between 1850 and 1870, the new structure of society began to take shape. Those peasants who could turn their status into that of 'proprietors' formed one class, and those who could not, another. However, without the abolition of the manor as the administrative unit of local government, it was still impossible for either peasant or labourer to gain true personal freedom. In fact, even in the last decade of the century, many peasants and labourers could still be called upon to perform certain communal works at the nobles' will. But things were not the same throughout the whole of Germany. In some places peasants could buy their freedom, and indeed did so between 1848 and 1870, by which time emancipation was complete;[46] in other parts, even the formal side of manorial jurisdiction had hardly been touched in 1870.[47] And yet, although the emancipation was far from being complete by 1870, the floodgates which had prevented the rush of people into the towns were now wide open. Within less than a quarter of a century both the demographic and the social structure of the country was transformed beyond all recognition.[48]

While it had not been easy for the peasantry to quit the land, there was also little to attract it to the towns. To be sure, the Freedom of the Trades (*Gewerbefreiheit*), i.e. the right of any man to enter the trade he chose, was proclaimed in some States (Westphalia, 1808, Prussia, 1811), but the predominance of the guild organisation remained untouched. A Commission, which was appointed in 1835 to study the labour problem with the aim of formulating a uniform labour legislation for the whole of Germany, finally submitted a report ten years later, in 1845, and recommended the introduction of State control where that of the guilds had already been abrogated. In fact, the position of the guilds was rather strengthened than weakened during the early forties. However, during the depression of 1845–47 the clash of interests between the free industries and their workers, on the one hand, and the guild-masters and the craftsmen, on the other, came out into the open for the first time when some guilds began pressing for legal restrictions on the use of steam in industry. It was in these years that one Congress, of craftsmen, in Hamburg, demanded the prohibition of *Gewerbefreiheit*, while another Congress, of free labourers, in Berlin, demanded a legally prescribed minimum wage rate, a twelve-hour work-day and freedom of movement. For the factory owners the labourers demanded the termination of the law which prohibited them to employ members of a guild who preferred to work for them.

With the Reaction, in 1849, the workers' views were silenced and those of the guild-masters became official policy. To enter almost any craft the worker had either to be a member of the guild, or, at least, to have passed an officially constituted examination; the employment of craftsmen in factories was made, legally, almost impossible. In fact, the law was too reactionary to be universally applied. Even the excellent Prussian administration was not in a position to overcome the requirements of the economy. The Commission which was set up to examine candidates for their technical qualifications had, in fact, very little actual influence, and restrained the changing trends only very little. Whole districts were built and plenty of houses were constructed, although, as Professor Clapham pointed out, not one legally qualified builder could be found in the region.[49]

In the sixties, even officially, the system was rapidly breaking down. The technological progress and the changing pattern of demand were already revolutionising the whole structure of production. The advantages of factory production under the new market conditions were too great to prevent its spreading for any length of time. This was particularly true when all the economically more advanced countries to the north and west of Germany had shed the remaining trade restrictions long ago. By 1869, then, the official 'testing' system was finally abolished in all but the trades in which it was required for the very nature of the work.

By this time, however, the government felt already threatened by a new source of 'troubles'. A Marxian Social Democratic party had just become a factor in German politics and seemed to undermine the harmony of the social structure of society. In 1878 they polled some 10 per cent of all the votes. In the following year, using a pretext which had little to do with the Social Democrats, Bismarck drove the party underground and employed the whole power of the State to crush it. In fact, he used the opportunity to try to break up all but a few working-class organisations. That such a policy can be of little avail in a period of rapid industrial progress seems in retrospect obvious, but Bismarck seems not to have been aware of this. When the Socialists reappeared in the 1880s as a legal party, they had grown into a far more formidable factor in German politics, but by this time Germany had already caught up with Britain in industrial production.

In France there were as yet few industrial workers in 1848; but these differed from their counterparts in Germany in that they were far more conscious of their status and far more aware of their interests.[50] This was true of both ordinary workers and craftsmen. Unlike the German, the French working-man never accepted the social hegemony and scales of value of the bourgeoisie, and never really tried to imitate it. The Revolution had swept away the guilds and with them the social element which in other countries had glossed over the true nature of class distinction and prevented a sharper form of socio-economic polarisation. Apprenticeship in France was, in the nineteenth century, merely a matter of tradition, and of professionalism, and no longer a legal requirement for anyone who wished to enter a trade. With the growth of the productive establishments—they could hardly be called industries in the first half of the century—the social gap widened. However, the revolutionary legislation which had prohibited any kind of association, whether of masters or of workmen, was not abolished until 1868, and prevented the gradually rising labouring class from turning its social consciousness into a powerful political force. Finally, there was also the 'workman's book', in which each employer had to write a reference for every employee, and without which no workman could be hired. For all these reasons, and in spite of its higher degree of social consciousness, the French working class, like the German, was unable to protect or raise effectively its living standard. As a result of this, French manufacturers were not only deprived of an effective market-demand, but also of the drive to substitute mechanical equipment for labour.[51]

The first serious attempt of the French working class to revise their legal position took place in 1848. In February a coalition of the liberal middle class, led by Lamartine, and of the socialists, led by Louis Blanc, succeeded in overthrowing Louis Philippe's July Monarchy and replaced it with the Second Republic. Yet, while Louis Blanc and Lamartine were united in their opposition to the monarchy and in their demand for the extension of the franchise, they were very far apart in their conception of the régime which was to replace the July Monarchy. In a second left-wing insurrection in Paris, during the same year, the Blancists were defeated, and not long after this Louis Napoleon was elected President, largely through the support of the provinces, which now began for the first time to take a more active part in national politics on the side of 'law and order'. Three years later, in 1851, the Second Republic came to an end when Louis Napoleon finally established himself as Napoleon III. The leaders of the socialist movement were sent to prison or went into exile and, for a time, it seemed as if nothing could be changed. But post-Republican France was very different from what it had been four years before. The brief period of the Republic, its political alertness, its Luxembourg Commissions, its political controversies and economic experiments, had left behind some institutionally irrevocable new trends. From a practical point of view, however, the movement had ended in complete failure as far as the organisation of labour was concerned. Only in the sixties did the pendulum gradually begin to swing back. Industry became a little more prosperous and the labour movement stronger though less militant. Even the government became aware of the need to grant more freedom, though the process was a gradual one and took place in two stages (the legislation of 1864 and 1868). The laws which for almost a century had prohibited the organisation of labour were at long last relaxed. With this, France finally entered the era of rapid industrialisation.

Then, however, came the ill-fated years 1870 and 1871. Once again progress came to a halt. The defeat of France by Germany filled prospective investors with gloom, and the terrors of the Paris Commune which followed added to it fear and uncertainty; together they led to industrial stagnation. Whether or not the fear was objectively justified is difficult to say, because the force which held the Paris Communalists together was, above all, resistance to 'the whole spirit of France's over-centralised government, as the first Napoleon had left it and all succeeding régimes had preserved it . . .' and to the 'suppression of journals, arbitrary arrest and the other beginnings of terrorism . . .'[52] which were, in fact, all demands to which the bourgeoisie could equally subscribe. However, as seen from the contemporary point of view, i.e. as an immediate situation, the bourgeoisie was left with little choice indeed. The Paris rising was 'the offspring of hunger, defeat, and armed idleness' for which, at least in the workers' view, no one but the bourgeoisie was to be blamed. They were accused of putting their own capitalist interests before those of the nation and of having capitulated; in the language of the Paris crowd they had turned from being *capitaliste* into *capitulard*. The class hatred, which had been fostered and rendered almost powerless to express itself throughout nearly a century of anti-labour legislation, now combined with the sense of injured national pride and the feeling of having been betrayed, and produced a social climate which left little room for a cold logical assessment of real considerations. The events of 1870–71 left a deep scar and may not only have led to a long delay in France's industrial progress, but may have also influenced its direction. Freedom of association was finally attained in 1884.

Perhaps the most important factors which prevented a more rapid emulation of the British industrial achievement on the European continent were the far-reaching differences in the cultural make up[53] of the societies. These socio-cultural differences were not merely the reflection of the greater degree of class mobility in Britain, but also part of the basically diverse scales of social values and priorities. The object of success or achievement in France and Germany was honour, i.e. the respect of others; the object of achievement in Britain was money and power. The Englishman's 'love of gain' was a means to an end, the German's and Frenchman's a way of life inextricably involved with the aim itself. The Englishman need have had no scruples in selling inferior goods—because his goods did not reflect upon the person of the producer; he need have had no scruples about underselling his competitors and driving them out of the business—because it was almost a sportsman-like thing to do. There was nothing wrong in competition; one side had to lose and one side to win. Finally, the Englishman was more an individual than the Continental and therefore much less restricted by family ties. The German or Frenchman could not mass-produce inferior goods because his product was 'himself'. Its quality reflected upon the kind of man he was, and money could hardly gloss over his professional failure. Moreover, he could not engage in what he and his society considered unfair competition. As honour and not profit was the first aim of his exertion, he could hardly do anything which would impair it. Socially he would not be forgiven if he owed his success to the downfall of some other member of his trade. In addition, in both France and Germany the cultural hegemony of the aristocracy had succeeded in imposing itself upon the way of life of the bourgeoisie so that they imitated it to the extent of feeling a collective responsibility for the actions and for the way of life of each and every individual member of their family. Thus, while the English industrialist, free from the bondage of the continental bourgeoisie's conception of honour, was able to mass-produce for a wide market because of the cheapness of his goods, and was stimulated to ever-higher efficiency of production by universal 'knockout' competition, and had far less pressure brought to bear upon him from a sense of collective family responsibility, the continental producer was very obviously in a different position. Being prevented by social pressures from engaging in cheap production, he could only very slowly increase the volume of his market; being prevented by social taboos from underselling his competitors he was not pressed towards efficiency and could survive by adjusting his prices and his rate of improvement by the standards set by the weaker links of his profession; finally, by identifying his honours with the quasi lineage of the name of his family, and having it identified by society with his business, the continental industrialist was not only far more restricted in his sources of finance than his English counterpart, but was also compelled to carry along on his payroll the most useless members of his 'tribe'. For a long time these facts held back the pace of continental industrialisation. It was because of them that the breaking of the continental tariff walls and the organisation of labour played such an important role in the progress of western European industry—the former, because it subjected industry to the pressure of competition, which it lacked at home, and the latter, because higher wage demands forced out of business the less efficient establishments and thereby raised the minimum level of productivity to which all other producers tended to adjust themselves.

Gradually both the outside pressure, i.e. foreign competition, and the pressure from below, i.e. the organisation of labour, forced the industrial class of entrepreneurs to adjust themselves to the changes. They became rich and began to realise their rising social importance and with this they began to shed the pseudo-aristocratic cultural hegemony and embarked upon the voyage which led to the substitution of their own new scale of values for the old. That from the moralist's point of view their scale has little to commend itself is obvious, but from the economist's point of view it is most certainly more suitable for the promotion of growth.[54]

A significant observation is that, having been released from the fetters of traditionalism, the economic performance of the continental countries quickly caught up with that of Britain. Even in France, where on the whole, as we have seen, industrialisation progressed more slowly or at least less irregularly than in Britain and Germany, the average real incomes were seldom far behind.[55] The rate of economic growth in France was lower than the British rate until about 1830, but in the following three decades, that is until 1860, France forged ahead, almost catching up with Britain on the eve of the Franco-Prussian war. In the seventies France's progress was slowing down again, and by the end of the century the rate of growth in Britain was exceptionally high.

THE INDUSTRIALISATION OF NORTH AMERICA

Conditions in North America were different from those of Europe. In the first place there were few traditions which had to be broken and no old-established institutions to be swept away before economic progress could be accelerated. Secondly, the population was particularly adaptable to new forms of life; the mere fact that in order to come to America the early settlers had to leave the relative security of their old environment and be ready to undertake the journey into an unknown future in a far-off land, had in itself a selective influence upon the immigrants, giving them a higher than average proportion of men with initiative, drive and ambition. Thirdly, the vast expanse of the uninhabited land, through which many of the settlers travelled and in which many of them eventually founded their isolated homes, forced upon them a much greater degree of independence and self-reliance than was common with the people whom they left behind in Europe. Finally, the great abundance of fertile land which was easily obtainable gave them the advantages of a higher living standard not only for the cultivators themselves but also for the rest of the people whose wages could hardly be diminished to the level of wage-rates paid in over-populated or quasi-feudal European countries. Thus, America was from the outset endowed with a high proportion of self-reliant, ambitious people who could avail themselves of fertile land and were free from the many restrictive institutional and social patterns of European society, and was also able to draw freely upon European technological experience in both agriculture and manufacture.[56] It was the combination of all these factors with its fortunate wealth of natural resources which helped the United States of America to develop from a thinly populated colony into the economically most advanced country in the world within the relatively short period of less than 150 years.[57]

Whereas emulation of Britain's industrial success on the continent of Europe was hindered by difficulties on the demand side of the market, the problem facing America was rather on the side of supply. Essentially the difference in this respect was that on the whole the Europeans were too poor to provide a stronger stimulus for market production (though, of course, labour was much cheaper in Europe than in America), while in the United States manufacturers had a much richer market but at the same time they were faced with much higher labour costs and interest rates. These were, at least initially, so high that, in spite of transport costs, American manufacturers were almost unable to capture their home market from the British competitors. The story of the great progress of the American economy is, therefore, above all the history of vertical and horizontal industrial integration leading to an unequalled fall in production costs. As labour and capital were relatively scarce, only those industries which had a good supply of raw materials and were suitable for the introduction of very far-reaching technological and organisational improvements had a chance to succeed. Indeed, they had to be so much more efficient from an organisational point of view than their more conventional competitors across the sea that their efficiency could offset both the high wage and interest rates. A good early illustration of the way this was done can be taken from the meat-packing industry. Cattle were readily available in the vast and thinly populated country and could be brought 'on the hoof' by a small number of men to the 'factory'. There they could be driven up an inclined plane to the top storey of a building to be slaughtered, 'after which each successive group of processes was carried out at a lower level, to which the carcasses dropped under their own weight, thus saving much effort. On the level they were moved in trucks and dumb-waiters and placed with the utmost regularity before those who constantly repeated the same few operations on each carcass.[58] In time, more of the operations on each successive level were further mechanised to save labour, and an increasing volume of the waste, bones, for example, which had previously been considered useless, now found uses in a variety of quickly developing subsidiary industries. However, even with all this rationalisation of the process of production, with the reduction to a minimum of the number of workers employed, and with a fuller exploitation of the materials and of their wastes, it is still doubtful whether the United States could have made such spectacular industrial progress had it not been for the high rate of population growth, the high living standards and wage rates, and the great influx of immigrants from abroad,[59] which at the same time stimulated demand and provided the labour force to satisfy it.

The earliest industries in America, as in most colonial countries, were those which were based upon the natural resources particular to the region, lumbering and shipbuilding. The shipbuilding industry enjoyed the twofold advantage of having a good supply of raw material nearby and of having easy access to a great market overseas which was ready to absorb its product. Other industries (with the exception of flour milling), which did not enjoy similar advantages on both the supply and the demand side, had very little chance to develop. In 1800 the country was too thinly populated and inland communications too poor to stimulate production. Even in the most densely populated parts[60] the number of manufacturing industries using modern methods was small, and the total volume of their output was of little significance. The change began in 1807 as a result of the American Embargo and the subsequent curtailment of imports. On the one hand the Embargo caused much damage to the traditional export industries, but on the other it not only freed some capital which had previously been invested there, and made it available to other industries, but also provided for these new industries an almost monopolistic market. Thus, while in the short run the Embargo brought about a depression in the American economy, in the long run it helped to lay the foundations upon which America's industrial future was built. Textile prices soared, and for a time America experienced a boom in industrial investment. The boom was short-lived; with the restoration of peace in Europe even a 25 per cent protective tariff could not save the 'artificially' developed American textile industry. Only the largest and most efficient enterprises managed to survive European competition, and these became the 'pace-setters' for American industry in later decades.[61] Revival began in the 1820s. By 1830 New England industries were already producing more than they had done before 1807. In the following decade progress was slow, but in the thirties it had accelerated to such a degree that even the depression, which followed in 1839, could no longer reverse the upward trend. There was, of course, a considerable reduction of output between 1839 and 1844, but no large-scale liquidation of businesses as had been the case during the depression of 1815. By 1845 the depression was over and industry progressed once more at an unprecedented pace, expanding very rapidly into new fields of production.[62] From Robert E. Gallman's estimates of the 'value added' by industry, it is possible to get a general impression of the outstanding pace at which the American manufacturing industry developed to the end of the nineteenth century.[63]

As in England, the textile industry was in America the main source of early industrial development after 1820. On the one hand it helped the expansion of men's and women's clothing industries and, on the other, it stimulated the production of machinery for use in textile plants.[64] In time the workshops in which textile machinery was made increasingly specialised in the production of certain machine components and left the production of others to other manufacturers. At the same time, however, they spread into new areas of machine production where similar components were required. The vertical textile-based machine industry was becoming more horizontally inclined by specialising in the production of parts which were used in a number of different industries; this change, which was both the cause and the effect of the advantages gained from the rising degree of specialisation, was soon felt by the rate at which new industries became mechanised and also by the iron industry upon which machine production was dependent. The resultant fall in the cost of machines, and consequently also in the cost of machine-produced consumer goods, raised the latter's chances of holding out against foreign competition. The earliest to profit in this manner were the textile and the shoe-making industries.[65] These were followed by the woollen industry and by furniture. In this sense, then, it is true that the economic progress of the United States was largely due to the abundance of natural resources, because had it not been for the large iron and coal deposits there would have been little chance for the machine industry to develop in the way it did. Thus, while industrialisation was becoming increasingly diversified in the North-east and was continually stimulated by the accretion and concentration of people, the South continued to be in a state of 'Colonial' production, i.e. producing primary materials mainly for export. (Since the end of the eighteenth century the South had more and more specialised in cotton, and to a smaller extent in sugar and rice.) However, while the North-east was specialising in industry, the South in cotton and other export crops, the West became the main source of the whole country's food supplies. All that was required now was a suitable transport system to bring the three areas closer together. The gap was filled by the spreading of the American railways in the second half of the nineteenth century. Hence, while railroads did not produce the rise of industry, they most certainly served as the catalyst which brought about the quantitative change in the rate of United States economic development.[66]

In addition to its natural resources, its lack of inhibiting traditions, and a rapidly increasing demand (as a result of the high rate of natural accretion and immigration of people) America had also an educational advantage. Since its very early days great stress was put on education in most States, and almost everywhere the schooling of all boys under 14 years of age, at least for three months in each year, was compulsory.

After the middle of the century, immigration (and with it the domestic market, and the rate of capital accumulation from both internal and external sources) increased very rapidly.[67]

The most significant change, from the point of view of industrial development in the second half of the nineteenth century, was the striking capitalisation of the American manufacturing industry. In the words of Professor Douglass North:[68] 'The changes typically consisted of relative declines in the consumer goods sector of manufacturing and relative rises in the manufacture of producer goods. . . .' These changes of emphasis not only reflected the increasingly more roundabout methods of production, i.e. the progress of technology, but also the rising demand for more durable and semi-durable consumer goods, i.e. the rising living standard.[69]

Thus, within the relatively short period of less than a century, America had become the most industrialised country, with the greatest total volume of industrial output, in the world. This growth was accompanied by a steep rise in productivity of labour which was due not only to the progress of technology but also to the shift of labour from the less highly into the more highly mechanised occupations. The resultant rise in *per capita* real incomes had never been equalled anywhere else in the world.[70]

In summary, within one century the United States developed from the colonial, i.e. foreign orientated primary and resource-bound stage of production (until 1814); through the early industrial stage of manufacturing industry with its forward and backward links, into raw materials and machine making (1820–60); towards a highly mechanised and specialised stage of production (1860–1914). In the first stage the process was stimulated, on the demand side, by foreign markets; in the second, by the growth of the domestic market, owing to the rapid natural accretion of people and to immigration; and in the third stage by the two last mentioned stimuli, which were further supported by the development of closer links with the domestic markets (through the expansion of the railway system) and by the rising level of real incomes. The latest of these growth-producing factors was to become the major stimulus for the even more impressive progress of the twentieth century.

In conclusion, the growth-producing factors in the United States were, on the supply side, the great abundance of free land which helped to maintain high wage rates; these, in their turn, forced upon entrepreneurs a high rate of mechanisation, which was made possible, on the one hand, by the relatively good supply of natural mineral resources and, on the other, by the comparatively high standard of education and the lack of cultural, i.e. socio-institutional, impediments; and on the demand side, the progressively increasing number of people living in the United States and their rising real incomes. Briefly, the combination of good natural resources, with a high rate of population growth and high wages, was responsible for the phenomenal rise of American industrial production in the nineteenth century.

INDUSTRIAL PROGRESS IN PRE-REVOLUTIONARY RUSSIA

Another country which was similar to the United States, in having rich mineral resources and vast areas of thinly populated land, was Russia; but unlike the United States, industrialisation there began much later.[71] The most obvious cause for the delay was the institutional structure which prevented the recruitment of a labour force for industry and reduced the standard of living of the greater part of the population to a bare minimum. To this must be added the scattered nature of the mineral resources (in particular, the distances separating the coalfields from the iron deposits), and the loss of the industrial exports market in the West when western Europe began to industrialise.[72]

Between the beginning of the last quarter of the nineteenth century and the eve of the First World War, total world industrial production increased more than fourfold; out of this the share of the United States rose from 23·3 per cent in 1876 to 35·8 per cent in 1913 (i.e. approximately sixfold (615 per cent)), whereas the share of Russia rose from 3·7 per cent in 1876 to 5·5 per cent in 1913 (i.e. also almost sixfold (595 per cent)).[73]

What, then, were the forces which helped to overcome the institutional and geographical obstacles to economic growth in Russia during the second half of the nineteenth and the early part of the twentieth centuries? In the first half of the nineteenth century, Russia had lost her external markets for industrial products, and in the absence of internal sources of demand[74] (due to the low level of incomes) her industrial development was largely dependent upon government expenditure. However, the latter was not only strictly restricted by fiscal limitations,[75] but also by the reigning view in government circles that industry should be left to follow 'a natural course' with as little State interference as possible. More than that, until the Crimean War the government was often as a matter of policy actively resisting industrialisation and even railroad construction for fear of the 'scourge of the proletatiat'. What was desired by the men who ruled Russia was increasing agricultural output, especially for export, which would not disturb the traditional way of life, and which, in the fullness of time, would also be of advantage to the 'safe' development of industry.[76] Industry, so it was assumed, would develop gradually out of the surplus earnings from the exportation of grains. In so far as the existing industries[77] were able to survive, they were heavily protected for fiscal and political reasons. These were to secure for the treasury an established source of revenue and to prevent unemployment—or, more precisely, the political disturbances which as a rule attended it. Yet irrespective of the reasons for the policy of protective tariffs, their results were not entirely negative, because they secured for the struggling Russian industry a domestic market which, though rather limited, was still big enough to serve as a stimulus for moderate industrial growth. After the middle of the century, however, both the State (for military reasons) and the great landowners (in order to buy cheap mechanised agricultural machinery and to increase their sales of grain abroad) changed their views and policies regarding railway construction and protective tariffs.

Such industries as were in existence at that time were located in the following manner. The metallurgical industry was located almost entirely in the Urals and in the 'central industrial area' between Nishni-Novgorod and Moscow. About 76 per cent of all the iron ore produced in Russia came from the Urals and about 16 per cent from the 'central industrial region'.[78] The two regions were linked together by the rivers Kama, Volga and Oka. By the middle of the nineteenth century about one hundred important metallurgical factories and almost as many smaller workshops were in operation in the Urals, and about the same number of family workshops were producing one kind or another of iron goods along the waterways connecting the Urals with the more densely populated 'central industrial region'. There, near Nishni-Novgorod and Moscow, the metallurgical industry was more complex and refined and had a higher standard of workmanship bred in the long-established artisan workshops. The remaining metallurgical industrial establishments were located in the north, near St. Petersburg. However, while in the Urals the industry could draw upon local mineral resources, and in the 'central industrial region' on local supply and on resources brought from the Urals, the metallurgical industry in the north was founded entirely upon imported raw materials. At the time, this gave rise to a good many complaints about 'the artificial nature' of the St. Petersburg industries, but in fact it was through them that new techniques and modern equipment eventually reached the rest of Russia. The textile industry was mainly concentrated in the 'central industrial region'. This was the most densely populated part of Russia, where the concentration of people was high enough to supply the necessary labour force and the necessary local markets for the industry. Indeed, more than half of all the textile industry, and about two-thirds of all the industrial labour force of Russia was concentrated there, between the three rivers Volga, Oka and Moskva. The food processing industries, and more particularly the sugar refining industry which was rapidly progressing in the forties, were located to the south of the 'central industrial region'.

Thus industrial Russia was broadly divided into four regions. In the south, the Ukraine was specialising in foodstuffs; in the east, the Urals were producing iron, gold and copper; the 'central industrial region' near Moscow was specialising in textiles and, to a lesser extent, also in metallurgy; and in the north, St. Petersburg was producing all of these things, but since it did not have the necessary raw materials, it was mainly dependent on foreign supplies.

Not unlike the textile industry in the United States during the twenties, the Russian textile industry made great strides forward, particularly in cotton, during the thirties; but, unlike that of the United States, the Russian textile industry had few 'backward and forward links' into other branches of industrial production. Its impact upon the industrialisation of Russia remained therefore merely marginal. More successful from this point of view, but not very much so, was the sugar-beet refining industry of the Ukraine, which began to develop in the forties and was fully mechanised and steam-powered by the middle of the century.[79]

But neither textiles nor beet-sugar were powerful enough to overcome the forces of stagnation in Russia. The abundance of wood and the well-established water-mills along the rivers of the Urals prevented a more rapid spread of coal and steam as sources of energy, and the low wage rates prevented technological progress and organisational rationalisation in the metallurgical industry. The Emancipation Act of 1861 marks the turning point. Though nothing very dramatic followed for some time, it set in motion a process which after gathering impetus for two decades eventually gave rise to the rapid growth of industry which began in the last quarter of the century.[80] Firstly, it reduced the bondage of serfdom and thereby greatly increased the flow of labour from the land to towns and industry.[81] Secondly, it gradually improved the general standard of living, and thereby the volume of demand for manufactured goods.[82] Thirdly, as a result of the previous two, and particularly because of the redistribution of the population in favour of the towns, the number of people who were able to produce their own necessities became relatively smaller while the number of those who were dependent on a cash-market was relatively increased. Fourthly, the general acceleration of population growth which accompanied all these changes, and which may well have been either their cause or their result or both, further stimulated the increase in the total volume of demand and production. Fifthly, the reduction in the outflow of money from the towns to the landed aristocracy in the form of various bondage-payments, which was one of the results of the Emancipation, helped to reduce the cost of industrial investments and to raise the level of industrial workers' demand. Sixthly, the inflow of money from abroad in exchange for grain exports raised the demand for manufactures, though only a small share of it from local producers, and lowered manufacturing prices moderately owing to the importation of some foreign-made modern machinery.

All these were long-term results of the Emancipation. The immediate consequence was a labour crisis in the industries which had hitherto employed serf-labour, and rapid progress where contract-labour was more common. Thus, the metallurgical industry in the Urals, and the textile industry in the rural areas, suffered a setback under the combined impact of the Emancipation and the liberalisation of foreign trade (which took place at about the same time), while in the Ukraine, and particularly in the greater towns, industry was expanding at a more than compensatory pace.[83]

Another element in the transformation of the Russian economy was the spreading of the railway system. Here, too, opportunities were similar to those of the United States, but they were left unexploited. Progress in railway construction was held back, as in industry, by the shortage of capital and by the resistance of the government, which regarded railways as the hotbeds of revolutions. By 1855 no more than 850 miles of railroad had been completed and not until the defeat in the Crimean War had revealed their military (and therefore political) importance did the government begin to offer some assistance. By 1867 the mileage had increased to about 2,500, and by 1882 to 15,000. Only after 1881, when the shortcomings of the merely assisted railroad-development had become too obvious to be further ignored, did the government itself finally take an active part in it. Even then most of the country had no railway services at all, while in a few regions there was acute rivalry between competing lines. Under the new system, and particularly between the years 1885–87, railway construction developed very rapidly however, and on the eve of World War I Russia had 46,000 miles of railroads.[84] Even then the railway system was far behind the country's economic requirements. It had neither grown organically, following the economic development of the country, nor had it been built with the deliberate intention of furthering industrial progress. Its primary object was military and political, its economic value was only of secondary importance to the planners—namely to facilitate the 'flow of surplus crops to the

Baltic and Black Sea ports and the distribution of grain within the country at times of regional famine'. It was not designed to stimulate industrialisation, although, in fact, it did so.[85]

Yet, though progress was slow and erratic, it helped to increase regional specialisation and domestic trade. It brought town and country into closer relationship, increased the number of people who depended upon a cash market for their supplies, brought the railway workers' more urban mentality into contact with the farmers', and created a new source of demand for the iron and steel industry which not only stimulated the latter's growth but also contributed to the increase in the number of skilled workers. More directly, however, railway construction gave an example in the raising of capital, which was followed by the other industries and eventually played a vital role in the industrial development of Russia. In the 1850s more than 100 joint-stock companies were established. Half their capital went to railway construction. But in the following decades capital requirements rose much more sharply and the role of the State increased, sometimes indirectly by granting the money for railway constructions, and other times merely as a guarantor. One important side effect of this process was the rapid growth of banks and of the credit system. This was particularly important as later it became the basis for financing the industrial establishments.[86]

In the seventies the industrialisation of Russia progressed at a moderately rapid pace. The increasing importation of iron and machines, and above all of rails and railway equipment, put a heavy strain on the country's foreign currency resources. This was being increasingly balanced by the exportation of grains and the progress of gold mining. Indeed, the expansion of the corn trade encouraged the government during the eighties to base its economic policy with regard to industrialisation in the belief that the exportation of corn could be made to pay for the whole process of industrialisation in Russia.[87] What was not fully taken into account was the fact that corn yields fluctuate from season to season and year to year much more violently than foreign currency requirements. Thus it often became necessary to fill the gap in the export quota caused by a bad harvest by reducing the volume of corn made available for home market consumption. In other words, the Russian people were made to pay for their future industrially produced prosperity by a low standard of living in the present. In fact, to a not insignificant degree, the means thus employed to stimulate industrial progress, by almost entirely ignoring the demand side of the problem, were defying their very ends. While on the one hand this policy was able to produce the real capital required for the equipment of modern industrial enterprises, on the other hand it prevented the growth of a domestic market which would stimulate production. In the United States, demand was fed from three sources: population growth, immigration and a steadily rising standard of living; in Russia only the first of these three was of true significance, while the last was confined to a very narrow section of the population. The savings which might have been produced by the reduction in the cost of some industrially produced goods, and which might have raised living standards, were periodically depleted through excessive exportation of corn, and consequently high food prices, in years of poor harvests.

There were, however, two other sources of economic change which impressed themselves upon Russia by the end of the nineteenth century: firstly, the rise of the petroleum industry, which suddenly gave new significance to the rich oil deposits of the Caucasus and thereby changed the 'industrial geography' of the country; and, secondly, the rise of the metallurgical industry in the Ukraine, which was initially the result, but later also the pillar, of the development of the Russian railway system. The completion of the railway lines connecting Moscow with the Black Sea ports and Krivoy-Rog with the Donetz basin finally made possible the bringing together of the Ukraine's rich coal and iron deposits at an economical cost for industrial production. Here was one of the few instances in the industrialisation of Russia where progress on the supply side was matched by an equal or even greater progress on the demand side of the national market.

The same source of development, i.e. the railways, which facilitated a rapid increase in iron and steel production, also served as their market. Orders for rails were for a long time continuously in excess of what the industry was able to produce. It provided a permanent stimulus on the demand side which led to a parallel effort to increase supplies. In just over a decade, from 1887 to 1900, Russia's pig-iron production increased almost fourfold, her coal production more than threefold, and her steel and iron production more than fourfold.[88] This sudden leap forward in the nineties was, of course, partly due to the gradual accretion of industrial strength which had been progressing, despite occasional setbacks since the time of the Emancipation Act, but its compression into such a brief period was mainly due to the deliberate policy of 'industrial nationalism' by which the country was governed at this time. This new policy did away with the legal restrictions which had hitherto been an impediment to industrial development, and substituted for them a high tariff wall to protect the national industry from foreign competition; and, at the same time, the spreading of the railway network and the increasing importance of hitherto neglected natural resources brought industry into parts of Russia where the impediments caused by traditional institutions and the demands of local rulers were less exacting and inhibitive on industrial enterprises. Finally, it was also during this period that foreign capital began to flow more readily into Russia and that the Russian banking and credit system began to take shape.

In summary, then, the main qualitative difference in the nineteenth century between economic growth in the United States and in Russia was in the fact that the former was demand-inspired, whereas the latter mainly responded to outside stimuli from the supply side. Both countries had vast areas of thinly populated farmland and were rich in natural resources. In America the abundance of land was an asset which assured high living standards for a great proportion of the people, and consequently a high volume of demand. In Russia it had the opposite effect. It gave rise to an institutional and political framework, developed by the landowners to safeguard their supply of labour, which prevented the great majority of the population from raising their living standards, and consequently the country's effective demand. The retention of the labour force by means of political and administrative government agencies at the command of the landed nobility brought with it periodical outbreaks of violence. On the one hand the nobility was in conflict with the peasants and on the other with the national movement, particularly in Moscow, which hoped for 'Emancipation from above' and for the industrialisation of Russia for political reasons. This essentially three-sided struggle had far-reaching consequences in the years to come. Firstly, it produced a considerable repressive police and spy apparatus for the suppression of peasants and students in the interest of the nobility. Secondly, as the Tsar, and also the national governments, could hardly rely upon traditional leadership in the country for support, they inflated the State bureaucracy, which was not only divorced from the general public but also dominated by family protectionism and fear of any person who betrayed signs of initiative. Thirdly, it gave to the central government the decisive influence in the direction of investment, and as this principally engendered investments in militarily and politically important industries Russia's industrial progress hinged upon government demand and not upon the development of a popular market.[89] In contrast to the United States, where the will of the consumer, through the operation of the price mechanism, directed capital investment first towards the consumer goods and only subsequently towards producer goods, investment in Russia was initially directed not towards the industries which were producing for a consumers' market but to the heavy industries which were able to raise the political and military potential of the country. This form of investment, however, contributed only gradually and in an indirect manner towards the improvement of living standards.

THE INDUSTRIALISATION OF JAPAN

The only country in Asia which has traversed the whole way towards industrialisation since the middle of the nineteenth century is Japan.[90] In the 1860s, on the eve of Japan's Industrial Revolution, conditions there were not very different from those prevalent on the eve of the British Industrial Revolution a century before. Japan in the 1860s already possessed a nucleus of skilled workers, a tradition of labour discipline, and a considerable rural manufacturing industry organised in a similar manner to the 'putting out' or domestic system in pre-industrial England.[91] Also Japanese industrialisation, like that of Britain, was accompanied by the growth of population, towns and foreign markets. During the last quarter of the nineteenth century the population of Japan increased by 30 per cent,[92] an increase which was to a great extent taken up by the simultaneous growth of towns,[93] and her exports grew by approximately 600 per cent.[94] There were, however, very important natural and institutional differences between the two countries which had very far-reaching consequences.

Firstly, in the 1860s Japan was already very densely populated by any standards; and, in absolute terms, the population engaged in agriculture did not begin to decline before the 1890s, and even then it fell only slightly. In fact there was less than one hectare of cropland per male worker in agriculture, while techniques of land exploitation were no better developed than in pre-industrial England.[95] During the three decades from 1878 to 1908 the net output of arable land rose by approximately 76 per cent, whereas the net increase in the productivity of farm labour rose by approximately 217 per cent.[96] This meant that the growth of the Japanese industry was accompanied during the last quarter of the nineteenth century by a rapid increase in the surplus of rural labour.[97] In other words, industry could count on a good labour supply while at the same time the flow of labour from the country into the towns was not great enough to stimulate directly a rise in the level of workers' real incomes in either sector of the economy. As a result of this the Japanese industry became increasingly obliged to look for markets overseas rather than rely upon the demand of the home market. (Obviously, in time, this led to the well-known political consequences.) In addition to this it directed industrialisation only towards those industries in which the superiority of mechanised over traditional methods of production were the highest. As a somewhat compensatory effect this saved a number of small labour-intensive workshops from going under and thereby prevented the disappearence of an industrial middle class: and it also prevented the destruction of a considerable number of rural trades which gave by-employment to families which could not make ends meet by farming alone.

Secondly, the deep-rooted cultural traditions of several centuries were carried over into the new era and influenced the organisation of Japan's rising industrial labour force in a unique manner. The Japanese worker continued to feel himself a member of his family, i.e. of an organisation which often retained its leadership in the countryside and in which each member had no rights as an individual except those granted to him by the head of the family. It may be said that the organisation of labour continued to be vertical, quasi-feudal, rather than horizontal, following class interests. Professor J. C. Allen,[98] describing this kind of paternalism, tells us that there were no recognised rates for jobs and that besides the basic wage current with each occupation, the workers' incomes were normally augmented by all kinds of extra allowances. There was an allowance for age, for education, for the length of service, for family obligations, for housing, for rises in the cost of living, etc. In modern industries the worker could expect, in addition to these, bi-annual *ex gracia* bonuses, and even unemployment pay if he was dismissed owing to bad business. In some trades the employer was also obliged to provide accommodation for his workers. Particularly in the spinning industry, where most employees were females, he had to provide their board and lodging. The girls, who were recruited by factory agents from their families in the villages, returned to their native places at the end of their contract, frequently after three or four years. The kind of accommodation and wages were usually agreed upon between the head of their families and the mill-owners. In most cases the agreement included provisions that payment was to be made in lump sums at the end of each contract, or at such intervals that would permit the girl to bring enough of it back home to her family. From this, Professor Allen concluded that conditions were not favourable for the growth of trade unions. Nor were they suitable for promoting a higher standard of living, except by the slow, indirect process of reducing the cost of industrially produced goods.[99] The absence of a more pointed and organised struggle between labour and employers may well have been another cause for the peculiar nature of Japan's development and for the great gap between the spectacular rise in output and the only very moderate rise in real incomes.

Thirdly, Japan was less rich in the necessary natural resources for industrialisation than Britain. Throughout the nineteenth century the country was greatly dependent upon America and Europe for machines; she did not possess adequate supplies of coking-coal, and for this reason she was far behind in iron and steel production. Indeed, it was not until the first quarter of the twentieth century that she managed, with the costly help of foreign experts, to develop a modern iron industry. Even then, Japan had to rely upon Korea and China for an adequate supply of ores.[100] It is also significant that most of Japan's capital was recruited from internal sources and that much of her rapid development was due to the determination of her leadership, which inherited a country with certain 'political and economic institutions that could be easily adapted to serving the nation in its new role. Her social organisation rooted in a special kind of family system, and the long centuries of feudal discipline, helped to produce a capacity for extreme self-abnegation on the part of individuals and an aptitude for corporate effort which served the country well in a time of rapid social and economic change, and the institution of an Imperial House which by mythology invested with divine attributes provided a focus for patriotic fervour.'[101]

Thus, in conclusion, when Japan started on her road as a major world power, she was already endowed with a politically suitable system and a psychological readiness for her new position. Unfortunately, however, she was not only overpopulated but also poor in the major industrial raw materials. Overpopulation resulted in an asymmetry between the more rapid rise of the country's industrial output and the only very slow improvement of the people's living standards; whereas the lack of the necessary resources led to her growing dependence upon other countries. The combination of both led Japan to look abroad not only for the supply of industrial raw materials but also for the markets in which she could sell her finished products. In fact, she had either to make sure of her markets overseas or to revolutionise her whole socio-economic structure. During the first half of the twentieth century Japan pursued the first of these two courses.

NOTES

1. F. Reuleaux, *Theoretische Kinematik*, 1875. Quoted here from Singer, Holmyard, Hall and Williams, Eds., *A History of Technology*, Vol. IV, p. 150.

2. Such as the utilisation of the skim milk from the Danish creameries to feed the pigs for the bacon industry and the utilisation of the pigs' bones in the artificial fertiliser industry, etc.

3. Urban population as percentage of total population in selected countries for available years around 1880 and most recent available years.

United Nations *Population Studies*, No. 17, 'The Determinants and Consequences of Population Trends', New York, 1953, p. 109.

Country	*Circa 1880*	*Most Recent Years*
England and Wales	67·9	80·0 (1931)
Belgium	43·0	62·7 (1947)
New Zealand	40·0	60·0 (1945)
Germany	29·1	56·6 (1933)
United States	28·6	56·5 (1940)
Canada	15·9	54·3 (1941)
France	34·8	53·2 (1946)
Denmark	28·0	48·2 (1945)
Sweden	15·1	42·3 (1945)
Switzerland	13·3	32·9 (1941)
U.S.S.R.	15·0	32·8 (1939)
Norway	18·3	28·4 (1930)

For earlier dates, *vide* Adna Ferrin Weber, *The Growth of Cities in the Nineteenth Century*, 1899, New York, 1963, pp. 144–145, Table CXII.

4. It is difficult to make a precise estimate, but Colin Clark's Table I, pp. 522–523, in the 3rd edition of *The Conditions of Economic Progress*, gives a clue to the degree of change.

5. For a more detailed description of the earlier stages of industrialisation in Britain and Belgium, see pp. 32–43.

6. Paul Mantoux, *The Industrial Revolution in the Eighteenth Century*, first published in English translation in 1928, quoted here from 1964 Methuen Paperback edition, p. 474.

7. David S. Landes, in *The Cambridge Economic History of Europe*, Vol. VI, Pt. I, p. 353.

8. D. S. Landes, *op. cit.*, p. 353n, remarking that her 'income cannot be compared precisely with that of continental countries', gives a list of estimates made by various authorities on the subject.

9. Sources: William Ashworth, *A Short History of the International Economy*, 2nd edition, pp. 21–22; Arthur Birnie, *An Economic History of Europe*, Statistical Appendix; *Annual Abstract of Statistics*, No. 96, H.M.S.O., 1959, p. 130 and p. 144; *Historical Statistics of the United States* (Bureau of Census), 1957, p. 356 and p. 416.

10. D. S. Landes, *op. cit.*, p. 518.

11. This is so because 14 per cent of 400x is still almost 56 per cent of 100x. (Estimates for production taken from William Ashworth, *op. cit.*, p. 24.)

12. The exceptions were Belgium, north-western and south-eastern Germany and Bohemia.

13. Serfdom, for example, was not abolished in France until the end of the eighteenth century, and in Prussia and Russia not until the nineteenth century. (See pp. 110–113 and 116 regarding the laws which prevented peasants from leaving the land and seeking industrial employment.)

14. Among other things this difference was due to the different laws of inheritance and to the more frequent and destructive wars on the Continent.

15. *Vide* pp. 150–151.

16. D. S. Landes, *op. cit.*, p. 361, '. . . it seems clear that along the wide spectrum of attitudes on this issue, ranging from the prodigality of an American family trained to look on a three-year-old automobile as unfashionable, even unpatriotic, to the parsimony of Maupassant's peasant bending to pick up a piece of string, the Englishman of the eighteenth

century was substantially closer to a psychology of abundance than the Frenchman or the German'.

17. D. S. Landes, *op. cit.*, p. 358.

18. In this respect the value of the guilds for the future economic development in Europe can hardly be overestimated, though its immediate effects were of course negative. For one who has lived in countries without a tradition of workmanship it appears almost incredible that a high degree of technology can be achieved in a consumer-goods industry without this transitional stage.

19. D. S. Landes, *op. cit.*, p. 360.

20. We shall follow here the factors in the same order as they were mentioned on pp. 150–154.

21. *Vide* pp. 23–32.

22. See S. Smiles, *The Lives of the Engineers*, 1861, for a detailed discussion of the technical difficulties in railway construction.

23. Christopher I. Savage, *An Economic History of Transport*, Cambridge, 1959. 1961 edition, p. 41.

24. *Vide* E. Cleveland-Stevens, *English Railways, their Development and their Relation to the State*, London, 1915, p. 164.

25. Figures quoted by J. H. Clapham, *Economic Development of France and Germany 1815–1914*, 4th edition, 1961, p. 339, are as follows:

KILOMETRES OF RAILWAY LINES

Year	*Belgium*	*France*	*Germany**	*Italy*	*Spain*	*U.K.*
1850	900	3,000	6,000	400	28	10,500
1870	3,000	17,500	19,500	6,000	5,500	24,500
1890	5,000	36,500	43,000	13,000	10,000	33,000
1910	8,500	49,500	61,000	17,000	15,000	38,000

* Germany in the area of 1871 frontiers.

26. See also progress of rail transport in the United States and in Russia, pp. 174 and 179–181.

27. In England, passenger traffic increased more than tenfold between the middle and the end of the century, according to Clapham, *op. cit.*, Vol. II, p. 182.

28. *Vide* pp. 150–152.

29. *Vide* pp. 154–159.

30. 'Bessemer was the inventor and manufacturer of bronze powder; Siemens was an engineer whose chief interest had been in electricity and the steam engine; Thomas was a police court clerk with a classical education and a hobby of chemistry . . . (Bessemer's revolutionary achievement was the converter). . . . The practical success of the converter was assured once it became possible to control accurately the low but vital carbon content of the steel it poured. One way to achieve this, but a difficult and unreliable one, was to stop the blast at the right moment. A far better way was to burn all the carbon out and then to restore just the right amount at the end of the process.' J. D. Bernal, *Science and Industry in the 19th Century*, London, 1953, pp 94–102.

31. Singer, Holmyard, Hall and Williams, *op. cit.*, pp. 54–57.

32. Sidney Gilchrist Thomas (1850–85) was assisted by his cousin Percy Gilchrist.

33. J. H. Clapham, *op. cit.*, p. 285.

OUTPUT IN THOUSANDS OF METRIC TONS

Country	*1880*	*1890*	*1900*	*1910*
United Kingdom:				
Pig Iron	7,873	8,031	9,103	10,172
Steel	3,730	5,301	5,981	7,613
Germany: (incl. Luxemburg)				
Pig Iron	2,729	4,658	8,521	14,794*
Steel	1,548	3,164	7,372*	13,149*
France:				
Pig Iron	1,725	1,962	2,714	4,038
Steel	1,354	1,407	1,935	2,850
Belgium:				
Pig Iron	608	788	1,019	1,852
Steel	596	716	927	1,857

* Indicates where U.K. output was overtaken by that of Germany.

34. *Vide* pp. 148–150.

35. Singer, Holmyard, Hall, and Williams, *op. cit.*, p. 62.

36. Singer, Holmyard, Hall and Williams, *op. cit.* Table on page 73.

WORLD PRODUCTION OF METALS (METRIC TONS)

	1850	*1875*	*1900*
Copper	55,000	130,000	525,000
Lead	130,000	320,000	850,000
Zinc	65,000	165,000	480,000
Tin	18,000	36,000	85,000
Nickel	20	500	8,000
Aluminium	negligible	$2\frac{1}{2}$	7,300

37. *Vide ibid.*, p. 86. An excellent example of the inefficient use of fuel is the well-loved English fireplace, where most of the heat usually escapes through the chimney.

38. J. H. Clapham, *op. cit.*, p. 96.

39. *Vide* Ch. Seignobos, *Histoire Politique de L'Europe Contemporaine* (Evolution des partis et des formes politiques 1814–96), Paris, 1908, pp. 440–445, for an excellent discussion of these trends.

40. The exceptions were the free towns of Hamburg and Bremen and their regions, while Alsace-Lorraine was annexed to Germany after the defeat of France in 1870–71.

41. Perhaps the government could not help acting in the way it did in a predominantly agricultural country which had just begun to realise the potential danger from a Black Sea trade in corn from Russia.

42. 'Neither rich nor poor were permitted to sleep under a bridge.' An often quoted example of equality before the law.

43. *'Schuhster bleib bei deinen Leisten.'*

44. Estate here is the translation of the German word *Standt* or French *Etat.*

45. Bavaria is a good case in point; and so are Wurtemberg and Saxony. *Vide* J. H. Clapham, *op. cit.*, p. 84.

46. For example, in Wurtemberg.

47. For example, in Bavaria.

48. J. H. Clapham, *op. cit.*, p. 278.

PERCENTAGE OF GERMAN POPULATION IN TOWN AND COUNTRY

Year	*Total Population*	*Rural Percentage*	*Urban Percentage*
1871	41,059,000	63·9	36·1
1880	45,234,000	58·6	41·4
1890	49,428,000	57·5	42·5
1900	56,367,000	45·6	54·4

49. J. H. Clapham, *op. cit.*, p. 325.

50. *Vide* J. H. Clapham, *op. cit.*, pp. 75–76.

51. J. H. Clapham, *op. cit.*, p. 77. 'The Civil Code was reinforced by the Penal Code. Under Articles 291–294 associations of more than twenty persons were prohibited; and under Articles 414–416 any concerted striking or picketing became a criminal offence. . . .'

52. J. H. Clapham, *op. cit.*, p. 270.

53. *Vide* pp. 150–152.

54. Although it is not directly concerned with the promotion of economic growth, it is interesting to note that the working classes in France and Germany were far less ready to accept the cultural leadership of the aristocracy than the middle class. Writing about the year 1847, Clapham, *op. cit.*, pp. 323–324, remarked, 'The master's right to speak for industry was disputed. First in Berlin and then in Frankfurt, meetings of journeymen (*Gesellen*), or, as they were beginning to call themselves, workmen (*Arbeiter*), claimed a voice in the settlement, as "the real producers" and "the core of Germany".' And speaking of France in 1851 Clapham, *op. cit.*, p. 266, says, '. . . although the French town workman of the time was seldom a factory hand, he had nevertheless the wage earners', the so-called proletarian, point of view. . . . No doubt he attached an economic meaning to the equality in whose name his father had fought after 1789. . . .'

55. In part this was, of course, due to the lower rate of population growth in France.

56. *Vide* pp. 102–103.

57. From approximately 1776 to 1914.

58. This example, quoted from William Ashworth's book, *A Short History of the International Economy since 1850*, 2nd edition, 1962, pp. 80–81, describes in fact not a cattle but a pig meat-packing industry in Cincinnati in the middle of the nineteenth century, but the example is representative of a number of similar establishments in various lines of production.

59. For more details see United States Department of Commerce, Bureau of the Census, *Historical Statistics of the United States Colonial Times to 1957*, Washington, 1960, pp. 7–8, 56–66.

Year	*Total Population of U.S.*	*Total of Foreign Born*
1850	23,261,000	2,244,602
1860	31,513,000	4,138,697
1870	39,905,000	5,567,229
1880	50,262,000	6,679,943
1890	63,056,000	9,249,560
1900	76,094,000	10,341,276
1910	92,407,000	13,515,886
1920	106,466,000	13,920,692
1930	123,188,000	14,204,193

60. For example Brown's, Almy's and Slater's cotton mills.

61. In contrast with France and Germany, where for cultural reasons

the pace was only too often set by the least efficient manufacturers. *Vide* pp. 152–154 and 169–171.

62. For example, the leather industry (shoes, etc.), the iron industry and the machine industry all had their beginning during these years.

63. Commodity Output in the United States 1839–99, in *Studies in Income and Wealth.* Quoted here from United States Bureau of the Census, *Historical Statistics of the United States, op. cit.*, p. 402.

VALUE ADDED BY MANUFACTURING

(In million dollars)

Year	*Current Prices*	*Prices of 1879*
1839	240	190
1849	447	488
1859	815	859
1869	1,631	1,078
1879	1,962	1,962
1889	3,727	4,156
1899	5,044	6,252

64. George S. Gibb, *The Saco-Lowell Shops*, etc., Cambridge, 1950.

65. Blanche Hazard, *The Organisation of the Boot and Shoe Industry in Massachusetts before 1875*, Cambridge, 1921, and Arthur H. Cole, *The American Wool Manufacture*, Cambridge, 1926.

66. This view does not differ from the view expressed by Professor Douglass North so much as it appears. (*Vide* 'Industrialisation in the United States', *The Cambridge Economic History of Europe*, Vol. VI, Pt. II, pp. 688–689.) Professor North wrote: 'It is important to note that this growing regional specialisation and inter-regional trade occurred before the railroad had become a significant influence in reducing transport costs. Falling ocean freight rates, sharp reduction in river freight rates, successful development of the steamboat on western rivers, the Erie of Pennsylvania canals, and other feeder canals throughout the West were the most important factor in permitting the rapid development of inter-regional trade. In the 1830s the railroad was just getting a start in America, and it still did not exert a significant influence upon the country's development. By the end of the 1830s the North-east, and particularly New England, had already developed manufacturing activity catering to a national market. The railroad was not the most important influence or indeed the proximate influence, in the development of manufacturing in the United States. This is not to suggest that the railroad was not an important factor in American growth in the nineteenth century. But the railroad was not "the leading sector" inducing American industrialisation. . . .'

67. For summary of immigration and general accretion of population see Statistics on p. 189, Footnote 59, or United States Bureau of the Census *Historical Statistics of the U.S. Colonial times to 1957*, Washington, D.C., 1960, p. 62, Series C. 133–138.

FLOW OF GOODS AND SERVICES TO CONSUMERS

(In billions of dollars) 1929 Prices

Year	*Total*	*Perishable*	*Semi-durable*	*Durable*	*Services*
1869–71	7·0	2·8	1·22	0·64	2·4
1872–76	8·5	3·5	1·37	0·77	2·9
1877–81	12·4	5·4	1·96	1·07	4·0
1882–86	16·2	7·1	2·49	1·50	5·1

Year	*Total*	*Perishable*	*Semi-durable*	*Durable*	*Services*
1887–91	18·1	7·5	2·92	1·95	5·7
1892–96	20·9	9·0	3·21	2·11	6·6
1897–1901	26·7	11·4	3·96	2·62	8·7
1902–06	34·3	14·1	5·02	3·27	10·8
1907–11	40·9	16·5	5·79	3·74	14·9

Source: United States Bureau of the Census, *op. cit.*, p. 144, Series F. 131–157.

PRIVATE AND PUBLIC CAPITAL FORMATION

(In billions of dollars)

	Producers' Durables (Current Prices)		*National Product (1929)*	
Year	*Gross*	*Net*	*Gross*	*Net*
1869–71	0·39	0·18	9·1	8·3
1872–76	0·41	0·16	11·2	10·1
1877–81	0·45	0·19	16·1	14·6
1882–86	0·53	0·18	20·7	18·7
1887–91	0·64	0·20	24·0	21·3
1892–96	0·60	0·13	28·3	24·9
1897–1901	0·84	0·20	35·4	31·4
1902–06	1·36	0·50	45·0	40·2
1907–11	1·62	0·39	52·5	46·6

Source: United States Bureau of the Census, *op. cit.*, p. 144, Series F. 104–132.

VALUE ADDED: TOTAL, AGRICULTURE AND INDUSTRY

(In billions of dollars, 1879 prices)

Year	*Total*	*Agriculture*	*Manufacturing*
1839	1·09	0·79	0·19
1844	1·37	0·94	0·29
1849	1·66	0·99	0·49
1854	2·32	1·32	0·68
1859	2·69	1·49	0·86
1869	3·27	1·72	1·08
1874	4·30	1·98	1·69
1879	5·30	2·60	1·96
1884	7·30	3·00	3·22
1889	8·66	3·24	4·16
1894	10·26	3·27	5·48
1899	11·75	3·92	6·26

Source: United States Bureau of Census, *op. cit.*, p. 139, Series F. 16–19; see also 18, 20 for mining and construction to make up the total.

NATIONAL WEALTH: REPRODUCIBLE TANGIBLE ASSETS

(In billions of dollars, 1929 prices)

Year	*Total*	*Year*	*Total*
1850	10·8	1900	139·0
1880	53·7	1912	186·3
1890	99·7		

Source: United States Bureau of Census, *op. cit.*, p. 152, Series F. 223.

INTERNATIONAL INVESTMENT POSITION

(In billions of dollars)

Year	*U.S. Investments abroad*	*Foreign Investments in the U.S.*
1843	Negligible	0·2
1869	0·1	1·5
1879	0·7	3·4
1908	2·5	6·4
1914	3·5	7·2
1919	7·0	3·3
1927	13·8	6·6
1956	49·5	31·6

Source: United States Bureau of Census, *op. cit.*, p. 565, Series U. 193 and 200.

INDUSTRIAL DISTRIBUTION OF GAINFUL WORKERS

(In Thousands)

Year	*Total*	*Agriculture*	*Mining*	*Manufacture and Construction*	*Trade and Transport*
1820	2,880	2,070	n.a.	350	n.a.
1830	3,930	2,770	n.a.	n.a.	n.a.
1840	5,420	3,720	15	750	n.a.
1850	7,700	4,900	90	1,260	420
1860	10,530	6,210	170	1,930	780
1870	12,920	6,850	180	2,750	1,350
1880	17,390	8,610	310	4,000	2,080
1890	23,740	9,990	480	6,190	3,520
1900	29,070	10,710	760	8,000	4,860
1910	36,730	11,340	1,050	10,530	7,860

Source: United States Bureau of Census, *op. cit.*, p. 74, Series D. 57–71.

68. *The Cambridge Economic History of Europe*, Vol. VI, Pt. II, p. 694.

69. Colin Clark, *The Conditions of Economic Progress*, 3rd edition, Table VIII, pp. 336–337.

I.U. OF NET INCOME PRODUCED PER MAN-HOUR IN MANUFACTURING

Year	*I.U.*	*Year*	*I.U.*
1849	185	1889–90	292
1859	266	1900–04	387
1869–70	231	1905–09	121
1879–80	271	1913	445

70. Colin Clark, *op. cit.*, Table XL, p. 169.

REAL INCOME PER CAPITA OF POPULATION IN THE U.S.

Year	$	*Year*	$
1850	362	1884–93	355
1860	357	1889–98	368
1869–78	232	1849–1903	411
1874–83	292	1898–1908	467
1879–88	337	1904–13	508
		(1952	**1,128)**

71. G. Warren Nutter, *The Growth of Industrial Production in the Soviet Union*, National Bureau of Economic Research, Princeton, New Jersey, 1962, p. 227, Table 61.

INDEX OF INDUSTRIAL OUTPUT PER HEAD OF POPULATION
RUSSIA AND UNITED STATES
(1913 = 100)

Year	*Russia*	*U.S.*	*Year*	*Russia*	*U.S.*
1860	19	22	1890	46	54
1865	16	22	1895	59	56
1870	21	29	1900	77	65
1875	25	30	1905	69	86
1880	31	38	1910	89	89
1885	36	39	1913	100	100

72. *Vide* pp. 109–118.

73. See Alfred Maizels, *Industrial Growth and World Trade*, Cambridge, 1963, p. 80, Table 4.1 and *The Cambridge Economic History of Europe*, Vol. VI, p. 25. See also League of Nations, *Industrialization and World Trade*, 1945. Quoted here from *The Cambridge Economic History of Europe*, Vol. VI, Pt. I, p. 25.

PERCENTAGE DISTRIBUTION OF THE WORLD'S
MANUFACTURING PRODUCTION

Country	*1870*	*1913*	*1936–38*
U.S.A.	23·3	35·8	32·2
Germany	13·2	15·7	10·7
United Kingdom	31·8	14·0	9·2
France	10·3	6·4	4·5
Russia	3·7	5·5	18·5
Italy	2·4	2·7	2·7
Canada	1·0	2·3	2·0
Belgium	2·9	2·1	1·3
Sweden	0·4	1·0	1·3
Japan		1·2	3·5
India	11·0	1·1	1·4
Other countries		12·2	12·7

74. See pp. 109–118.

75. The main items here were military equipment, railway construction and a number of other State-protected industries.

76. In fact, grain exports and industrial growth progressed in almost parallel lines during the first half of the nineteenth century.

77. Mostly survivors of the great days of industrial development under Catherine II, in the eighteenth century.

78. The term 'central industrial region' is taken from Professor Roger Portal's article, 'The Industrialization of Russia', in *The Cambridge Economic History of Europe*, Vol. VI, Pt. II, p. 806.

79. According to Professor Portal, *op. cit.*, p. 809, in 1861, 85 per cent of sugar production in Russia came from refineries equipped with modern machinery and working on steam, which produced 62,000 tons of sugar.

80. For details see f.n. 71.

81.

Year	*People Living in Russian Cities*	*Percentage of Increase*	*Percentage of Total Population*
1815–25	827,000		1·8
1856	1,583,300	94	2·2
1870	2,383,000	50	2·8
1885	3,541,865	68	3·2
1897	2,641,395	31	3·6

Adna Ferrin Weber, *op. cit.*, p. 108, Table LXII.

82. See, for more detailed discussion of these points, pp. 109–118.

83. Total cloth manufactured by Russian industry in 1858, 24 million roubles; and in 1862, 26 million roubles.

84. For more details see Professor R. Portal, *The Cambridge Economic History of Europe*, Vol. VI, Pt. II, p. 813.

85. R. Portal, *op. cit.*, p. 813, mentions as examples of the contribution of railway construction the Perm-Ekaterinburg, and the Ekaterinoslav railways, which brought together iron and coal.

86. R. Portal, *op. cit.*, p. 813.

87. This policy was also suggested for the Gold Coast when it seemed as if cocoa could pay for the industrial development of Ghana after independence.

88. See R. Portal, *op. cit.*, Table 74, p. 837.

THE DEVELOPMENT OF PRODUCTION

(In million poods)

	1887	*1890*	*1900*
Pig-iron	36·1	54·8	176·8
Coal	276·2	366·5	986·4
Iron and Steel	35·5	48·3	163·0
Oil	155·0	226·0	631·1
Cotton (requirements)	11·5	8·3	16·0
Sugar	25·9	24·6	48·5

89. In fact, it led to a situation where the production of popular consumers' goods increased only as a result or reflection of the progress made in the military industry and in railway construction, both of which were themselves greatly subject to the fluctuations in the international corn market.

90. For an excellent description of the rise of Japan, see G. C. Allen, *A Short Economic History of Modern Japan*, London, 1946, 2nd Revised edition, 1962, and the same author's contribution in *The Cambridge Economic History of Europe*, Vol. VI, Pt. II, Ch. X. For a different view see W. W. Lockwood, *The Economic Development of Japan*, Princeton, 1954.

91. This point is, in the present author's view, too often forgotten. For example, W. W. Lockwood, *op. cit.*, begins his study with the following statement: 'The speed with which Japan emerged from Quasi feudalism . . . is in striking contrast to the centuries of evolutionary growth characterising the process in the West.'

92. According to Lockwood, *op. cit.*, p. 155, the population of Japan increased from 35,929,000 in 1880 to 44,826,000 in 1900; according to G. C. Allen, *op. cit.*, Stats. Table No. I, it increased from 35,200,000 in 1873 to 46,100,000 in 1903.

93. According to G. C. Allen, *op. cit.*, App. III, it appears that the number of people employed in agriculture was 14,501,000 and in manufacture and mining was 833,000 in 1872 and 17,481,000 and 2,873,000 (respectively) in 1895.

94. G. C. Allen, *op. cit.*, App. Table XXVII, gives data on the volume of Japan's foreign trade based on the work of K. Kojima.

95. For international comparisons, *vide* Folke Dovring's article in *Monthly Bulletin of Agricultural Economics and Statistics*, Vol. VIII, pp. 1–11, F.A.O., Rome, August–September 1959.

96. *Vide* Kazushi Ohkawa and Henry Rosovsky in *Economic Development and Cultural Change*, Vol. IX, Pt. II, October 1960, pp. 43–68.

97. In Britain the compound rate of total population growth 1831–1901 was about 1·5 per cent, and of agricultural employment 0·6; whereas in Japan between 1890–1915 the total annual rate was 1·1, but of agricultural employment 1·5 per cent.

98. *The Cambridge Economic History of Europe*, Vol. VI, Pt. II, p. 898.

99. This is an interesting problem from the point of view of the historian of the Marxist school because, in effect, this means that progress in Japan took the form of only one set of 'capitalistic contradictions'—namely, the contradiction between employers, whereas the second set, between exploiters and exploited, does not assume a conscious form.

100. This is noteworthy because it shows how, in spite of Japan's long tradition in metal craftsmanship, she was unable to develop a metallurgical industry earlier, and shows how Japan's expansionist policies were closely related to the growth of her iron and steel industries.

101. G. C. Allen, *A Short Economic History of Modern Japan*, p. 107.

Chapter V

THE NEW ERA

THE RISE IN LIVING STANDARDS

Perhaps the most important change which has taken place in the developed countries during the last fifty years is the tremendous rise in *per capita* output and consumption.[1] The rising output was not only due to the much better organisation and division of labour and the wider use of power-driven mechanical equipment,[2] but also to the discovery of new materials, new uses for the familiar ones, and improved ways for their exploitation.[3] Man not only learned to use by-products but also 'wastages' which occurred in the processes of production. He learned to shorten his labour time, i.e. to increase the time during which he was free to produce more goods or to avail himself of more leisure and services,[4] and to increase the volume of materials upon which he could productively spend the extra time. In other words, man not only increased his *per capita* output but also the per unit yield and total quantity of the available economically exploitable resources.

What were the motive forces behind this process? What was the force that drove entrepreneurs to go on improving the organisation of their establishments? What led them to purchase ever newer, better, and increasingly costlier equipment?[5] What made them look for new raw materials and for new uses for their by-products? Basically it was competition. The capitalist system, once it has developed, does almost automatically drive out the entrepreneurs who are not efficient enough to compete with others. If an entrepreneur learns of the existence of a new piece of equipment which can reduce his production costs, and introduces it in his factory, he will almost certainly be able to undersell all other entrepreneurs in the same line of business, and by doing so he will eventually either drive them out of it or force them to follow his example.[6] If the information about the availability of such a piece of equipment becomes common knowledge, all other employers who have the capital to do so will also introduce it and deprive the first entrepreneur of his initial advantage. For this reason it is not the equipment alone upon which 'the survival of the fittest' rests. The efficiency of the organisation of the business is of equal importance. If it is badly organised, if with one employer the labourers waste time (if they have to move around fetching things, if there are bottlenecks in the flow of work between the various stages of production, etc.), production costs will necessarily be high; in any case higher than with other employers, in the same industry, who organise their plants more efficiently. Consequently, side by side with the continual efforts by employers to introduce new kinds of equipment, there also exists a scientific approach towards improved plant and labour organisation. Indeed, with increased utilisation of mechanical equipment the importance of the organisational problem increases. It was very early recognised that the potential advantages from the technological innovations can only be fully exploited when the labourers' working pace is well adjusted to the rhythm of the machines he makes use of and when not too much of his time is lost in handling operations.[7] However, production costs are also determined at an increasing rate by other factors besides the efficiency of the power-driven mechanical equipment and organisation. Transport, the cost of raw materials, and the various uses to which their by-products can be put play an ever greater role in the determination of the profitability, i.e. competitiveness, of an enterprise. Taking petrol as an example, we find that the value of the by-products or 'wastages', such as kerosene, fuel oil, tar, asphalt and the oil-based plastic industries, often outweigh in importance the original object of production. Therefore, the production cost of petrol is less dependent upon the cost of crude oil, its raw material, than on the prices which the by-products will fetch which occur in the refining processes. The latter become new sources of profit and contribute to the reduction in the former's production costs. Hence, the modern entrepreneur is increasingly forced not only to plan his own industrial sector, but also the utilisation of his by-products. At times he may be forced to set up a whole line of industries to do so; other times he finds it necessary to combine or at least co-operate with other producers in order to be able to plan the utilisation of 'wastages' for maximum efficiency, so that he can survive.[8]

Another factor which contributed to the rise in efficiency was the competition, if one may call it competition, between the entrepreneurs on the one hand and the workers on the other. The specific conditions of industrial factory production bring into close daily contact great numbers of workers and thereby make it less difficult for them to resist effectively their ruthless exploitation. They can, within given limits, prevent the prolongation of their working day, and more often than not even reduce it. When conditions are favourable they may also force employers to raise their wages. In this way, looking at it from the employer's point of view, production costs are heightened and he can only compensate himself by introducing new and more efficient technical equipment.[9]

The history of this struggle, the competition between workers and employers for the greater share of the product, is not unknown. In the early stages of industrialisation most urban workers had little leisure and lived in extreme poverty. Until the middle of the nineteenth century strikes rarely achieved their objectives. Only in the second half of the century did the position gradually begin to change.[10] The growing mechanisation of industry was accompanied by other changes which were rapidly transforming society. The old vertical, quasi-patriarchal, allegiances of employer and employee gave way to a new kind of horizontal class stratification. Thus, with relations between workers and employers becoming less and less personal, workers were becoming increasingly conscious of the fact that only collective action can effectively protect them against injustices at the plant, hardships of unemployment, and sickness or disablement at home.[11] By the beginning of the twentieth century the labour movement had already grown powerful enough to support its demands by large-scale strikes and even by the threat of a general strike. In the United States unions were demanding official recognition in wage negotiations, and in France, at least the radicals, were thinking of a general strike with the object of securing the total surrender of industry to the workers. By 1914–18, in the face of a mounting wave of nationalism, unionism suffered a severe setback. After the war, however, the threat of 'the Soviet example' and the increasing political influence of the workers' organisations in the democratic countries greatly strengthened labourers' bargaining power. In the years between the two World Wars, employers also tried to regain their former commanding position, and this was one of the major causes for the rise of Fascism in its various forms. When Fascism in Europe was finally defeated, the struggle assumed new forms, but by now, with employers very much on the defensive.[12] Piece-rates being no longer practicable, and with employers no longer in a position to shift upon the employees the cost of time wasted by poorly organised production, management too was becoming more and more professional. At the same time an increasingly systematic search for new time- and labour-saving inventions and innovations was stimulated by the rising wage rates. Thus, whenever possible and economical,[13] employers replaced workers by machines, but where automation was too costly or could not be applied for technical reasons, and efficiency continued to depend upon the goodwill of the workers, new methods of inducement, like profit sharing and social benefit schemes, were becoming more and more common.[14]

In summary this then was, on the supply side, the economically[15] progressive element in capitalism that for more than a century the competition for markets between the producers themselves, and the competition for a greater share of the produce between employers and employees, served as the driving force which stimulated higher efficiency through technological and organisational progress. There was, however, yet another force, on the demand side, by which the organisation of labour stimulated progress. Wherever the workers succeeded in securing, through higher wages or other advantages, a greater share of the produce, and the employer managed to recover the higher cost of labour by one or all of the three earlier-mentioned methods (i.e. better organisation, more capital equipment, fuller utilisation of resources), the higher wages, perhaps paradoxically, also served as stimulus for producers to increase production. This is so because a full circle is created in which the higher wages force producers to introduce better methods of production, while at the same time they also help to expand the market which can absorb the higher output per unit of labour and resources. As entrepreneurs do not produce for charity, although now and then they may be ready to give away a surplus, demand in a free enterprise economy is always as important as supply. Once the demand abates there is no incentive for the entrepreneur to go on producing and increasing his efficiency. The growth of demand is therefore indispensable; but demand can be of two kinds. Firstly, it can be domestic, i.e. demand which originates from the employment of labour in agriculture and industry within the country, and, secondly, it can be external, i.e. originating in foreign markets to which a surplus of production is diverted. In the early days of the Industrial Revolution, when Britain was in the forefront of developments, a good part of British production was directed towards such external markets in Europe, in India and in Africa.[16] Japan's development followed a similar course in the last quarter of the nineteenth and early part of the twentieth century. She too directed a great share of her industrial product abroad to the Chinese mainland.[17] And though the majority of people living in Asia were poor indeed, their numbers were large enough to present an attractive market. Even though each individual Indian or Chinese had very little to spare, the great multitude of people taken together produced an exchangeable surplus which was tempting for a European or Japanese industry which itself was only in its early stages. Yet, when all over Europe and in America other industrial countries joined the 'new era', the colonial markets soon became too small to absorb the rising volume of goods which were offered to them. The surplus which the economically backward countries produced was no longer large enough to pay for all the goods which the industrial countries were able to export.

There was, however, during the same time, another development which took place in the industrialised countries. Production for export had led to a high rate of employment and had in this way contributed to the strengthening of the workers' position in pressing for higher wages.[18] In addition, competition amongst employers led from time to time to reductions in the cost and price of goods. Consequently, domestic demand became more and more significant in the make-up of production in the industrial countries. With each new rise in real incomes the range and volume of demand increased, and with it production kept rising. The best example for this kind of domestically inspired growth can be seen in the economic history of the United States of America. There specific conditions, i.e. the abundance of land, had from the outset raised the cost of labour above that which was common in Europe at the time.[19] In turn this led to a very high degree of industrial organisation and to the early introduction of the most important labour-saving equipment. With this, competition between employers for markets led to a considerable cheapening of finished products. The relatively low prices of the industrial products and the relatively high wages in the United States created a far wider domestic market than in other countries. In time the widening of this market was futher stimulated by the rising wave of immigration and became much more attractive to most industrialists than the possibility of capturing poorer Asiatic and African markets.[20] To be sure, one did not exclude the other, and most industries in America and elsewhere sold on both domestic and foreign markets, but the trend was rather towards more exchange between the industrial and semi-industrial countries themselves.[21] For example, Japan, having exhausted the Chinese effectual demand, and having made the attempt to exclude competitors from this market by war and the occupation of parts of China, eventually tried to cash in on the growth of incomes in Europe.[22] Managing to maintain a very low domestic standard of consumption, i.e. by keeping wages low, and at the same time introducing the most advanced technology, the Japanese were able from time to time to under-sell Europeans even in Europe. In this way they were able to attract a share of the extra income generated in Europe. Obviously, this practice met with a good deal of opposition in the industrial countries and, in effect, eventually led to the siding of Japan with the Axis in the Second World War.[23]

Another system, which came into existence in eastern Europe, made an effort, in order to stimulate industrial growth, to replace competition by planning. The basic idea was that competition is not really necessary for the introduction of the most modern time- and labour-saving equipment and for the optimum exploitation of resources. All this could be done by decrees from above, by State policy, i.e. by deliberate State intervention, with the object of doing all that is necessary to divert resources directly to highest productive efficiency. The supporters of this idea believed, and still believe, that: 'In a planned economy, ignoring external factors . . . the role of competition, which enforces progress by the threat of punishment (the progress may even be fictitious but has to be effective from the standpoint of getting market results) is replaced by the positive incentive of realising the overall economic aims. The compulsion exercised by competition plays, however, a positive role with regard to foreign trade; this is particularly important for countries which remain behind in the top achievements of world technology and organisation.'[24] Theoretically this appears to be very sound. What it does not take into account are political circumstances and the human element.[25] If society had reached that stage of education in which each person is of himself trying to do his best for the community, without the fear of the economic penalties of competition, there would have been undoubted success in eastern Europe. However, as the new system fell upon a population which was not at that cultural and educational level, the results did not really substantiate the theoretical predictions. In addition the process of planning itself, and particularly the division of resources between the production of the 'means of production', i.e. of producers' goods, and the production of consumers' goods, is a very complicated matter and necessitates a great deal of precise information.[26] In fact there was neither statistical equipment sufficiently developed to make the required precise assessments, nor were the political forces which interfered with planning of a neutral nature.

In summary, therefore, there were three patterns of development. The first, which was mainly experienced by the countries in north-western Europe, combined export production with an increasing domestic demand which resulted from the cheapening of products and the rising wages; secondly, there was the pattern of export production, as experienced by Japan, where to a great extent growth took place at the expense of home consumption and at the risk of running into international difficulties by infringing upon other countries' markets; and thirdly, the pattern of rapid, planned, industrialisation in all spheres of production. This method, which was tried in Russia, ran into a great number of political and cultural difficulties. The country in which progress was most marked was the

United States of America, where it was mainly dependent upon the domestic market. Obviously, this means no more than that so far and in particular circumstances the highest rate of development has occurred in a country where the domestic market was predominant.

The question which remains to be answered is whether it was the fast development of industrial equipment which, by reducing production costs, led the way to higher real incomes and to the rapid growth of demand or whether it was the rise in incomes which led the way and pressed along the progress of technology. It is obvious that the two (the demand and the supply) can never be entirely separated; but it may be significant to note that the rapid progress of industrialisation in America was preceded by relatively high incomes, which themselves were probably due to the abundance of land.[27] In Europe, and particularly in England, conditions were different. There, with no abundance of land, the majority of people were poor and hungry, and domestic demand was relatively small.[28] The masses did not participate in the advantages of industrial production, at least not in the early stages of the industrial revolution,[29] and demand was augmented by the expansion of English foreign trade to both the continent of Europe and the colonial territories overseas. The fact that science had progressed in ancient Greece and Rome, and in late medieval and eighteenth-century continental Europe, but did not produce a technological revolution, appears to bear evidence to the tremendous importance of demand in the process of changing pure scientific knowledge into applied technology. It is for this reason that the idea of introducing highly efficient equipment into backward economies and leaving the social or demand side unattended 'to look after itself' when, due to the better methods of production, products become cheaper does not really seem to be very reliable. There seems to be in existence a vicious circle which makes demand dependent upon the efficiency of supply, and supply cannot really become efficient as long as the demand is not brisk enough. The idea that the State may set up a number of highly mechanised and efficient industries and then protect their markets in order to give the first stimulus to economic growth has been tried, but the results so far have not really been satisfactory. If the workers employed in these industries were to become the market for agricultural products and the farmers the purchasers of the industrial goods, the number of industries which would have to come into existence simultaneously would have to be very large indeed. In fact it would have to be larger than is practicable.[30]

We may then summarise the position of developed countries in the new era as follows. Firstly, the productivity of labour has very much increased; secondly, the efficiency of the exploitation of materials has similarly increased; thirdly, the redistribution of incomes and profits, which accrued from the two earlier mentioned developments, has been in favour of the majority of the population and has raised domestic demand for both consumer and capital goods; fourthly, the profits, which resulted from the replacement of labour by machines and from the better exploitation of materials, were large enough to stimulate reinvestment in ever better means of production. Altogether, therefore, ignoring temporary business fluctuations and trade cycles,[31] it is obvious that in the developed countries the demand for both capital and consumer goods has been rising for several decades at a rate which was out of all proportion with the demand in underdeveloped countries. In addition to this it must be noted that in the developed countries the State has taken upon itself an ever greater share in the provision of capital (which it skims off the population as taxes), and has thereby taken an ever-growing responsibility for pursuing a deliberate directive policy towards stability and economic growth.[32] As most of the developed States have a more or less democratic system of government, the process of development, in so far as governments were able to influence it, was directed towards satisfying the greatest number of the electorate. Indeed, unless a government was able to provide employment and a reasonable standard of living it stood the risk of being turned out of office. Unwilling to abdicate, governments were continually forced to strike a balance between their principles and long-term aims and the more immediate requirements and demands of their electorates. Yet, while the organisation of labour exerted a major influence upon the division of the national product in favour of the masses, the capitalists, too, managed from time to time to rid themselves of this labour pressure and of the need for ceaseless innovation. Sometimes they were able to gain control over labour organisations, other times they managed to get them outlawed. Fascism in Italy and Nazism in Germany are excellent, though not the only examples of this kind of effort.[33] Employers were also successful in freeing themselves from competition altogether in some places by managing to control the government, and partially by getting governments to impose tariffs and high customs duties on certain competitive imports. In a number of instances they were also able to set up monopolies and cartels. Usually such efforts were veiled by some kind of nationalistic patriotic phraseology. Frequently a mixture of truth and half-truth was also employed to justify the inequity in the division of the national product between employers and employees. As the concentration of capital is a prerequisite for the introduction of new and more efficient industrial equipment, it seems at least initially not undesirable that profits should accumulate in the hands of enterprising capitalists. In time the workers also benefit from this, as the more intensive capitalisation of production will lead to lower production costs and cheaper products. In other words, the capitalist may be pictured as a mere agent performing the function of transforming that part of the workers' incomes that, if it were distributed, would only cause inflation, into productive growth-producing capital which in time will cheapen the price of goods and thereby compensate the workers manifold for their initial 'apparent' loss. A very idyllic picture indeed.[34] In theory, this may appear very sound, but in practice it is unlikely that the entrepreneurs will out of their own free will reduce the price of their products unless they are forced to do so; nor will they introduce new and costly equipment while they are protected from competition and can make good profits without risks in an easy and unadventurous way. This is at least what the historical evidence appears to indicate. For this reason it can be said that, above all, it was the struggle of the workers to raise their standard of living which helped more than anything else in the capitalist countries to achieve the high rate of economic growth which they experienced. Without this stimulus from below, the demand for higher wages and the organisation of labour, and without free competition amongst the employers and the resultant price reductions, there would have been little progress and less economic efficiency.

THE UNITED STATES OF AMERICA: COMPETITION AMONG CAPITALISTS AND THE RISE OF ORGANISED LABOUR

In an earlier chapter[35] it was said that the United States owe their riches to the combination of an abundance of land and agricultural products which formed the basis for the development of some of the most important manufacturing industries; a multitude of natural mineral resources such as iron, coal and oil; and a rapid growth of the labour supply as a result of both the high rate of natural accretion and of immigration. In addition, it has also been said that the relatively high wage rates in America, which were also due to the abundance of fertile land, were in the nineteenth century only slightly affected by the influx of foreign labour, and that because of this manufacturers were for a long time, i.e. until the beginning of the present century, unable to compete for large markets with others in the industrialising countries.[36] Thus, with manufacturers dependent upon their domestic markets, one government after another kept up the high protective tariff wall against foreign competition,[37] and promoted free trade inside the country.[38] In fact all governments made it their policy, at least until the 1930s, to interfere as little as possible in domestic economic affairs. In this way American manufacturers were freed from foreign competition and at the same time at liberty to exploit fully their national market. A market which has been described as 'the largest area in the civilised world which is thus unrestricted by customs, excises, or national prejudice, and its population possesses, because of its great collective wealth, a larger consuming capacity than that of any other nation'.[39] Then, between the years 1870 and 1900, competition amongst American capitalists became so brisk that there was a general feeling that profits were falling off at such a rate that all but the most efficient enterprises were threatened with destruction.[40] Capitalist reaction to this was a growing trend towards consolidation, i.e. the creation of larger units which were able to benefit from economies of scale and monopoly. In some cases, where the consolidation of businesses was achieved without creating a monopoly, it served the general good, but where it resulted in monopoly it had as a rule, at least for some time, a retarding influence on the growth of the economy. Eventually, however, monopoly usually united competitors with the general public and stirred them into concerted action, leading in a good number of cases to the breaking up of the monopoly and reintroduction of competition. A good example for such a struggle is the case of the Standard Oil Company. The attempts of this company in the 1880s to free itself from competition with other oil producers took the peculiar form of a railroad war, that is of a battle for the command over the means of transport. Finding itself in a geographically more advantageous position than its competitors[41] the Standard Oil Company was able, by some rather unscrupulous manipulations, to reduce its transport costs so far below those of its competitors that by the end of the decade it remained in almost sole control of the oil market.[42] Only then did Rockefeller and his associates of the Standard Oil Company encounter a new adversary—namely the State. The creation of The South Improvement Company gave the competitors of Standard Oil the opportunity to organise public opinion to support them in their campaign. What they had been unable to achieve economically they now tried to achieve with the support of the general public by political means. The South Improvement Company had contractually agreed with the two other transport companies to divide amongst themselves the whole of the oil carrying business, but with the additional proviso that Standard Oil shipments should be allowed rebates while all other oil companies would be made to pay the full price. The charter of The South Improvement Company was revoked under the combined pressure of the public and the competitors, but the old rebate system continued. By 1880 Standard Oil was virtually in a position to dictate its own transport rates. Ten years later, in 1890, another series of attempts was made to break up the Standard Oil monopoly by State legislation, which again resulted in nothing but the reorganisation of the company to suit the new legal position. Only in 1911 was its monopoly shaken, when the Supreme Court ruled that the company had conspired by many and devious methods to build up a monopoly and was not, as the company argued, the natural product of the growth of a single business, that had never 'conspired or combined in restraint of trade'.[43]

The success in reducing the power of monopoly at this time was undoubtedly the result of the successful co-operation between the competitors and the press,[44] which kept informing the public about the evils of 'big business'. In 1912 competition became *the* election issue. The Democratic candidate, Woodrow Wilson, stated that American industry was no longer as free and competitive as it had been half a century before, and that something ought to be done by way of new legislation to 'prevent the strong from crushing the weak'.[45] This the Congress tried to achieve by passing, in 1914, the Clayton Antitrust Act prohibiting price discrimination and deals forbidding the parties to handle competitors' goods and the acquisition of competitors' stock in order to reduce competition, and other similar monopolistic practices.[46] The extent to which this and similar legislation was really successful in restraining monopoly is difficult to assess. It certainly had some degree of success[47] but it did not restore the kind of 'free for all' which characterised the American economy in the late 1860s and early 1870s. For a time business consolidation abated, and the partnership between businessmen struggling for survival and the general public came to an end. In the decade that followed the end of the 1914–18 war, consolidation set in once more at an even faster rate. The leading sectors, in which most of the new mergers took place, now were the metallurgical industries and public utilities. Virtually thousands of small enterprises were driven out of business within one decade. And yet, although small business was going under, the general public was not really aroused. It was a time of prosperity. A popular song of the period said:

> The rich get richer
> and the poor get poorer
> in the meantime
> in between time
> We're having fun.

In fact the poor were not getting poorer. Only the traditional middle class was being deprived of its place in society by big business. The country as a whole was experiencing a period of widespread industrial prosperity and rising living standards (1923–29) and there were no real immediate grounds at the time for the workers to renew the old antitrust coalition with the middle class.[48]

In Professor Faulkner's view the causes for the relaxation of public opposition to the new wave of business consolidation were:[49] 'An appreciation of the inevitability of consolidation in a capitalist system, the futility of antitrust legislation to prevent it, the rising standard of living which has made the masses less keen to scent evils in the movement, and finally, the incessant propaganda of big business interests.'

However, while the competition between the capitalists themselves abated, and big business was emerging victoriously from one kind of competition, the other kind of competition—between workers and employers—was becoming increasingly powerful. Until the middle of the nineteenth century this seldom led to widespread tension. As long as labour was scarce and not concentrated in towns, and land was abundant, there was neither much need nor opportunity for the organisation of labour. After the middle of the century things were changing very fast. In the 1880s already a quarter of the population of the United States was in one way or another dependent on industry for their livelihood and settled in towns of more than 8,000 inhabitants. Moreover, the total population of the United States was increasing at a rate of some 20 per cent and that of cities at a rate of close to 40 per cent per decade,[50] while the pattern of the employment structure also showed a relatively faster growth of enterprises employing great numbers of workers than that of small workshops.[51]

Thus while, on the one hand, the traditional safeguards for the American working class's standard of living (the scarcity of labour and the fertility of the land) were waning, on the other, new ones, in the form of workers' associations, were rising as a result of the growth of towns and the concentration of labour. It has, in fact, been observed that the years in which cities grew most rapidly closely correspond with the periods of greatest activity in the labour movements.[52] The two other factors, which were of no little importance for the rise of the American labour movement, were the development of the press and the spreading of education, which had already become a part of the American way of life. The most important immediate cause which led to the organisation of labour in the United States was probably the Civil War and its aftermath. Firstly, because the objective conditions of the working class had become worse during the war. Prices had risen and wages had not. Many of the returning soldiers could find no work because their jobs had been filled in their absence either by new immigrants or by contract labour,[53] or had become redundant altogether because of the introduction of new labour-saving equipment. Secondly, the climate of opinion among the workers themselves had changed. They had learned a lesson in the use of violence, which deprived the employers of their hitherto almost unrivalled monopoly over it through their control of the police force; they had learned a lesson in co-operation and concerted action; and they had also learned a little about their economic reality from the Southerners' propaganda telling them, what many must have eventually recognised as the truth, that the economic position of the slaves, whom they were fighting to liberate, may not have been much worse than their own as 'free and white' men.

Thus, with the fetters of traditional attitudes falling, with little need to fear an American Peterloo, and with the dawning recognition of the economic reality in a period of falling living standards and rising unemployment, the stage was set for a new era of labour relations in the United States. Before long membership of the local unions rose and their number increased. In time some of them joined together to form national associations and to publish their own newspapers. With this the struggle for better labour conditions was being carried on in both the professional and the political spheres.

A very good example for the political struggle is provided in the activities of the Knights of Labour,[54] a good example for the professional struggle in those of the American Federation of Labour.[55] The Knights of Labour had their antecedents in at least two earlier great unions with similar objectives. These were the National Labour Union (which was essentially a political organisation for the legal enforcement of an eight-hour working day and restriction of immigration, especially from Asia),[56] and the Knights of St. Crispin (a very powerful shoe-makers union). However, both the National Labour Union and the Knights of St. Crispin, and many other unions, were virtually destroyed in the great economic depression which took place in the 1870s. Business prospects were indeed so low at the time, and unemployment so widespread, that even where union pressure was possible, and there were few industries where this was the case, there was little hope of achieving anything but perhaps the closure of more business enterprises. Whether consciously from the examination of the situation, or merely by intuition, a number of union leaders recognised this and came to the conclusion that if something was to be done successfully it had to be on a political level. There was indeed little to be gained from a struggle for the redistribution of the 'fruits of production' when there was no production; but there was much to be gained from making the government take active steps to restore national prosperity. Here, too, was a platform which united part of the middle class and small employers with the workers against the growing economic and political strength of big business. The franchise, together with the shift in the distribution of population between country and town in favour of the latter, gave the leaders of the movement the necessary means for influencing the government's economic policies. These were the sources of the considerable success of the Knights of Labour.

Originally the Knights of Labour had been 'a Noble Order', a secret society, of a small number of garment makers in Philadelphia. They had much less in common with traditional European socialism than with the co-operative movement, though it is true that they did advocate the public ownership of public utilities. They did not believe in strikes but were rather inclined towards the 'banishment of wage slavery' altogether by political means. In 1883 their membership counted about 50,000, by 1886 it had risen to almost 1,000,000. By that time, however, the American economy was beginning very steadily to recover and the old divergency of interests between wage-workers and self-employed re-emerged. This led to considerable changes in both the aims and the organisational structure of the movement. The small businessmen and the farmers continued to be in favour of reform through political action, whereas the wage-workers, who accounted for about three-quarters of the membership, demanded direct action in the form of strikes to raise the workers' standard of living. The break became inevitable. The opportunity arose when anarchists threw some bombs after a riot. The middle-class minority was quick to use this as an excuse for its withdrawal from the union, though it was fairly obvious that the union had nothing to do with activities of this kind. After this the disintegration of the 'Knights' was very rapid, almost as fast as its rise had been only a few years earlier. By 1888 most of its middle-class membership was leaving because for them the organisation had become too radical, and most of its radical membership had left to join the new more militant American Federation of Labour. The middle class felt disillusioned with union politics and the workers demanded more direct industrial activity. It would, however, be a mistake to underrate the importance of the 'Knights' to the development of American industrial relations and politics. Firstly, they helped to put new life into the many smaller local unions which had almost been extinct by the end of the depression; secondly, they indicated the possibilities which are inherent in the American political system for using the working men's vote as an instrument for securing certain economic advantages; and thirdly, they showed the way which half a century later led to Franklin D. Roosevelt's 'New Deal'.

While the Knights of Labour had been primarily concerned with the political opportunity which the system offered to labour, another organisation, the American Federation of Labour, was pressing the case of labour along the traditional lines of industrial action. Their policy was more purely unionistic. They did not advocate political action, though in their early days they too had demanded the abolition of contract emigration and conspiracy laws.[57] After 1887, with the decline of the Knights, the Federation absorbed a great part of its radical membership. In 1890 it had about 100,000 members, in 1900 almost 1,000,000 and in 1910 close to 2,000,000. The years 1898 to 1904 were perhaps the most important in the history of American organised labour. It was during these years that it received widespread recognition by the employers and during which it showed its greatest drive and its members displayed a great deal of self-sacrifice and idealism.[58] Needless to add, these were also years of prosperity and rapid economic growth.[59]

Together with the growth of the labour movement[60] other radical changes in the economic structure of the United States were taking place. Though it may never be possible to separate cause from effect, there can be little doubt about the close relationship between this growth of organised labour and the rate of technological progress in industry during the period 1897 to 1929. The rapid increase in the use of labour-saving equipment and its displacement of labour undoubtedly raised the membership of unions, while the resultant strengthening of the same enhanced their success in wage disputes with employers. In return, this stimulated further the tendency of employers to replace labour by machines whenever and wherever possible. In fact, we are told[61] that in the years 1899–1914, '2 per cent of industrial workers in the United States lost their jobs every five years as a result of being displaced by new machinery. But this rate of separation was counteracted by the rate of addition of jobs yielded by the rapidly expanding economy. In the same period, 15 per cent more jobs were created every five years. This expansion took care not only of the technologically displaced but of the rapid growth of population as well.'

In the twenties, American industrialists had managed to improve their technological equipment so much that the expansion of industry into new products was no longer sufficient to absorb the 'displaced' labour force.[62] In addition to this, the persistent influx of new immigrants further increased, at least until the middle of the decade, the disproportion between the rising employment opportunities and the much more rapidly increasing labour force; and finally, the slow rise in employment opportunities and the more rapid increase of the labour force were both overtaken by an even steeper rise in the national output.[63] Had there been less immigration during the first half of the decade, and had the organisation of labour not suffered so much from the patriotic enthusiasm of the war years, it is more likely than not that the discrepancy between the rise in the rate of productivity and the rate of increase of the labour force would have resulted in a fall in prices and higher wages. As it happened, and excluding the first two years of the decade, prices did not fall but were gently rising[64] and wages rose only very slightly from 1923 to 1928.[65] The difference between the sharp rise in productivity and the slow rise in real incomes was taken by the employers as profit. This redistribution of income in favour of the latter led for some time to the deepening of investment which made possible the rapid rise in productivity and the displacement of labour with its resultant effects on the wage level, but at the same time it also starved the market of its effective consumers' demand. Eventually this maladjustment between the production of producers' and consumers' goods had to come to light. It did so with the Great Depression of the 1930s.[66]

Another section of the population which did not share in the prosperity during the twenties were the farmers. This was because the rapid development of farming equipment during and after the war had led to considerable overproduction, especially when, with the coming of peace, Europe was once again in a position to provide for her needs. The position was finally made even worse for the farmers by the rising taxation of farm property.

In 1921 the Farm Bloc was formed in the predominantly agricultural States to press for legislation in the farmers' interest.[67] Firstly, they demanded, and received, various tariffs to protect them against foreign competition. This policy, which might have been of some value in a country with considerable agra imports, 'backfired' in the United States with its vast agra surplus. Secondly, the Bloc wanted, and managed, to improve rural credit facilities. These they hoped would not only stimulate exports but also encourage further co-operative efforts. Here again the originators of the idea failed completely to recognise the changes which had taken place in the position of the United States in the world economy and of American agriculture in particular. Thirdly, the Bloc demanded, without success, that the government should buy up agricultural surpluses for export, at a 'fair' price, and then, after selling them abroad, balance the profits from some against the losses from others by way of an equalisation fee.[68] Though unsuccessful in the immediate present, the efforts initiated and acquainted the public with the idea of government price fixing in agriculture which was eventually introduced by F. D. Roosevelt's government. In summary, the agricultural problem in the United States had shifted in the decade 1921 to 1930 from production to marketing.[69]

The most perplexing problem, regarding the twenties in the United States, is to explain the inability of the labour movement, which had been so formidable before the war, to see to it that the American workers acquired their full share in the gains from the rapid rise of industrial productivity. This was particularly surprising if one remembers that outside the United States, i.e. internationally, the position of labour was rather stronger after than before the war. One cause for this was undoubtedly the atmosphere which the American Federation of Labour had itself helped to produce during the war. Throughout the war the shortage of labour had given the workers a potentially very strong bargaining position, but, because of the patriotic fervour, the opportunity to exploit this was ignored. The executive of the American Federation of Labour not only neglected exploiting the situation but publicly declared that the war against Germany and her allies 'is labour's war'.[70] In this the Federation was as good as its word and did all in its power to raise the efficiency of production. Its leadership confined its activity to ensuring that living standards were not actually reduced.[71] Gompers, of the American Federation of Labour, was elected chairman of the Labour Committee of the National Defence Council and called a representative conference of both workers and employers, at which all sides agreed not to take advantage of the situation. As a rule, with only a few exceptions, the workers kept the agreement;[72] employers had no reason not to keep it.

In line with this 'one-sided truce' a War Labour Board was set up, early in 1918, to act as a kind of tribunal between employers and employees. This too helped to prevent friction. At the end of the war labour was rewarded for its patriotic loyalty by the establishment of the League of Nations International Labour Organisation, and by a number of other similar achievements (the legal recognition of the unions, etc.). On the whole, however, the effects of the war were rather detrimental for the American labour movement. It is true that it received international recognition and that the eight-hour day became an established fact, but real wages had fallen and were lower than during the last pre-war year. However, more important than this were the lasting losses, namely the weakening of the socialist party and the disappearance of the I.W.W. and other left-wing groups from the labour movement and from the political platform. Thus, while the war had taught employers a lesson in violence and in intolerance, labour emerged from it with reduced vigour and received only a minor share of the economic benefits which accrued to the financiers and manufacturers as a result of the war.[73]

The reaction, which began after the war, was as bad as had to be expected. The unions, having lost their experience in the struggle, were unable to cope with the combination of economic depression from over-expansion; unemployment, as a result of demobilisation; and the return to a peace economy with the reorganisation of industry which attended it. A number of ill-organised and ill-timed strikes collapsed and where the economic pressures did not suffice the Federal government stepped in to break the workers' resistance. The demoralisation which followed these failures was so depressing that it rendered the American labour movement impotent for almost a decade to defend the workers against the mounting inequality of the distribution of wealth.[74] To these almost objective difficulties other less necessary ones were added. The courts which had during the war become accustomed to ignoring civil and human rights continued to do so and paid little heed to the demands of labour, and several industrialists did not shun the use of *provocateurs* to justify the calling up of the militia for support in labour disputes.[75] Thus, while labour was getting weaker, capital was becoming stronger and better organised.[76] Two other very important factors which contributed to labour's inability to capture a greater share of the national product were the increasing differentiation between skilled and unskilled workers, and the general climate of opinion that held that things were getting better all around. The first of these two, i.e. the divergence of status within the working class, was due to the fall in prices of some products and the skilled workers' relatively rising standard of living after the depression of 1921. (Unfortunately the skilled workers used to be the hard core of the movement before the war and their lack of enthusiasm in the twenties was a severe blow to it.) The second factor, namely the illusion of prosperity, had its roots partly in the fact that the conditions of one group in the working class were really improving its living standard, and partly in the subtle psychological effect of the capitalist propaganda which pretended that a redistribution of wealth in favour of the wage earners was actually taking place. The basis for this completely unfounded idea was the greatly advertised invention of the 'employee stock ownership'.[77]

Thus, by temptation on the one hand and threats on the other,[78] organised labour in America was rendered harmless, while employers were increasing their capital out of proportion with the growth of effective consumers' demand. Had labour been more successful in checking the accumulation of wealth—and had employers been less greedy in exploiting the inactivity of the labour movement—they might, perhaps, have saved the United States from the severity of the collapse which ended the decade.

The collapse, which in the course of a few years changed the 'free for all' into 'state regulated' capitalism, began with the famous stock-market crash of October 1929. Within three years unemployment rose to 25 per cent of the labour force[79] and pay-rolls fell to less than 45 per cent of their average 1929 level. Out of the total labour force of between 45 and 48 million workers, the unemployed numbered in 1930 more than four-and-a-half millions, in 1931 approximately seven-and-three-quarter millions, in 1932 about eleven-and-a-half millions, and in 1933 over thirteen millions. For the majority of the American people, even those who were working, the depression meant wage cuts, insecurity, and frustration. Human dignity fell to a very low ebb.[80] With the reduced demand for goods there was little to stimulate production. It decreased to about half of its pre-1929 level. Agriculture and foreign trade suffered worst of all. The former because it had already been depressed before 1929, and the latter partly for truly economic reasons (the depression in Europe, the lack of American loan money, and the new exchange situation), and partly because of the European retaliations in 1930 against the high American tariffs.

Thus, unless the government wished to risk a revolution, it was bound to take some initiative in economic affairs. With this the era of almost unrestrained free enterprise, the period of the American laissez faire, came to its end. Initially, President Hoover tried to stimulate the economy by tax reductions and state support to agriculture. Both the tax relief and the support of agra prices cost the taxpayers a lot of money but were of very little avail. Equally unsuccessful were his appeals to private enterprise to keep up production.[81] Of some use were similar appeals to State governments and municipalities, i.e. elected bodies, which were called upon to put forward some of their construction programmes in order to create employment. And yet, though all and every one of these measures did little to cure the depression, they were of very great importance in creating a new state of mind. They did in fact acknowledge that government has certain responsibilities regarding the economic welfare of the people. They paved the way to the new deal of regulated capitalism. As the elections drew closer the government became increasingly aware of the need for a more progressive and active economic policy if it wished to remain in power. One factor which had a strong though mostly indirect influence in this direction during the depression was the rapid re-emergence of the socialists and communists. 'The Russian example' not only frightened the old guard of conservatives but seemed to show to those who wished to see it that where production was aimed at 'the satisfaction of social wants' rather than 'the accumulation of profits' (with the satisfaction of social wants merely as a coincidental result), unemployment could be totally eliminated. It was true that not all that one heard about Russia was very pleasant, the standard of living was lower than it had been in pre-1929 America, and civil liberties were at a very low ebb, but who really cares for civil liberties when he is unemployed and starving? Indeed, how much of these celebrated liberties had survived in the United States?[82] In 1932, the socialists polled close to a million votes in the American election—a large vote indeed. Their political influence, however, went far beyond their strength in numbers. Their growth had opened the eyes of even the most stout supporters of laissez faire to what might happen to capital if no drastic steps were taken by the government to improve the economy. Unconsciously, by scaring the opposition with the alternative to the New Deal, they helped Roosevelt to win the elections which were to begin a new phase in American socio-economic relations.[83] What the New Deal was to be was far from clear to anyone in 1932, but it had the right ring about it to stir the imagination of the people and it implied a change—a change for the better, as it was hoped. As Professor Arthur Lewis wrote:[84] 'No single chapter can contain the New Deal. Here combined in one administration were innumerable great measures grappling with innumerable problems.' On the economic plane alone, and there were also New Deals in the foreign and domestic political planes, there was 'a New Deal for the unemployed, for farmers, for debtors—a Relief New Deal. A New Deal for Labour, for trust-busting, for control of Wall Street, for progressive taxation —a *left* New Deal. A Recovery New Deal, designed to *prime the pump* and to send the economy once more vigorously upward. A social security New Deal. Each pursued in detail with vast expenditure through an ever growing network of government agencies; . . .'[85]

The two main problems were, of course, how to put an end to the depression and how to eliminate the 'piratical methods and practices which . . . not only harassed honest business but also contributed to the ills of labour'.[86] Initially, so it appears, Roosevelt was not quite aware how indivisible the two problems—economic revival and socio-economic reform—really were. At least, in so far as revival was concerned he continued the traditional supply orientated methods of 'priming the economy by the encouragement of higher profits'. His early advisers, drawn from the camp of private enterprise, believed, or made the government believe, that support for high prices would lead to more profit and this would set the economy upon an upward trend because rising profits would be followed by increasing production and employment. When the futility of this policy had been sufficiently demonstrated, Roosevelt's new advisers, the famous Brains Trust from the Universities, suggested a new, demand dominated, policy which bridged the gap between the efforts towards social reform and towards the revival of the economy. In fact, the new policy aimed at a redistribution of the national wealth in favour of the less privileged part of the population. In the monetary and financial sphere Roosevelt eased the burden of deptors by inflation—i.e. by 'increasing property values until they were greater than the debts'; in the sphere of agriculture he introduced crop restrictions—i.e. payments for restricting the planted acreage[87] and better credit facilities. In industry, the solution was not found until some abortive attempts had been made to revive the World War I spirit of co-operation between government, capital and labour.[88] As time went by, labour became more and more critical of these efforts, or rather of the evasion of the arrangements which were to be made for their representation. Eventually, by the end of 1934 the system was reorganised and by mid-1935 abolished altogether, when the Supreme Court of the United States ruled it unconstitutional. Throughout this time the actual position of labour continued to deteriorate. Yet, together with this further deterioration, the foundations were laid for a complete change in American labour relations. For the first time the government became fully concerned with the problems of labour. It provided unemployment relief, stimulated insurance and pension schemes, and, above all, viewed with favour the organisation of labour in the defence of its interests. Unemployment was attacked on a wide front by the initiation of many public works and construction schemes[89] and by making large sums of money available to the State governments to follow the federal government's example. These schemes did much to relieve unemployment in the country.[90] Yet with all this the problem was not really solved before the war turned unemployment into a labour shortage. In the long run, however, the most important aspect of these efforts was the principle involved; namely, that man has a right to work, and that it is part of the job of government to see that work is obtainable. This point cannot be overstressed.[91] It upheld the dignity of man and the dignity of labour. It may well rank as the greatest contribution of this century to western civilisation. It abolished the degrading patronising attitudes of charity. Whether the critics of his schemes, who accused Roosevelt of introducing them for merely vote-catching political reasons, were right or wrong makes no difference whatsoever, the net effect is clear, it introduced a new dimension into the socio-economic relations—dignity.

More directly, the economy was affected by Roosevelt's legislation aimed at increasing the social security of wage-earners, unemployment insurance, old-age pensions, etc., and the introduction of minimum wage-rates and maximum working hours. Yet Roosevelt's success could not have come without the support of the workers by helping themselves. Had it not been for the revival, or perhaps re-birth, of the American labour movement, things could hardly have turned out the way they did. Had it not been for the reorganisation of labour, Roosevelt could hardly have successfully pursued his labour policy. Had it not been for Roosevelt's labour legislation labour would have found it much more difficult to organise and assert itself. This, then, was the real importance of section 7 of the National Industrial Recovery Act, that it gave government sanction to labourers' right to organise and to bargain collectively through their freely elected representatives. The monopoly of capital over the instruments of government was broken and the free competition between employers and employees for the greater share of the fruits of production was restored. The traditional growth-producing factors in the capitalist economy were once again called into life. In the political field capital was henceforth on the defensive.

THE SOVIET UNION: GROWTH WITHOUT CAPITALISTIC COMPETITION[92]

Marx foresaw a socialist revolution in a highly industrialised society. As a result of this the theoretical problems of communism were mainly concerned with the redistribution of wealth. The creation of an industrial society was supposed to be the historical task of the capitalist stage of development. However, contrary to Marx's theoretical assumption, the first successful communist revolution took place in a quasi-feudal and backward country with no developed industry in which capitalism had not fulfilled its 'historical' task. In addition to this, the Bolshevik Revolution was followed by an armed intervention staged by some capitalist countries to overthrow it which, with or without justification, left behind the feeling of the existence of a permanent capitalist plot to restore the old régime in Russia. The combination of these two factors, the absence of industry and the shadow of an impending capitalist attack, together with the urgent need to raise living standards, was the main factor affecting the specific policies of accelerated industrialisation in the Soviet Union. The more the feeling of danger from another intervention mounted, the greater was the stress upon the development of a military industry; whenever the danger seemed to abate, a larger share of the resources was diverted to the development of the civil industry. Moreover, the Soviet Revolution took place within a war and was accompanied by a deep rift within the Russian working class and by a feeling that it had been betrayed by the other working classes of western Europe and especially by the German Social Democracy. This too exerted an important influence upon the course of developments in Russia in the years to come.

The first task the revolutionary government set itself was to bridge the gap between Russia's economic backwardness and her newly achieved progressive political system. It had to bring the infrastructure into accord with its political superstructure—a task hardly provided for in orthodox Marxian theories. Communists used to be proud of having succeeded in fulfilling the task of turning Russia into an industrial country. The history of the industrialisation of capitalist countries offers ample illustration of the real cost in terms of human sufferings of this process. It demands an enormous concentration of capital, the transfer of labour from the countryside to the cities, and the termination of traditional institutions. In other words the construction of an industrial society was always linked with the destruction of earlier forms of relative social security. In the western countries this transition from rural ways to those of an urbanised industrial society was accompanied by a great many hardships suffered by the majority of the working people. It led, at least temporarily, to sinking living standards, greater insecurity of livelihood, and recurring periods of mass unemployment. These ills, which appear to be the natural by-products of transition, were also unavoidable, with the exception perhaps of mass unemployment, in the Soviet Union. On the road to industrialisation Russia had to face most of the problems Britain faced a century before. In fact, early twentieth-century Russia was at a disadvantage in comparison with nineteenth-century Britain because she lacked Britain's technical and economic basis. Britain's industrialisation had progressed gradually from export manufacturing towards a growing domestic market. In Russia, industrialisation was taking place 'in a race against time'. The fact that the process of industrialisation required by its very nature great human sacrifices has already been mentioned, and Russia was no exception. On the contrary, the accelerated pace at which industrialisation was forced forward in that country added aditional difficulties and left a deep mark on the emergent socio-political structure.

In the western countries the opposition of the working class to the hardships which accompanied the process of industrialisation gave birth to the gradual evolution of trade unionism and of the socialist movement. However, the same factors and sources for discontent which were present in the capitalist countries during their era of early industrial development and gave rise to socialist opposition there were also present in the Soviet Union. The need to prevent the growth of such an opposition, which would threaten the rapid development of Russia's industry, was at the roots of the heavy-handed suppression of all real or apparent oppositions. In other words, the feeling was that a higher standard of living and the security of the country were dependent upon rapid industrialisation, and that all other issues were of only secondary importance. This paved the way for the system which is usually associated with the name of Stalin.

The great European socialist movement was unable to prevent World War I. Only the Bolshevik party had rejected the war outright. Outside Russia the Bolshevik attitude to the war was only shared by a number of small socialist groups. In Russia herself, Lenin made great efforts to secure an alliance with other workers' parties but was unsuccessful. His famous slogan 'All the rule to the Soviets' was in effect a call to all other workers' movements for unity. Right up to the peace treaty of Brest-Litovsk he never ceased in his efforts to lead the revolution in full partnership with the L.S.R.[93] Unfortunately the Mensheviks and the Cadets were against the revolution, and the L.S.R., too, turned against him at the time of, and because of, the Brest-Litovsk agreement. Thus history prevented the Russian Revolution from acquiring some of the other non-Russian or Bolshevik workers' movements traditions. Worse than this, the Bolshevik leadership developed an attitude of suspicion towards all other working-class movements which culminated in accusations that German and French social democracy was saving European capitalism from its doom. All, even left-wing, independent thought was suppressed, and all the achievements of other socialist movements outside Russia ignored. The fact that British and French social democracy had put an end to the war of intervention was overshadowed by the treachery of the German social democrats in the early part of the century. Yet there were also other more direct factors which contributed to the rigidity of Soviet policies. The opposition which everywhere is brought to life by the hardships which accompany industrialisation developed, in the capitalist countries, in the form of the growth of the socialist movement.

This was a gradual process which coincided with the rise of the bourgeoisie. The growth of the working class preceded the rise of its class consciousness, and both only followed in the wake of industrialisation.

In the Soviet Union the process was reversed. Industrialisation had to be achieved by a working class which was already becoming class conscious and had just emerged victoriously from a revolution: a working class which now, after the old régime had been toppled, was expecting to reap the fruits of its victory. Returning from the battlefields each and every worker must have had his small private hopes and dreams about his future to be fulfilled now that things were going to be different in Russia. Yet what was the reality? The country's economy was in a state of utter chaos. The government was neither able to follow the traditional line of financing the country's industrial progress out of the sale of agricultural surplus to the capitalist countries, nor do anything else but pursue its policy of industrialisation at any but the most accelerated pace. To finance the development of industry from export earnings would have made its growth dependent upon the 'good will' of the hostile camp of capitalists who could engage in price fixing or refuse to sell to Russia the most necessary goods. To slow down the rate of industrialisation and permit a gradual and staged transfer of labour and resources from the agricultural to the industrial sector was also out of the question, because, unless the government was able to industrialise the country very rapidly, it would soon have to succumb to internal or external pressures. For these reasons the government could do little else but tell the workers to wait and in the meantime tighten their belts even further, and then stress and overstress the pace of industrialisation in the hope that through the accelerated rate of capital production it would soon reduce the cost of consumer goods and raise the real incomes of the population. This policy, however, required first of all that at least initially as much as possible of the national product should be diverted to the production of capital goods, i.e. to the production of 'the means of production'. But this also meant that as little as possible could be spared for the direct satisfaction of consumers' demand. In fact, the government was forced to pursue the policy of sacrificing present needs for future gains. Such a policy, which is difficult to implement at any time, even with a well-educated society, was hardly easy to pursue at a time when armed men were returning from a war and from a victorious revolution full of hopes and expectations for a brighter future. The communist leadership was therefore caught up in a paradox. The innocent and just demands of the revolutionary workers, which in the west had contributed so much to economic development, were undergoing a metamorphosis in the Soviet Union and became objectively damaging to socialist development. There was, of course, a hard core of socialists who understood all this, but most of these lived in the towns. The rest of the country was far from happy with this policy of consumers' restraint. Particularly the richer peasants, who had been relatively well off in pre-revolutionary Russia, were unwilling to reduce their standard of living after the years of war and devastation. In the hands of Stalin this lack of enthusiasm to take part in the building of the future at the expense of the present was easily translated into treason and hostility towards the working class. To accelerate the rate of industrial growth Stalin tried to extract from the agricultural sector as much as possible. In the years before the revolution, agriculture had contributed close to 17 per cent to the national product by sales of grains to western countries. Assuming that this surplus could be increased and diverted to industry by way of lower food prices in the cities, Stalin devised a whole list of measures aimed at forcing the peasants to increase production and reduce their consumption. The justification was that the accelerated production of producer goods would later also increase the production of consumer goods, and lower their cost of production and prices, so that the farmer would be able to buy more though his nominal income might be reduced. Following this line of thought Stalin not only taxed the farmers to the extent that skimmed off the 17 per cent but heaped taxes upon taxes to force them to work harder and consume less.[94] As events came to show, this was not a well-conceived policy. Apparently the farmers did not improve their production and had no wish to do so. It did not have the psychological result that Stalin supposed, namely to make them work harder, but depressed them to an extent that they had no wish to produce more; on the contrary, they tried to hide as much as possible of their economic capacity for fear of being forced to produce more and more and more, and have an ever smaller share of it.[95] Suddenly, the farmers, who had also hoped to benefit from the revolution and were the majority of the population, found themselves under a constant threat of having their living standards further reduced.

Thus the tremendous centralisation of the economy not only required a growing apparatus to enforce central planning but also to suppress possible outbreaks of discontent. Together with the bad traditions inherited from the pre-Revolutionary bureaucracy, this soon gave rise to the development of officialdom into a class by itself; a class which was content to carry out orders and instructions from above, without worrying about the nature of those orders and their content. At the same time this class was also suppressing all criticism of those instructions from below, killing as it were all germs of independent reasoning. In time Stalin alone remained capable of thought and decision making. The party, its apparatus, and the whole body of State bureaucracy, were merely there to carry out instructions. All criticism became tantamount to an attack on the party and its leadership. The natural by-product of this state of affairs was the well-known 'cult of the personality', i.e. the rule of mediocracy. As independent thought was taken to be heresy, only those with no imagination could serve their party well. Christianity had given to the world the idea of charity; socialism set out to replace it by the rule of right and responsibility. This attitude was based on the idea that each and every human being was entitled to an equal share of material and spiritual well-being, and that every member of society was individually responsible to all his fellow men. The Russian writer Maxim Gorky opposed Christian charity because he believed the concept of charity to be at cross purposes with justice. Wherever there is room for charity, he claimed, there is no place for revolt against injustice. Charity and dignity cannot be housed under one roof, the one degrades the other. It prevents society from revolting against those who do injustice to it; who take for themselves an unequal share of the fruits of the labour of others. Yet again, what a peculiar twist did these ideas receive under the Stalinist tutelage! While Soviet education was successful in discrediting charity and hypocritical manifestations of pity, it did not succeed in raising responsibility and human dignity to the required higher moral plateau. Both justice and responsibility were denuded of their moral values and transformed into a system of technology. The rights of the individual were reduced to a minimum—barely to the right to work and eat. The idea of responsibility to ones fellow men was transformed into a mere scheme of figures of output and production. Certainly, it stimulated economic growth, but it did little to raise socialist morality to a higher level.

Thus, ill equipped to withstand the perversion of socialist morality and dominated by the by-product of the cult of the personality, the rule of mediocrity, Russian literature and philosophic thought were also brought to stagnation under Stalin's heavy hand. After having flourished by the end of the nineteenth century and in the early days following the Revolution, Russian and socialist literature and political thought were reduced to propaganda. In an ill-fated attempt to use it as an educational instrument, literature became primarily concerned with the description of society as it should be rather than as it is. The heroes became all-round ideals and the villains all-round vicious enemies of the people and the party. No room was left for development of characters and circumstantial influences. Literature became therefore increasingly estranged from life, and in the main hardly worthy to be called literature at all. In this form it could hardly have played its valid role in the education of the people. Not dissimilar was the fate of communist philosophy. All that remained of it in Stalin's time were scholastic exercises quoting and explaining Marx without taking any notice of the changing reality since his and Lenin's days. History, too, was made to share the fate of literature and philosophy. Regardless of the fact that all Marxist and socialist analyses were supposed to be founded on detached historical objectivity, the party wilfully distorted historical facts to serve imaginary interests. By this it brought the development of socialism to stagnation. The harm done in this way to communism went far beyond the boundaries of the Soviet Union. As Russia was the first socialist State and its communist party was the first of its kind to bring about a successful revolution, all other communist parties were modelling their tactics after the Russian pattern. The sad experience with other labour parties at the time of the Russian Revolution cast a dark shadow upon the relations between communist and socialist parties in the west too, even when the suspicions were no longer justified. The fear of an impending Fascist attack upon the Soviet Union in the thirties, which was justified, further increased the tendency among western communists to take the lead in all matters from the U.S.S.R. For these reasons it is difficult to speak of Russia's economic development as the necessary universal example for socialist inspired economic growth. It was a process specific to Russian conditions which may or may not be repeated elsewhere.

Returning now to the growth of industry in Russia, it can be seen that progress there was far from smooth and from optimum performance. It is, of course, a fact that in some heroic years, when the enthusiasm of the workers for the creation of a new Russia was high, a peculiar combination of communism and nationalism produced some very outstanding results; but this patriotic or socialist fervour did not and could not last continuously. In years without this heroic fervour things did not go so well. Moreover, there were many objective mistakes in the methods of industrialisation and in its bureaucratic administration. In 1928, Stalin formulated the policy for Russia's economic development. It required 'a fast rate of development of industry and the production of the means of production in particular, as the basis and key to industrialisation and to socialist development of the economy as a whole'. 'Socialist industrialisation,' he said, 'is the development of large-scale industry, and primarily heavy industry, to a level where it becomes the key to the reorganisation of the entire national economy on the basis of advanced machine technology, [and] ensures the victory of socialism and strengthens the country's technical and economic independence and defence capacity in face of the capitalist world.'[96] The realisation of these policies requires 'huge material and financial outlays which cannot be obtained through capitalistic exploitation'. It was to be obtained through 'socialist accumulation'. This meant through the utilisation of that part of the national product which had previously been wasted on 'parasitical consumption by the exploiting classes', and through the exploitation of the revenue from State enterprises and foreign and domestic trade. Finally, Stalin also prescribed maximum taxation and price fixing as the method for getting the difference between the 'potential and the actual savings' in the agricultural sector. The division of the economy into two distinct sectors, agriculture and industry, was deepened, and industrial investments were made into a function of technological progress with little regard for actual market demand.

In summary, then, the general strategy of development was the separation of agriculture from industry, and the separation of consumers' actual demand from investment decisions. To this were added scales of priorities which graded industry above agriculture, heavy industry above light industry, extractive above finishing industries, etc. As Lenin wrote:[97] 'Accounting and control—that is the main thing required for arranging the smooth working and the correct functioning of the first phase of communist society'. Thus, planning (accounting and control) was in the socialist State to take the place of the capitalistic price mechanism. In other words, Soviet economic growth was to be advanced through scientific planning. In accord with this, P. Popov, for example, published in 1926 his *The Balance of the National Economy of the U.S.S.R. for 1923/24* which was an attempt to quantify the volume and structure of the output which flows into the national economy from its different branches and its distribution among the individual branches and the various groups in the society. But such works as Popov's were not taken seriously. The contention that prevailed, and was labelled 'scientific planning', held that 'pragmatism' rather than the 'accuracy upon which strict science insists' is necessary for practical purposes.[98] The law of planned development, which came to replace the price mechanism, was expressed in the plans of the State planning commissions in accordance with the directives of the Communist Party and the government. However, as the law of planned development may or may not be well observed in the process of actual planning, the original plans and the whole system was continuously being 'corrected' and 'improved in the light of experience of the most advanced practice'.[99] In fact, this kind of 'pragmatic'-continuously-corrected-planning came very close to chaos. In 1936 Stalin proclaimed that socialism had been achieved in the Soviet Union and that economic growth could henceforth only come as a result of policy directives and their execution. Output targets ceased to be technological predictions and became government instructions which had to be carried out. Organic growth was no longer considered of importance as it was part of the discarded capitalist economic structure. Consequently all cost accounting was abandoned and losses were hidden in the lump sums of the general averages. It became a system of maximum rather than optimum planning. There was no method by which the profitability of any specific investment could be judged and this led frequently to the utilisation of barely marginal units of production, 'empire-building', nepotism, inefficiency and general maladministration. These observations, which were made by no other than Mr. Khrushchev[100] and repeated by Mr. Brezhnev,[101] well illustrate what went wrong in Russia. However, the fact remains that, if not because of then at least in spite of Stalin's policies, the Soviet economy achieved a phenomenal rate of industrial growth.[102] How this came about seems fairly well documented, at least as far as the later period is concerned; why is a point still very much debated.

The lowest point in the production of industrial materials in the Soviet Union, after it had been falling steadily since 1916, was reached in 1920.[103] In the following year the civil war came to an end, and with the initiation of the new economic policy the country's economy recovered at an unusually rapid pace.[104] By 1924 production, measured by volume, had once again reached the pre-war level, though not the same quality. Moreover, in accordance with the prescribed policy of stressing the production of the means of production the structure of the output was also changed in a way which makes a strict comparison with the pre-revolutionary period very difficult. This is so because, if measured from the point of view of the final consumer of consumers' goods, industrial production in 1927 was considerably below that of 1913–16, whereas from the point of view of capital construction, growth was considerably greater than before the war.[105] The most valuable aspect of this change for the future development of Russia was, of course, the fact that owing to this shift away from 'present consumption', *per capita* output rose very considerably indeed (between 1 per cent and 33 per cent according to the particular nature of the industry).[106] In addition to this the total industrial output *per capita* of the population increased even more significantly because the rise in productivity was accompanied by a high rate of transfer of labour from the agricultural to the industrial sector and by the drastic reduction of un- and under-employment and by the labour accretion from natural population growth.[107] In the period that followed, that is between 1928 and 1937, the growth of industrial production continued at an accelerated rate from over 8 per cent annually in the early part of this period to close to 15 per cent towards its end.[108] Partly this rate of growth is overstated because it does not take due account of the deterioration in quality of goods and of the rapid depreciation for lack of spare parts production which resulted from the tendency to measure and reward success by quantity rather than quality of output.[109] Professor Warren Nutter goes as far as suggesting that the output of food which statistically increased by some 13 per cent may have in actual fact declined. The output of some other consumer goods, textiles for example, declined even statistically. However, the production of the means of production increased very greatly, and most of all that of military equipment particularly after the rise to power of the Nazis in Germany. As in earlier periods the higher output was due to a combination of more labour employed in industry and higher *per capita* productivity. In the period following the first and second Five Year Plans, that is from 1937 to 1940, industrial growth was very much retarded,[110] although it was during the same period that the territory and the manpower of the Soviet Union were augmented. Partly this was undoubtedly the result of the great purges, which with one stroke deprived the Soviet Union of most of her most experienced leadership, and replaced it by often totally unsuitable and inexperienced graduates; and partly it was due to the diversion of more resources, including manpower to the military industry.[111] On 22 June 1941, Germany attacked the Soviet Union on a 2,000-mile front. Relentless German advances brought them to the outskirts of Moscow and Leningrad and to the banks of the Volga, causing as they advanced the almost entire destruction of the Russian economic potential this side of the Urals. The legacy of the invasion was such that it reduced output in a way that even in 1946 it fell well below what it had been in the years before the war.[112] Lend-lease shipments from the United States and reparation payments from the enemy countries, and the transfer of some assets from eastern Europe after the war, helped a little. So did the employment of prisoners of war. Yet, altogether, if measured by the volume of the destruction, and not by pre-war yearly production figures, their long-term value appears rather small.[113] By 1949 the Russian industry regained once more its pre-war level of production. Military industry was reduced and the civilian industrial sector accordingly increased. Much of the progress was due to improved technology.

In the fifth Five Year Plan (1951–55) the production of consumer goods increased more rapidly than in any of the earlier planning periods, but the output rate of all industries taken together was not as high as it had been during the second (and highest) Five Year Plan. The shift towards the production of more consumer goods was certainly appreciable during Malenkov's government but may have started earlier, even before the death of J. V. Stalin;[114] the release of more resources and labour from the military to the civilian industry was connected with the termination of the Korean hostilities. The sixth Five Year Plan was abandoned soon after it was started and replaced by a Seven Year Plan (1959–65) which stipulated a less strenuous rate of growth.[115] Since then, Soviet experts have begun to speak of diminishing returns and some have even become publicly critical of 'command planning'. Professor Yevsei Liberman, of Kharkov University,[116] for example, claimed that the Soviet economy has become far too diversified to be usefully encompassed by the old system of material balances. Other Soviet experts who are also dissatisfied with the old planning techniques put the responsibility for failures less on the old material balances than on Stalin's aversion to precise mathematical economic analyses—to 'playing with funny figures' as he called it. These economists appear to be convinced that with the aid of modern and more improved computers, planning could be more scientific, accurate, and meaningful. In addition there has been some experimentation in recent years with a partial introduction of an effective market system through which 'each firm would operate within the market and rely on the provided efficiency prices'.[117]

In summary, then, throughout the fifty years since the Revolution the Russian economy has above all concentrated upon the production of capital goods and devoted far less attention and resources to consumer goods. From time to time the production of the latter was postponed, and postponed again, so that in effect it never reached the level equal to the growth of consumers' demand and capital formation. In addition to this there were of course the major catastrophes, like World War II, which led to the physical destruction of most of what had been achieved in the 1920s and 1930s. Therefore, although the Soviet 'growth of production figures' are surprisingly high, the reality measured by the standards of living may not fully equal this height. Firstly, because it presents a statistical elusion, for the rate of growth measured in percentage and based on an early period of industrialisation is always misleading[118] (if you have one factory and you build a second you have 100 per cent increase, if you have a hundred factories and you add one, you only add 1 per cent).[119] Secondly, the gross figures sometimes hide the fact that the registration is done by the product without due recognition of quality and the availability of spare parts, etc.[120] Thirdly, and most important of all, it would be necessary to compare the rise in personal expenditure of the average Soviet family if one would want to have a true picture of the progress of the Soviet economy; that is, if one agrees that after all it is not the concern of the modern economist to record high rates of output but to stimulate a rising living standard. The Soviet Revolution took place in 1917, over fifty years ago, and it is true that World War II destroyed many of the earlier Soviet achievements; but since the war, over two decades have passed; how far, then, can the policy of reducing production costs really be assessed from the point of view of the final consumer as successful? This is one question which has never really been answered. It is particularly difficult to answer it because living standards inside the Soviet Union seem to vary so very considerably from one place to another. However, it seems fairly justified to say that, with the great means and scientific achievements and knowledge at their disposal, Russian society should by now have done better. This was, of course, recognised by the leaders of Russia, and they are taking active steps now to raise the level of consumption.

We are now faced with an interesting historical development. In the capitalist States, including the United States of America, we find an ever-growing degree of control by the government over the means of production, whereas in the socialist States we find a gradual weakening of government control over a number of production processes. In other words, it appears as if the Marxian prediction about the waning of the capitalist system, and the concentration of the means of production in the hands of the people, as represented by their governments, is coming true in the United States and in other capitalist States, while at the same time, fifty years after the Revolution, the Russian economy is beginning to reach that stage in which it is catching up with its political superstructure. It is therefore possible that the political tensions which accompanied the Stalinist era may well have been the same birth-pains, in their particular Russian form, that, in a different form, were present in the bleak ages during the industrial revolutions in England and western Europe. In conclusion, it seems true that the process of economic growth is a genetic or biological process which has its rules which cannot easily be avoided one way or the other. Once the society has reached a certain cultural standard and achieved a certain level of technology, its wants and the ability to satisfy them increase and the economy is set upon an upward path. Until this state is reached, society does not progress at an accelerated pace. It may therefore, perhaps, be said that not because of, but in spite of, Stalin's economic policies, the Russian economy managed to reach the heights that it actually did. Even if one was to adopt a more generous attitude towards Stalin's 'forced development', one would still have to ask whether the cost of this sort of development was really equal to the achievements; whether, indeed, the subjugation of the whole country to a tyrannical system of penalties was really necessary to achieve the rate of growth which might perhaps also have been achieved through the encouragement of competition.

JAPAN: INDUSTRIAL GROWTH AND INTERNATIONAL COMPETITION

Another country where the process of industrialisation was not dissimilar to that of the Soviet Union was Japan. Here, too, rapid economic progress took place within a relatively short period, i.e. in less than a century. It began in the last quarter of the nineteenth and reached full development (in the generally accepted sense) by the middle of the present century. Here, too, much of the development took place at the expense of domestic living standards;[121] and here, too, as in Russia, the gross national product increased very strikingly, while the general level of incomes and domestic consumers' demand did not advance at a similar pace. Another similarity between the two countries was that, as in Russia so in Japan, certain traditions had already developed before the great acceleration of economic progress due to which the Japanese were able to adopt quickly American and European techniques of manufacturing and to produce with highly capitalised industrial methods very soon after the beginning of the modernisation of their economy. The fast rate of population accretion helped here because the resultant low wage rates could be maintained, even though industrial employment and production was rising very rapidly. This also enabled investors to receive high profits, although they often had to sell their production at relatively very low prices. For these reasons it appears correct to assume that if the Japanese investors had been dependent on the domestic market alone growth could not have continued for long. Thus deprived of a domestic market as a result of the low wage rates, they turned abroad to the densely populated Asian mainland as the natural outlet for their produce.[122] Like England in her early days of industrialisation, Japan capitalised on the relatively enormous number of foreign consumers. This was possible because, although the individual consumer in Asia had very little to spare, the total of the many small amounts was still large enough, for a time at least, to continue the growth of Japanese production. Eventually, of course, Japanese exporters found themselves in competition with those of other countries[123] and subject to protective tariffs. The advantages of shorter transport routes and of low wages were not always large enough to outdo the quick capitalisation of industry in Europe and America. This, together with the protective tariffs imposed in some colonies, did not stop the growth of Japanese industrial production but changed the direction of her export trade.[124]

Japan, as England before her, suffered from a shortage of raw materials. In order to be able to control the necessary raw materials and to monopolise markets, Japan set out to occupy part of the Asian mainland. In 1894 she invaded Korea, which was then a dependency of the Chinese Empire. In the war that followed, Japan annexed Formosa and the Pescadores. In 1904 she attacked Russia and received Karafuto and Russia's concessions in Port Arthur and her mining rights and railroads in South Manchuria; in 1910 she finally annexed Korea; in 1915 she took Kiaochow from the Germans. In 1918 Japan was finally in full control of Shantung, Manchuria, Inner Mongolia, North Sakhalin and parts of Eastern Siberia. However, by 1925 she was forced to retreat from the Chinese and Russian territories and to adopt the 'Open Door' policy imposed upon her in the Pacific by the Americans and British. A few years later, in 1929, the world economy collapsed and with it the Japanese economy. The old aggressive forces which had lain dormant for some time found new supporters among the worried rich and hungry and jobless poor, who were told that 'If the Yamato race wishes to distinguish itself', Japan must adopt a policy of 'blood and iron'. They must first crush the great competitor—the United States—in order to be able to control China. 'But in order to conquer China', Premier Baron Tanaka had told them in 1927,[125] 'we [the Japanese] must first conquer Manchuria and Mongolia. In order to conquer the world, we must first conquer China. . . . Having China's entire resources at our disposal, we shall proceed to conquer India, Asia Minor, Central Asia, and even Europe. But to get control of Manchuria and Mongolia is the first step. . . .' In 1931 the Imperial Army seized Manchuria and was preparing the way for an attack upon the Soviet Union. After a number of unsuccessful border skirmishes it abandoned this idea and launched a full scale assault upon China. The war with China 'proved endless and hopeless'.[126] In 1940 Germany, Italy and Japan signed a treaty recognising the former two Powers' right to establish a New Order in Europe and Japan's domination of 'Greater East Asia'. The three countries also undertook to assist one another with all means at their disposal when one of them was attacked by a Power (i.e. the United States of America) not involved in the European war or in the Chinese–Japanese conflict.[127] A year later, in December 1941, Japan was at war with the countries that 'conspired' against the 'New Order in East Asia', namely, the United States, Britain and the Netherlands (government in exile). Within a year and a half of relentless advance more than 500 million people were brought under Japanese rule, but by June 1942 the tide of war began to turn, ending with Japan's total military, economic and moral collapse in 1945. With this the first phase in Japan's history of economic progress came to an end.

Summarising this phase, W. W. Lockwood writes,[128] 'that Japan's great external opportunity arose not so much from her priority in Far Eastern industrialisation, or her seizure of territory, as from the whole conjuncture of circumstances which enabled her to enter and trade peacefully in an expanding, relatively free world economy'. The 'conjuncture of circumstances' were the tremendous growth in the world's primary production and the relatively free flow of 'factory technique and capital with little political interference'. With Europe, Japan exchanged products which required cheap labour, little capital, and special skills, for certain raw materials; with the United States she maintained a very lucrative silk trade; and with the east she exchanged her industrial products for food and the raw materials to feed her industry. She had, of course, an exceptional advantage in being linked to the world by her excellent natural suitability for water transport. Her main disadvantage, according to some historians, was the political anxiety which was enhanced by the generally nationalistic aggressive climate of the thirties, and which drove the people of Japan, with those of other countries, into the arms of an economically ignorant and politically chauvinistic leadership. Whether in reality, in the face of the protectionist policies of the old colonial powers in the east, Japan was or was not left any alternative but to pursue an aggressive line, is still open to debate. William W. Lockwood, for example, appears to think that although 'the spread of economic nationalism in the thirties was putting brakes on further Japanese trade expansion for the moment, and clouding its outlook in the future . . . Japan's real economic interest could only lie in combating, not reinforcing, this inimical drift to trade restriction and bilateralism'.[129] G. C. Allen is of the view that 'during the half-century before 1937 Japan's economic expansion was unquestionably influenced by her success in war. The Sino-Japanese War of 1894–95, the Russo-Japanese War of 1904–05, the First World War and the campaigns against China in the early and middle thirties, all led to the enlargement of territory under her control and opened up opportunities for investment and trade in areas where she enjoyed special advantages. This,' Professor Allen continues,[130] 'is not to deny . . . that the real costs of preparing for, and fighting, these wars had outweighed their economic benefits, nor that the diversion of so much of Japan's energy and resources to imperialist expansion had been at the expense of economic welfare.' Whatever the area of agreement and of disagreement between these views, both accept for a fact that as long as Japan continued to base her development upon foreign trade she was bound to clash with powerful competition from some of the most developed countries. From this point of view, however, protectionist colonialism was no less aggressive than Japanese expansionism. Conquest had merely come earlier to India than to Manchuria, but the aims were the same—monopolistic control over the countries' economic potentials. Obviously, the fact that Britain already had such a monopoly and exploited it, and Japan was first to gain it, cannot be accepted as evidence for differences between the economic policies of the two countries. In fact, therefore, the choice the Japanese had to make was not between war and peace, but between war and economic stagnation and collapse. The last would probably be followed by a social revolution. In accord with the spirit of the times the rulers of Japan chose the first alternative. In the words of Professor Schuman,[131] writing about 1941, 'What choices were available to Japan's policy makers . . .? A policy of restoring and maintaining peace was not among them, for the Fascist combine of Big Business and Big Brass had brought into being an economy and a polity dependent for viability on armaments, war, and conquest.' Consequently, Japan got involved in a war with the United States of America, Britain and the Netherlands, while Hitler and Mussolini declared war on the United States. Only Russia and Japan remained at peace for the time. Now it was up to Japan to cut off China and Russia from their American and English allies. If this was possible both could be crushed and America and Britain left without the necessary support. The error in these calculations was, however, that neither Russia nor China could be conquered while America was able to pour out enormous quantities of military equipment which was more than a match for either Germany or Japan.

Defeat left Japan with no 'spheres of influence' and no investments on the continent of Asia. Moreover, her world-wide commercial network and a great part of her industry was shattered. What had remained of it was also to a great extent useless for peace-time production. Morale was low and so was the spirit of enterprise; raw materials were scarce and in most towns even food was in short supply. There was no confidence in the country's leadership and the foreign occupation forces were consciously undermining what had remained of the old social order. Paradoxically it was this utter defeat which extricated Japan from the cul-de-sac into which her pre-war leadership had led her. Without this crushing defeat it would have become almost impossible to break away from the unholy alliance of Big Capital and Brass and to find a way out of the vicious circle of economic growth leading to foreign military ventures and foreign military ventures stimulating economic growth. It would not have been possible to raise wage-rates—the effective domestic demand which was the only alternative to the old-style export orientation of production. The change in the socio-economic structure and the ensuing reorientation of production policies showed very soon their favourable results. Five years after the end of the war the gross domestic product per head of the total population had already regained its 1937 level, and two years later, in 1952, it had risen above it by no less than 19 per cent.[132] The estimated net value of manufacturing also grew from 2·75 billion dollars (at 1955 prices) in 1937 to 4 billion dollars in 1955 and to 5·84 billions in 1957;[133] whereas the consumption of manufactures per head of population was more than twice as high in 1957 than at the eve of World War II.[134] At the same time exports of manufactures were reduced by over 15 per cent between 1937 and 1955.[135] In summary, then, the post-war period in Japan was marked by a high rate of population accretion, a high rate of addition to the capital stock of the country, a high rate of growth of manufacture, and by rising living standards.[136] It further appears that by 1953 the Japanese economy had recovered and surpassed her pre-war peak years. In the decade that followed her rate of growth may well have been greater than that of West Germany, France and the Soviet Union.[137] An analysis of the estimated national income figures, given in the United Nations *Statistical Yearbook* for 1964,[138] strongly supports this possibility. If the year 1953 is taken as the index base, Japan's national income in the following decade should have increased in this manner:

NATIONAL INCOME

Year	*Index*	*Year*	*Index*	*Year*	*Index*
1953	100	1957	146	1961	243
		1958	148	1962	272
1955	116	1959	171	1963	313
1956	131	1960	204		

This trend was accompanied by increasing employment in the manufacturing and service industries, by decreasing unemployment, and by a steady reduction in working hours.[139] At the same time industrial production as a whole rose far more rapidly than employment and the production of metal products, basic metals and chemicals increased most of all.[140] However, agricultural production, food in particular, did not increase at a similar pace, though the structure and composition of food consumption shows a definite improvement.[141]

NET FOOD SUPPLIES PER CAPITA

Year	*Calories per Day* (Total)	(% of Animal origin)	*Proteins, Grammes per Day*
1948–50	1,900	4	49
1954–56	2,100	6	64
1957–59	2,220	8	68
1960–62	2,270	9	69
1962	2,280	10	70

For comparison calory and protein consumption was:

	Calories per Day (Total)	(% of Animal origin)	*Proteins, Grammes per Day*
In the United States (1962)	3,090	41	91
In Denmark (1963)	3,310	42	93
In India (1962)	2,000	6	51

Internal retail trade increased more than threefold (from 67 of the 1958 = 100 index in 1955 to 212 in 1963)[142] and foreign trade has, with no empire, grown far beyond the pre-war level.[143] It is also significant to note the change which has taken place in the direction of Japan's foreign trade since the war.[144]

POST WAR RE-DIRECTION OF FOREIGN TRADE

Japan's trade (million U.S. dollars) 1938 compared with 1963

	1938	%	*1963*	%
Total	1,110	100	5,450	100
United States	125	11·26	1,520	27·89
Latin America	14	1·26	320	5·87
Western Europe	75	6·75	710	13·04
Eastern Europe	1	0·09	181	3·32
Asia	470	42·34	1,605	29·45
China	330	29·73	70	1·28
Others	95	8·57	1,044	19·15

Finally, the rising living standards are reflected in the following comparison of earnings and prices.[145]

WAGES AND PRICES
(1958 = 100)

Year	Earnings in Manufacturing	Consumer Price Index All Items	Consumer Price Index Food
1948	23'	58	66
1955	87	97	99
1956	96	97	98
1957	100	100	101
1958	100	100	100
1959	109	101	101
1960	118	105	104
1961	129	110	111
1962	143	118	120
1963	157	127	131

How, then, did these surprising changes in the Japanese economy come about? Until the end of 1948 the country was in confusion with industry making only little progress towards recovery and the government desperately pumping 'investment' money into the economy and causing violent inflation. There was no export trade worth mentioning. It was during this period, however, that under the direction of the foreign occupation authorities the foundations for the new economic structure of Japan were laid. Firstly, tenants were given titles to their holdings which hitherto had been the property of great landlords. Secondly, a number of labour reforms broke the traditional patriarchal relationship between employers and employees. Thirdly, anti-trust laws were imposed upon industry and the old guard of economic leaders were prevented from recapturing political and economic control. Taken together these were irreversible structural changes which helped to put the country on her new course of development. Although it may be true that these reforms 'made no immediate contribution to economic recovery',[146] it is equally true that it was during this period that the new social relationships took shape which prevented the revival of the pre-war industrial growth pattern even when the Americans tried to achieve this in 1949, when a complete change took place in their Japan policies.

The immediate cause for this change in American attitudes was the Cold War and the growing strength of Communism in Asia. Further socio-political reform schemes were shelved and the reconstruction of an industry which could serve the interests of the American policy-makers was given first priority. Suddenly inflation was checked and production, which had been stagnating during the reform period (1945–49) leapt up. In the following year (1950), the war in Korea, in which Japan did not take part but merely served as the nearest industrial base behind the United Nations forces, enormously boosted industrial production. Once again,

Japan was prospering because of war and the resultant favourable export trade. In 1952, when sovereignty was restored to the Japanese, it looked as if the old system of the pre-war era was coming back 'under new (United States) management'. By 1953 industrial output rose higher than it was in 1938 and foreign trade more than doubled. Yet there was a great difference between the pre-war and post-war period in the distribution of the gains from these favourable developments. In fact, the old alliance between big capital and the military could not be revived. This was so not only because the latter had been very much discredited by the defeat but also because the Americans, though able to rely upon the capitalists' anti-communism, had less confidence in the military who might or might not change their allegiances at will. This deprived capital of its 'patriotic' hegemony and of its actual control over the means of coercion. At the same time the workers themselves had gained a much greater degree of self-confidence and of actual bargaining power as a result of the early post-war period of socio-political reforms. Thus, while Japan's share in production for the supply of the United Nations Force in Korea increased, her own military expenditure remained small; and when, after the termination of hostilities, the Americans continued to maintain bases in Japan, they brought in a considerable additional income. It is true that the end of the Korean War brought with it a recession, but it was very short and was followed in 1955 to 1957 by a rise in production which was even sharper than the one of the war boom. The most significant facts, however, in this period, were the rise of incomes, which rose much more than prices, and the growth of the domestic consumers' market and of the natural foreign trade which began to replace the artificial stimuli for production of the earlier years. The most important industrial reforms which survived the restoration of sovereignty, and formed the basis for the re-distribution of the national income, were the creation of a trade union movement, and the considerable body of labour legislation.[147] Most persistent among the latter was the workers' right to organise, to bargain collectively, and to strike, and the employers' obligation to recognise the unions and to introduce certain welfare provisions, including a strict regulation of the length of working days.

According to Professor G. C. Allen[148] 'the result was startling. The number of trade unionists rose from none at the end of the war to nearly 6¾ million in 1948, and the unions quickly launched themselves on a career of militant activity which SCAP[149] soon had to restrain in the interest of economic efficiency.' However, with the change in American policy, in 1949, many of the legally sanctioned improvements were modified; and with the re-emergence of the old guard of Japanese industrialists during and after the Korean War the position of the unions became more and more difficult. But, the chance of relegating labour to its pre-war status seems to have passed for ever.[150] Of more lasting importance were the achievements of SCAP in the rural communities. As the tenant farmers were buying their farms from the great landlords, paying for them in instalments over a number of years, their debts were almost entirely wiped out by inflation. Consequently, by 1949 Japan had become a country of well-established peasant proprietors, and little was left of the traditional great landlordism. Unlike the industrial workers' unions, the farmers' unions gained considerably from the Korean War boom. It not only reduced the surplus of farm labour but greatly raised food prices; the former deficiency was rapidly made good by the introduction of modern farm equipment, while the latter advantage encouraged very considerable improvements in the exploitation of the land, such as the wider use of fertilisers and the more selective growing of crops.

In summary, then, the Allied occupation put Japan's economy on a completely new footing. On the one hand, the occupation changed certain traditions and social patterns and helped to organise labour so that it could take a share in the profits made by industry, and consequently created a growing domestic market; on the other hand, it deprived the Japanese economy of her pre-war markets and sources of raw materials. These losses were, however, mitigated; during the first post-war years by the great need for production to make good the damage done to the country in the course of the hostilities, and in the years that followed by renewed war production to supply the United Nations forces in Korea. Finally, when the Korean War came to its end, the Japanese economy had already gained so much impetus, and its domestic demand had already grown so far, that growth continued in the normal capitalistic pattern. In this Japan was aided by the general prosperity of the 1950s, in which she shared with most other capitalist countries of the world. Essentially, however, the history of Japan's economic progress does not very much differ from that of the Soviet Union. The difference between the two was that in the Soviet Union the people were forced by political power to 'tighten their belts' as part of a deliberate design of building a better future; and that in pre-World War II Japan, the political power was not needed to coerce the population to retain its low living standard because the Japanese had not yet had their social revolution. In addition, economic development in Japan was rather the consequence than the cause of political developments, while in the Soviet Union all policy decisions were at least in theory aimed at promoting economic growth.

ISRAEL: A SPECIAL CASE

It is also interesting to note how Palestine, later Israel, was rapidly transformed from a backward area with a colonial economy into a modern one with a well-developed economic structure. Here some unique factors coincided and produced a particular pattern of development. Firstly, there were the immediate requirements of World War II, namely the fact that British forces had to be maintained in the Middle East to fight the Italian and German armies which were attacking Egypt from Libya. As these forces had to be supplied and the routes of communication with the rest of the British Empire were under heavy threats from the enemy, Britain was less insistent in the early forties than in normal times upon her traditional colonial policy of preventing the growth of industry in Palestine. For a short time Britain was even forced to encourage it. Secondly, the great inflow of European Jews before, and particularly soon after the war, brought into the country an educated population with cultural patterns akin to those of the industrially developed countries. Thirdly, there was a continuous inflow of capital, first from generous contributions from Jews all over the world, and particularly from American Jews, and later from German reparation payments. Thus, in the case of Israel, there was a stimulating combination of a population with a suitable attitude to industrial development and with the necessary technical education, together with a great inflow of capital from outside sources. In fact, it may be correct to say that, rather than an indigenous process of natural growth, it was a direct transfer of people and capital to Palestine, and Israel, which was the source of its industrialisation. In this sense Israel is similar to Australia, New Zealand and other settlements, where Europeans settled and continued their European way of life. It has also much in common with the European settlement in North America, differing from it only in so far as the process in Israel took less time than in the United States and in that the Israelis had at their disposal all the technological and scientific knowledge gathered since the days of American colonisation. Moreover, the Jewish community, being used to a European living standard, soon organised its trade union movement and defended its high level of income and expenditure. Sometimes this led to the unpleasant result of cheap Arab labour being excluded from Jewish working places, but at the same time it prevented the development of a South African economy where the new immigrants became an upper class and the non-European population was relegated to the manual and badly paid jobs. The high wage rates in the Jewish sector and the high rate of industrial efficiency which resulted from the level of education and technical knowledge, which the immigrants had brought with them from Europe, supported each other and created the necessary closed circle of economic growth. The influx of Jews into Palestine which continued for over a decade[151] kept both demand and industrial production at a rising level. At the same time it was the influx of unearned capital from abroad which helped the growing economy to overcome certain of its initial capital difficulties which were bound to arise from the disproportion between population accretion, colonial manipulations, and the accelerated rate of economic growth.[152]

The fact which to the student of economic progress appears to be of particular interest about Israel is that until fairly recently her economy was neither socialist nor really capitalist in the accepted sense of these terms.[153] Moreover, even today, after two decades of outstanding economic progress following her attainment of independence in 1948, the Israeli economy still displays some characteristic features of a typically colonial economy. The most obvious of these are the relative weakness of her privately owned productive sector and its concentration in the light and consumer goods industries; and the predominant position of the unproductive elements who do not reinvest their profits in the producing sectors of the economy, but engage in finance and commerce, and whose affluence continues to be guaranteed, as it is in colonies, by favourable credit, tax, foreign-exchange, and trade laws.[154] Together with these colonial features, the Israeli economy also exhibits a great many characteristics inherent in a highly developed capitalist structure. These are the progressive social organisation, the relatively high rate of mechanisation in both industry and agriculture, and consequently also the relatively high rate of productivity[155] and a very well-developed education and health service, a reasonably good system of social security, and a developed pattern of consumption.[156] In addition, the Israeli economy has a high rate of development investment from abroad.

Yet, side by side with these colonial and capitalist features, there are some distinctive socialist characteristics in the Israeli economy. These are to be found in the public and co-operative sectors. The public sector includes State enterprises, enterprises owned or controlled by municipalities, by the Federation of Labour and by the Jewish Agency. This sector 'embraces enterprises, services and institutions which are owned by all the citizens collectively or by a large part of them organised in a collective framework. The profits obtained by these enterprises belong to the public and are utilised for the public benefit, according to the understanding and decisions of the authorities in charge of their management.'[157] The cooperative sector 'includes enterprises which are owned by the workers in these enterprises, such as producers' co-operatives, or institutions and services belonging to members. These are organised for mutual aid in the fulfilment of definite economic needs, such as consumers' co-operatives, credit unions and co-operative housing projects.'[158] The essential point about these two socialised sectors, and particularly about the former, is that although, like the capitalist sector, they are designed to make profits, profits are not their only raison d'être and not the main factor in making investment decisions.

The true significance of this national sector comes to light from the fact that, for example in 1953, it produced and owned no less than 47·7 per cent of the total net national product of the country and 80 per cent of all the land fit for cultivation, and contributed close to 75 per cent to all new investment.

The organisations which together make up this national sector are, firstly, the Jewish Agency which uses mainly funds collected as voluntary contributions from Jews all over the world. This organisation finances the transportation of immigrants and their settlement as farmers. It also has a share in the greatest irrigation company in Israel, and in the national air and shipping companies, and in a number of investment banks. In addition the Jewish Agency owns 40 per cent of all the country's farming land,[159] which is leased to farmers at the nominal rent of approximately 1 per cent of his average earnings. During the first ten years of Israeli independence this organisation financed 42 per cent of all investment in agriculture and established close to 550 new agricultural settlements. Secondly, there are the Israeli government enterprises. These include, in addition to the usual State responsibilities such as the post office, harbour and airport authorities, etc., the railways, the water supply, a number of formidable housing companies, electricity, and mineral extraction. The government further owns 40 per cent of all the country's arable land[160] and provides about half of the country's investment funds out of its special development budget. In addition, the State owns a number of development companies, the greater part of the military industry, and a considerable part of a great number of other enterprises, such as chemical and fertiliser industries, etc. The true significance of this sector may be estimated from the fact that almost 70 per cent of the workers employed by the State-owned companies are engaged in basic industries. There is, thirdly, the General Federation of Jewish Labour (*Histadrut*), which uses members' dues and the profits from its own enterprises. This union, with its membership of more than a quarter of the total population of the country, and more than three-quarters of the country's entire labour force, has, since its foundation in 1920, not only carried out the normal union tasks of protecting workingmen's interests but 'has been inspired by the aim to sidestep the stage of capitalist development by means of the immediate realisation of the establishment of a Socialist Workers Society, composed of the workers' collectives in the different branches of the economy'.[161] In this respect the influence of the *Histadrut* comes from two sources: from its directly owned enterprises, which are mostly concentrated in basic industries, construction, irrigation, transport and finance; and from the co-operatives, which are owned by their members but form an integral part of the *Histadrut's* central co-operative organisation. These are in agriculture, the collectives (*Kibbutzim*) and the smallholders' co-operatives (*Moshavim*), and in manufacture and services, a number of consumers', producers', transport and banking co-operatives. All the activities of this sector, which in essence is the only truly labour-controlled part of the Israeli economy (because a change of government may, of course, lead to a 'denationalisation' of the State enterprises but cannot directly affect these), are directed by the 'roof organisation' of the *Histadrut*, the Worker's Society (*Hevrat Ovdim*), whose management is elected by the General Convention of the *Histadrut* for the purpose of formulating the policies and co-ordinating the activities of the various enterprises and sections of the movement 'in accordance with the aims of the Workers' Society and for the safeguarding of its co-operative character'.[162] As a rule one of these aims has always been the development of the country's economy. The share of the *Histadrut* in Israel's net national product, in 1953 for example, amounted to 21·5 per cent, of which 7·9 per cent came from the directly owned part and 13·6 per cent from that of the co-operatives. Yet again, the real weight of this sector is much greater than its percentage share. According to the evidence collected by Dr. Darin-Drabkin for the year 1956,[163] the percentage of workers employed in *Histadrut* enterprises, compared to the whole labour force, was a follows: in agriculture 73 per cent, in industry (including mining) 17 per cent, in construction 33 per cent, in transport 28 per cent, and in commerce, finance and other services 12 per cent. Altogether, 24 per cent of all those employed in Israel worked within the *Histadrut* sector. Moreover, the economic strength of the General Federation of Jewish Labour goes much further than its actual control over resources and establishments for the following reasons. It has the direct control over most of the national labour force in its capacity as trade union. It has so great a share in the total employment of labour that it can indirectly influence wage rates in the private sector, particularly in times of prosperity. It has accumulated so much capital that, at least in some trades, it can set the pace of efficiency for the private entrepreneurs if they hope to be competitive. And finally, it had for a long time a considerable moral ascendancy over the private sector in the eyes of the working class and the national middle class because of its tremendous contribution to the reconstruction of the country and the attainment and defence of her national independence. The main weakness of this sector, however, which arose much more recently, is that it has begun to suffer from the same illnesses of many other nationalised industries elsewhere, namely from less keen cost accounting and unnecessary inflation of its administration and other overheads. This is due to the fact that since independence this sector has been under less strain from competition or from hostile State policies, because the same political party (*Mapai*) which dominates the Federation of Labour has also been continuously the major partner in each coalition government in Israel.

Historically it was this sector that was decisive for the foundation of Israeli economic development and national independence. Neither the colonial government, with its traditional economic policies, nor the bourgeoisie, were willing or able to industrialise the country and give the Jewish community its territorial basis. Why the British Mandatory Government[164] was unwilling to help the industrialisation of Palestine is obvious and does not require further explanation here;[165] the reasons for the inability of private capital to fulfil the 'historical tasks of capitalism' are more complex. Firstly, without at least some degree of assistance from the State, it has always been difficult to nurse into life an industry and it was even more so in the face of a hostile government which could and did use its legal and administrative powers to discourage it, while encouraging one-crop-export-farming, primary production, money lending and commerce. Secondly, as Palestine is poor in national resources, there were few objective advantages in the establishment of industries there from the point of view of profitability.[166] Thirdly, as the object of capitalist production is above all profit, there is of course always a tendency for capital to flow where profits are highest, and in underdeveloped countries where they can be made in the shortest possible period. For these reasons, too, private capital in Palestine shied away from basic and long-term investments and was inclined to react violently to many sporadic changes in the demand on the world markets.[167] Fifthly, private agricultural capital was also affected by the same conditions and motives as industrial capital, and consequently concentrated in plantations for export crops, particularly citrus-fruit, and in land speculations.

The position of the labour-owned sector of the economy was very different. Here for the sector as a whole investment decisions were taken by the political leadership of the Workers' Society (*Hevrat Ovdim*), whose main objectives were national and social, whereas the direction of the individual establishments was strictly in accordance with the criteria of cost accounting and profitability. Thus, while the political management made sure that workers' enterprises were established where they were most necessary for the development of the country, and where private capital was neither able nor willing to take the risk, the management of each individual firm was forced to maximise efficiency of production in order to be equal to the hostile conditions, and, in a number of cases, to foreign and private competition. In the general atmosphere of rising Jewish nationalism, which combined in Palestine with the socialist aspirations of a great part of the earlier immigrants from eastern Europe, this bred a particular kind of dynamic leadership with a high sense of national and social responsibility which was invaluable to the whole process of development. In agriculture the tasks of the Workers' Society were not very different. As much of the land was not really suitable for immediate profitable cultivation, and therefore unattractive to the ordinary farmer; and as at the same time the leadership of the Jewish labour movement was aware that only the actual settlement of the land could establish the de facto ownership and frontiers of the National Home, they pursued a deliberate settlement and investment policy which was reinforced by long-term loans and irrigation projects often financed by the Jewish Agency, in all areas which appeared to them to be of strategic value.[168] Finally, it was also this sector which had the greater share in the maintenance and equipment of the Israeli defence force and its military industry during its period of illegality before the departure of the British.

Yet with all this it is not really correct to call this sector the basis of a socialist economy. At its best it is merely a labour-owned sector within a capitalist economy which is linked to, and dependent upon, the western world. Like any other big and powerful trust, its enterprises are subject to the ebb and flow of the economic fortunes of the rest of the capitalist world.

The attainment of independence brought new problems and new dangers to the existence and progressive role of this sector. Throughout the colonial period it had been the only economic factor able to combat effectively the various restrictions the British Government placed in the way of Jewish aspirations. On the one hand, this reduced the opposition of the private sector to its growth, and on the other hand, it earned its wide popular support from both workers and members of the nationalist middle class. In other words, there was no real contradiction between the requirements of national private capital and the growth of workers' economic combines.

By 1949 this 'honeymoon' between capital and labour was rapidly coming to an end. The Israeli working class was ill equipped for the class struggle that followed. The workers organised in the General Federation of Jewish Labour had grown in an atmosphere of national construction and had developed a tradition of constructivism. They were more experienced in evading the punches of colonialism than in industrial battles, they were more attuned to the construction of socialism than to the usual practices of the class struggle. These legacies deeply impressed themselves upon the nature of the class struggle which therefore only gradually began to assume more conventional forms after independence.

Capitalism in Israel was hostile to the workers' economic sector (*Histadrut*) not only because of the support it could lend to the workers in their struggles for higher wages and better working conditions, but also because of the differences between the economic policies which were suitable for the prosperity of commerce and banking in the private sector and for its foreign partners, and the policies which favour the productive national capital of which the workers owned the greater share. However, as the workers' enterprises were functioning within a capitalist framework this sector was wide open to grave dangers from both internal and external sources. From inside, the main risks arose out of the contradictions between the day-to-day requirements of the workers in matters concerning wage rates and working conditions etc. on the one hand, and the needs of the establishments which had of necessity to engage in capitalistic competition on the other.[169] In addition, not unlike the process which took place in the communist countries, there also arose in the Israeli socialist sector a considerable antagonism between the management—which was rapidly turning itself into a class, and as such, progressively assimilating itself to its capitalist counterparts—and the workers, who were gradually developing an attitude of growing suspicion towards both. In fact, less than a decade after the termination of the British Mandate in Palestine, it became difficult to distinguish the capitalist employers and their imitators from the managerial strata of the *Histadrut* sector. Unfortunately, therefore, the workers' economic sector was no longer able to continue its constructive role in the development of the country in the same way as it had done during the colonial rule. It was unable to regenerate itself as its leadership, the managerial labour bureaucracy, was able, due to the enormous funds at its disposal, to free itself from almost all supervision. The fact that the political leadership of the country was in the hands of the same party which created and upheld this bureaucracy further encouraged these tendencies. Even in their capacity as trade union officials they became more and more concerned with the execution of government policies, usually presented as national emergency measures, then with normal trade union responsibilities.[170] The reason why the Israeli working class was, and still is, putting up with this kind of workers' representation is partly due to the relatively high incomes of most of the organised workers,[171] but its main cause still remains the Israeli workers' constructive traditions and powerful nationalism.[172] It is, of course, a fact that the State of Israel is surrounded by Arab States which made it their official policy to prepare for its destruction, and that as long as this situation remains as it is the nationalist element will continue to outbalance the class conscious element in the Israeli working class. However, even more important than nationalism is the legacy of pre-independence constructivism. The same constructive contribution which had made the working class into the real creator of the State and had given it its economic potential that prevented both colonialists and local capitalists from reducing Jewish labour to the low standard of living common in colonial and pre-industrial countries, became with the attainment of independence its Achilles heel. The feeling of responsibility towards its creation, the national industry and the new State, made the Israeli working class unfit during a long period to engage in the normal methods of class struggle. Had it not been for the great influx of capital from abroad, this truce could not have lasted as long as it did. Thus the economic growth of Israel was neither the result of socialist planning nor of capitalist competition. In the words of David Horowitz:[173] 'The central feature of the development of Israel is that whole communities have been transplanted to, and established in, the country, with all the prerequisites of capital, manpower and skill as well as puchasing power for the creation of an internal market, which are necessary for such resettlement. The various elements of economic growth, the dynamic reaction of the economic structure of the immigration country to the process of migration, released new economic forces. The settlement of Israel was therefore not a colonisation venture following the traditional pattern of production of primary commodities for the world market. It was a transplantation of population, a transfer in sudden, large, wavelike motions of an immigrant population possessing the prerequisites of skill and capital and automatically providing its own internal market. This rapid movement of people within a short period of time constituted an artificial non-economic driving power.'

JEWISH IMMIGRATION AND TOTAL POPULATION OF ISRAEL AT END OF YEAR—1948–64

Year	*Immigration*	*Total*
1948	101,828	879,000
1949	239,576	1,173,871
1950	170,249	1,370,094
1951	175,095	1,577,825
1952	24,369	1,629,519
1953	11,326	1,669,417
1954	18,370	1,717,814
1955	37,478	1,789,075
1956	56,234	1,872,390
1957	71,224	1,975,954
1958	27,082	2,031,072
1959	23,895	2,088,685
1960	24,510	2,150,400
1961	47,638	2,234,200
1962	61,328	2,331,800
1963	64,364	2,430,100
1964	54,716	2,525,600

NOTES

1. *Vide* W. A. Cole and Phyllis Deane in *The Cambridge Economic History of Europe*, Vol. VI, Pt. I, Ch. I, Cambridge, 1965; Colin Clark, *The Conditions of Economic Progress*, London, 1960, p. 201 and Chs. III–VI; W. Arthur Lewis, *Economic Survey 1919–1939*, London, 1960, Statistical Appendix, Table XVI, p. 203; Alfred Maizels, *Industrial Growth and World Trade*, Cambridge, 1963, Appendix E, p. 537, Table E4. Alfred Maizels' estimates of the rise in the net value of manufacturing production per head of total population, in dollars at 1955 prices, between 1899 and 1957, were (in selected countries) as follows:

Country	*1899*	*1913*	*1929*	*1937*	*1950*	*1955*	*1957*
Belgium-Luxemburg	170	240	315	310	355	460	485
France	100	165	215	190	210	265	325
Germany	125	180	205	245			
West Germany				275	230	405	450
Italy	40	65	85	90	100	150	170
Netherlands		105	155	145	205	270	280
United Kingdom	175	200	230	295	380	460	455
United States	175	245	380	370	605	695	695
Japan	10	10	25	40	20	45	65
India	1	2	3	4	6	7	8
Pakistan					2	5	6
Nigeria						2	

As defined by Alfred Maizels, *op. cit.*, the industrial countries 'contained 28 per cent of the total population of the world outside the Soviet countries in 1959, but consumed about 82 per cent of all non-food manufactures in that year'. P. 23.

2. Colin Clark demonstrates this rise in his Table VIII, I.U. of Net Income Produced per Man-Hour in Manufacturing, in *The Conditions of Economic Progress*, 3rd edition, p. 336.

Year	*U.S.A.*	*U.K.*	*France*	*Denmark*	*Japan*	*Sweden*
1913	·445	·177	·180	·376	·137	
1920–24	·622	·293	·180		·172	·418
1925–29	·760		·235	·512	·236	·484
1930–34	·911	·327	·253	·620	·289	·585
1935–38	1·029	·344	·305	·648	·286	·675
1948	1·308	·377	·277	·532	·172	·820
1950	1·404	·412	·296	·575	·236	·879
1952	1·429	·409	·342	·561	·321	·909
1953	1·493	·421	·337	·566	·362	·945

3. World production of plastic materials, for example, rose from 1,349,000 metric tons in 1950, to 5,133,000 metric tons in 1959, and of chemical fertilisers from 8,002,000 in 1937–39 to 22,980,000 metric tons in 1958–59. *Vide* Alfred Maizels, *op. cit.*, Table 11.10, Production and trade of industrial countries in plastic materials, p. 300, and Table 11.11, World production, consumption and trade in chemical fertilisers, p. 301. During the last three decades the supply of the traditional chemicals (i.e. the organic and inorganic chemicals, the medical and pharmaceutical preparations, the fertilisers, the early plastics, pigments, paints, perfumery, cosmetics, soap, coal, tar, dyestuffs, tanning extracts, oils and explosives), which had all been known on the eve of World War I, were further supplemented by a great number and volume of new chemicals, particularly by antibiotics, sulphonamides, hormones, vitamins, tetra-ethyl lead, synthetic detergents and the very many new plastic materials. According to Alfred Maizels, *op. cit.*, p. 299, 'Chemicals which can readily be identified as technically new products developed during, or since, the last war accounted for 20 per cent of world trade in chemicals in 1955, 22 per cent in 1957 and 24 per cent in 1959. . . . Of these, plastic materials have grown most rapidly in recent years, followed closely by synthetic detergents, though the latter are much smaller in total value.' The production of other materials on which man could spend his new won time was, of course, also very impressive. World production of cement, for example, increased from 81,000,000 metric tons in 1937 to 292,000,000 in 1959. (*Vide* Alfred Maizels, *op. cit.*, Table 14.7, p. 381.)

4. For example Colin Clark, *op. cit.*, p. 127, quotes the following table of Average Hours per Day, calculated from Returns of 'Conseils de Prud'hommes' for Paris and France:

	Paris		*Rest of France*	
Year	*Males*	*Females*	*Males*	*Females*
1896	9·5	10·0	10·4	10·2
1901	9·8	10·5	10·3	10·3
1911	9·7	11·7	10·5	9·9
1921	8·6	9·9	8·2	8·1
1930	8·7		8·2	8·2

In the United States the average weekly hours of employment fell from about 60 in 1900 to 35 in 1960, while productivity rose from about 100 cents per man-hour in 1900 to almost 270 in 1960. (*Vide* J. F. Dewhurst and Associates, *America's Needs and Resources*, New York, 1955, and United Nations Yearbook. See also John W. Kendrick, *Productivity Trends in the U.S.*, New York, National Bureau of Economic Research, 1960.) In Britain the average hours worked weekly in all industries rose from 45·6 in 1950 to 46·3 in 1959. (*Annual Abstract of Statistics*, No. 96, 1959, London, H.M.S.O.) For other countries, see *Annuaire Statistique* of the United Nations Table of Manpower. Hours of Work. Note also the rising share of the service industries in the total of the gainfully employed population.

5. For an excellent account of capital formation, see National Bureau of Economic Research, New York, *Capital Formation and Economic Growth*, A Conference, Princeton, 1955. Note particularly contributions by Professor Bert F. Hoselitz and Professor Thomas C. Cochran.

6. See 'Technical Change and Capital Formation', by Abbott Payson Usher, and 'Innovation and Capital Formation in Some American Industries', by W. Rupert Maclaurin. Both in *Capital Formation and Economic Growth*, Princeton, 1955, National Bureau of Economic Research, New York.

7. Initially the adjustment problem was probably settled empirically. When, however, substantial progress in book-keeping was made, and when cost accounting became detailed enough to show the particular bottlenecks of high production costs, the organisation problem too was gradually being treated more and more systematically. The earliest progress of this kind took place in the United States, where labour costs had always been high, and in Europe, in periods of particular scarcity, as, for example, in times of war. One pioneer in this field was F. W. Taylor, who recognised how much of the average labourer's working time was wasted through faulty managerial arrangements and lack of workers' enthusiasm for exerting themselves to enrich their 'betters'. He suggested that employers should plan each worker's daily tasks in advance so that he be given exact instructions regarding the work he ought to do and the method he was to employ by the beginning of each day. This gave the employer the opportunity to assess the precise time which was to be allowed for each task or unit of produce, so that by the end of the day he was able either to reward the worker by a bonus for doing more than the expected average or penalise him by short pay for not having fulfilled the quota. (This method, under the name of 'Stachanovite Work', is still widely applied in the Soviet Union, where workers are also given medals as a reward for outstanding performance.) The details into which Taylor went, to assess what he considered a fair day's work, were such that they required the study of the relative advantages of tools for different though superficially similar tasks. Other pioneers in this field, also in the United States, were F. B. Gilbreth and H. L. Gantt. The former is now recognised as the father of 'time and motion study', and the latter as the initiator of the modern bonus and promotion system. A more systematic 'all round' approach to the problem of industrial organisation came from France. There, Henri Fayol, as general manager of a large coal combine (1888–1918), devised the first centrally directed enterprise which was only surpassed in its detailed planning and control, in the United States, by Henry Ford's great motor-car industry. Altogether, however, to this very day, most of the scientifically managed businesses are the large-scale enterprises, while in the smaller establishments only such improvements have been introduced as were coincidental to the requirements of the mechanical equipment. The trend, however, is towards the larger kind of establishments. For a brief summary of management see William Ashworth, *The International Economy Since 1850*, 2nd edition, pp. 83–84; for a more detailed discussion, see L. Urwich and E. F. L. Brech, *The Making of Scientific Management*, Vol. I–III, London, 1945–48.

8. See, for examples, *Report of the Federal Trade Commission on Changes in the Concentration in Manufacturing, 1935 to 1947 and 1950*, Washington, 1954. This is also illustrated by Alfred Maizels, *op. cit.*, Table 4·1, p. 80. World trends in population, production and trade, 1876–1959. (Index numbers, 1913=100.)

		Production		*Trade Volume*	
Year	*Population*	*Manufactures*	*Primary Produce*	*Manufactures*	*Primary Produce*
1876–1880	79	25		31	31
1896–1900	90	54	76	54	62
1911–13	99	95	93	94	97
1926–30	111	141	123	113	123
1936–38	124	158	135	100	125
1948–50	145	238	156	132	116
1954–56	158	341	191	216	156
1957–59	166	381	203	251	182

According to the United Nations *Statistical Yearbook* for 1964, Table 162, Trends in world trade since 1938 compared with trends in population and production, the volume of exports grew as follows (Index 1958 = 100).

	1938	*1948*	*1955*	*1958*	*1960*	*1962*	*1963*
All commodities	57	55	89	100	118	131	141
Food and raw materials	83	66	90	100	119	125	132
Fuel	41	49	89	100	111	130	142
Manufactures	42	50	86	100	122	137	147

9. He may, of course, also resort to monopolistic agreements and price-fixing with other producers, and thus compensate himself for the higher labour cost through higher prices, but this is in practice only possible in a minority of cases. In some countries, and at various times, employers were, however, able to suppress the labour movements through gaining political control over the governments, or by diverting workers' attention away from their economic interests. So far, however, these 'successes' were never entirely successful and long lasting.

10. For the history of the early struggle, see the brief but very useful summaries in H. Hearder, *Europe in the Nineteenth Century 1830–1880*, London, 1966, pp. 121–132; Ch. Seignobos, *Histoire Politique de L'Europe Contemporaine 1814–1896*, Paris, 1908, pp. 44–60. (For later period, see next footnote.)

11. For the history of the labour movement, *vide* S. and B. Webb, *The History of Trade Unionism*, London, 1920; W. A. McConacha, *Development of the Labour Movement in Great Britain, France, and Germany*, Chapel Hill, 1942; E. H. Phelps Brown, *The Growth of British Industrial Relations*, London, 1959; P. S. Foner, *History of the labour Movement in the United States*, New York, 1947–55.

12. See further discussion of this period in Japan and the U.S.A. on pp. 229–233 and 204–217.

13. 'Economical' here means the relationship between the wage packet expenditure and the cost of the required machines. It is significant to note that in this connection the cost of the machine depends upon the current rates of interest on loan capital and on the specific rates of depreciation. *Vide* Joel Dean, *Managerial Economics*, New York, 1951, Chapter 10, Capital Budgeting, pp. 551–610.

14. See J. Henry Richardson, *An Introduction to the Study of Industrial Relations*, London, 1954, pp. 83–136, or Sidney Pollard, *The Development of the British Economy 1914–1950*, London, 1962, pp. 289 and 290. In the United States, in 1959, the distribution of the National Income (at factor cost) was: from wages and salaries 258·2 billion dollars, and from supplements (of this welfare kind) 19·6 billion dollars (together this makes 69·6 per cent of the total national product). *Vide United States Department of Commerce, Survey of Current Business*, July 1960. Contributions for social insurance in the United States increased from 0·2 billion dollars in 1929 to 2 billion dollars in 1938, to 5·2 billion dollars in 1948, to 14·5 in 1957, and to 17·3 billions in 1959. In Britain both employers and employees do as a rule contribute to the insurance schemes. The total incomes under the National Insurance Acts from employed, self-employed and non-employed contributors were as follows (in millions of pounds): 1951, 23·96; 1952, 23·96; 1953, 24·04; and 1958, 24·54. Out of this more than 19·00 million pounds were paid annually in the same years as unemployment benefit. See *Annual Abstract of Statistics*.

15. The *politically* progressive element was liberalism, and the *socially* progressive element was individualism. The past tense (was) is used here advisedly because, since the beginning of the Cold War, very little but lip-service to liberalism and respect for the rights of individuals has survived.

16. *Vide* Alfred Maizels, *op. cit.*, Tables A.I and A.II, Exports from industrial countries, pp. 426–428; and Phyllis Deane, *The First Industrial Revolution*, Cambridge, 1965, pp. 51–68; Arthur Birnie, *An Economic History of Europe*, London, 1930, 1964 edition, p. 272; and A. J. Youngson in H. J. Habakkuk and M. Postan, Eds., *The Cambridge Economic History of Europe*, pp. 170, etc.

17. See a more detailed account of the progress of the Japanese economy on pp. 183–185.

18. Consequently it raised domestic demand, not only directly through the greater share of the national product which workers managed to secure, but also through the rise in the labour requirements in the capital producing sector of the economy, and at times through a fall in prices when colonial markets were unable to absorb all exports.

19. For fuller discussion of this period see pp. 102–103.

20. Immigration is of particular importance, because it not only increased the demand for goods, but also helped to prevent too steep a rise in wage rates which might have disrupted the smooth course of the economy.

21. See Alfred Maizels, *op. cit.*, p. 178, Table 7.12, Changes in 'imports' of manufactures into industrial and semi-industrial countries and the rest of the world by major commodity group, 1899–1959. $ billion at 1955 prices. (Totals)

Years	*Industrial Countries*	*Semi-indust. Countries*	*Rest of World*	*Total*
1899–1929	+ 6·18	+3·13	+4·61	+13·92
1929–59	+11·33	+1·61	+6·62	+19·56

22. See Alfred Maizels, *op. cit.*, p. 435, Appendix A, Table A6, Exports of Manufactures . . . at constant prices. $ millions.

Values at 1913 prices			*Values at 1955 prices*				
1899	*1913*	*1929*	*1929*	*1937*	*1950*	*1955*	*1957*
61	153	330	759	1890	816	1748	2482

23. See G. C. Allen, *A Short Economic History of Modern Japan*, 2nd edition, London, 1962, p. 218, Table XXVII, The Volume of Foreign Trade, 1873–1937 (1913 = 100). See particularly column Terms of Trade. The persistent fall from 1932 onwards. See a more detailed discussion of Japan, pp. 229–233.

24. Wlodzimierz Brus (University of Warsaw), 'Problems of Economic Incentives in Technical Progress in a Socialist Economy', *Co-Existence*, Vol. 3, No. 2, July 1966, p. 138.

25. See more detailed discussion on pp. 217–229.

26. This problem was again made abundantly clear by the contributors to the United Nations Seminar on Planning Techniques for participants from Asia, Africa and Latin America in Moscow in July 1964. The papers of the contributors were published by the U.S.S.R. Academy of Sciences in 1964. K. N. Plotnikov, *The Political and Economic Basis for Planning National Economy*; N. M. Oznobin, *The Basic Principles and Methods of Long-term Planning in the USSR;* L. Volodarsky, *Planning and Statistics*; B. C. Urlanis, *Demographic Factors and Planning of Economic Development*; A. I. Notkin,

Planning of Rates and Proportions of National Economy Development (From the Experience of Socialist Countries); V. S. Nemchinov, *Models in National Economic Planning* (Modelling of Economic Processes); M. Y. Sonin, *Manpower Balance in the USSR*; Y. I. Koldomasov, *Material Balances*, System and Classification of Material (natural) Balances; G. F. Dundukov, *Financial Balance*; M. L. Terentyev, S. S. Shatalin, L. Y. Mints, Y. Y. Finkelschtein, and others.

27. American wages were continually rising in terms of their purchasing power since the late 1860s. See *Statistical Abstract*, 1899, p. 92.

28. See Y. S. Brenner, *Theories of Economic Development and Growth*, London, 1966, Ch. I, for Mercantilist attitudes.

29. See W. G. Hoffmann, *British Industry 1700–1950*, Oxford, 1955; and E. H. Phelps Brown and Sheila V. Hopkins, 'Seven Centuries of Building Wages', *Economica*, November 1956, and 'Seven Centuries of Prices of Consumables, etc.', *Economica*, August 1955.

30. It is on this point that the present author disagrees most strongly with Professor W. W. Rostow's theory about the 'break-through', and with the late Josef Stalin's theory of the preferential treatment of industry at the expense of agriculture. See Y. S. Brenner, *op. cit.*, pp. 165–174 and 223–247.

31. These short-term problems are discussed in connection with individual countries.

32. For example, the Gross National Income in the United States (in billions of dollars) was divided as follows (United States Department of Commerce, *National Income*, 1954, and *Income and Output*, 1959, in rounded figures).

	Year				
	1929	*1938*	*1948*	*1958*	*1959*
Disposable Personal Income	83·1	65·7	189·3	317·9	337·3
Disposable Business Income	11·5	8·3	26·6	44·6	50·5
Disposable Government Income	10·4	12·6	44·4	83·4	96·1

33. G. H. Sabine, in his *History of Political Theory*, 2nd edition, London, 1951, gives a good description of these efforts in his chapter on Fascism.

34. This point of view was well expressed in the famous remark that 'what is good for General Motors is good for the American people'.

35. See pp. 171–176.

36. With the exception of a number of industries in which they had a natural advantage. For example, meat packing.

37. The tariffs had initially been introduced as a mere temporary measure during the Civil War.

38. Until the 1930s this policy was fairly successful.

39. *Twelfth Census of the United States*, VII, lvii (quoted from Harold Underwood Faulkner, *American Economic History*, 8th edition, New York, Evanston and London, 1964, p. 398).

40. For illustrations, *vide Preliminary Report of the Industrial Commission of 1899*. For example, competition between rail-road companies had become so brisk by 1873 that they were reducing fares even below the actual transport costs. In sugar, too, competition led to the closing down of eighteen out of the thirty-seven refining plants, and there are many other examples. According to W. Ashworth, *op. cit.*, p. 94, 'In thirteen leading manufacturing industries in the United States the average amount of capital of each manufacturing plant was multiplied by thirty-nine between 1850 and 1910, and the value of average output was multiplied by nineteen.'

41. Unlike other companies, they were not entirely dependent on the railroads, as they could ship their oil by way of the Great Lakes and the Erie Canal.

42. H. U. Faulkner, *op. cit.*, p. 432, quotes the following paragraph from a *New York Assembly Document*, No. 38, of 1880, describing the position of the Standard Oil Company: 'It owns and controls the pipe lines of the producing regions that connect with the railroads. It ships 95 per cent of all oil. . . . It dictates terms and rates to the railroads. It has bought out and frozen out refiners all over the country. By means of the superior facilities for transportation which it possessed, it could overbid in the producing regions and *undersell in the markets of the world.* Thus it has gone on buying out and freezing out all opposition, until it has absorbed and monopolized this great traffic, this great production which ranks second on the list of exports of our country. The parties whom they have driven to the wall have had ample capital, and equal ability in the prosecution of their business in all things save their ability to acquire facilities for transportation.'

43. For more details, see H. U. Faulkner, *op. cit.*, p. 441.

44. Writers like Upton Sinclair, I. M. Tarbell, L. Steffen, Thomas Lawson and Charles E. Russell were in the forefront of this struggle against monopoly and had a very great influence upon the attitudes of the American workers towards big business in the years that followed.

45. Woodrow Wilson, *The New Freedom*, p. 15.

46. United States *Statutes* 38, §730.

47. For example, see the results of the work done by the Federal Trade Commission.

48. For the progress of consolidation in this period, see H. U. Faulkner, *op. cit.*, pp. 609–611.

49. H. U. Faulkner, *op. cit.*, p. 613.

50. The following table is based on H. U. Faulkner's, *op. cit.*, Table of the growth of City Population in places of 8,000 inhabitants and over, p. 450. [My approximations. Y. S. B.] (Index numbers base 1860 = 100.)

Year	*Growth of Total Population*	*Growth of Town Population*	*Per cent of Town Population of Total*
1860	100	100	16·1
1880	166	220	22·7
1900	250	500	32·0
1920	353	920	43·8
1940	440	1300	49·3

51. See H. U. Faulkner, *op. cit.*, p. 424, Table, Manufacturing Establishments classified by Value of Products, etc. Wage Earners.

52. See H. U. Faulkner, *op. cit.*, Ch. 22, The Labor Movement to 1914.

53. Foreign workers to whom the fares were advanced by employers or their agents abroad, to be recovered from their wages in instalments.

54. *Vide* N. J. Ware, *The Labour Movement in the United States.*

55. *Vide* L. L. Lorwin, *The American Federation of Labour*, 1933.

56. The National Labour Union later became the National Labour Reform Party in 1872.

57. H. U. Faulkner, *op. cit.*, p. 455.

58. H. U. Faulkner, *op. cit.*, p. 456.

59. Daniel Hamberg, in *Principles of a Growing Economy*, New York, 1961,

pp. 43–45, writes: 'From 1897 until the 1930s our economy entered a period of renewed expansion, marred, as always, by periodic downturns. [1907; 1908; 1919; 1921; 1922; 1924; 1927; Y. S. B.] The basic characteristics of this period of expansion were provided by the introduction of a wide array of new or improved productive *techniques* (motorisation, electrification, standardisation, the spread of assembly-line production), new *products* (automobiles, telephones, household electrical appliances, industrial chemicals, radio, movies, etc.), an upsurge in immigration (18 million, 1897–1924), and stabilisation of markets (consolidation of formerly competing rail-roads into a few basic systems, and the spectacular merger movement in manufacturing, mining, and the public utilities). In the years following 1897 the economic atmosphere was basically sunny and optimistic. Indeed, the panic of 1907, initiated by a crash in the stock market, led not to general despair but to the rise of the Sunshine Movement—whose motto was "Think prosperity and we'll have prosperity". In the depression of the 1930s similar slogans were greeted with angry derision.' It is perhaps worth noting that the American farmer did not share in the prosperity during the 1920s. (Professor Hamberg's data for this period are taken from F. C. Mills, *Economic Tendencies in the United States*, New York National Bureau of Economic Research, 1932, and from George Soule, *Prosperity Decade*, New York, 1947). *Vide* Footnote 3, p. 45, of Hamberg, *op. cit.*

60. There were, of course, other unions besides the two mentioned here which were selected to illustrate the different approaches to the labour problems. There was for example the I.W.W. (Industrial Workers of the World) which, as its name suggested, favoured an international association of workers 'founded on class struggle' in more or less the European socialist manner. In 1908 they proclaimed that 'a struggle must go on until the workers of the world organise as a class, take possession of the earth and the machinery of production and abolish the wage system'. Their methods were also the traditional European ones of general strike, boycott and violent or non-violent demonstration. They were, in fact, part of the rising world movement of socialism. The main core of their support came from the camp of unskilled labour. The union lost much of its strength when in the war its membership was faced with the alternatives of nationalism and socialism. After the war, in 1918–20, what was left of its membership mostly joined the Communist party.

61. *Vide* Daniel Hamberg, *op. cit.*, p. 45.

62. 'In the years 1923–1929, the *rate of separation* as a result of technological displacement was 5 per cent of workers every two years; the *rate of addition* of jobs was 4½ per cent every two years.' D. Hamberg, *op. cit.*, p. 45.

63. Employment rose between 1920 and 1929 by 16, the supply of labour by 21, and the national output by 46 per cent. *Vide* D. Hamberg, *op. cit.*, p. 46.

64. They rose by almost 5 per cent between 1922 and 1929. *Vide* P. F. Gemmill and R. H. Blodgett, *Economics: Principles and Problems.*

65. The Real Income *per capita* measured in 1929 prices rose from $634 in 1923 to $676 in 1928. *Vide* Simon Kuznets, *National Income and its Composition*, N.B.E.R., 1941.

66. A great deal has been written about the phenomenon of alternating periods of prosperity and depression, and this is not the place to discuss this again. In the present author's view the student interested in this very important subject would be well advised to start with the excellent little book by R. C. O. Matthews, *The Trade Cycle*, Cambridge, 1959, and then read G. von Haberler's book *Prosperity and Depression*, 1943. The problem is

particularly of interest to students concerned with the planning of growth in underdeveloped countries, because it appears that the twenties in the United States are a good example for a case study of growth through capitalisation at the expense of 'present' consumption, which is too often held in front of African students as the quintessence of all economic wisdom. In fact, in America, it led to a depression which lasted until the equilibrium between supply and demand was restored. The question which remains to be answered is, therefore, whether it should not be possible to regulate the accumulation of capital through a better division of the national product between employers and employees in such a way that a steady equilibrium rate of growth can be achieved. In other words, whether the stop/go development cannot be replaced by a gradual rise which on the average would over time reach the same height of capitalisation as the growth which is interrupted by periodical depression and is achieved at the cost of a low standard of living for the workers. The various theories dealing with this aspect of development have been discussed by F. H. Halm and R. C. O. Matthews in their article 'The Theory of Economic Growth: A Survey', in *The Economic Journal*, Vol. LXXIV, 1964, and have been summarised by Y. S. Brenner in *Theories of Economic Development and Growth*, London, 1966. The history of these fluctuations in the period following World War I has been summarised by Professor W. Arthur Lewis in his *Economic Survey 1919–1939*, London, 1949, Pt. I. It may perhaps be pointed out here that the main difference between Britain and the United States regarding the *social cost*, i.e. the price the workers had to pay for the rapid economic development, seems to have been that in Britain the working class paid for the accumulation by long periods of deprivation in the nineteenth century, whereas the Americans paid in sporadic but shorter depressions in the twentieth.

67. *Vide* J. D. Black, *Agricultural Reform in the United States*, 1929.

68. For details, *vide* McNary-Hangen Bills of 1927 and 1928.

69. *Vide* J. C. Malin, *The United States After the World War*, p. 247. Quoted from H. U. Faulkner, *op. cit.* 'Prior to 1913', says Malin, 'United States agricultural policy was focused upon the problems of production. In that year a new departure was inaugurated which for the first time placed systematic emphasis upon the problem of marketing.'

70. Gombert here quoted from H. U. Faulkner, *op. cit.*, p. 595. It is noteworthy that Lenin took in Europe precisely the opposite view. He said that this is a war between capitalists and should be of no concern to the working class.

71. H. U. Faulkner, *op. cit.*, p. 594, gives the following table, illustrating how the working class in the United States really fared during the war.

Year	*Wages per Hour*	*Cost of Living*	*Real Wages*
1913	100	100	100
1916	111	118·3	93·8
1917	128	142·4	89·9
1918	162	174·4	92·9
1919	184	188·3	97·7

72. There were a few strikes, but most of them terminated in conciliation.

73. H. U. Faulkner, *op. cit.*, p. 596.

74. A good example for the state of mind with which the labour leadership emerged from the honeymoon of co-operation with the employers during the war was the *naïveté* with which Gompers expected that labour

would be rewarded for its loyalty. This, more than anything else, gave the impression that only the capitalists are truly patriotic Americans, whereas the workers may or may not follow their example.

75. H. U. Faulkner, *op. cit.*, p. 631.

76. The 'American Plan', a scheme organised by the employers to combat organised labour, which met with a considerable degree of success, and the alienation of the middle class from the labour cause, by clever capitalist propaganda, and finally, labour's incompetence in fighting it, were among the other causes which weakened the workers' movement.

77. According to H. U. Faulkner, *op. cit.*, p. 633, 'A Federal Trade Commission investigation made in 1922 and covering a cross section of American business found that employees comprised 7·5 per cent of the common stockholders of corporations in which they were employed, and 3·5 per cent of the preferred stockholders, but held only 1·5 per cent of the common stock and 1·9 of the preferred. A later study made by the Industrial Relations Section of Princeton University found that only 4·26 per cent of the stock of twenty important companies which had vigorously encouraged employee stock ownership was actually owned by employees. (A large proportion of these were doubtlessly held by superintendents and by the salaried office and executive force.) While the actual number of shareholders has increased, the technique whereby a small group may maintain control of an industry has been perfected.'

78. H. U. Faulkner mentions specific judiciary decisions like the abolition as unconstitutional of the child-labour laws and the minimum-wage law for women in the district of Columbia. In addition to this a Supreme Court decision held union members responsible for the actions of their officials and permitted employers to force their employees not to join a union.

79. Committee on Economic Development, *Economic Growth in the United States.*

80. Daniel Hamberg, *op. cit.*, p. 49, summarises the situation beautifully in the following paragraph: '. . . for the engineer, the depression might mean that he would waste his talents in a gas station. For the doctor, it meant unpaid bills; for the patient, unattended medical needs. For the very poor, it meant starvation. For the unemployed, the alternatives to starvation were few in number, none allowing the maintenance of human dignity: begging, soup lines, apple-selling, leaf-raking in the park. For parents the depression meant watching children go hungry, without adequate medical care, and without the kind of material and nonmaterial environment that would allow them to develop into secure, healthy, dignified individuals. The depression meant an intensification of all social evils: crime, juvenile deliquency, broken homes, the growth of racial and religious hatred, lapses into violence, a growing audience for demagogues. . . .'

81. It is interesting to see how little capital was willing and able to react to the requests of the President in this national emergency and to compare it with labour's full support for the government during World War I.

82. It would be very interesting to examine how much freedom for the individual is left over these days in the countries which advertise this as their national commodity.

83. It is interesting to note that had the rate of growth of the period 1915–20 continued it would have reached the 1937 level in the same year. See data in J. F. Dewhurst, *op. cit.*

84. *Economic Survey 1919–1939*, London, 1949, p. 104.

85. W. Arthur Lewis, *op. cit.*, p. 105.

86. National Industrial Recovery Act, 1933.

87. Because of a Supreme Court decision in 1936, which declared this practice unconstitutional, it later took the form of payments to farmers to improve the soil by leaving it fallow, etc.

88. The National Industrial Recovery Act of 1933 was aimed to introduce self-regulation of business through fair competition codes. These were to be worked out by co-operative efforts of all the interested parties—employers, workers, consumers and the government. As it turned out, it merely represented the views of employers, unless the workers were well enough organised to make their views also heard.

89. The Civilian Conservation Corps employed in the first year of its operation alone more than a quarter of a million young men in various land improving schemes.

90. In 1938, schemes of this sort created close to four million jobs, i.e. employment for one-third of the total unemployed labour force.

91. If Judaism had contributed the rule of justice 'an eye for an eye', and Christianity had tempered it with charity, the new approach added dignity to justice and took the stigma out of charity.

92. The material of the following seven pages is a record of a conversation the author had in 1955 with Dr. Chanoch Baszosza, one-time leader of the Palestine Communist Party (EMET), on the subject of the origins of Stalinism. Dr. Baszosza was later 'purged' from the Israeli Communist Party (MAKI) and published an independent journal called *New Ways.* In the March 1957 issue his record of the conversation was published under the title 'The Renaissance in Communism.' The two versions differ very little.

93. Left Social Revolutionaries.

94. For more details of the theoretical background of these policies, see Y. S. Brenner, *op. cit.*, Ch. VII, pp. 223–247.

95. This was later one of the reasons for the establishment of *Kolchozes* and *Sovchozes* to 'industrialise' agriculture.

96. *Vide Fundamentals of Marxism–Leninism*, Moscow, 1964, p. 559.

97. *The State and Revolution*, F.L.P.H., Moscow, 1961, p. 161.

98. *Vide* N. Spulber, *The Economics of Communist Eastern Europe,* Cambridge, Mass., 1957, p. 222.

99. *Fundamentals of Marxism–Leninism*, *op. cit.*, p. 574.

100. *Pravda*, 14 November 1958.

101. *Pravda*, 26 March 1965.

102. The explanation for this, for what it is worth, can be divided into three categories. Firstly, the explanation of those who claim that such progress as there was did only take place in a limited number of sectors of the economy and that in fact the Soviet statistics are misleading. Secondly, the explanation of those who claim that, with all its efforts, the government did not succeed in eliminating unplanned autonomous 'genetic' growth, and that this must be held responsible for the progress. The argument is that had it not been for Soviet planning, genetic growth would have made Russia progress even more. The adherents of this argument speak of two economies which existed side by side in the Soviet Union, the successful autonomous one and the far less successful planned one. As evidence they point to what appear to be common practices in the Soviet Union, the hiding of accumulated reserves and equipment from the authorities by enterprises and their utilisation outside the plan. Likewise they stress the discrepancies between production figures collected by the Soviet Statistics Office from managing directors and from government ministries [*Vide*

Pravda, 4 July 1957] and the frequent complaints about spontaneous activities and lack of planning discipline which appear in Soviet publications. Finally, they cite the example of the practice of ministries of drawing up plans without taking into consideration what is being done by other ministries [*Vide* Nikita Khrushchev's speech of 8 April 1957, and Theses of 30 March 1957], and naturally, the Kolkhoz markets which were legalised and produced even by official accounts some 20 per cent of the country's farm product, to which they add the yield of the 1·6 million hectares product of the Workers' Allotments. Thirdly, and here all critics of 'super-planning' are in agreement, the great improvements which followed the removal of some restrictions on the spontaneous growth must be attributed to decentralisation. (Y. S. Brenner, *op. cit.*, pp. 235–236.)

103. According to G. Warren Nutter, *The Growth of Industrial Production in the Soviet Union*, Princeton, 1962, p. 185, Table 47, the fall was (at 1913 weights, index 1913 = 100) as follows:

1916	111	1919	24
1917	92	1920	22
1918	40		

104. G. Warren Nutter, *op. cit.*, p. 185, Table 47.

1921	24	1925	73
1922	35	1926	91
1923	43	1927	101
1924	53	1928	103

105. *Vide* G. Warren Nutter, *op. cit.*, Table 53, pp. 196–197

106. *Vide* G. Warren Nutter, *op. cit.*, Table 40, p. 172.

107. *Vide* G. Warren Nutter, *op. cit.*, Chart 16, and pp. 173–176, 191–192.

108. G. Warren Nutter, *op. cit.*, pp. 195–198, according to Table 53 (Moving-weight Indexes of Production, 1913 = 100), the total rate of growth of all products was as follows:

1928	102	1931	143	1934	182 (Civilian only)
1929	116	1932	144	1935	216 ,,
1930	134	1933	153	1936	252 ,,
				1937	268 (Civilian) 285 all

109. There were a number of articles on this in the Soviet Press during 1965. See also Y. S. Brenner, *op. cit.*, pp. 241–245.

110. According to G. Warren Nutter, *op. cit.*, p. 196, 1913 index = 100, growth of all industries was as follows: 1937, 285; 1938, 298; 1939, 311; 1940, 318.

111. There seems now to be a good deal of controversy about the development of the military industry in the period 1939–41, with some observers taking the view that Stalin in fact neglected stepping up military production, relying on his treaty with Germany in the last years before the war; and others taking the view that Stalin merely signed the treaty to gain time for raising his war potential. The evidence available so far can substantiate both points of view.

112. According to G. Warren Nutter's index, production stood at 180 as compared with 311 in 1938 and 318 in 1939.

113. G. Warren Nutter's view differs here from that of the present author. Warren Nutter writes, *op. cit.*, p. 216, that the earlier mentioned factors considerably mitigated Russian economic losses.

114. There is a more detailed discussion of this in Gregory Grossman's contribution to *Capital Formation and Economic Growth*, Princeton, 1955, 'Some Current Trends in Soviet Capital Formation'.

115. *Vide* A. W. Haslett, *Soviet Seven-Year Plan 1959–1965*, 1959. According to G. Warren Nutter, *op. cit.*, p. 126 (1913 index = 100) the growth of all industries in this period was as follows:

1940	318	1948	276	1953	516	
		1949	343	1954	563	
1945	264	1950	393	1955	620	
1946	180	1951	448	1956	(625)	civilian only
1947	219	1952	488	1957	(686)	,,
				1958	(715)	,,

116. Reported in *The Times*, London, 13 January 1965.

117. *Vide* article by A. Zauberman of the London School of Economics, 'New Phase in Soviet Planning', published in the London *Times*, 2 February 1965.

118. A. Zauberman, *op. cit.*

119. This reasoning does, of course, equally apply to growth in other latecomer countries such as Japan, for example, with which Soviet economic growth is frequently, and legitimately, compared.

120. For the reductions which are necessary it is sufficient to see the great number of articles devoted to this subject in *Pravda* in 1965.

121. See p. 183 for the development of Japan in the nineteenth century.

122. *Vide* William W. Lockwood, *The Economic Development of Japan, Growth and Structural Changes 1868–1938*, Princeton, 1954, Table 34, p. 395.

OVERSEAS TRADE OF JAPAN PROPER

Exports in millions of yen	*1893*	*1913*	*1936*
All Countries	88	716	3,585
Asia	27	360	2,263
China, Korea, Formosa, Manchuria, Hongkong	23	302	1,608
India	2	30	259
South-east Asia		24	302

123. *Vide* G. C. Allen, *A Short Economic History of Modern Japan*, London, 1962 edition, p. 217, Table XXVI.

CHANGES IN EXPORT MARKETS (IN PERCENTAGE OF TOTAL EXPORTS)

	1934–36	*1955*	*1959*
China, Korea, Formosa and South East Asia	58%	34%	26%

124. *Vide* Alfred Maizels, *Industrial Growth and World Trade*, Cambridge, 1963, p. 486. Table A68. Exports of manufactures from Japan in $ million f.o.b.: 1899, 48; 1913, 153; 1929, 476; 1937, 645; 1950, 697. *Vide* also G. C. Allen, *op. cit.*, p. 217, for growth of United States and other countries' share in absorbing Japanese exports.

	1934–36	1955	1959
U.S.	= 17%	22%	30%
Europe	= 8%	10%	11%
Other countries	= 17%	34%	33%

(See also footnote 123 above.)

125. In a memorial to the Emperor on July 25th. Quoted here from Professor Frederick L. Schuman, *International Politics*, New York, 1953, p. 364.

126. F. L. Schuman, *op. cit.*, p. 369, writes: 'The ensuing war proved endless and hopeless, despite vast slaughter and devastation—verbally deplored but tacitly connived in by Western statesmen who were favourably impressed with Japan's "anti-Communist" crusade.'

127. This is the Ribbentrop—Ciano—Saburo Kurusu agreement which was signed in Berlin, 27 September 1940.

128. William W. Lockwood, *op. cit.*, p. 402.

129. William W. Lockwood, *op. cit.*, pp. 403–404.

130. D. C. Allen, *op. cit.*, p. 170.

131. Frederick L. Schuman, *op. cit.*, pp. 371 and 372–373.

132. Alfred Maizels, *op. cit.*, p. 533, Table E2, Appendix E. Estimates of gross domestic product per head of total population . . . 1899–1957 $ at 1955 prices.

1899	*1913*	*1929*	*1937*	*1950*	*1955*	*1957*
65	90	145	185	135	185	220

133. Alfred Maizels, *op. cit.*, p. 537, Table E4, Appendix E, shows that the net value per head of population (1955 prices) changed from $40 in 1937 to $20 in 1950 and to $45 in 1955 and $65 in 1957. Table E3, Appendix E, p. 535, shows the estimate net value of manufacturing production in billion dollars at 1955 prices as follows:

1899	*1913*	*1929*	*1937*	*1950*	*1955*	*1957*
0·45	0·63	1·59	2·75	1·71	4·00	5·84

134. Alfred Maizels, *op. cit.*, pp. 538–539, Table E5. Estimates of apparent consumption of manufactures in billion dollars at 1955 prices.

1899	*1913*	*1929*	*1937*	*1950*	*1955*	*1957*
0·54	0·73	2·05	2·85	1·92	4·89	7·58

Table E6, Estimates of apparent consumption of manufactures per head of total population in dollars at 1955 prices.

1899	*1913*	*1929*	*1937*	*1950*	*1955*	*1957*
10	15	35	40	25	55	85

135. Alfred Maizels, *op. cit.*, p. 515, Table C1, Appendix C, Volume indices of exports of manufactures by country.

136. Tables (a) to (f) are from G. C. Allen, *op. cit.* Table (g) from United Nations *Statistical Yearbook*, 1964. (a) Appendix B, Table I. (b) Table IX (p. 200), Indices of Agricultural and Fishery Production (1933–35 = 100). (c) Table XIIb (p. 203), Indices of Industrial Production (1934–36 = 100). (d) Table XXXII (p. 222), Index of Real Wages in Manufacturing Industry (1934–36 = 100). (e) Table XXVIIb (p. 218), Post-War Volume of Trade (1934–36 = 100). (f) Table XXIX (p. 219), Foreign Exchange Reserves in million of United States dollars. (g) United Nations *Statistical Yearbook* Table 170 (p. 527), Estimates of National Incomes in 1,000 million yen. (h) Figure for 1951. (i) Figure for 1953. (j) Figure for 1959.

Year	*Population*[a]	*Agricultural Produce*[b]	*Industrial Produce*[c]	*Real Wages in Manufacturing*[d]
1950	83,200,000	99	84	85
1955	89,300,000	130	181	115
1960	93,400,000	139	410	146

Year	*Exports*[e]	*Imports*[e]	*Foreign Exchange Reserves* (M.$)[f]	*National Income*[g]
1950	30	33	930[h]	5,647[i]
1955	72	90	839	6,535
1960	117[j]	148[j]	1,824	11,504

137. It should be noted that these figures represent the rate of growth and not the relative economic welfare of the countries. The fact that the rate of growth in the United States was lower does of course not signify that the Japanese or Germans were better off than the Americans. G. Warren Nutter, *The Growth of Industrial Production in the Soviet Union*, Princeton, 1962, Table 58, p. 220, compares industrial production in France, Japan, West Germany and the Soviet Union and gives the following results (1953=100).

Year	*France*	*Japan*	*West Germany*	*Soviet Union*
1954	110	108	112	109
1955	118	116	128	120
1956	130	144	138	n.a.
1957	140	167	147	n.a.
1958	146	168	151	n.a.

138. Table 170, p. 527.

139. *Vide* United Nations *Statistical Yearbook*, 1964. For Employment (excluding agriculture), Table 7, p. 55; for Employment in Manufacturing, Table 8, p. 57; for Unemployment, Table 10, p. 61; and for Working Hours, Table 9, p. 59.

EMPLOYMENT

(1958 = 100)

	1948	*1955*	*1956*	*1957*	*1958*
Employment (excluding agriculture)		82	89	95	100
Employment in manufacturing		77	86	95	100
Unemployment (in thousands)		760	710	590	630
Hours of Work (per week)	49·0	45·7	47·2	46·9	46·5

	1959	*1960*	*1961*	*1962*	*1963*
Employment (excluding agriculture)	105	110	116	122	127
Employment in manufacturing	102	110	118	126	131
Unemployment (in thousands)	650	500	440	400	400
Hours of Work (per week)	47·3	47·8	47·0	45·8	45·5

140. *Vide* United Nations *Statistical Yearbook*, 1964, Table 15, p. 96.

INDUSTRIAL PRODUCTION

(1958 = 100)

	1938	*1948*	*1953*	*1956*	*1957*
All	57	22	60	86	99
Metal products	27	15	40	67	93
Basic metals	52	21	64	93	105
Chemicals, coal and petroleum products	45	14	51	82	96

	1958	*1959*	*1960*	*1961*	*1962*	*1963*
All	100	124	156	186	201	222
Metal products	100	144	207	267	300	329
Basic metals	100	132	170	211	210	235
Chemicals, coal and petroleum products	100	116	140	162	184	217

141. *Vide* United Nations *Statistical Yearbook*, 1964, Table 21, p. 128, and Table 137, p. 374.

INDEX OF FOOD PRODUCTION

(1952–53 — 1956–57 = 100)

1958–59	*1959–60*	*1960–61*	*1961–62*	*1962–63*
117	121	125	125	133

ALL AGRA COMMODITIES

(including fibres, tobacco, indust. oilseeds, etc.),

1958–59	*1959–60*	*1960–61*	*1961–62*	*1962–63*
116	120	123	123	131

142. United Nations *Statistical Yearbook*, 1964, Table 159, p. 455.
143. United Nations *Statistical Yearbook*, 1964, Table 160, pp. 464–465.

FOREIGN TRADE

(Value in millions U.S. dollars)

Year	*Imports*	*Exports*	*Year*	*Imports*	*Exports*
1938	1,070	1,109	1958	3,033	2,877
1948	684	258	1959	3,599	3,456
1953	2,410	1,275	1960	4,491	4,055
1955	2,471	2,011	1961	5,810	4,236
1956	3,230	2,501	1962	5,637	4,916
1957	4,284	2,858	1963	6,736	5,452

144. United Nations *Statistical Yearbook*, 1964, Table 161, pp. 476–477.
145. United Nations *Statistical Yearbook*, 1964, Table 167, Earnings in manufacturing, p. 512, and Table 169, Consumer Price Indexes, p. 523.
146. This is the view taken by Professor G. C. Allen, *op. cit.*, p. 172. As can be seen from the following, the present author does not entirely agree with this view for different reasons.
147. The few unions which existed in pre-war Japan were dissolved in 1940. *Vide* G. C. Allen, *op. cit.*, pp. 184–185.
148. G. C. Allen, *op. cit.*, p. 185.

149. Supreme Command Allied Powers, i.e. The Occupation Authorities.

150. *Vide* G. C. Allen, *op. cit.*, p. 185, for payment methods in Japan.

151. The population of Israel since 1948 has increased as follows: 1948, 770,000; 1951, 1,577,825; 1954, 1,717,814; 1957, 1,975,954; 1961, 2,232,300; 1965, 2,525,600. Jewish immigration alone rose from 101,828 in 1948 (May to December) to 239,576 in 1949. In the following years immigration subsided: 170,249 in 1950, 175,095 in 1951, and only 24,639 in 1952.

152. *Vide* Y. S. Brenner, 'The Stern Gang, 1942–1948', *Middle Eastern Studies*, Vol. II, No. 1, London, October 1965.

153. Dr. Hanoch Bz'oza, in his excellent article (Hebrew), 'Is There an Israeli Road to Socialism?', *New Ways*, May 1957, writes: 'There are those who define Israel as a typical Capitalist State and there are others who take offence at such a definition. There are some who see in the labour-owned sector of the economy nothing but disguised capitalism and even a branch of foreign capital, and there are others again, who see in it the germs of socialism which in the course of their development will by themselves bring about socialism in the country. . . .' His own conclusion is that Israel is a capitalist State.

154. Of Is. £ 446 million total profits in 1955, profits from trade and finance were Is. £ 161 million and from industry only Is. £ 66 million.

155. *Vide* Alfred Maizels *op. cit.* p. 59, Table 3.2, Degree of industrialisation in production and in exports in 1955. Production of manufactures per head ($) United States = 695, Switzerland = 480, Sweden = 465, Belgium–Luxemburg = 460, United Kingdom = 460, Canada = 440, West Germany = 405, Australia = 350, Denmark = 325, Norway = 315, Netherlands = 270, France = 265, New Zealand = 325, *ISRAEL* = 170, Italy = 150, Argentina = 145, South Africa = 115, Chile = 75, Mexico = 60, Yugoslavia = 85, Brazil = 50, Japan = 45, Colombia = 45, Turkey = 30, India = 7, Egypt = 15, Pakistan = 5, etc.

156. According to the United Nations *Statistical Yearbook*, 1964, the rate of illiteracy among the population of 15 years and over was 15 per cent. (In India it was 72·2 per cent, in Turkey 61·9 per cent, in Yugoslavia 19·7 per cent, in the USSR 1·5 per cent) (1961). The number of inhabitants per physician in 1962 was 400. (In India 5,800, Turkey 5,700, Yugoslavia 1,400, USSR 500, United States 760, United Kingdom 960.) The consumption of calories and protein per day in 1962–63 was: total 2,800; of this, of animal origin 19 per cent, and grammes of protein 85. (The figures for other countries in same order of presentation were: India 2,000, 6 per cent, 51 gm., Turkey 3,111, 10 per cent, 98 gm., Yugoslavia 2,940, 19 per cent, 99 gm.

157. H. Darin-Drabkin, *New Outlook*, Israel, January 1958, p. 22. Dr. Darin was economic adviser to the Israel Ministry of Labour (Housing and Immigrant Absorption Section).

158. H. Darin-Drabkin, *op. cit.*, p. 22.

159. That is, north of the town of Beersheba in the southern desert called Negev.

160. See previous footnote for definition of arable land.

161. H. Darin-Drabkin, *op. cit.*, p. 26.

162. H. Darin-Drabkin, *op. cit.*, p. 26.

163. H. Darin-Drabkin, *op. cit.*, p. 27.

164. Strictly, Palestine was not a British colony but a mandatory area given to Britain by the League of Nations after World War I.

165. Mainly they had to do with various political pressures from the Arab world, and with the traditional conception of economic imperialism. The present author discussed this problem very briefly in an article about the Stern Gang, in *Middle Eastern Studies*. An excellent, much wider and detailed account is given by Aharon Cohen in his book (Hebrew) *Israel and the Arab World*, Israel, 1964.

166. This was, of course, the main justification of the Mandatory Régime in Palestine for its colonial economic policies.

167. For example, investments in the plantation of orange groves (it is seven years until they yield incomes) boomed at the time of the Spanish Civil War, when Britain could not be supplied with citrus fruit from its usual source. Light industry, and especially food processing, was very successful during the African campaign in World War II.

168. Here they also had to overcome, in addition to the natural obstacles, until 1948, the legal restrictions on Jewish settlement in parts of the country imposed by the British.

169. For this reason it was private capital which, paradoxically, clamoured in Israel for nationalisation, meaning, of course, the nationalisation not of their own but of the workers' enterprises.

170. When one of the leaders of the great Israeli unofficial seamen's strike met one of the senior government and union officials, the latter's argument against the strike was that, whatever the seamen's grievances, 'one does not paralyse the nation's fleet'.

171. Which was also made possible by the great influx of United States and German capital.

172. Which the incompetent leadership of the left was unable to turn to labour's advantage.

173. David Horowitz, *The Economics of Israel*, London, 1967.

Chapter VI

THE UNDERDEVELOPED COUNTRIES

THINLY AND DENSELY POPULATED AREAS

Let us define underdeveloped countries as countries which have not yet entered the process of self-sustained economic growth. These countries must be divided into two different groups. Countries which are densely populated, and countries which are too thinly populated to make investment directly effective. For the first group we may take India as an example and for the second West Africa.

In Europe the accretion of people since its low in the fifteenth century progressed gradually and was accompanied by an equally slow rise in the accumulated capital. In addition, this slow process of population accretion and concentration of capital was accompanied by a particularly European marriage and family pattern. Whenever the economic capacity of an area increased, population growth became more rapid because marriages were contracted earlier and people had more to eat, were healthier and died less frequently from diseases and starvation. Whenever the cumulative effects of the accretion went beyond the economic capacities of the area, a reversal set in and disease and hunger spread the famous Malthusian checks and the balance between the economy and the population was restored. Thus, over a prolonged period of several centuries, there was a parallel progress of population growth and rising economic capacity in northern Europe. This parallel was so obvious that the classical economists viewed population as any other factor of production reacting as it were to the simple mechanism of demand and oversupply. In their opinion, population growth was dependent upon the economic capacity of the country, i.e. on the requirements of the entrepreneurs.[1] The first real change which interfered with this regulative Malthusian process came from outside the system in the late nineteenth century with the discoveries of Pasteur and Koch. The drastic reduction in virulent diseases, and the consequent prolongation of life, increased the labour force manifold and greatly accelerated the whole process of population growth. Yet, this 'outside' interference with the Malthusian regulative mechanism only began in the last quarter of the nineteenth century when industrial progress, and with it the economic capacity to absorb a greater labour force, had already progressed in the countries concerned out of all comparison with earlier periods. By that time the accumulation of capital had risen to such heights that the additional labour force could be more or less easily absorbed in the production processes. In addition to this, transportation had also improved to an extent that it made possible the transfer of part of the surplus population to the thinly populated areas outside Europe. In other words, the great increase in European population, which only began to abate towards the middle of the twentieth century, was matched by an equal, and sometimes even higher, growth of economic capacity and capital accumulation. Truly there were periods when excess population was felt rather severely, in the form of business fluctuations and the resultant spells of unemployment. Yet these were mere temporary setbacks which originated from the economic structure and the organisation of the society. It was in fact, more the result of maladjustments in the production of consumers' and producers' goods than of the rapid increase in population. From a long-term point of view the accumulation of caitpal, or the growth of employment capacity, was climbing as rapidly as, if not more rapidly than, the accretion of people.

In countries like Egypt or India the position was very different indeed. No prolonged period of balance between capital accumulation and its translation into economic capacity and social change had taken place. The outside interference, that is the reduction of mortality from virulent diseases and the consequent population accretion, impinged upon them suddenly. No gradual social change had preceded which in the absence of economic capacity could have reduced the size of families and rate of childbirth. Unlike over much of Europe in the eighteenth century, there was no marriage pattern which reacted to economic conditions. As soon as a girl was ready to bear children she was helping to increase the population problems. As the incidence of death among children continued to be high, the number of children born had to be many if the family hoped for some to survive. For each individual family the survival of as many children as possible was necessary in order to afford some economic security once the elders grew too old to work. They simply had to have many surviving children to afford their elders with some measure of physical security and the prestige which often depended on the size of the family. Thus, the immediate needs of the people were directly contrary to their future wellbeing in the long run and on the national level. In summary, the reduction of mortality from virulent diseases impinged in parts of the economically backward areas upon a population which was not prepared for it.

Naturally, this led to a fall in living standards and to a further differentiation between the social classes in these societies. It rapidly eliminated any kind of 'middle income group' and divided society into a great mass of people living at the very frontiers of starvation and a small number of people who were economically so far above them that there was no social fluency left. Had it not been for the rich countries' readiness to divert food and sometimes capital surpluses to help these areas, population accretion would have been checked by the Malthusian predicaments. With foreign aid, the number of people living on the frontiers of starvation increased, and grew so numerous that the capital required to absorb them as a labour force has gone far beyond that which the rich countries are able and willing to supply. Moverover, poverty has reduced the people in the poor countries to such a state of health, education and apathy, that even given the necessary capital their efficiency would still be so far below their competitors, in the developed countries, that the amount of real capital required to make up the difference might have to be manifoldly higher than that required for an equal number of people in a developed country. This is not all. The populations of these countries continue to live on the frontiers of starvation, as any increase in income for the earlier mentioned social causes will continue to be followed by an increase in their numbers, rather than in the rise of their *per capita* income. The vicious circle which was, in fact, due to the impact of better health on people who were too poor, is one of those roads paved with good intentions which lead to 'the other place'. Nowadays, even large sums of capital cannot effectively overcome the needs for both improved living standards and the creation of more capital capacity to employ labour.

In this sense, then, and in this sense alone, the advocates of the contraception schemes may be right. Yet they tend to simplify the problem. They ignore the social conditions and the economic necessity, and therefore, also, the wish of the people to raise big families. Poverty breeds its own social structure, part of which is the need for large families, and large families breed poverty. It is a closed circle. One solution may be emigration. But is it? The emigration of people from overpopulated countries, as was the case in the nineteenth and early twentieth centuries in Europe, is now no longer possible. The receiving countries do not want people of low economic capacity. They are only ready to accept those who have reached that level of education which enables them to live and earn a living in their new homelands. For this reason it is rather the most productive element which may be able to emigrate from the overpopulated countries, whereas the economically most useless are left behind. New poor will be born to take the place of the better educated who leave.

The prospect here seems to be slender indeed. One solution would be to bring about a social revolution, a revolution in attitude towards family and childbirth. Can such a revolution really be brought about? It is very unlikely! Social habit and cultural patterns change very slowly, certainly more slowly than production techniques. There is, of course, the possibility that, with the progress of capitalisation in the developed countries, a point may be reached there when capital will be in such surplus that it will be invested at the low rate of profit at which a very, very high capitalised industry may be set up in one or more of the overpopulated countries. This industry may be so highly specialised and capital equipped that it will be able to absorb even uneducated population. Certain operations can be taught to people who do not have a full technical education. Yet, with the development of lunar rockets and spacecraft, enough of the surplus capital can be rocketed into the skies to prevent a surplus on our earth, and it is also true that the higher capitalised an industry becomes, the less labour it requires to be operated. The only rational solution remains the creation of a closed market, comprising of the various underdeveloped thinly populated and the underdeveloped densely populated countries, and the development of an internal economic system between them, protected, at least initially, against outside competition. This is in effect the idea of the closed African economic community. For example, if the African continent was closed to European products, Egyptian concentration of labour would find a ready market in the vast hinterlands of Africa for industrial products, whereas the agricultural hinterland of Kenya, for example, would be able to supply the Egyptian industrial worker with his nourishment and raw materials. However, this would not only require political unification of the Continent, and effective resistance to pressures from the developed countries, but also an enormous amount of capital from the latter to unite the Continent by means of railroads, roads, air communication and any other kind of transport facilities, which are extremely costly if one remembers the enormous areas over which they would have to be stretched. Even then, the problem of population accretion beyond the rate of a capital accretion in the overpopulated areas may not be solved. Perhaps only a combined ideological, educational and social attack upon the backward populations, supported by enormous propagandistic efforts and well directed real capital investment may bring some relief in this direction. Short of this the problems in the overpopulated areas seem almost insoluble.

THINLY POPULATED COUNTRIES

In the thinly populated countries the problem may be less severe. Here a great capital influx could, at least in certain parts, bring about some real change. The connection of isolated villages by roads, or the stimulation of certain industrial enterprises, could have far-reaching results. It may, of course, merely result in a rapid accretion of people and perhaps even in an over accretion of people, but this is not absolutely necessary. The time over which such change would necessarily spread may bring with it some social readjustments if the rich countries would make it their concerted deliberate policy to assist such social change. Yet, here too, the amount of capital required and the degree of agreement of policy in the rich countries is far from being adequate. Private capital would hardly flow to most of these areas unless it could hope to have returns, so that initially it would be up to government to supply the capital. The main difficulty lies in the socio-political implications. The dangers involved in foreign aid may be much greater than one may realise from superficial observations. The productive employment of capital depends upon the available labour force. If this labour force is not prepared to join in the productive process, the capital will be of little use. However, a labour force which is not used to engage in any productive employment which has not the specifically 'European' or 'Christian'[2] spirit of acquisitiveness, which does not feel that its 'time-off' may be, on balance, worth less than its 'disutility' from labour, may look upon capital merely as an income and not as a productive resource. In other words, it is not alone a problem of the ability to make productive use of a population, but also the problem of the wish of the population to be productively engaged. A starving population may wish to work to survive, but no more. A population which gets foreign aid may even lose the wish to work in order to survive, as it has found a way to survive without doing anything. It is not correct to assume that the mental mechanism of the acquisitive society in the developed countries operates in a similar form in other different societies. Buddhism does not look upon the poor man as poor in a moral sense. The wish to work may be mere mutation of the mind in some societies, therefore only a combination of a social and cultural revolution, with the simultaneous availability of capital resources, may produce a rapid economic change, akin to that which has taken place in the developed countries.

But man's wish and ability to work may also have to do with climatic factors. Tropical climates have certain advantages and disadvantages in this respect. The advantages are that, for example, in the forest belts men can often survive without having to do much work. There is no obvious need for shelter, because there are no cold periods during which he might freeze to death; there is no obvious need to grow food, as fruit grows wild, and the earth gives certain fruits which need no deliberate farming and there are still animals or fish which can be hunted without the developed 'labour discipline'. At the same time the accumulation and storage of food to accommodate for periods of drought is made almost impossible. Weevils on the one hand, and fungi on the other, destroy all food crops very rapidly unless they can be protected. It is not surprising, therefore, that in many tropical areas people are used to great feasts, during which all food reserves are consumed. There is no way of storing food in these regions unless it can be done with modern highly capitalised storage facilities. But then, distances are preventing the real exploitation of silos, etc.

It is perhaps easy to see why the slave traders succeeded in West Africa, where the surplus labour which in Europe would have been exploited in the production of capital and other stored wealth was simply exported. If local chiefs in Africa, like lords in Europe, could have exploited their tenants, it is hardly likely that this peculiar type of export from West Africa, the slave trade, could have developed. Moreover, the abundance of land, in relation to people, is similarly not as straightforward as one expects it to be from a superficial observation. The abundance of land is only a reality if it is utilised in a modern way. On the average, only one-seventh of the tropical forest land is in use wherever it is in use at all. This is due to the system of shifting cultivation. Yet to use any other system of cultivation, instead of burning the overgrowth and waiting for the land to be burned again after five or ten years so that it can be re-exploited for cultivation, would require the levelling and crushing and ploughing in of the natural vegetation, for which highly technical equipment of great cost has to be used. In other words, the surplus of land would only be a surplus if the equipment were available that could turn it into utilisable land year after year.

Another point is that, even if capital was available for storage facilities and for the improvement of transport, there may still be difficulties arising out of the mental and physical status of the people. Medical experiments conducted in Europe after World War II showed that protein deficiencies influenced men's capacity to work. Protein-underfed children were also tested. Tests of their ability to trace lines or tap with a pencil so many times on a table and of their stamina were examined. The results of these tests showed the obvious, i.e. that protein malnutrition weakens physical and mental capacity to do productive labour. The widening gap between the rich and poor countries is accompanied by a trend towards increasing protein consumption in the rich countries, and a decreasing protein consumption in the poor countries. A substitution takes place in the latter, where they are forced to switch over to cheaper starchy food (cassava). It has been pointed out that there may be a difference between the effects of the withdrawal of proteins from a diet which was usually rich in protein and between the withholding of protein from a diet which has been poor in it for a very long time. Indeed, the organisms of the protein-underfed people may have adjusted in a way which makes the lack of proteins less effective, but this theory is far from proven. As a matter of fact, some encephalographic examinations of brain rhythms seem to contradict this possibility. But, whether protein deficiencies reduce the capacity to work or not, it is a minor problem in comparison with the effects of the subclinical tropical diseases. Hundreds of tests which have been conducted in West Africa on university students have shown that almost all of them are suffering from subclinical malaria. Again, there may be here a difference between the clinical malaria experienced by European settlers and the age-old subclinical malaria which may have evolved some defensive reactions. However, doctors seem fairly convinced that it must have an effect on people's ability to work, and some are suspecting that it may also affect mental ability.[3] Again, in some encephalographic tests, peculiar rhythms are dissimilar in people who do and do not have malaria in their blood.

As important as the physical ability to work, whether it is impaired by climate, disease or malnutrition, is the attitude to work, i.e. the wish to work. It is quite possible that the peculiar acquisitiveness common to the economically developed societies is not attractive to the societies in underdeveloped countries. There are, for example, societies which glory in the splendour of their 'betters' and have very little use for property for themselves as individuals. This is not the place to raise the question whether these are the results of their economic condition or whether their economic conditions are the results of these attitudes. However, in as far as the leaders of the underdeveloped countries are concerned, they appear to want to enter into the European or American pattern of development, and therefore they will have to find a way to overcome the impeding factors.

In thinking of these impediments, let us begin from the problem of the income gap. Even if a man wishes to improve his personal lot, he may find this a very difficult thing to do anywhere, but even more so in an underdeveloped country. Not only because any income he may gain may be taken away from him by his extended family, but also because the margin of income above his immediate needs is so small that he would have to save for an extremely long time until he could buy anything of value that he really desires. The gap between what he can save and what he needs is so enormous that, acting rationally, he may rather not save at all. He may rather drink away the meagre extra penny and enjoy himself. This attitude was very common in mercantilist England—it is common in Africa today. As long as incomes are so low that they do not permit the breaking away from the closed cycle of poverty, people are bound to react in this manner. This provides the excuse for the employer to keep wages low, because a rise in wages would only make the worker drink more, and the supply of labour less secure, while it might very well also reduce the absolute labour force.[4] Thus we are told that higher wages lead to less labour, while we may also find that low wages make economic progress almost impossible. The mercantilist argument that low wages, i.e. the fear of starvation, are the best incentive to make people work, may apply to underdeveloped societies today as much as it applied to mercantilist society in England. However, the opposite argument, i.e. that high wages may be an incentive-creating factor resulting in better and more work, may be equally true, if the price of commodities which are within the range of wants in these societies can be brought within the reach of the workers. This is, of course, very difficult to achieve in the face of the low productivity of labour and capital. Colonial systems were maintaining low wage rates in the colonies because this was one way of cheapening the supply of raw materials. Local leaders in the colonies were interested in keeping wages down in order to profit as much as possible from the difference between the production costs of the colonial products and what they fetch from the allies abroad to whom they sold them. The history of this unholy alliance between foreign and local exploiters created an atmosphere of hopelessness amongst the workers and is therefore also responsible for the depression in the underdeveloped countries. The gloom also contributed to the inefficiency of labour. But until this mood can be effectively diminished there is little hope for a change in workers' attitudes. The attempts which have been made here and there of paying by piece rates rather than by daily rates can only affect people employed in the cash market, and then, too, only if rates are really high enough to encourage workers. But piece rates, based upon labour alone, rather than upon the combination of capital and labour, cannot really result in revolutionary change in incomes. It cannot suffice to revolutionise the whole framework.

Saving and a raising of the living standard are also made difficult by the traditional social environment. For example, most African societies live in extended families, or in similar forms of organisation. These families afford the individual a degree of economic security, while they also put upon him obligations which make him give the same economic security he receives, to the other members of his family, whenever he is in a position to do so. In other words, if an individual member of the family wants to improve his own lot, he has to improve with it, and at the same time, that of all other members of his extended family. His individual effort, which might perhaps double his income, would have to be divided amongst so many others that there would be little real effect felt on his own living standard. For this reason, only the co-ordinated effort of the whole family to improve can make progress really possible. Otherwise, the slight improvement of the standard of living of the family merely permits the survival of more children, and increases the number of persons amongst whom the slightly greater income is distributed. Thus, on the whole, effective change from this directly economic side can only be brought about if the subject of improvement is the family or tribe and not the individual. This means that the incentive-producing factor has to be a whole enterprise which would have to be based on the traditional social organisation. The alternative to this is the breaking up of 'the family', a process which is indeed taking place here and there in some underdeveloped countries. But here, too, new problems are created which are no less complex. In addition to this family impediment to economic growth, there are the no less important impediments which originate from the State. Here, too, the legacy of the colonial governments must be held greatly responsible.

The colonial governments were interested in the maintenance of peace, i.e. law and order, in their dependencies. This was in their own interest. Without peace there would be no certainty of the supply of natural resources and no security for whatever markets there were to dump upon the surplus industrial products of the 'mother countries'. In addition to this there was, of course, the Christian duty of peace making. The best and easiest way of maintaining law and order was by strengthening the hands of the local leaders. The traditional leadership, which sometimes had quite democratic origins, imposed itself ever more tyrannically with the assistance of the colonial overlords, who were putting their political power at its disposal. What had before been accepted in much the same way as the responsibility of the father of the family for its members in Europe, now became institutionalised in Africa as a new kind of law. For all practical purposes the chief became the owner of the land, i.e. the owner of the most important means of production. In this capacity he dealt with the colonial government and foreign trader. The colonial representative, on his part, believed, or would have others believe, that if the chief became rich, this would benefit the rest of his tribe as well. The chief soon learned to copy the European's paternalistic attitude towards the people and let them glory in his own advantages. In fact, the bond which was forged between the colonial interests and the chief's interests in exploiting the land and labour in the dependent territories became almost inseparable. As long as the family, or the extended family, or the tribe, was closely knit, and small enough to let the individual really share in the enrichment of the tribe's leadership, there was no clear-cut contradiction of interest. With the growth of the tribes or families, and with the ever growing institutionalisation of relationships within the tribes and families, the true contradiction became increasingly apparent. By this time, however, another new group had risen to prominence out of the traditional society. This was the colonial administration. The foreign overlords needed a kind of local, educated labour force to handle the administration of their interests. These administrators were soon living a dual existence. On the one hand they were recruited from the tribe or family of which they were part, and on the other they joined a new kind of 'tribe'—that of the civil service. They owed, therefore, a double loyalty, first to their tribe and secondly to the civil service.[5] The responsibilities, the duties and the way of life imposed by the one were very different and often in contradiction to the other. They were paid a salary by the one master, and this salary grew with each higher stage they rose to in the hierarchy of the service, and this affected their behaviour in one way. However, the road to enter this service and to gain this salary, and incidentaly to use their position in the service of the other members of their family, required another set of manners.

The prerequisite for entering this new social class of government employees was the ability to read and write, i.e. to pass through the foreigners' education system. The advantages of being a civil servant, or of having a civil servant in the family or tribe, became quickly obvious. Not only was the man able to bring a cash income back to his tribe, but it also opened new avenues for gaining certain advantages from the central government. Often it opened the possibilities of having more members of the family employed in the service. In time more and more people were ready to put the savings of the family together, to push one of their members through the foreign education system in order to have him in the civil service. This was a reasonable and good investment. Once a civil servant the man was, of course, in a peculiar position. He adopted many of the values of the foreigners, while at the same time he was obliged to give a return on the investment in his education to his fellow tribesmen. Whereas in the schools, which led up to his place in the civil service, he was instructed against nepotism, he felt it his duty towards his family, who had saved and suffered to put him through these schools, to engage in such practices as nepotism. He had to strike a fine balance between his own culture and the 'civilisation' of the foreign civil servants who were, only too often, the misfits of the societies from which they came and who adopted a patronising attitude towards the local population. Naturally, the local administrators also imbibed enough of their foreign colleagues' attitudes (of the colonial patterns) to develop an arrogance towards their own tribesmen. Soon they felt united with their other fellow civil servants as a class by itself. Unfortunately, conditions were not very favourable for the colonial civil servant to see more of the real values which civilisation outside the colonies had managed to produce. There were, of course, exceptions to this rule; there were civil servants who went for their education to the so-called mother countries and came back full of the best intentions, and who had excellent human and organisational qualities. But these were only the exception to the rule. They were, and indeed still are, under continual pressure to leave their country and service.

Now, since the decline of the direct subjugation of the colonisers in the colonial dependencies, a threefold struggle begins to develop. There is the colonial administration, and the traditional local leadership which try to hang on to power; there is a demand for higher living standards from below; and there is an African civil service which moves between these two exponents and which is trying to replace the foreign administration and put itself in its place. The decline of interest of colonial powers in their dependencies is partly due to the substitution of the old traditional raw materials by man-made materials (which come from other places), and partly due to the growing richness of the European markets, which make the colonial export market rather marginal in significance, and to the change in attitudes towards the once dependent but now independent areas. However, after the war the atmosphere was favourable for a display of goodwill towards the underdeveloped peoples, and political expediency made the liberation of these people a necessity. The struggle for independence in the colonial countries themselves took the form of a struggle for mastery between the civil service on the one hand, and the old vested colonial interests, as represented by the chief and other local dignatories, on the other. The traditional leadership was, of course, reactionary; they were satisfied with the continuation of the trade association with their old colonial allies. The new and rising class of the administrators was progressive in the sense that they wanted to free themselves from the old links, and wished to substitute them by rapid industrial development. The great mass of the people who were hoping for a higher standard of living, which only the new class could promise and to whom the colonial bonds were shown to be the cause of their poverty, supplied the mass backing for the early success of the national movement led by the administration. Here and there the demarcation lines between the various groups were further confused by the fact that the civil servants were often themselves chiefs and landowners. But on the whole the division was clear. On the one side were those with interests in trade and in the production of raw materials, and on the other the new generation of civil servants united by the wish to change the old ways of life. The most significant aspect of this 'three cornered' struggle was that none of the groups was, in fact, able to promote real and immediate improvements. The traditional leadership had nothing better to offer than the continuation of the old relationship with the colonial countries which they supplied with raw materials. In perspective, this meant that they could really offer nothing but a gradually declining living standard for their labourers, as the market value of the raw materials which they supply was falling.[6]

The civil service could, of course, promise industrial progress, i.e. progress through the development of industry, but could they really fulfil this promise in the face of the prevailing gap between the efficiency of capital in the developed countries and in their own? Certainly not; unless they could get the capital required for the industrialisation from outside sources, or from their own upper classes of landowners, who, of course, are reluctant to part with their property. Moreover, the civil service, i.e. the class which was to bring about the industrialisation, was itself closely related by tribal and family ties to the old landlowing groups, thus tying their hands and making it almost impossible for them to bring about the necessary revolution. Even worse than this, they were educationally ill-suited and ill-equipped to lead this movement. They had been brought up on the worst traditions of colonial administration; they had been trained to despise those whom they call 'illiterates'. They were, in fact, not truly interested in and did not really believe in the rapid assimilation of the poorer of their society. What they were and still are interested in is their own advancement and their own social position, and being accepted as equals or superiors by the traditional leadership and the people in their countries. Thus, materially ill-equipped to produce the industrial revolution and mentally ill-equipped to revolutionise the masses into a fervour of constructive enthusiasm, they used up a great share of the foreign aid and the foreign investments to inflate their own ranks. Held back by their social traditions, which made them use, or rather misuse, their position of power to help their families or tribes, and unable to produce a new economy, they merely held the whole country to ransom. In other words, while the traditional leaderships skimmed off whatever profits could be made from the production of raw materials and export trades to enrich themselves, occasionally letting some of it trickle down to those who worked for them, the new class is using the instrument of government to skim off whatever other incomes may accrue to their country. In some places they have managed to take away some of the money earned by the traditional leadership by taxation; more often they have only managed to appropriate the foreign aid and investments and to transform them into incomes of ever greater armies of administrators. On the one hand they begin to free themselves from their traditional family ties and begin to look after their individualistic interests. On the other hand their numbers have grown to an extent that the national income has to be divided between so great a number of aspirants that nothing is left over for capital accumulation. Yet both these trends could still be advantageous in some ways were it not for the great confusion prevalent in the ex-colonial countries between the outside symbols of civilisation, as represented by the colonial foreign administrators (such as large motor-cars and similar devices), and real consumers' demand.

In summary, the ancient prestige symbols of leadership, the cattle, lineage, etc., of the tribal leaders, are being replaced by new prestige symbols of only too often misunderstood foreign origin. The only part of the population which does not participate in any of these old and new sources of income, in the sharing of the government revenue, the foreign aid, and the income from raw materials and trade, are the workers and farmers. The growing requirements of the civil service, and the reduced income of the traditional leadership, further help to reduce the real income of the productively employed. This reality sometimes leads to discontent and to violence. But more often it seems to lead to disillusion and a mood of general hopelessness. There simply seems no point in trying to work more or harder. It is therefore true that the elimination of colonialism in underdeveloped countries, which was partly the result of a reduced interest of the colonising countries in their colonies, and partly also the result of the struggle for mastery between the new administrative classes in the colonies and traditional leaderships which were backed by the colonialists, was not the result of the rise of new productive economic forces but merely a political struggle. From this point of view independence did little but transfer the leadership from one group to another. It did not transfer the wealth of the nations to their productive forces, but it put it into the control of a class which under suitable circumstances could use it for development. The success of the administrative class in this struggle was due to its ability to combine the aspirations of the working people for a higher living standard with their presentation of the colonial system as the source of the immediate evil. Although historically this is well founded, politically this fact is not very useful. Unless independence was gained 'from below', by the rise of a productive class, there was little hope for a revolutionary change. It is, of course, true that the best people in the civil service were and are trying to bring about an economic as well as a political change, by using their political position to industrialise their countries, but their possibilities to succeed are rather limited. The need to look after their extended families prevents them from judging the success of industrial enterprises by profitability and forces them to judge them by the number of people they can employ. At the same time they also accepted the colonial attitudes towards the cheapness of labour. That is, they were led to believe that a sure course towards high profits is 'low wages'. Their concern with employment, and with the supply side of development, their complete neglect of the demand side, and their unwillingness to permit a new class to rise which would compete with them for leadership are, of course, severe hindrances to their efforts to bring about economic modernisation. Even in a country like Ghana, under Nkrumah's political system, administrators' wages continued to be higher than those of qualified workers.[7]

It was the administrative class which won independence for Ghana and gained political power. As a class, it was not ready to share the fruits of the revolution with another class, which it had become used to treating as its inferiors, as the colonialists had taught it. In fact, the success of the administrative class, and the high income which it was able to ascribe to itself because of the foreign aid, and often unearned incomes, drained all the people with initiative from other productive spheres towards itself. As long as any member of the civil service could earn a salary which was above that of any qualified productive worker, the drain from the productive labour sector was bound to continue, and indeed did so. It was in this sense that misdirected foreign aid did direct harm to the development effort of some underdeveloped countries. It made possible the continuation of this flow of the potentially productive élites towards unproductive employment. It prevented the growth of that part of society which might have brought about, and still may bring about, the necessary change in labour attitude and in the actual economic conditions. Moreover, investment without due stress on cost accounting, and unprofitable employment of labour, was also the result of the influx of unearned funds. Nationalisation, too, in the sense that the government rather than the private entrepreneur was made the source of national enterprise, further accelerated these economically dangerous trends. The civil servant who is receiving a salary is obviously less interested in the profitability of the enterprise than in its prestige, and in his own power over his fellow men. In other words, to put development projects into the hands of civil servants became a great source of underemployment of labour.

Here, too, the new trends combined with the traditional attitudes in a peculiar manner. New industries did not destroy the traditional attitudes of collective responsibilities which were bound to cause inefficiency and nepotism, but strengthened them by evading the need for strict profitability accounts for each enterprise. There was no government which was strong enough to prevent these trends in any of the emergent new States. Each of these governments was ruling because a social group brought it to power. Almost everywhere this group was led by the civil service, including teachers, etc. Any attempt, therefore, to bring about a readjustment of income structures, i.e. to raise the wages of productive labour at the expense of the standard of living of the civil service, was automatically bound to clash with the violent opposition of this group. For example, one attempt to readjust salaries in this direction in Upper Volta led to a coup d'état overnight. As a working class had not yet come into existence as a class, there was no force behind the leadership in the government which could prevent the old administrators, including the military, from ousting the government from power. Nkrumah, in Ghana, also tried various ways of bringing about industrialisation. He, too, eventually discovered that the only way to protect such a development plan would be by using foreign forces to defend his position in government, at least until such time as a working class in the European sense of the concept could emerge. This policy, as events have shown, was as ill-conceived as many others he tried because it is impossible, in this time and age, and in isolation, to 'sit on the bayonets' of foreign watchmen. Moreover, neither Nkrumah, nor any other leader in any underdeveloped country, has an efficient, or even inefficient but experienced, well-organised secret service or police which could suppress opposition as Stalin did during the years of Russia's rapid industrialisation. A policeman in Africa is more loyal to his tribe than to the central government, and any policeman who is policing anywhere but in his own tribe is completely useless because he will get no answers or any information which the people are not willing to give to him. Briefly, progress depends on the growth of a qualified working class, but the growth of this working class depends upon it assuming political power in order to be able to grow.

There was one serious attempt to break away from this vicious circle. This was the effort in Mao Tse Tung's China. It was the policy of the great leap forward and of the great propagandistic effort to convert nationalism into an economic incentive. It may have gone some way towards solving some of the most pressing economic difficulties in China, but even there the results are far from clear. It appears that the great upheaval which was taking place there in 1966 was another effort to overcome the stamina of mental inertness and to change labour attitudes and make workers again work more efficiently. It was, perhaps, once more an effort to bring about mass enthusiasm, the readiness to work hard for a better future without expecting immediate benefits. That such a national upheaval is possible has been shown, for example, by the people of Russia during the spells of heroic construction, and, again, by the British people in 1941–44. Indeed, during wars people are often doing things which are directly contrary to their immediate interest. They endanger their lives for ideas, for the attainment of future aims, or because the social environment is pushing them in this direction. The release of such forces can, of course, go a long way towards economic development. But the background is not the same everywhere. Not all societies are susceptible to such mental attitudes, and not all societies can at all times find the leadership which is able to harness these forces. Even if they do, this kind of attitude may last for only relatively short periods, which may not be sufficiently long to transform an economy. Even assuming that here and there economic development could be presented as the direct continuation of a struggle for independence, to which certain people have become accustomed, it is far from certain that this kind of stimulus alone could be enough to produce results. In fact, it is not only the wish to work but also the tools which are necessary. Perhaps it was, indeed, the particular combination of the European tradition of religious scruples, in the acquisition of wealth, and the obvious greed in the right mixture which created a society that was able to develop economically. A society whose representatives are merely greedy, without the 'right mixture', may be too acquisitive to be really economically progressive, because it will 'kill the goose that lays the golden eggs'. In addition to this, although it is perfectly true that capital can be replaced by labour inasmuch as labour can often be replaced by capital, that a dam can be built by the labour of thousands of underemployed workers, instead of by the utilisation of foreign capital equipment, a solution of this kind is only practicable where the population is numerous enough to bring it about. Thus, while this attitude may be fruitful in, say, China, it will perhaps be useless in the vast areas of Africa or South America.

In summary, assuming that a population can be animated by some nationalist incentives to the urge to develop, this could only bring good results if enough people live within an area to make the results felt. In addition, the change would have to be accompanied by the growth of a market which could absorb the produce. However, the gap between the rich and poor countries has become so wide that in effect there is not much chance of finding that market anywhere outside the poor countries themselves. At the same time the linkages between the poor countries themselves are of a nature which does not permit the easy growth of such a market. Most producers in the underdeveloped countries have become accustomed to produce for a developed market. That is, not for their own hinterland, but for 'overseas'. The products they have become accustomed to are those which are relatively abundant in the tropics and scarce in Europe and North America. Production for a home market would, therefore, require a complete review of customary attitudes. It requires the elimination of foreign competition and the raising of the prestige of locally produced goods in the developing countries themselves. It would require the development of new industries and new lines of production next to the traditional ones, because it is unlikely that the old productive enterprises could or should switch over to new products. Yet how should the new industries be selected? So far, most of the new industries have been constructed with at least one eye on an international market. However, demand for the goods which can be produced in the underdeveloped countries is strictly limited in the developed ones. The aim must therefore be to produce goods which can find a market in the underdeveloped regions. And, in fact, there are several lines of production which would have a market in these areas if foreign competitors could be discouraged by political means. For example, there is a ready market for tins of meat and fish in many parts of Africa. Meat and fish hold a certain prestige value for the African consumer, and it is not an entirely new product for them. Radios and bicycles and motor-cycles too have a similar attraction for people in underdeveloped countries. It is in the stimulation of the production of goods like these that some hope does exist for the growth of locally based industries. In other words, it might be expedient to use obtainable capital for the creation next to the old existing export industries of intermediate industries, with the deliberate intention of stimulating local market demand. The idea here is not to substitute consumer-goods industries for producer-goods industries but to support the growth of consumer-goods industries in the hope that they themselves will, in the process of competition, give rise to the production of producer goods as a second stage of development. If such a policy could be accompanied by changes in the income structure of a country, there might be a good chance for demand to set in motion a cycle of production which may, eventually, lead to the production of capital goods. How this may, perhaps, be brought about is beyond the scope of this analysis and will be discussed elsewhere. However, one need only remember that in Europe, not so long ago, there was a feeling that the rich were getting richer and the poor poorer, and that there was no escape from this situation. The reality, at least as far as the latter are concerned, never materialised. In late nineteenth- and early twentieth-century Europe the division between 'have and have nots' stimulated the political organisation of the workers to the point which eventually led to the redistribution of wealth in the form of the Welfare State. May it not be that the apparently hopeless situation of the underdeveloped countries will produce a similar reaction? It may bring about the political organisation of the underdeveloped countries which will enable them to resist effectively the maldistribution of the wealth of our world. It took the various workingmen's movements in the developed countries over a century to co-ordinate their efforts to bring down the old class structure and open up the avenues for the achievement of a higher living standard; and it took even longer to recognise the dependence of the rich on the rising living standards of the poor to keep up their production. Why should we not hope for a similar process to take shape in the relationship between the poor and the rich nations? As Victorian charity in England was eventually replaced by the just demands of the workers, so we may hope to see the foreign-aid projects replaced by the politically organised efforts of the peoples in the underdeveloped countries. Such a change can only come about once the leaders of the developing countries realise their true positions, once they are ready to forgo 'Victorian' aid and make themselves masters of their destinies. Progress cannot be imported, it must grow and be cultivated by the leaders of the underdeveloped countries. It is their responsibility. After all, and with all the gloomy aspects of what is still happening and what has taken place in the underdeveloped countries in recent years, any traveller who visited some of these countries in the past and comes back today cannot help but admit that a change for the better has taken place. True, this improvement has taken place only in isolated parts of the big continents, and has benefited only parts of the population, but in Europe, also, modern farming and traditional farming, for example, existed one next to the other for several decades, if not centuries.

THE 'OVERPOPULATED' COUNTRIES

The terms densely populated and overpopulated are too often used as if they were synonymous. This is certainly not the case. The former term merely expresses a fact—such as London is densely populated; the latter immediately implies a judgement of the economic capacity of an area and of its population. For example, India, with a density of population of 151 persons per square kilometre, is more 'overpopulated' than the Netherlands with 356, Monaco with 14,765, and Italy with 168 persons per square kilometre.[8] In addition, the term overpopulation is also dependent upon the territorial division to which it is applied. London as the centre of the Commonwealth economy is perhaps less overpopulated than London as the capital of England alone. South Asia as a whole has a density of population of 58 persons per square kilometre, while Europe's density of population is 89. There are only 28 persons per square kilometre living in Egypt if the country is taken as a whole, but if the inhabited areas are taken by themselves the density becomes no less than 803 persons per square kilometre. If we were to define overpopulation as a term describing a situation in which at a given time and in a given political entity, for instance a country, the population exceeds the means of its sustenance at a dignified level, we would have to include in effect all the underdeveloped countries of the world. It is therefore necessary to add a qualification to this definition to exclude the countries where, for example, an addition to the population would rather increase than reduce the economic capacity to raise living standards. From this point of view overpopulated countries must be defined as countries in which increments of capital lead to further increases in population, and not to rising *per capita* real incomes and higher living standards. Consequently, the definition of overpopulation must be taken out of the realm of demography and geography and put in its proper socio-economic context.

From this point of view, India can certainly serve as a good example of an overpopulated country. There are at least two obvious ways by which, theoretically at least, an overpopulated country can readjust. Either through the termination of the rapid accretion of people, or through the redistribution and/or accumulation of capital at a rate which is greater than that of population growth, or by both these ways together.

The record of recent years shows that neither of these methods which were both attempted in India can be easily implemented. The fact is that, over the last decade, India's population increased by approximately 2·2 per cent annually (and birth rates continue rising), while the national income has only risen by approximately 2 per cent per annum. The failure of the national income to keep pace with population growth, in spite of the foreign aid which the country received each year, was primarily due to the complete failure of the Indian Government in the sphere of agriculture.[9]

Almost three-quarters of India's population are employed in agriculture, which produces close to half of the country's national product. In order to catch up with the current needs and to dispense with foreign food supplies, farm production would have to increase by no less than 4 per cent annually. This would have to take the form of higher yields per acre rather than of an extension of the cultivated area, as there is little fertile land left that is unused. For this reason any significant increase in India's farm production is closely connected with socio-economic change. In other words, only a cultural or social and educational revolution may bring about a radical improvement in the country's food situation.[10] Unfortunately, however, there is little evidence of such a revolution taking place. For almost two decades since independence was achieved the per acre yield of India's farmland has increased by no more than 1·7 per cent per annum. With the population increasing during the same time by approximately 2·2 per cent per annum, the food situation is rapidly getting worse rather than better. The only encouraging sign in this depressing picture is the fact that the yield of some of the most important crops, such as rice and wheat, has not shared as much as other crops in this relative decline but has increased by more than the overall percentage for all crops. Yet, even so, both rice and wheat yields have shown a tendency to fall below those of the three last decades before 1948.[11] One gets the impression, in fact, that population growth is pressing agriculture on to ever poorer land, with no improvements in farming taking place to compensate for this. That this state of affairs is not 'an act of God' but the result of the human condition is fairly obvious, especially if one takes into consideration that not more than half a century ago other countries were also experiencing per acre yields of a similar order as India today and have since managed to raise them two and threefold. Moreover, some countries which have soil conditions which are not dissimilar with those of India produce twice as much (Greece, Yugoslavia) and more than three times as much (Japan, Czechoslovakia) per acre.[12]

It is, of course, true that a strictly arithmetical comparison, covering the last sixty years, of rising per acre yields, from one year to another, in the more developed countries, shows an annual compound rate of growth of no more than 1·2 per cent, i.e. less than that which is taking place in India today (which is about 2 per cent), but this comparison is not really justified. In the past the per acre yield could in the best case only rise at the rate at which the science of agronomy progressed. There is, however, no reason why India today should not adopt at once the whole accumulated knowledge of the past. There is no scientific reason why she should not emulate Japan, where yields are more than threefold. As a matter of fact, it appears that some countries, notably Yugoslavia, have recently experienced annual rates of growth of close to 8 per cent. A similar rate of increase in per acre yields has also been held not unreasonable for India.[13]

According to the evidence quoted by Dr. S. K. Nath,[14] the potential growth of India's agricultural production is demonstrated by the fact that she 'produces only 1,400 kilogrammes of rice per hectare, whereas Japan produces 4,620 and Australia, 5,950. Again, India produces only 790 kilogrammes of wheat per hectare, whereas France produces 2,600 and Denmark 4,130.' Obviously, it is the cultural background and its socio-political implications which prevent India from escaping her predicament.

On the political level, one significant impediment to more agricultural development is what may be termed the 'anti-colonial' mentality—a state of mind, through which most leaders of newly independent countries pass, which equates agriculture with colonialism and industry with independence and development. These ideas do not only result from the fact that colonial governments favoured primary production and did nothing to encourage industry (and in a number of cases even deliberately prevented its growth), but also, because to any observer it must be obvious that industrial countries are rich, while in all poor countries the great majority of people are employed on the land.[15] This superficial anti-colonialism is often accompanied by a socialist-inspired trend of thought which is too much influenced by the Russian approach of the Stalinist period, i.e. by the idea that industrial progress will eventually also help agriculture. Finally, again on the political level, it was as a rule the urban population which brought about the withdrawal of colonialism and first gained the political hegemony in their countries. Naturally. industry was closer to their heart than agriculture. Moreover, the concentration of the unemployed (as distinct from the underemployed) in the towns constituted a far more immediate political problem for the new governments than the solution of the age-old problem of the condition of the peasantry. In addition, and again for immediate political reasons, economic progress needed to be seen, an effect which is easier to accomplish through the construction of impressive works than by the slow and unglamorous process of rural development.[16] Next to all these more or less political reasons for the relative neglect of agriculture there was also a genuine assumption that, 'on the basis of comparative advantage, India should probably be an importer of foodstuffs and an exporter of products of heavy industry'.[17]

For these reasons the new leadership in India was politically and mentally ill-equipped to treat the agra problem with the same sense of urgency as it treated industry. Thus, while the First Five Year Plan (1951–56)'still clearly recognised that substantial development of agriculture is a precondition of viable industrial development . . . the Second Plan (1956–61) shifted the emphasis strongly towards industrial development, especially the development of heavy industry and the necessary ancillaries such as transport',[18] and the earlier emphasis on agricultural improvement, education and roads was very much reduced. This trend continued in the Third Five Year Plan (1961–66).

Yet it is difficult to pass judgement on the wisdom of this policy because, against the earlier quoted views, of the Ford Foundation experts, which estimated the potential of India's agriculture to be extremely promising,[19] there are no less respectable views which differ in their assessment. No less an authority on development than Professor W. Arthur Lewis[20] holds the view that until 1980 the best that can be expected from India's agriculture would be a 1·5 per cent per annum rate of increase, and that for this reason the best practical policy would be to follow the Japanese example and concentrate upon an export industry. Export could then pay for the rising food imports. He believes that if manufacturing can be increased to supply a growing export market, then the over-populated countries could solve their difficulties without increasing radically their agricultural output. This, together with the underlying assumption that such countries will not be able to increase agricultural production at the same rate as their population grows, leads him to concentrate attention upon the export manufacturers rather than on anything else. In other words, what he means to say is that it is the growth of exports which sets the limit to internal expansion.[21] Hence, the basic difference between the supporters of a more agriculture-orientated development policy and the supporters of an almost entirely industry-orientated development policy for India springs from their different assessments of the ability of the world market to absorb India's industrial output and of the practical possibility of removing India's cultural, social and political impediments to rural progress. The industrialists believe that world markets will absorb enough of India's industrial produce to pay for her growing needs of food, while the agriculturists are of the opinion that investment priority to agriculture, education and community development, together with the vigorous pursuit of land reform, holds more promising prospects for India's future. In fact, neither side totally excludes the other, but in practice even the little attention which was given to agriculture under the past three industrially orientated Five Year Plans was, perhaps with the exception of community development, never supported wholeheartedly. S. K. Nath[22] writes that, in effect, the Ministry of Agriculture has remained in some respects one of the minor ministries in Delhi and that there is less glamour attached to being an officer in that ministry than in some others. The officials appointed for the community development projects which were in charge of trying to increase the per acre yields were poorly paid and given a status far below that of other members of the administration. No wonder they were less respected and showed little initiative and ability. Those who were appointed at village level, in other words those who were the most crucial link between the villagers and the government, were poorly trained and even more poorly paid. The most important impediment, however, was the lack of enthusiasm on the part of the farmers. To show this, Dr. Nath quotes the results of an intensive study of two villages, which showed that a great proportion of the villagers had little interest in increasing their incomes, added to which, he also noted, more often than not a great part of the population in these villages did not realise the connection between a greater output and higher incomes.[23] The causes for this, as Dr. Nath sees them, are apathy, bonds of religion, the class structure of the rural society and the system of land tenure.[24] He goes so far as saying that any farmer who would engage in activities which might raise his income in an appreciable way runs a risk of incurring upon himself, to say the least, the displeasure of his betters. So that, notwithstanding the propaganda about land reforms, its effects have gone almost unnoticed. This is particularly true where the landlords have close ties with the government and where they are particularly strong.

However, there appears to be yet another good reason for the farmers' apparent 'lack of enthusiasm'. This is the fact that their assessment of their real chances to improve under the prevailing circumstances may well be more realistic than those of the specialists and experts. This is so because essentially the First Five Year Plan differed very little, in so far as agriculture was concerned, from the old 'Grow More Food' campaign. It, too, was supply-orientated with only little if any regard for profitability. To be sure, it included major and minor irrigation projects, the distribution of fertilisers and some insecticides and improved seeds, but it did not provide for adequate prices and price stability and for sufficient profit incentives. This fact was recognised when the Second Five Year Plan was formulated and the item about the necessity for 'an appropriate price policy' was added.[25] Yet in reality nothing substantial was done about it. Therefore, and bearing in mind that in India the unit of agricultural production and entrepreneurship is as a rule the family, and that any change in the volume of production can only be brought about as a result of the individual decision of millions of such family farming units, the true significance of the absence of an effective price policy should be obvious. When this became too clear to be further ignored, the government's answer to the problem was the complete decontrol of agra prices, including even those of food grains. The immediate result of this was a rapid rise of their prices. However, as it is the universal experience in all underdeveloped countries that food prices fluctuate vigorously from their lowest ebb immediately after the harvest to their highest level just before the following one, and only very few farmers have the resources and facilities to store and withhold their crops from the market until prices become reasonable, the decontrol of food prices did little to help the farmers but did much to help the traders who had the necessary storage facilities. Indeed, the latter reaped the full advantage of the decontrol, while it did nothing to encourage farmers to produce more than they had done before.[26] The absence of an effective government scheme for the stabilisation of prices to accompany the decontrol led to 'the discomfiture of peasant and consumer and at the same time assured good fortune to the traders'. As a distinguished Indian expert observed,[27] this 'not only exemplifies the inability of the government . . . to make up its mind regarding basic issues in plan-policy, but also raises serious doubts regarding the real social objectives pursued by those in authority'. In view of this, it appears obvious that all the talk about the application, or rather about the lack of application, of the considerable scientific information collected in India for which the farmers' 'unworldliness' and 'apathy' is usually blamed merely comes to hide the basic social reality that India's policy-makers are animated by a class conception which puts the interests of their own class before that of the country as a whole.[28]

The only truly hopeful signs for the future of Indian agriculture can be seen in the gradual emergence and growth of the co-operative system. Here and there the co-operatives are beginning to organise not only to improve their crop storage, land use, and marketing arrangements, but also in order to exert political pressure on the government. Though only very timidly, they are already pressing for 'a completely integrated State-sponsored co-operative organisation throughout the country as the initial step for making effective planning for agriculture possible'. The idea itself is not new. It was already put forward in 1959, when the Ford Foundation Team stressed the need for transferring the responsibility for the distribution of seeds, fertilisers and for the marketing of farm produce, into the hands of the co-operatives. However, no action was taken upon these recommendations. That this inactivity was less the result of some policy decision than of the inherent class orientation of the government seems fairly obvious. It may be demonstrated by the pattern of Indian taxation. Between 1951 and 1961 domestic savings rose by approximately 3·5 per cent. This was much less than what was potentially possible and a direct result of the fact that India's rich were severely undertaxed. According to Professor H. L. Lydall,[29] 'only if a further 8 per cent of national income is taxed away from the top 10 per cent of the population of India will the taxation of that part of the population be as progressive as it is in the United Kingdom'.

The sector in which India's progress was least disappointing is industry. Here net investment rose from approximately 5 per cent of the national income in 1951 to 8 per cent in 1956 and to 11 per cent in 1961. The annual rate of growth was about 3·5 per cent and the rate of growth of *per capita* incomes was about 1·5 per cent (with the remaining 2·0 per cent being taken up by population growth). In comparison with agriculture, where overall growth during this period reached only 33 per cent, the overall increase of industry by 70 per cent appears quite formidable. But then, only 17·8 per cent of India's population is employed in industry, and a large part of this is employed in services. Even less impressive is this achievement if it is compared with that of China.[30] Moreover, much of India's industrial achievement was also due to foreign assistance, which increased steadily from 10 per cent of the total investment during the First Five Year Plan to 24 per cent in the Second, and to 34 per cent in the Third. From a purely impressionistic point of view, looking at a number of specific industries, India's achievements appear, of course, to be much more impressive. The production of diesel engines increased more than ninefold in the course of the 1950s; of electric motors more than tenfold; of steel almost threefold; and of all consumers' goods together, almost double. Yet in relation to the low point from which this percentage growth was started, and in view of the great preference given to industry in the development plans, it appears very questionable indeed if the achievements justify the hopes that the country's industrial growth will be equal to the expected export trade surplus to pay for India's food imports. In fact, the results of the three Five Year Plans seem to show that at least at this stage of development in India the 'take-off' is less likely to result from a 'break-through' in a number of highly capitalised industries than from a balanced investment on a broad front including agriculture.[31]

Thus, in India, as in most other underdeveloped countries, a considerable difference is evident between the objective needs and the politically possible. Addressing the 42nd Convocation of Nagpur University in 1962 on the subject of the socio-economic situation in India, D. R. Gadgil[32] made this crystal clear. 'To begin with,' he opened his excellent address, 'there appears to be very general agreement among qualified observers that there has been since independence, an increase in corruption, and that this is specially in evidence among the highest and most powerful strata in society. It is also widely reported,' Gadgil goes on, 'that among large sections of our population and over wide areas a sense of frustration and a feeling of disillusionment prevail. The advent of independence and the responsibility for self-direction that it threw on the nation should have made us keenly conscious of social obligations. The changed circumstances should also enthuse and invigorate us in efforts at all-sided improvement and advance. That this has not happened points to some fundamental defects in the existing situation.' In his examination of the nature and the extent of the changes which took place since independence, he pointed out that the necessity to raise the country from its depressed social, educational, political and economic state had been recognised by the country's national anti-colonial leadership of the pre-independence period and had affected its scales of values and prestige, and the moral tone of the society at large. This enabled the pre-independence leadership to be both critical of the people and yet enthuse many of them to work for the advancement of their country, against heavy odds and at the risk of incurring the wrath of the foreign rulers. The coming of independence changed the situation, at least in so far as there was no longer the need to overthrow the foreign government. From here on, the responsibility for the solution of the large social, economic and educational problems of the country became the problem of the government and people of India themselves. The lead in these efforts was appropriately taken by the State. However, the peaceful change-over from colonial rule to independence affected on the administrative level the political posts alone. The one-time political outcasts and detainees became, and justly so, the occupants of the offices vacated by the British, while the rest of the administration remained unchanged. Yet even in the political offices the changes of rulers did not bring about any changes in the manifestation of authority. In effect, the new leadership very rapidly adopted all the outward manners of the foreign rulers which were intended to keep them apart from and above the people they were ruling. The whole administration continued to uphold the colonial structure which united the characteristics of a caste society with that of class. Consequently, the interests of the superior service personnel in the civil services, whose members continued to be carefully selected by the old colonial criteria, had a very great influence in all national policy decisions. As in colonial times, the government continued to attach more importance to the good standing and prestige of its officials than to telling the truth to their public. Consequently, all public arrangements became a kind of privileged sphere of government officials who need pay little attention if any to the requirements, demands or criticisms of the people. Briefly, although the administration may grow, and widespread welfare programmes may be initiated, the machinery for their implementation remains as before and certainly does not fit the objectives.

The most important positive change which Gadgil can see is the programme of planned economic development, which has indeed become the main national goal. That this process of industrialisation and urbanisation will also have a powerful impact on the structure of society in the future is obvious. What form this change will take is, however, far from certain. Before planning 'all growth of modern industry in India . . . has been brought about under a protective régime, major cost of which has been borne by the Indian consumer'. In planned industrialisation too, claims Gadgil, 'protection is continued in a variety of ways, and the plan is articulated through selecting particular capitalists for particular fields and enabling them to acquire highly scarce resources of every type. Whatever the financial skill of the capitalist, his success and progress are mainly due to conditions created by State policy and maintained at public cost.'

If this assessment of Gadgil is correct, as it appears to be, it indicates that, even with the best success, India's industrial growth can only follow the pre-war pattern of Japan, that is, development through exports without due consideration for the rise of a domestic market. This policy is indeed well reflected in the slogan, 'Production before Distribution'. But can such a policy still succeed in the post-war world? It seems very unlikely. What it may succeed in is the transfer of the wealth of the country even more into the hands of the rich without, however, laying the foundations for its truly productive employment. Therefore, more likely than not, India's industry will in this way never become competitive on the world market, and should protection at one time or another be terminated, it will stagnate or even altogether decay. Yet the rise of the new group of protected capitalists appears to be the most important social phenomenon in modern India. In colonial times there was a considerable gulf separating Indian businessmen from civil servants. This gulf no longer exists. Failing to create their own new scale of social values the civil service came increasingly under the influence of the business community. This trend has by now gone so far that senior civil servants no longer aim at the highest rank in the service, but search for administrative posts in both foreign and Indian business concerns, if not for themselves then for their children and other relations. Since much of the success of business in present-day India depends upon the goodwill of the government and its administrators, the consequences of this situation are fairly obvious. Not very different is the relationship between businessmen and politicians. In the pre-independence days a good number of patriotic businessmen helped India's political parties, at some risk to themselves and to their businesses, in the struggle against the colonial power. They had no hope of getting any immediate tangible rewards for their contributions. This situation has altogether changed. Now that the politicians are all-powerful, the contributions from businessmen continue, only the motivation has changed. At their best they contribute to support their party's election campaigns, at their worst they resort to outright bribery to secure direct advantages. Thus, at least in the towns, is India's traditional leadership being replaced by a new kind of leadership, that of businessmen who manage to concentrate in their hands an enormous amount of economic and political power. Unfortunately, however, these businessmen, with their great concentration of wealth, have little in common with their American or western European counterparts, but are much more akin to the old colonial types. Their roots are still in finance and in commerce and their whole organisation is still powerfully influenced by family and community ties. Nepotism is therefore but a natural phenomenon for this 'new-old' socio-economic strata of India's urban society.

In the words of D. R. Gadgil, 'The Indian businessman happens, at present, to be at a particularly unattractive stage of his development. He was never noted for any highly puritanic or moral qualities. . . . He has also not been imbued with that high sense of social and national responsibility which characterised the Japanese businessman in the Meiji era. However, some generations ago he was, at least, frugal and unostentatious. Recently, he has shed these characteristics and is now rapidly adopting the consumption standards of European and American businessmen. As a result, on the large surplus margins that State policy places in their hands, the high consumption standards of owners and managers of modern business constitute a first charge; and expense accounts, air-conditioned restaurants and hotels and night clubs figure as essential lubricants in the progress of Indian industrialisation.'

All this raises a highly controversial issue. Can social justice and economic growth move forward simultaneously in a planned Indian society, or can they not? In the view of the present author there is no hope for economic development without social justice, because only the latter can promote the growth of the domestic market. Taking into consideration the highly competitive conditions of world markets today, there is little hope for India's economic development unless a domestic market can develop. Hope therefore remains in the fact that in some rural sectors policies are now actually beginning to be based on a fundamentally new and different approach,[33] for example, that the new tenancy legislation ignores much of the traditional property rights. If, indeed, the ideology which is implied in the new approach should strike roots in the rural sector, it is unlikely not to spread to other sectors as well. Perhaps it will result in a modest redistribution of incomes which may lead to the growth of the domestic market for Indian industry.

AN AFTERTHOUGHT

It appears that economic progress may well be an organic process similar to others which take place in various forms of biological development. Once started, it will grow and spread its seed in ever-growing circles over ever greater parts of the earth wherever and whenever conditions become suitable. Studying economic growth from this point of view, one comes to ask questions about the nature of the impediments which prevent mankind from making more general progress towards greater material affluence rather than about the positive forces which make for economic growth which may then be taken for granted. If, further, one agrees that the main driving factor behind these positive growth-producing forces is competition of one sort or another, one must begin the story of development from the era of the Reformation in Europe. However, as one cannot explain why this new seed of growth should have first germinated just where and when it did, and why man the 'spiritual being, who, in order to survive, must devote a reasonable attention to economic interests' should have almost suddenly become an 'economic animal who will be prudent, nevertheless, if he takes due precautions to assure his spiritual well-being'—one must resort also to the naturalists' 'trick' of giving the phenomenon a name rather than an explanation. Thus we may call it a mutation, a particular, perhaps fortunate, coincidence of co-operation between forces which are within human control with forces which are not. The coincidence of 'the contraction of the territory within which the writ of religion was conceived to run' and the decline of chivalry, without its entire extinction, together with the expansion of trade and the rise of new classes, i.e. the combination of religious and socially imposed restraint with natural mercantilistic greed, may well be the specific mixture which produced the capitalistic state of mind which became the moving force for economic progress. Having struck roots, it was only a matter of time for the new state of mind to grow and spread. From north-western Europe it spread to the rest of the Continent, and the European settlers and Asian visitors to Europe carried it with them to other parts of the world. There, when conditions were suitable, it affected other people of non-European stock as well. However, as cultural traditions and socio-political conditions had prevented a more rapid emulation of Britain's economic achievements in the late eighteenth and during more than half of the nineteenth century on the continent of Europe, so do similar and perhaps even stronger impediments prevent its more widespread growth in the economically backward parts of the world today.

In fact, it must appear as if nature has given to mankind a world pregnant with riches to suffice for all, while man in his sinfulness has created for himself a socio-political edifice which alone holds back his progress to universal affluence. To those who are taking active part in freeing themselves from these man-made impediments to progress I dedicate this study.

NOTES

1. *Vide* Y. S. Brenner, *Theories of Economic Development and Growth*, Ch. I, London, 1966.

2. I am using the term 'European' or 'Christian' in a vague form to describe the mixture of greed with moral scruples so widely accepted in capitalist society.

3. There is an excellent example of a study of two similar villages in one of which people had the means, but not the wish to improve, and in the other people had the wish but not the means, in Theodore W. Schultz, *Transforming Traditional Agriculture*, New Haven, 1964.

4. It is a common claim of South African foremen in the mines that if the workers earn enough to buy a bicycle they will go riding all over the country and not return to work until the thing is broken. This is their justification for paying a bonus at the end of the contract rather than higher wages.

5. Excellent illustrations of this kind of problem can be found in the writings of the Nigerian writer, Chinua Achebe, particularly in his two novels, *No Longer At Ease* and *Things Fall Apart*, London, 1958 and 1960.

6. More and more of them are being replaced by synthetic materials from the developed countries and the market for the remaining ones;

cocoa, for example, is strictly limited to population growth in the developed countries.

7. For example, the official schedule of daily rates of pay in accordance with article 10 of the collective agreement, dated 20 October 1960, rates clerks at 12s. 2d. to 16s., messengers at 7s. and labourers at 6s. 6d. per day. Senior administrators' salaries begin at £800 per annum.

8. The data illustrating density of population are for 1963, taken from Table 2, in the United Nations *Statistical Yearbook*, 1964.

9. Food production has decreased both relatively and absolutely since the middle of the 1950s.

10. The alternatives are, of course, increased food imports, which would have to be paid for through a very rapid expansion of industrial exchange-goods production which, as we shall see, is very unlikely, or birth control, or mass emigration.

11. The yield rates in quintals per hectare as estimated by Colin Clark, *op. cit.*, Table XXVIII, pp. 296–299, are as follows:

	1909–13	*1925–29*	*1934–38*	*1949–51*
Rice	16·6	14·2	13·6	10·8
Maize		9·0	7·4	6·0
Wheat	8·1	6·8	6·9	6·5

12. Denmark produces six times as much wheat per acre as India.

13. This is the view of the Ford Foundation team of experts.

14. Published in Walter Birmingham and A. G. Ford, Eds., *Planning and Growth in Rich and Poor Countries*, London, 1966, p. 150.

15. The fact that there are rich countries where agriculture is itself industrialised, or the basis of a powerful industry, is often not recognised. The fact that industrial growth depends on agricultural progress also goes unrecognised.

16. This is, of course, one of the dilemmas of democratic and even undemocratic rule, that the need to show achievements may clash with the real concern for progress.

17. Benjamin Higgins, *Economic Development*, New York, 1959, p. 717.

18. William H. Nicholls, 'The Place of Agriculture in Ecomonic Development', *op. cit.*, in Eicher and Witt, p. 33.

19. See Footnote 14.

20. 'India's Economic Prospects for 1980—The Need to Develop Export Manufacture', *Capital*, Supplement, 16 December 1954, p. 7.

21. W. Arthur Lewis. Quoted from W. H. Nicholls, *op. cit.*, p. 35.

22. In Birmingham and Ford, Eds., *Planning and Growth in Rich and Poor Countries*, pp. 142–170.

23. It is necessary to add that Dr. Nath here warns the reader that these findings need not be exactly representative for the country as a whole.

24. S. K. Nath, *op. cit.*, p. 151.

25. *Second Five Year Plan*, Government of India Planning Commission, New Delhi, 1956, p. 261.

26. This is, of course, only relevant to the regions where the natural conditions permit an increase in the yield per acre.

27. D. R. Gadgil. Address to 13th Annual Conference of the Indian Society of Agricultural Statistics, Poona, 8 January 1960.

28. We shall return later to these connections in more detail. See p. 290.

29. Professor Lydall is quoted here from S. K. Nath, *op. cit.*, p. 154.

30. *Vide* Wilfred Malenbaum, 'India and China: Contrasts in Development', *American Economic Review*, June 1959.

GROSS INVESTMENT AS PERCENTAGE OF GROSS NATIONAL PRODUCT

Year	*India*	*China*	*Year*	*India*	*China*
1950	9·3	9·7	1956	13·2	19·2
1952	9·8	14·2	1957	13·6	23·9

31. Cynics can, of course, claim that without serious investment in agriculture India's population problem will solve itself when the ultimate limits of land use at present conditions are reached. But a Communist-led revolution seems then more likely.

32. All subsequent quotations from D. R. Gadgil are taken from this Convocation address, which was reprinted in the Gokhale Institute Studies (No. 39), *Planning and Economic Policy in India*, Poona, 1962 edition.

33. D. R. Gadgil, *Planning and Economic Policy in India*, Gokhale Institute of Politics and Economics, Poona, Bombay, Calcutta, New Delhi, Madras, London, New York, 2nd edition, p. 247.

INDEX

Q

R

For Product Safety Concerns and Information please contact our EU representative GPSR@taylorandfrancis.com
Taylor & Francis Verlag GmbH, Kaufingerstraße 24, 80331 München, Germany

www.ingramcontent.com/pod-product-compliance
Ingram Content Group UK Ltd.
Pitfield, Milton Keynes, MK11 3LW, UK
UKHW040855180926
475701UK00001B/6
* 9 7 8 0 7 1 4 6 4 0 1 6 7 *